3ds Max Modeling for Games

Volume 1

Praise for *3ds Max Modeling for Games, 2nd Edition*, Volume 1

"This book is a must-have resource for anyone wanting to learn how to make game art in 3ds Max. It has great support on the forums which is a testament to the author's enthusiasm for the subject. My students would be lost without it. If you want to understand how to really make 3d art for games then this is the book you need."

—**David Wilson,** programme leader, BA (Hons) Computer Games Modelling and Animation, University of Derby, UK

"This is a great book covering most aspects of modeling for games including the basics of 3D, Ambient Occlusion, Normal Maps, Character, Vehicle, Scene Creation and much, much more. It covers everything you need to get you started for your career in games."

—**Andy Manns,** lead artist, THQ

"An extremely comprehensive book covering all the basic theory and techniques with 3ds Max, currently used within the best game development studios in the industry."

—**Alex Perkins,** art director, Sony Computer Entertainment Europe

"For a beginner, getting to grip with 3ds Max is a daunting prospect, but this book picks on the relevant features and aims to get you producing usable 3D game art quickly and efficiently. It gives you a great understanding of what goes into make good 3D video-game art and will give you the vocabulary needed to talk with confidence about in-game models."

—**Don Whiteford,** creative director THQ Digital UK Ltd.

"This book is one of the most comprehensive, straight-forward, and easy to follow guides for modeling precise and efficient 3D game assets and environments. Andrew Gahan has heard everything every educator has said about what a textbook needs to do to meet the broad stroke of students' needs and abilities in learning how to master 3D modeling with 3ds Max. With simple understanding and imagination, this text can be used to transform modeling for games into modeling for animation or modeling for simulation."

—**Tim Harrington,** national assistant dean, Game and Simulation Programming, DeVry University

3ds Max Modeling for Games

Insider's Guide to Game Character, Vehicle, and Environment Modeling

Volume 1

Andrew Gahan

AMSTERDAM • BOSTON • HEIDELBERG • LONDON • NEW YORK • OXFORD
PARIS • SAN DIEGO • SAN FRANCISCO • SINGAPORE • SYDNEY • TOKYO

Focal Press is an imprint of Elsevier

Focal Press is an imprint of Elsevier
225 Wyman Street, Waltham, MA 02451, USA
The Boulevard, Langford Lane, Kidlington, Oxford, OX5 1GB, UK

Notices
Knowledge and best practice in this field are constantly changing. As new research and
experience broaden our understanding, changes in research methods, professional practices,
or medical treatment may become necessary.

Practitioners and researchers must always rely on their own experience and knowledge in
evaluating and using any information, methods, compounds, or experiments described herein.
In using such information or methods they should be mindful of their own safety and the safety
of others, including parties for whom they have a professional responsibility.

To the fullest extent of the law, neither the Publisher nor the authors, contributors, or editors,
assume any liability for any injury and/or damage to persons or property as a matter of products
liability, negligence or otherwise, or from any use or operation of any methods, products,
instructions, or ideas contained in the material herein.

Library of Congress Cataloging-in-Publication Data
Application submitted

British Library Cataloguing-in-Publication Data
A catalogue record for this book is available from the British Library.

ISBN: 978-0-240-81582-4

For information on all Focal Press publications
visit our website at *www.elsevierdirect.com*

11 12 13 14 15 5 4 3 2 1

Printed in the United States of America

Typeset by: diacriTech, Chennai, India

Working together to grow
libraries in developing countries

www.elsevier.com | www.bookaid.org | www.sabre.org

ELSEVIER   BOOK AID
             International   Sabre Foundation

Contents

Contents

Contents

Acknowledgments

Thanks to:

Anthony O'Donnell for the update and the new content.

Laura, Anais, and Lauren at Focal Press.

Dave Griffiths, for the low poly truck tutorial.

Tom Painter, for the character tutorial.

Everyone at UVLayout (http://www.uvlayout.com).

Ben Cloward, for the use of the shaders (http://www.bencloward.com).

Ryan Clark at Crazy Bump (http://www.crazybump.com).

The superstars of www.3d-for-games.com/forum: Frap, Cyphris, Willster, Kinesis, Harry P, Nathdevlin, Jeskalade, Henry Ham, Mr. Bluesman, Drecks, Swiss, Sanguine, Ruchitajes, Elliot, Dave, Theia, Stocko2k, Aidyfuzz, A. Cherry, Sebastian K, Ashley, Jtec, Fossman, Tokyogamer, Caio1985, McMonkeyBoy, Punnuman, Glode, Jason-NivEous, Seth, Neil_P, XaKu, Thudo, Airone, Jono23, DexterXS, Abubaker, Thomas, Dav, Ibrahim, Starfrogsplash, Jamie, Boffy, Commandercloin, EddyBrown, Memorex, Bogas, Gheist, Timex, and everyone else who makes this all worthwhile—thanks all!

Everyone at Autodesk (www.autodesk.com)

And a special thank you to everyone else who helped me along the way.

Finally, thank you for picking up the book.

About the Author

I'll keep this short and sweet, as I know your primary interest is how to model the scene on the cover and start making money as a professional modeler, not to hear all about me.

I started in the games industry in 1992 as a junior artist for Digital Image Design. They came to my college, and after seeing my graphic design work, they offered me a summer job making games. I jumped at the chance and without any portfolio or experience at all, started training on my first game. I progressed to senior artist, developing flight simulators and military training systems, until the studio was bought by Infogrammes around 1998. I became lead artist when Infogrammes sold the studio to Rage, then left and became art director at a small startup called Lightning Interactive. I switched again to join my old friends at Evolution Studios (Evolution was set up when Infogrammes bought D.I.D., with Martin Kenwright leaving and taking six people with him). I progressed through the ranks again at Evolution Studios, becoming art manager on some of the later World Rally Championship games on PlayStation 2, then producer and outsource manager, and then to my current role as senior development manager. At the time of this writing, I have just completed work on MotorStorm: Apocalypse, for PS3, and am currently working on a number of unannounced projects.

If you're interested, here is the list of games that I have helped develop:

- Robocop 3 (Amiga)
- TFX (PC)
- Inferno (PC)
- EF2000 (PC)
- F22—Air Dominance Fighter (PC)
- Total Air War (PC)
- Wargasm (PC)
- GTC Africa (PS2)
- World Rally Championship (PS2)
- WRC II Extreme (PS2)
- WRC 3 (PS2)
- WRC 4 (PS2)
- WRC 5—Rally Evolved (PS2)
- MotorStorm (PS3)
- Pursuit Force 2 (PS2)
- MotorStorm 2: Pacific Rift (PS3)
- MotorStorm: Apocalypse

Also, here is the list of other training titles that I have put together:

- *3ds Max Modeling for Games* (Book)
- *Game Art Complete* (Book)
- *3D Automotive Modeling* (Book)
- *Max in Minutes* (Videos)
- *Maya in Minutes* (Videos)
- www.3D-For-Games.com (Website and Forum)

About the Book

There is so much information crammed into just one book, I have had to keep it as concise as possible. I cover only what you need to complete each tutorial and nothing else. This book is designed to get you up to speed as quickly as possible producing great artwork and is not designed to teach you how to use all aspects of 3ds Max. If you're looking for a book to teach you the ins and outs of Max, then there are plenty to choose from. Personally, I'd rather keep my hard-earned cash and press the F1 key—the built-in help can show you all the functions you'll need to get started.

The book is arranged over eleven chapters, starting from getting to grips with the basics, moving onto some low-poly modeling, and culminating into a couple of fairly advanced builds. I've arranged the content of every chapter to be part of a similar theme to enable you to use most of the assets that you learn to build the final showpiece scene at the end. I realize that this approach is slightly limiting, but I decided that it would be best to teach you to model a number of things in the same style rather than a whole load of different things in different styles, just for consistency.

About the Contributors

Here are the guest writers, in their own words.

Anthony O'Donnell—All the New Content

I'm an Irish artist currently living in England. Like most artists in the games industry, the job of creating games was one I wanted since a young age. Initially, I wanted to work in comics or in feature animation, so in the pursuit of this goal, I attended Ballyfermot College of Further Education (BCFE) for three years in Dublin, Ireland. I graduated in June 2004 with a HND in Computer Animation.

For almost three years after college, I worked hard improving my skills and trying to attain a position within a commercial art industry while working other full-time jobs. I had finally caught a break and started at Evolution Studios in May 2007 working as a junior artist on the DLC for the first MotorStorm title creating objects.

Since then, I have had the pleasure of working on MotorStorm: Pacific Rift and MotorStorm: Apocalypse as an environment artist/level designer. Currently, I'm still working at Evolution Studios by day and by night attempts to one day turn paper into published comic art continue. I also helped to produce the Max in Minutes and the Maya in Minutes series of training videos for Focal Press.

David Griffiths—Low-Poly Vehicle Tutorial

I have been in the games industry now for over 10 years. I graduated from Blackpool and The Fylde College (part of Lancaster University) in the United Kingdom with a degree in technical illustration. I started my career in the automotive industry, working freelance on-site for a company called I.V.M. in Germany. I moved naturally into games, starting out with flight simulators. Some of my notable roles in the games industry have been working as a lead artist for Pandemic Studios in Santa Monica, California, when I worked on Star Wars: The Clone Wars. On Clone Wars, I was able to add to the Star Wars Universe, where I designed the TX-130 Fighter Tank and the G.A.T. vehicles (among many others), which were used in other games, comics, story books, and have even been made into model kits. The Fighter Tank has a very strong fan base, which is cool. Mercenaries was another great game to work on for Pandemic and Lucas Arts; it hit every major console. I have also had the privilege to work on the smash PS3 franchise MotorStorm, including the latest release MotorStorm: Apocalypse.

Tom Painter—Character Tutorial

As a child, I would waste many a sunny day on my ZX spectrum and Amiga; by the time I was a teenager, I had developed an addiction to Street Fighter 2 that was roughly equivalent to that of a bad drug habit. Encouraged by my father, I decided I would pursue a career in games.

After my studies, I got my first break in the games industry as a pixel artist working at Tiertex on Nintendo Game Boy Advance titles. When Tiertex dissolved, I joined Evolution Studios as an environment artist for the WRC series of games on the PlayStation 2.

In 2005, I moved to Pandemic Studios in Australia to work on Destroy All Humans! 2. I changed roles to become a character artist working on Saboteur and two top-secret titles in progress (project B and project Q).

Now, it's 2011 and I'm the owner of Big Man Production, a specialist 3D outsource production company working for clients in the video game and advertising industries.

I love working in 3D because the job never gets boring—there's always something new to learn or new ideas to implement.

Introduction

Why a Second Edition?

After meeting so many readers of the original book on the forum that supports this book (www.3D-For-Games.com/forum), as well as a lot of them in person, we came to the decision that a bit of an update to *3ds Max Modeling for Games* was in order. Not only had the software moved on but so had the expectations from employers looking to hire staff. With lots of companies closing down and it becoming harder than ever to break into the industry, we decided that it would be a good idea to bring the book up to the present day and to include more of the essential skills that every professional 3D artist must master.

I worked with Anthony O'Donnell to bring you all of the new content, which we believe is worthy of buying this book again if you have the original. About 60% of the content is new, and focuses a lot more on professional skills, which we believe will really give you the helping hand to stand out from the crowd.

Why This Book Was Originally Written

This book was written with one single goal in mind: to teach people who are relatively new to 3ds Max how to produce great results in the smallest amount of time possible.

The idea of writing a book came about when I had purchased yet another *How to Use 3ds Max* book online without flicking through it first. I purchased the book because I was keen to start researching training for 3ds Max and how people are currently going about learning Max. I started to read through the book and was amazed at what they were teaching but also overwhelmingly shocked at what they were getting the readers to produce—the end results were shocking, even laughable. I thought to myself, "If that's the way they are teaching how to use 3ds Max, I don't want to learn it."

It's great to know how to do something, but if what you ultimately produce is unusable, then what's the point?

So, I managed to get in touch with Laura Lewin at Focal Press, and she just happened to be looking for writers. After pitching a few ideas, this was the one that was accepted.

As you become more experienced in modeling, you'll discover that there are many different methods of producing the same piece of work. All that I am offering in this book is one particular method for each tutorial: the one that I believe is either the fastest or the easiest or the one that I think produces the best results for the least amount of time.

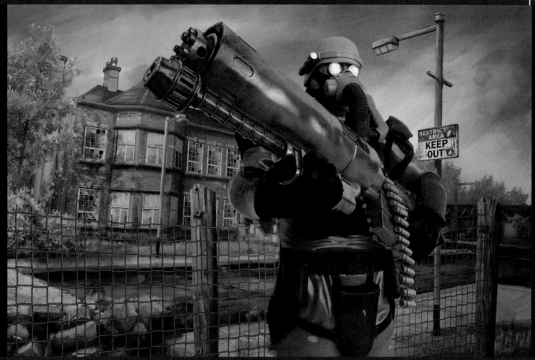

CHAPTER 1

Introduction to 3ds Max

The first part of this chapter is designed to get complete beginners up to speed with an overview of the 3D Studio Max user interface, tools, and some functions. The version we'll be covering is Max 2011; if you happen to have an earlier version, a lot of this information will still be accurate.

A trial version of the latest release can be downloaded from the Autodesk Web site. Just go to www.autodesk.com and look in the Products tab.

First of all, let's have a brief look at the layout of the *User Interface* (or UI). Figure 1.1 is a screen grab of how 3ds Max appears when it's launched. Let's have a look at each of the main areas of the interface.

1. In the top left corner, we have a button which is the 3ds Max logo. Click on this to bring up the *Application menu*, which provides the file-management commands such as opening or loading a scene and the saving options.
2. To the right of this is the *quick access toolbar*, and it contains icons for saving, creating new scene, opening file, and the undo and redo commands.
3. Just below these we have the *menu bar*. This gives you access to all the tools and their settings in 3ds Max along with the create options for creating 3D shapes. It also contains all the preferences and software settings under Customize > Preferences.

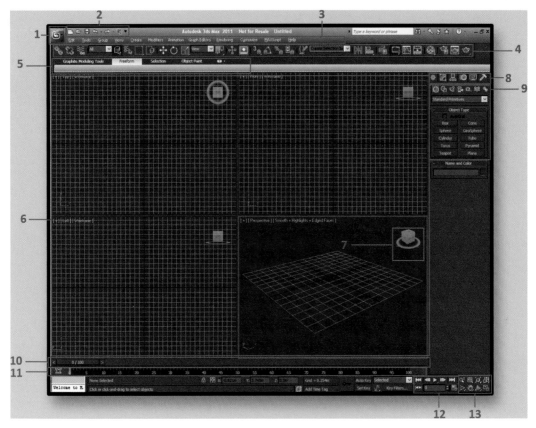

FIG 1.1 Layout of the user interface.

4. Below the menu bar is the *main toolbar*, which contains a lot of the basic tools we will need. Highlighted in the grab of the toolbar below are the select, move, rotate, and scale buttons. These are the tools we need to manipulate objects and meshes within 3ds Max.

   Other options on this bar include the snap settings for snapping components using different methods. The selection options are also available here. Including the selection filter, a useful dropbox, will allow you to restrict selections to certain object types. This is very useful when dealing with complex scenes with many types of objects.

   On the right side of the toolbar as seen in the image are the buttons to bring up the material editor and the rendering options.

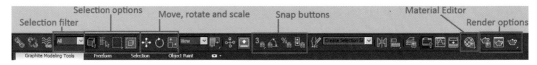

FIG 1.2

5. Beneath the main toolbar are the Graphite Modeling Tools. This section gathers all the standard edit tools related to polymodeling in one place. It really helps to speed up the modeling process.

6. The four windows highlighted by number 6 are the four default viewports. From the top left, these are the TOP view, FRONT view, LEFT view, and the PERSPECTIVE view. It is possible to arrange the viewports whichever way you want. To maximize or minimize the active viewport, the shortcut is ALT + W. The currently active viewport will always be highlighted by a yellow border.

    You can also left-click and drag in the intersection between viewports to resize them. Right-click in the intersection again and select reset layout to restore the default four panel view.

7. Highlighted here is the viewcube. This is a very handy tool for quickly changing the orientation of a camera or changing the viewport with one click. You can do this by clicking on either a direction on the compass around the viewcube or clicking on the cube itself.

    When the cube is displayed in a 3D viewport, you can select any corner, side, or face to position the camera. To change to a standard view, click on the center of a face.

    When in a standard view, four arrows will appear around the viewcube allowing you to cycle through all the standard viewports; for example, front, back, and top. To go back to a 3D view, click on a side or a corner.

    You can also hold the LMB (left mouse button) and drag to rotate the viewcube and viewport.

    Below is an image of the viewcube. The viewcube on the left is from the perspective viewport, and the right one is from the front viewport.

FIG 1.3

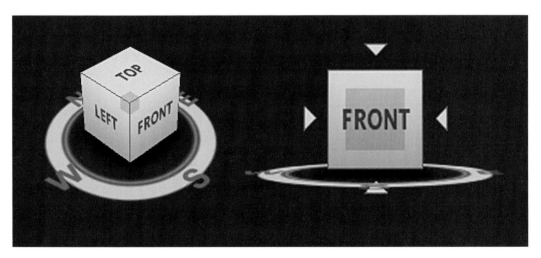

8. This is the command panel, and it consists of six panels that give you access to most of the modeling features of 3ds Max. To display a different panel, you click its tab at the top of the command panel.

The most important panels for beginners are the create panel and the modify panel.

Create panel: The create panel gives you access to the primitive shapes which are good starting points for creating models. Also featured within this tab are shapes, lights, and cameras. There are seven categories. All of these can be created by selecting what you want in the menu with the LMB and then clicking the LMB in the viewport. Then the item will appear.

Modify panel: The modify panel is where you can change the creation parameters of an object and also where you can apply modifiers to objects to reshape them. The modify panel's contents will contain different parameters, depending on what category or type of object is selected. We will be dealing with all these various parameters as we encounter them throughout the book.

9. These are the *object categories* within the *create panel*. This is the panel which contains the basic primitive objects. The drop-down box below the icons allow you to access more advanced shapes and items. By default it is on standard primitives.

10. This is the *time slider*. This displays the current frame the time slider is on and how many frames are in the total range. To move the slider, you can either select it and hold the LMB and drag it along back and forth or you could use the playback controls to the right (12).

11. The *track bar* sits below the time slider and is a timeline displaying frames in increments. It is mainly used for adjusting keys. Moving, copying, or deleting them.

12. These are the *animation playback* controls and do as they say. You can use them to either jump to the start and end frame on the time slider or move one frame at a time.

13. To the right of the animation playback controls are the *viewport navigation controls*. Some of the options here will vary and change depending on the type of viewport that's active, for example, whether it is a standard one or you are looking through a camera or light.

To use the controls, select the option you want from the navigation controls with the LMB, and then use the LMB in the viewport to carry out this action. If you hold the LMB on the navigation buttons with a triangle in the bottom right-hand corner of the icon, you will get more advanced options for that function.

One example is the rotate tool. You have the following three options:

Arc rotate: This will rotate the camera within the viewport using the view as the center of rotation.
Arc rotate sub object: This will use the component selected, that is, a vertex as the center of rotation.

Arc rotate selected: This will use the selected object as the center of rotation. I tend to leave it on arc rotate selected, as this makes sure that you are always focused on what you have selected.

Viewport Navigation:

To navigate the viewport in 3ds Max holding the MMB and moving the mouse will pan the camera. Using the MMB to scroll will zoom in and out. ALT + W will maximize or minimize the active viewport.
There are also hot key options to switch between views. Press P to change it to a perspective view, F for a front view, B for a bottom view, and T for a top view.

The Quad Menu

I'm going to briefly mention the Quad Menu now as it can help to speed up your work rate when you get used to it.

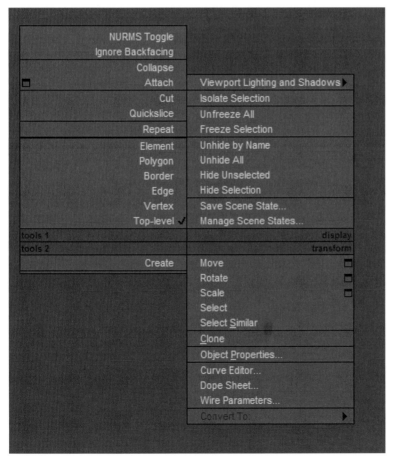

FIG 1.4 The quad menu.

The Quad Menu will give you access to most commands needed by clicking the RMB in a viewport. If there is no object selected, it will display generic commands seen in the right two quadrants of the image above. The two left quadrants will appear when an objected is selected, and as it is context-sensitive, the contents will vary depending on what's selected.

The Quad Menu can be heavily customized, and it is worth looking into this further as you develop a workflow and get more experienced with 3ds Max. Max's help section can provide further information on this if you are interested.

Setting Up 3ds Max

To begin with, we'll start with some basic settings for 3ds Max. Go to Customize > Preferences > Files > Enable Auto Backup, and set the number of Auto Backup files to 9, and set Backup Interval (minutes) to 10, then click OK.

Next we'll set up the units we'll be modeling in; these vary from studio to studio, but in this book, one unit equals 1 cm. Go to Customize > Units setup … and, select Metric, and then click OK.

Don't forget the in-depth help section is always at hand on the main menu or by pressing F1 or just log onto the free help forum at www.3d-for-games.com/forum and we'll answer your questions as soon as you've registered and logged in.

Game Art Terminology

I'd like to introduce you to the key terms used in the games industry relating to the creation of 3D assets. I am not going to go into great technical detail, as there are plenty of resources online which will explain these terms in greater depth. 3ds Max has a wealth of information in the help section, so don't be afraid to use that F1 key to search for anything that you'd like to know more about. As you progress through this book, you will encounter all the elements listed below, clearly explained in context, and you'll learn how to implement them.

Geometry

3D geometry is made up of vertices, edges, triangles, and polygons. These are the elements that define the surface of a 3D model. We can manipulate each of these in 3ds Max.

Vertex (plural of vertices): A vertex is a single point. It contains information of its position in 3D space using the X, Y, and Z co-ordinates system found in 3ds Max. Vertices form the basic structure of geometric objects in 3D. Figure 1.5 shows a vertex on the corner of a cube.

Edge: An edge is a line that connects two vertices. The edge is highlighted in red in Fig. 1.6.

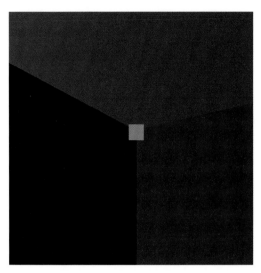

FIG 1.5

FIG 1.6

Triangle (face): A triangle is created when three vertices all have edges connecting them. In relation to a 3D model, a triangle is the surface between these three vertices/edges. It is this surface that defines the form of a model. Triangles could also be called faces as these usually have three sides. Figure 1.7 shows a triangle selected on the face of a cube.

FIG 1.7

Polygon: A polygon is typically the surface between four vertices/edges. This could also be referred to as a quad. Polygons are also referred to as faces as they can have three or more sides. Polygons with more than four sides are referred to as n-gons. A quad consists of two triangles; you can see this in

7

Fig. 1.8. On the left, I have selected a polygon on the side of the box which has two triangles counted in the selection. In the right of the image, I have selected an n-gon. Note it's still counted as one polygon but three triangles or tri's.

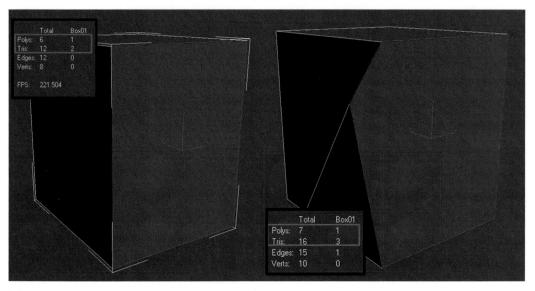

FIG 1.8

When creating 3D models for games, 99% of the time they should be made up of tri's or quads. You can create a model with a mixture of triangles or quads or n-gons, but in the end, game engines and 3ds Max, all polygons are broken down into triangular faces. It's good practice to measure your models complexity in triangles as this is more accurate.

Stitched Geometry and Floating or Intersecting Geometry

These terms refer to two techniques of constructing a model.

The first, "stitched geometry" or "stitched in geometry" is when every vertex in the model is connected to another creating a water-tight solid mesh. The example on the right of Fig. 1.9 is a cylinder sitting on top of a cube which is stitched to the cube at a vertex level. All of the faces that are not visible between these meshes have been deleted.

The example on the left of Fig. 1.9 where the cylinder sits on top of the cube is referred to as floating or intersecting geometry. Leaving geometry floating will mean that you use less triangles overall, but there is some overdraw in the face of the cube at the point where the cylinder sits over it. This surface area will be calculated in rendering, but it is never visible. The stitched in example has no unrendered surface area as it has been deleted during the stitching process.

The decision on which method is best can be determined by a game engine or a project's needs. As a general rule and guide though small objects are ok to be placed on meshes as they cause little overdraw. Some examples are handles on doors, switches, posters, or fire alarms.

Large objects such as buildings connected to each other are best using the stitched method as the saving in overdraw is worth the extra triangles when the overdraw consists of a large surface area on screen.

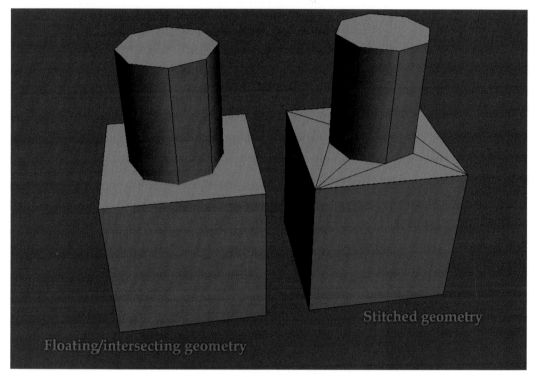

FIG 1.9

LODs

LOD is the acronym for Level of Detail. LODs are used in almost every game today. A LOD is a version of an asset which is lower in polygon count than the original. Sometimes, LODs have smaller texture maps or simpler shaders too.

For an artist creating LODs, you should aim to reduce the polygon detail to around 50% per LOD, more if possible without destroying the outline of the asset.

There will be a chapter discussing this topic in detail later. Figure 1.10 shows a model of an old fire extinguisher with two LODs and the polygon counts of each reduction.

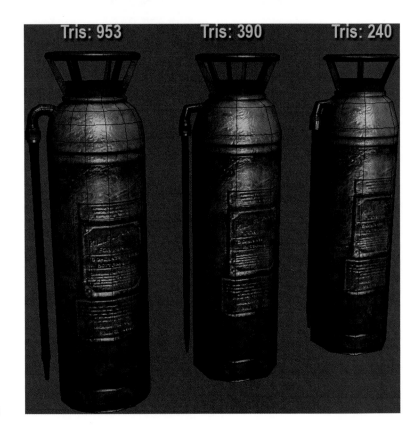

Tris: 953   Tris: 390   Tris: 240

FIG 1.10 An old fire extinguisher.

Textures

The terms textures or texture maps in game art refer to 2D images that are projected onto or wrapped around a 3D mesh. We'll discuss this more in the tutorials later on in this book.

These texture pages can be cropped from photographs, be hand painted, or created using a combination of both. The purpose of texture maps is to define an object's surface, color, or texture and to visually describe any extra details that are not modeled in polygons.

Here is a brief description of the most common texture types.

Diffuse map: A diffuse map is the main texture applied to most 3D models. This texture should define a surface's main color and detail. A good diffuse map should not have any directional lighting in it. The only lighting that should be present in this texture should be from an ambient light source as if it's being lit evenly from all directions. This means that recesses in the texture will appear darker and raised element would be lighter. No shadows or highlights should be present in the texture.

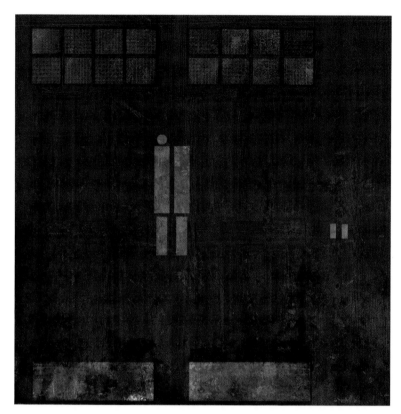

FIG 1.11 An example of a diffuse map.

Bump map: A bump map is a gray scale image, which affects the shading over a surface. A game engine or 3D program will interpret dark values as recessed areas and lighter values as being raised areas. Bump maps are used less frequently now because of other more advanced techniques like normal mapping.

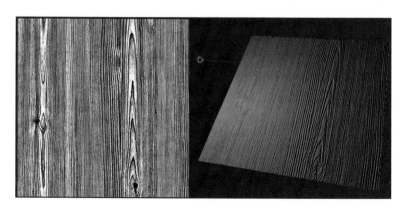

FIG 1.12 An example of a bump map.

Specular map: A specular map can be a gray scale or color image. Specular maps define a surface's shininess and highlight color. If you use a gray scale specular map the lighter the value in the texture the shinier that area will be. Darker values will be less shiny with pure black resulting in a matte surface. A gray scale spec map will give you a white highlight. The example below is of a door. The metallic and glass surfaces are almost white, whereas the wood and dirt are much darker. You should be able to see the benefits of a specular map in the render.

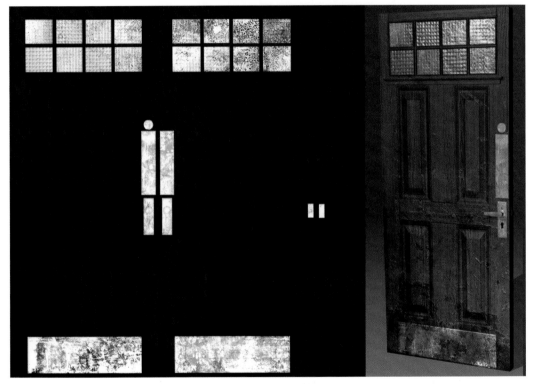

FIG 1.13 An example of a specular map.

Normal map: Normal maps have become a standard in most current games. A normal map is an RGB texture used to give an object the appearance it has a lot more detail than it really has. Each color channel contains information that represents the direction of a face's surface normal in 3D space using the X, Y, and Z co-ordinates. This means normal maps work with dynamic lights and will light as if it were geometry. Normal maps can be generated from high resolution models or can be created from gray scale images. We'll be discussing this in more depth later.

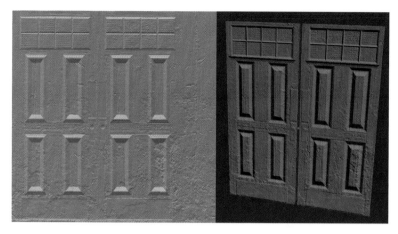

FIG 1.14 An example of a normal map.

Alpha map: An alpha map is a gray scale or black-and-white texture which controls the transparency on a surface. Black pixels appear transparent (or see-through) and white pixels appear opaque (or solid color). Common uses for alpha maps in games are leaves and foliage, wire mesh fencing, glass, cloth, decals, and particles. The example here is a small plant.

Alpha Map

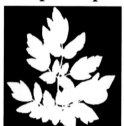

Diffuse Map

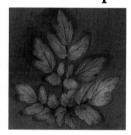

Both on model

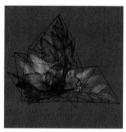

FIG 1.15 An example of an alpha map.

Shader: A shader or material in 3D is what we input all these textures into and then it's applied to a model. A basic explanation for a shader is that it is a set of instructions for the GPU (general processing unit) or a mini program for the software telling it how to render a surface. Shaders can have a lot of parameters that we can adjust further to increase the effects of the assigned texture maps. We'll be using 3ds Max's material editors later in the book.

Types of Texture Layouts

The space where we will layout our texture, the *edit UVWs* window has three axes just as the viewport does. They are referred to as UVW rather than XYZ. The *U*- and *V*-axes correspond to the *X*- and *Y*-axes. The *W*-axis corresponds to the *Z*-axis and is generally used for procedural maps. For now, we'll be referring to the *U*- and *V*-axes.

Tiling Texture

A tiling texture is one that is seamless and can be repeated across a surface. It needs to be seamless in at least one or both of the *U*- and *V*-axes to work. The following image shows the different directions a tiling texture can tile in.

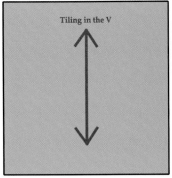
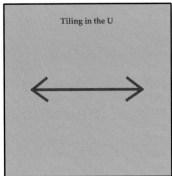
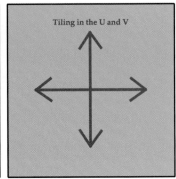

FIG 1.16

Tiling textures are commonly used in games to cover large surfaces or surfaces that do not require any unique details such as the ground, brick walls, or landscape. Here are some examples.

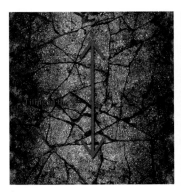
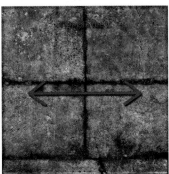
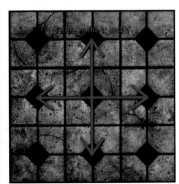

FIG 1.17

Unique Texture

A unique texture is one that contains no tiling elements but many uniquely unwrapped UV shells laid out into the UV space. This type of map is commonly used for objects that require specific details or characters. Figure 1.18 is an example of a unique texture layout.

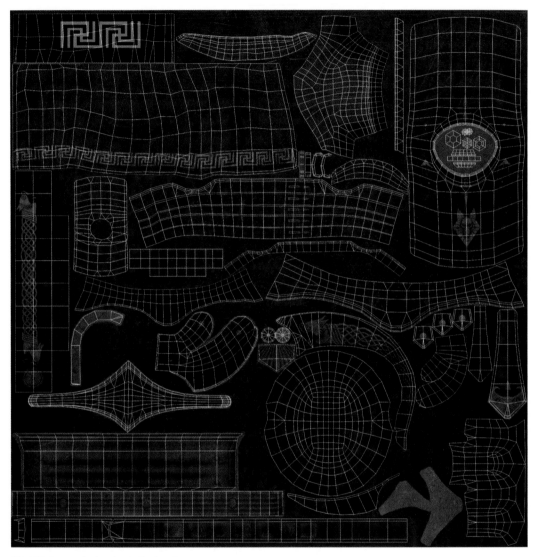

FIG 1.18 An example of a unique texture layout.

A Unique Texture with Tiling Elements

This type of texture layout utilizes both tiling elements which need to tile in at least one axis and uniquely unwrapped elements all laid out in the texture sheet. The following example has three strips running along the bottom of the texture sheet tiling in the *U*-axis. The top half of the texture is made up of several uniquely unwrapped elements.

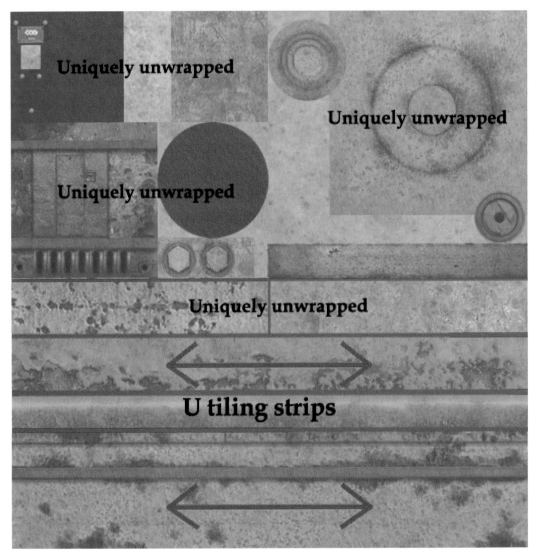

Uniquely unwrapped

Uniquely unwrapped

Uniquely unwrapped

Uniquely unwrapped

U tiling strips

FIG 1.19

Think about how you will create your own texture pages in the future using these techniques.

This concludes our brief introduction to the most common terms used when creating art for video games. There are many more things to learn, and we will be dealing with some of these later in the book. It's now time to start making some objects, so let's move on to Chapter 2.

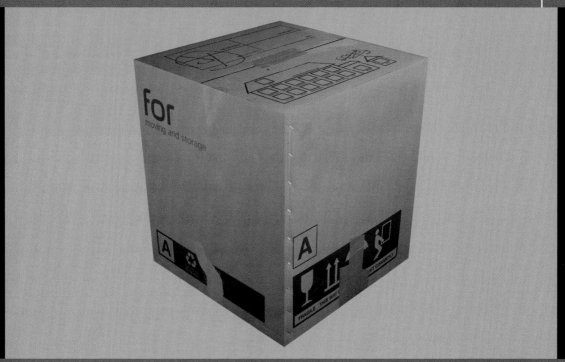

Creating, Unwrapping, and Texturing Simple Models

Model 1—Cardboard Box

For our first model, we're going to create a box. Go to the Main Menu > Create
> Standard Primitives > Box.

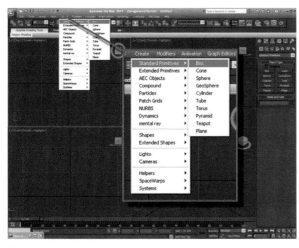

FIG 2.1

3ds Max Modeling for Games

17

Left-click and drag in the viewport to create the box. Click again to finish. Now set the dimensions to 45 × 45 × 50 in the modify panel to the right. If your box is being displayed in wireframe in any of your viewports, just click on the viewport and press the F3 key.

You can also create primitives from the create panel to the right. Ensure standard primitives appear in the drop-down box. Then choose box from the object type panel and left-click and drag in the viewport to create the box the same way as in the previous method.

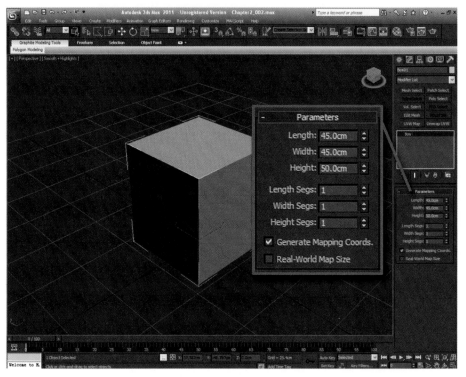

FIG 2.2

With the box selected, right-click it and select Convert to Editable Mesh from the Quad Menu.

Now you need to save your progress. Always name your files with a relevant name to make it easier to find your assets later on. As this is the first save file, we'll create a few folders to store all the files that you'll be working on while using this book. Go to save the file (File > Save as …), create a folder called 3D Modeling for Games, then create another folder inside the one you've just created called Chapter 1. Now save your file as Cardboard box1.max or Chapter1_001.max.

We have completed the modeling part of this tutorial. Now we have to apply the texture maps to the faces of the box and our first asset will be complete.

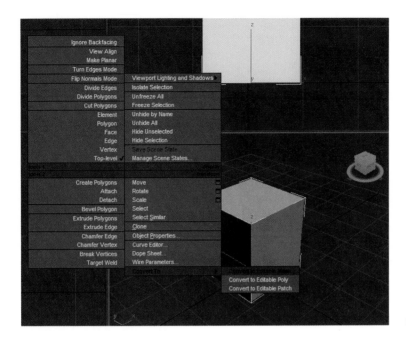

FIG 2.3

3ds Max Shortcuts

There are a few viewport configurations to help you to speed up the mapping of the box. Go to Modify, click the Configure Modifier Sets button, and select Show Buttons from the menu as shown in Fig. 2.4. Then select Configure Modifier Sets (Fig. 2.5).

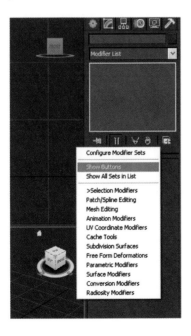

FIG 2.4

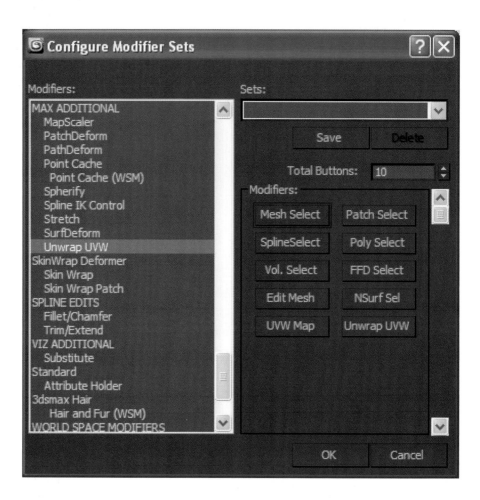

FIG 2.5

This action displays a set of buttons beneath the Modifier List rollout menu that can be configured to have all your most often used modifiers. Set the Total Buttons value to 10 and add Edit Mesh, UVW Map, and Unwrap UVW to the buttons, as we will use these modifiers the most in the first few chapters of the book. Do this by finding the modifier on the alphabetized list and drag it onto the button. To find a modifier on the list easily, just keep typing the first letter of it on the keyboard and you will cycle through all the modifiers with that letter (e.g., press "E" for Edit Mesh). Then click OK to close the Configure Modifier Sets window.

Texture-Mapping Your Box

With your box still selected, go to Selection section of the modify panel and click Element, and select the box. This should highlight all the faces (press F2 to toggle the highlighted selection).

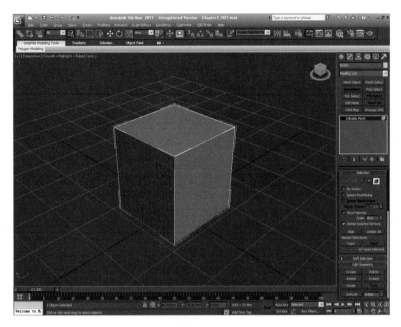

FIG 2.6

Now click UVW Map from your newly created modifier set and check Box Mapping from the Parameters menu.

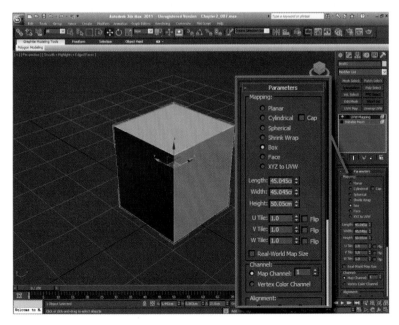

FIG 2.7

Next, right-click UVW Map in the Modifier stack and select Collapse All from the pop-up menu, then click Yes; you want to continue at the prompt, as we don't need to preserve the stack in this instance.

With your box still selected, click on the Material Editor (on the top toolbar or press "M") and change the standard material to a multi-sub object material as shown in Fig. 2.8, and click OK to discard the old material. If you keep the old material by accident, don't worry; it doesn't matter either way in this instance, as we are creating new ones.

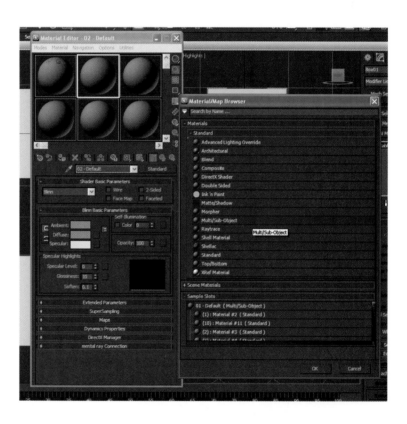

FIG 2.8

To keep this tutorial simple, I have already prepared the texture maps that you'll be using from photographs. Later on in the book, we will discuss creating textures from photographs and applying them to models.

To add the textures into the Material Editor, select the material ID from the vertical list and load in the texture map for each side of the box. Although there are 10 materials displayed in the editor, we'll just use the first six listed: Material #2 through Material #7 in my case. Yours could have different names, depending on how you have used 3ds Max previously. Don't worry if your names don't match mine at this point, as they can be renamed.

Click on the first material in the list, next to ID 1 (Material #2 in my case) and assign a Bitmap material to it. To do this, first click on the Sub-Material (Fig. 2.9), click the small square button to the right of "diffuse" in Blinn Basic Parameters (Fig. 2.10), select Bitmap from the top of the pop-up menu (Fig. 2.11), and click OK.

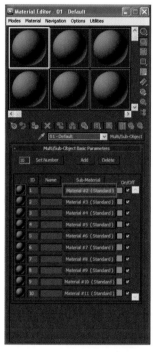

FIG 2.9

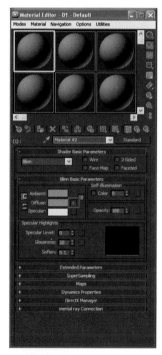

FIG 2.10

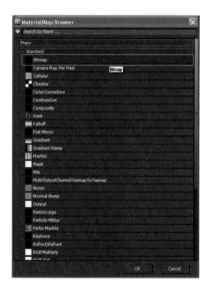

FIG 2.11

Now load Box1_top.jpg from \Chapter 1\Textures\ from the download area on the Web site. Please refer to the introduction in this book for full instructions, or go to www.3d-for-games.com, click on the Books and Media tab, and then click on *3ds Max Modeling for Games 2nd Edition* and the downloads for each chapter will be in yellow at the bottom of the page.

There are two ways to assign the next material to ID 2. The first way is to click on the Go to Parent button (Fig. 2.11a), and then select the second material in the list or click on the Go Forward to Sibling button (Fig. 2.11b), which will go straight to the Blinn Basic Parameters of the next material.

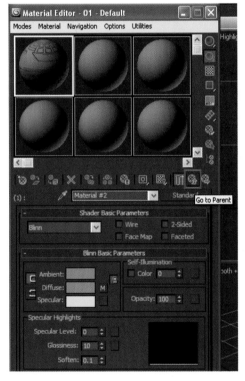

FIG 2.11a

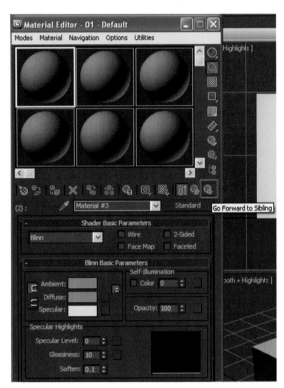

FIG 2.11b

Then repeat the process of clicking the small square button to the right of "diffuse" and selecting Bitmap from the top of the pop-up menu, and clicking OK.

As you assign each material a texture map, click the Show Standard Map in Viewport button (⚙) so that when you Assign Material to Selection, the textures are visible on the object.

Repeat this process for ID 2 through ID 6, loading the remaining five texture maps into the Material Editor and ending with Box1_base.jpg being assigned to ID 6.

Here's how they should be assigned:

> ID 1 — Material #2 — Box1_top.jpg
> ID 2 — Material #3 — Box1_sid1.jpg
> ID 3 — Material #4 — Box1_ sid2.jpg
> ID 4 — Material #5 — Box1_ sid3.jpg
> ID 5 — Material #6 — Box1_ sid4.jpg
> ID 6 — Material #7 — Box1_base.jpg

Remember that your Material number may differ from the numbers I have. As long as you match the ID (number)—for example, ID 1 goes with the corresponding texture map, in this case Box1_top.jpg—you'll be okay. Also *make sure* that you remember to select Show Standard Map in Viewport 🔳.

Now that we have assigned texture maps to all of the materials, we will apply the material set to the box and apply the material IDs to the faces of the box, allowing us to see the texture maps.

With the box still selected as an editable mesh, click the Assign Material to Selection button to assign the material set that you've just set up to the box you're mapping (Fig. 2.12). At this point, you should see that a lot of the box's faces now have texture maps on them. These currently correspond to the default face IDs, which are not necessarily the ones we want, so let's go through and check each face of the cube individually to make sure that the correct texture map is applied to the correct face on the box.

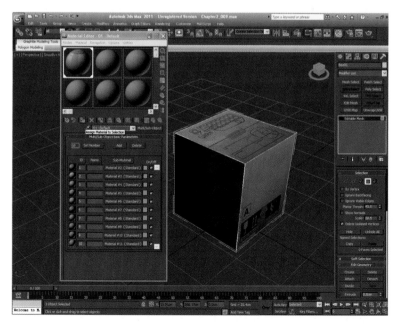

FIG 2.12

For this model, we must do this carefully, as some of the packaging tape on the box wraps around onto the adjacent faces. Look out for mistakes when you complete the model.

To get the correct map onto the correct face, first select the face of the box that is on the top of the box in the Perspective viewport. Go to Selection and select Polygon. Scroll down from selection until you get to the Surface Properties rollout box and in Material, make sure that Set ID is set to 1.

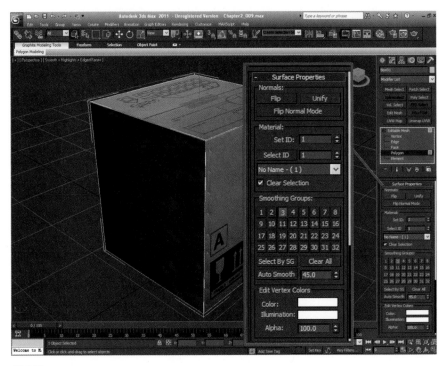

FIG 2.13

In the Perspective view, select the polygon on the left-hand side and assign the ID to 4. Depending on how the box mapping oriented each of the box's faces when we mapped it, the texture map may not be oriented the correct way. If this is the case, we'll need to modify the UVW Mapping co-ordinates to correct it.

From the Modifier List, click the button Unwrap UVW, which adds the Unwrap UVW modifier to the modifier stack (Fig. 2.14). Below the modifier stack, adjust the vertical scrolling menu until you find Parameters. Once you have found the Parameters section, click Edit. The Edit UVW window will pop open.

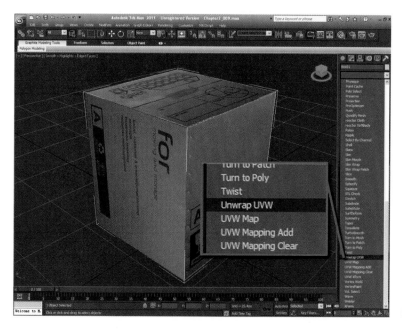

FIG 2.14

From the pull-down menu at the top right of the new Edit UVW window, click on the rollout, and select Map#1 (Box1_side1.jpg).

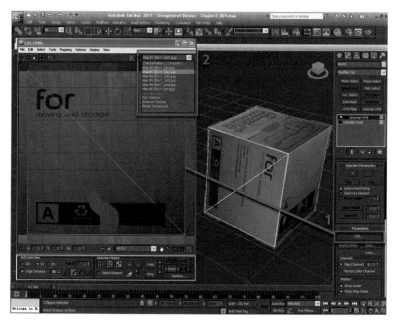

FIG 2.15

Now we need to select all of the vertices (left-click, drag bounding box around all vertices, then release the left mouse button). You'll know if you've selected them all as they all change to a red color.

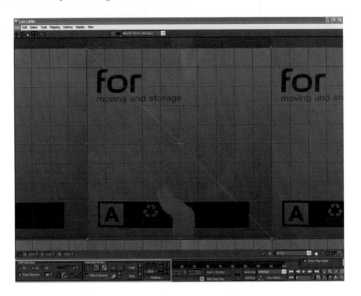

FIG 2.16

Now we need to rotate all the vertices to the correct orientation on the cardboard box, but first press the "A" key on the keyboard to activate the angle snap shortcut. We rotate the vertices (select Rotate at the top left of the Edit UVW window) until the text on the texture map is the right way up on the cardboard box model in the viewport.

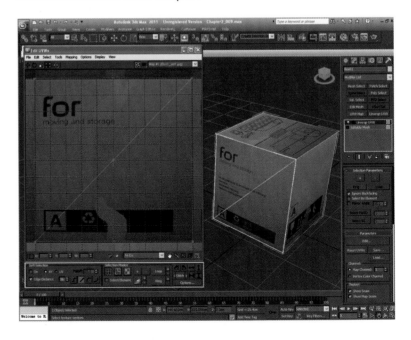

FIG 2.17

There are a few options that I like to set to help me see the map more clearly when doing this type of mapping. At the bottom right-hand corner of the Edit UVW window, click Options. This step brings up some extra settings for editing the UVWs. Uncheck Tile Bitmap and set Brightness to 1, which is useful in that it will help you see the texture sheet a lot more clearly. This option can also be set from the top menu, by selecting Options > Preferences (Ctrl + 1 + O) and adjusting it in the Display Preferences menu.

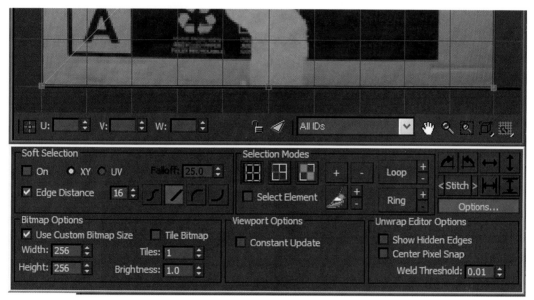

FIG 2.18

Next, right-click Unwrap UVW in the modifier stack and select Collapse All, then select Yes, to clear the stack.

Now we'll continue mapping the rest of the cardboard box. Left-click on Editable Mesh in the Modifier Stack and press the "4" key on the keyboard, which is the shortcut for Select Polygon.

Other useful shortcuts of this type are as follows:

1 Select Vertex, 2 Select Edge, 3 Select Face, 4 Select Polygon, and 5 Select Element.

With Edit Polygon selected, select the other visible front polygon in the Perspective view, repeat the mapping and unwrapping procedure on the second side that you can see in the Perspective viewport, but this time, set the ID of the face of the box to ID 3.

To see what you are doing more clearly in each of the viewports, right-click on the name of the viewport and select Smooth and Highlights from the pop-up window.

On this occasion, the second box side texture map on my model is the correct way up, so there is no need for me to unwrap the UVs. If yours doesn't match this, repeat the previous process.

To help you to see the model more clearly while in the Perspective view, click on the Maximize Viewport Toggle (bottom right of interface). Now click on Arc Rotate Selected (to the left of the Maximize Viewport Toggle) and rotate the object so that you can clearly see the rear two sides of the cardboard box. You can also close the Material Editor or minimize it for a good look at all sides too. Feel free to have a play with the new floating controllers (in the top right) of each viewport to change your view, too.

Select the polygon on the left and assign it ID 2. If the texture map is not orientated correctly, quickly correct it by following the mapping procedure from mapping the first side of the box (Unwrap UVW, Edit, Select Map#2 box_sid1.jpg, select vertices, rotate to correct orientation).

Collapse the stack again, press "4," and select the fourth side to map. This time, set the ID to 5 and adjust the UVW Mapping, if necessary, so that it matches the example.

Finally, rotate the Perspective view (Arc Rotate Selected button) and select the bottom polygon of the cardboard box. Set the ID to 6 and adjust the mapping, if necessary. On this side of the box, pay close attention to the packaging tape on the texture map and make sure that it lines up correctly with the tape wrapping around onto the sides of the box. Once you're happy with it, that's it—you're done.

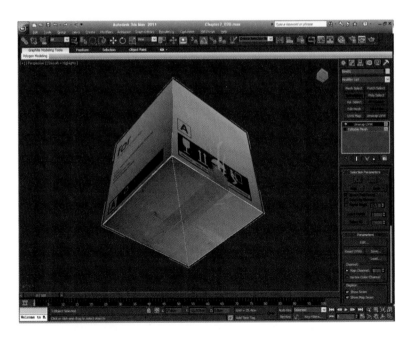

FIG 2.19

Common Problems

When building assets like this one, always make sure that all of the texture maps are the same size and resolution. Differences in resolution have a massive impact on the quality of your finished model, and even if the maps are supplied to you, always check their size and color depth to make sure that they match where they should.

With models containing patterns that wrap around the object, make sure that they line up correctly on all sides.

Rendering Your Model

To produce quick renders of your model for an object database or for a progress portfolio, first we need to set up the environment.

At the top of the screen, select Rendering then Environments and Effects from the drop-down menu, or alternatively press "8" for the shortcut.

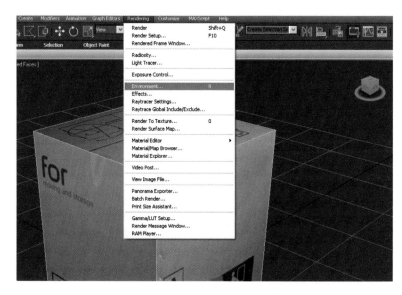

FIG 2.20

For this type of quick render, I usually set the Global Lighting Ambient to around 150, the Tint to approximately 200, with the intensity at 0.5, and the background color set to something neutral or close to white (around 230). In this case, as I'll be using the render just to put in a progress portfolio, I'll be using 230 for the background. It will help the object stand out and will be a lot less messy to print in color.

Once you're happy with the settings, close the Environment and Effects window, and rotate the viewport until you're satisfied that the view is showing off the best of the model. I like the detail in the cardboard on the top of the box, and I also like the staple details with the rips on the sides, so they will be most prominent in my render.

Go to Rendering > Render Setup or type F10 as a shortcut, opening up the parameters for the scanline renderer. In Output Size, click the 800 × 600 button, and click the Render button (bottom right of parameters pop-up). You should now have a render of your cardboard box. If you want a render that is of a slightly higher resolution, instead of clicking the 800 × 600 button, click the Image Aspect lock button and type in 1920 (or whatever size you like) and press Return and then the render button. You can render images at any size you like.

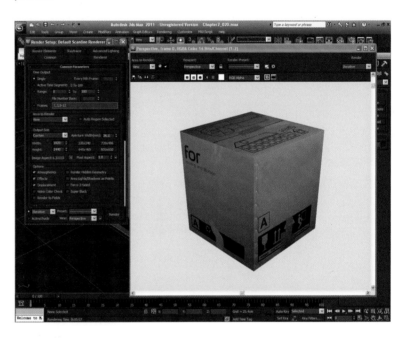

FIG 2.21

Try adjusting the Ambient Light, Tint, and Background color settings until you render an image that you're happy with. But keep the render nice and clean if it's for a portfolio. You can always add it to a themed style sheet in Photoshop for your final portfolio later. Keeping it clean will enable you make any style changes later on a lot more easily.

Congratulations on getting to the end of this build. If your final model is slightly different to mine, don't worry too much, as long as you understand the process, and that's the main point.

If you didn't quite manage to understand everything, or if you have any questions, just log onto www.3d-for-games.com/form, and we'll answer your questions as soon as you've registered and logged in. Start by saying hello in the welcome thread, and then post up your questions in the support thread.

Model 2—Creating a Plastic Barrel

Ok, so hopefully you've managed to complete the cardboard box tutorial in part 1 without encountering any problems.

If you skipped the tutorial, try to at least flick through it so that you know what we've covered just in case we've mentioned something we don't go back to again.

As we have so much great content to cram in this one book, we'll really try not to repeat things, so that you get the absolute best value for your money. Because of this, I advise you to complete the tutorials in order so that you don't miss anything; even if you know what you are doing, at least skim read them as there could be something important that you miss, which could cause problems for you later on.

Ok, let's move on with the modeling.

This time, we will be creating another primitive object and using a lot of different actions, including Editable Poly, Select and Uniform Scale, loading background images, keyboard shortcuts, object properties (See-Through and Backface Cull), Boolean (Cut & Union), deleting faces, and Target Weld for vertices.

For this tutorial, we will use some reference photos. These photos have already been provided for you and can be downloaded from the Web site. Please refer to the introduction of the book for details on how to get these.

To build this model, we will be doing slightly more modeling than the first tutorial and a little more complex mapping; but don't worry, we'll guide you through this, step by step.

We will use the reference photos as a guide to model from, and we will use them again to create the texture map.

First, open up 3ds Max and start with a new scene (File > New, select the New All, and click OK). The first thing we need to do is load the first photo into 3ds Max to use as a guide. To do this, while you're in the Top viewport, press Alt + B to import a background image.

Make sure that you check the options Match Bitmap, Display Background, and Lock Zoom/Pan. From the chapter files, open **Img_0301.jpg** from **Chapter2\ CH002_Textures**, and then click OK. You could also create a flat plane of polygons and map the image to it for reference if you prefer.

You should now see the photograph of the top of a dirty plastic barrel in your Top viewport. Go to Create > Geometry, make sure that Standard Primitives is selected, and click on Cylinder.

Then click in the Top viewport, approximately in the center of the barrel in the photo, and create a cylinder that is roughly the circumference of the barrel. Don't worry about the height at this point, as we will adjust it in a moment.

Next, set the parameters to 12 Sides and 3 Height Segments. Click Select and Rotate and rotate the cylinder so that the top and bottom edges are horizontal as shown in Fig. 2.23.

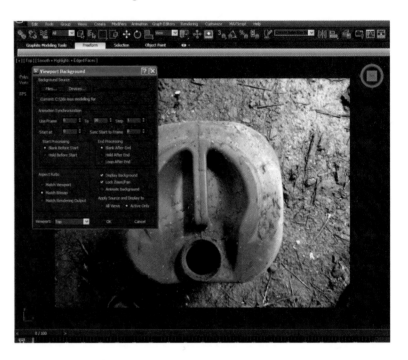

FIG 2.22

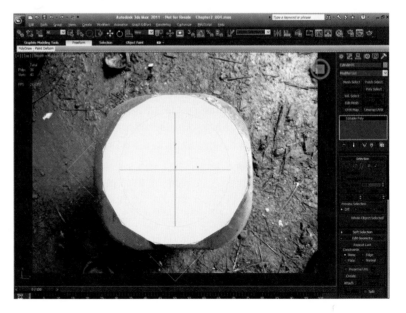

FIG 2.23

Now maximize the Top viewport (Alt + W) so that the top view is full-screen. Go to Modify and right-click on the cylinder and select Convert To: Editable Poly.

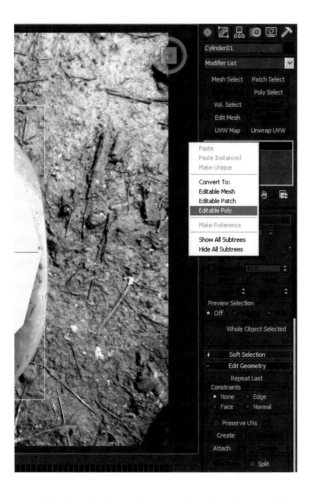

FIG 2.24

Feel free to modify the cylinder so that it matches the photograph more closely (as pictured in Fig. 2.25) using Select and Uniform Scale and Select and Move from the top toolbar.

Next click Editable Poly and select Vertex if it's not already selected. We need to make the cylinder slightly squarer to match the photo by selecting groups of vertices and moving them either horizontally or vertically.

The completed shape doesn't have to be perfect, so don't spend too much time getting the form right. I used Select and Uniform Scale and selected four groups of vertices at a time. When you're finished, the object should look roughly like Fig. 2.25.

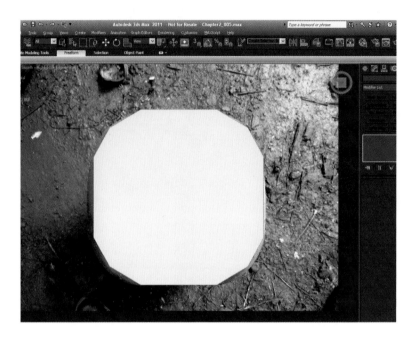

FIG 2.25

Click Alt + W again to reveal the other viewports and we'll open up another image to use as a guide. While still in the Top viewport, click Alt + B and uncheck Display Background (because we are finished with that image).

Next, right-click on the Front viewport and zoom out from the barrel using Zoom Extents (in the bottom-right corner) and the left mouse button. If you aren't sure what any of the buttons on the toolbar are, just hover your cursor over them for a second and a pop-up dialog box will tell you.

Now we've zoomed back from the image slightly, we need to import another background image (Alt + B).

Load in **Img_0300.jpg** from **\Chapter2\CH002_Textures**. This time, uncheck Lock Zoom/Pan and then click OK.

As this photograph was taken from a different angle to the model we're building, I've unchecked Lock Zoom/Pan to let me rotate the object and zoom in and out. This will allow me to set the right height for the cylinder, which we'll now call the "barrel."

Click Select and Rotate from the top toolbar and rotate the barrel 90°, so that it lies on its side. If angle snap is off, turn it on (by pressing the A key) before starting to rotate the barrel.

You should be left with something that looks like Fig. 2.26.

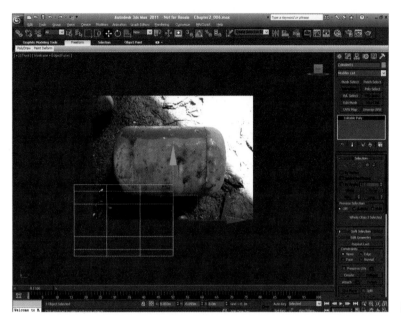

FIG 2.26

Using Select and Move, as well as Select and Uniform Scale, move the barrel over the photograph and set the height of it, so that it matches ours.

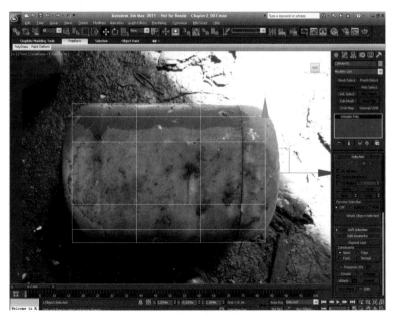

FIG 2.27

We have the basic dimensions of the barrel; we can start to model the details and make it look a bit more realistic.

As this is a low-poly object, we won't be adding lots of details—just enough to round off the edges, and we'll add the handle shape on the top. The rest of the detail will come from the texture map.

We need to create the slight curves to the top and bottom of the barrel.

To do this, we will scale the center vertices on the *x*-axis. Click Editable Poly, go back to the Front viewport, and drag-select the center vertices. Click Select and Uniform Scale and drag them out so that they look something like Fig. 2.28.

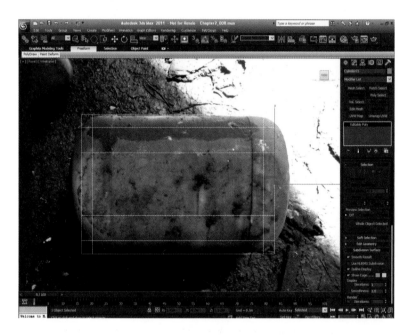

FIG 2.28

Click Editable Poly again to turn it off. Click Select and Rotate and rotate the barrel back 90° into the upright position that it was in earlier. Then click Alt + B and turn off Display Background. Finally, click Zoom Extents All (Shift + Ctrl + Z).

If you like, you can click in each viewport, and click F3 to toggle Wifeframe/ Smooth + Highlight and also click F4 to toggle View Edged Faces, so that you can see the work you've completed so far, more clearly.

For details on the other shortcuts on the F (function) keys and all the preset shortcuts in 3ds Max, go to Customize > Customize User Interface and scroll down the list to see what the default hotkeys are.

You can also assign your own here, but remember, if you make any changes, save the settings.

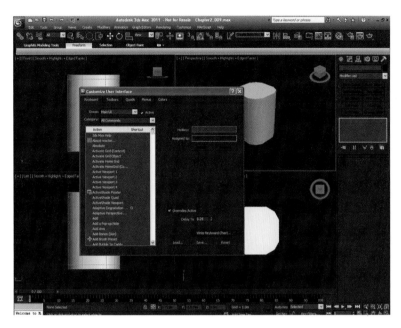

FIG 2.29

Ok, let's continue with the model.

In the Front viewport, type 1. This selects Vertex in Editable Poly (try pressing the keys 2, 3, 4, and 5, one at a time, to see how these work as shortcuts). Type Alt + W and then drag-select all of the very top row of vertices, and then Ctrl + drag-select the very bottom row of vertices. Click T for Top viewport, and click Z for Zoom Extents.

Click Select and Uniform Scale and scale the vertices in to give a slight bevel to the top and bottom of the barrel. If you drag toward the center of the barrel when scaling, look at the co-ordinates at the bottom of the screen (just right of center). Drag until you hit 90%, which should look about right. Again, you don't have to be especially accurate on this.

Click F to go to the Front viewport and scale the same set of vertices a little on the y-axis until your barrel looks something like Fig. 2.30.

There are two ways we can go with the build at this point. We could leave the model as it is now and create a texture map for it, and call that complete (which would be reasonable for a low-poly object), or we can model some detail on the top. In this case, we'll model the detail on the top, as I want to show you a really cool tool called Boolean.

Type T to select the Top viewport, and then press F3 to see the wireframe of the barrel. Click Create > Standard Primitives > Cylinder and make sure that Height Segments is set to 1 and Sides is set to 12. Click in the center of the barrel and create a cylinder that is about half as wide as the barrel.

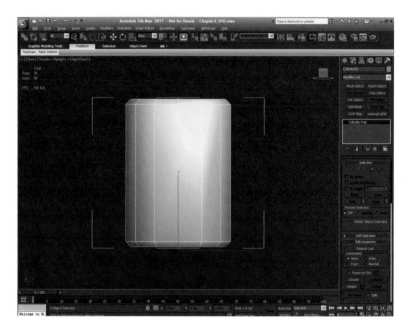

FIG 2.30

Type F for the Front viewport, and then press Shift + Ctrl + Z to Zoom Extents. You should now have the barrel and also a cylinder in the scene. Click Select and Move, and move the cylinder up so that it intersects with the top of the barrel.

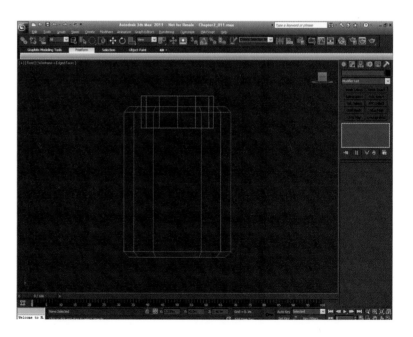

FIG 2.31

Remember to regularly save your work as you model. It's really easy to get swept away with the progress, and you can spend many hours on something—only to lose it all in a crash. Try to save regularly and have the autoback function set. We all usually only remember to save just as our computers crash, which is obviously too late.

Performing the Boolean

Let's move onto Boolean. Select the barrel and press P (for the Perspective viewport) and F3 if the meshes aren't Smooth and Highlight–shaded. Click Create, where Standard Primitives is displayed, click on the rollout menu, and select Compound Objects.

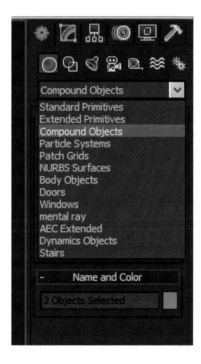

FIG 2.32

You should see Morph, Scatter, Conform, ShapeMerge, Boolean, and others. Boolean is a powerful tool and can be quite confusing until you get the hang of it. First, you need two objects; it works best with solid "closed meshes," that is, where there are no holes in the mesh.

These are called Operand A and Operand B. Think of these as Shape A and Shape B. There are four different types of Boolean in 3ds Max 2011—Union, Intersection, Subtraction, and Cut. If you search for "Boolean Compound Object" in the 3ds Max 2011 help (F1) or the InfoCenter, it explains what all these are in detail. It is well worth reading the explanation and then creating

41

two objects in a different file and playing with the different types to see what results you can get.

For this model, we will be using Cut. With the barrel still selected, click Cut from the Operation selection on the right of the workspace, then click Pick Operand B (choose the other shape), and then click to select the cylinder, as shown in Fig. 2.33.

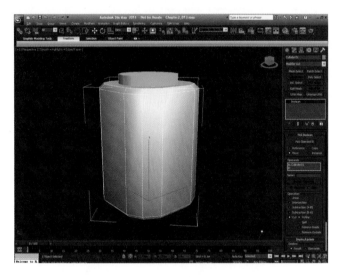

FIG 2.33

This step will cut the barrel with the shape of the cylinder, but leave you with a solid mesh.

To finish off the Boolean work, click on Modify, right-click on Boolean, and select Editable Mesh.

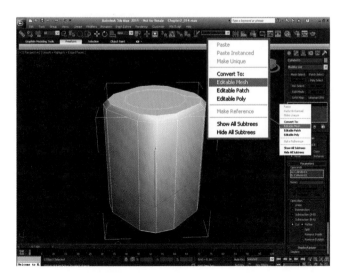

FIG 2.34

42

Fixing Your Mistakes

One of the most important parts of modeling something that you haven't modeled before is that you may not build it perfectly from start to finish, and you may have to modify your work. This approach can be a lot quicker than going back to a save file or (even worse) rebuilding something. If you've followed the tutorial accurately up to this point, you will have made a small mistake that was included deliberately on the last action. Before we performed the Boolean, it would have made progressing easier if we had rotated the cylinder that we were using to cut, so that the top and bottom edges were horizontal. Rather than going back to a previous save file, we'll just fix it at the polygon level.

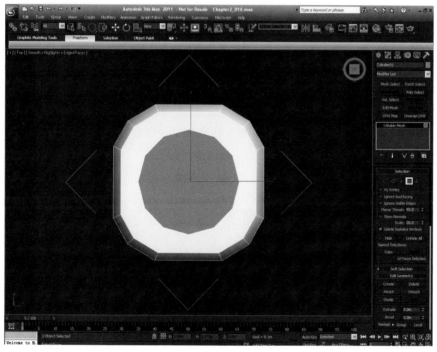

FIG 2.35

First, you need to be in the Top viewport. Make sure that the barrel is still selected and type 4 to go into polygon mode. To make sure that you have the center polygons selected, press F2 (Shade Selected Faces Toggle) to display what you've got selected. If you don't have a mouse with a scroll wheel, it's a good idea to get one, as the wheel can be used to zoom in and out of the scene.

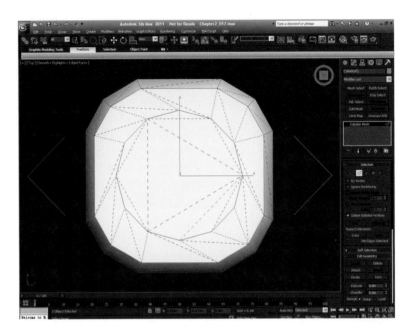

FIG 2.36

We need to rotate the polygons only a small amount, but looking at the barrel, it's impossible to see which way it should be. So we need to have a look at the edges of the polygons. Press 2 and drag-select the whole barrel. This step will show you where all the hidden edges are.

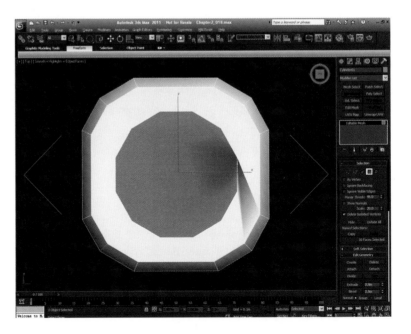

FIG 2.37

44

There are two ways to line the polygons up the way we want them. The first is to select just the edges we want to rotate and then rotate them, but the quicker way is to press 4, make sure the center polygons are selected, and rotate them making sure that angle snap (A) is on.

As you can see by the shadows that have appeared on the surface (smoothing), we have turned some of the polygons so that they now overlap. We just need to type 2 to modify the edges again and then select Turn from the Edit Geometry toolbar on the right.

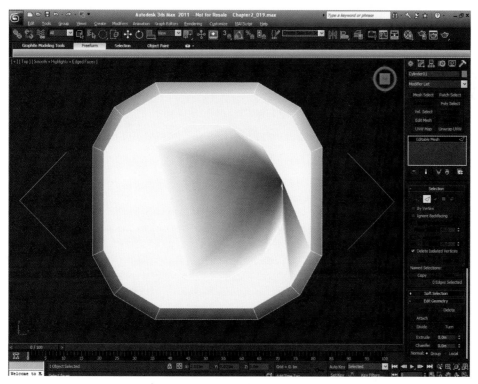

FIG 2.38

Then we just need to click on the edges that are cutting through the corners of the central circle of polygons on the top of the barrel, turning them so that the polygons no longer overlap. If you see any other particularly long and thin triangles, you might want to turn the edges of those too, to tidy up the mesh.

Next, we will add the final details to the top of the barrel. First, let's extrude the center polygons to create the dip in the top of the barrel; then, we'll create a simple handle form.

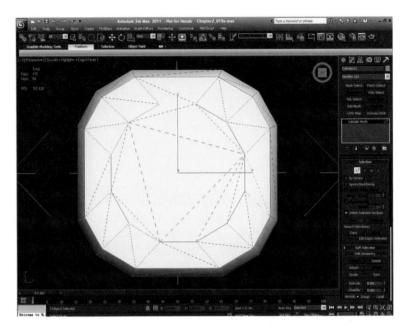

FIG 2.39

Press P to jump into the Perspective window, and then press Z (Zoom Extents) so that you can see what you're doing. Buttons like Zoom Extents (Z) have a small triangle in the corner to show that they have multiple options. Left-click and hold on the triangle and the various options will be made available. In this case, there are two options: Zoom Extents and Zoom Extents Selected. I usually prefer Zoom Extents Selected, as it zooms into the selected part of the model only, usually making it easier to work. Have a look at all the other buttons and get familiar with what they do—getting up to speed with these early will save you a lot of time.

Next we need to extrude the top center polygons to create the sunken form of the top of the barrel. Still in Editable mesh, select Extrude from Edit Geometry, then click on the center polygons (select them if they have been unselected), and drag the mouse toward yourself. This will create the extrusion. Obviously, if you had clicked and pushed forward when extruding, you would have created the same form, but as an addition to the geometry rather than a subtraction. Next, just scale the polygons to create the indentation on the top.

Now, we need to create a handle. We'll use Boolean again, as it's nice and quick.

From the Top viewport, create a new cylinder in the center of the barrel. Give it eight sides and one height segment, and rotate it so that the top and bottom edges are horizontal. Then convert it to an Editable Mesh and scale it to the rough shape of a handle.

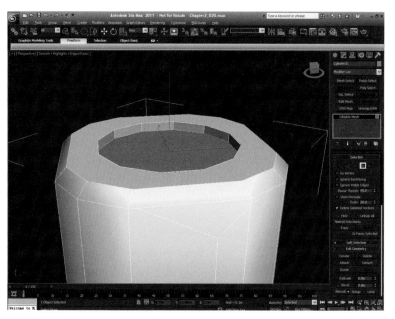

FIG 2.40

Make sure that the handle shape intersects with the barrel shape, as we will be using Union, but also that it stays in the center of the barrel and doesn't overlap the sloped edges of the indent. Just before performing the Boolean, select the barrel instead of the handle.

As before, select Create, Compound Objects, Boolean and make sure that Union is selected, click Pick Operand B, and then click to select the handle. Don't worry if the barrel suddenly changes color. It is just picking up the material from the cylinder (meaning that you didn't select the barrel before picking the handle as the Operand B). If this happened, just undo and try again. As we'll be texture-mapping the barrel, the color of the base material doesn't matter, but you may pick up some properties from the handle that could affect the way we map the barrel, so make sure you have the barrel selected before you click Operand B.

As we left a small gap between the handle and the edge of the barrel on the top of the barrel, let's join that up next. First select Modify, and then right-click Boolean and convert to Editable Mesh.

As we're not sure what the Boolean has done to the mesh, let's have a look by going to Edge select (press 2) and drag-selecting all the edges on the top of the barrel (or using Ctrl + A). As you can see, there are a few of really thin polygons around where we join the handle and the barrel together, so let's clean them up by selecting Edit Geometry and Turn. We'll turn each of the long edges until we get something that looks like Fig. 2.42.

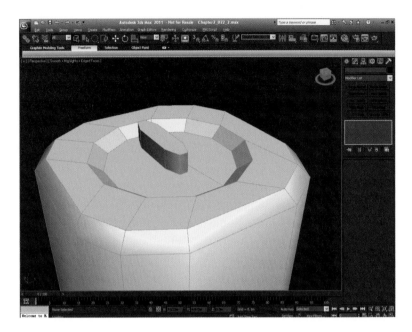

FIG 2.41

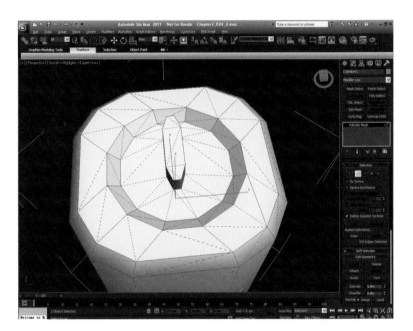

FIG 2.42

Remember to confirm that Ignore Backfacing is selected so that you don't accidentally turn edges on the back of the object by mistake. Errors like this can be quite time-consuming to fix if they go unnoticed—as you won't really want to use Undo if you've done a lot of modeling. Extra care should also be taken when welding vertices, as the errors can be difficult to undo if unnoticed.

Now we're going to weld a couple of vertices to make the handle look a little more realistic and like the reference.

First, select Edit from the main toolbar at the top of the screen and select Object Properties to open a pop-up box. In Display Properties, check Backface Cull, and click OK. By checking Backface Cull, all the polygons will be displayed only as one-sided. Next, we need to delete a few polygons and weld the vertices to fill the hole. If you weld the vertices first, you may unknowingly create some inner-facing polygons. Not only will these affect the smoothing on the object, but they can also make some of the UVW unwrapping confusing.

Now let's delete the unwanted polygons. Rotate the barrel until you can clearly see the far side of the handle. Now we're looking to delete the three polygons that make up the join between the handle and the edge of the barrel. Type 3 to select Face Selection and make sure that you can see which faces you have selected. Select the six faces, and click Del to delete them.

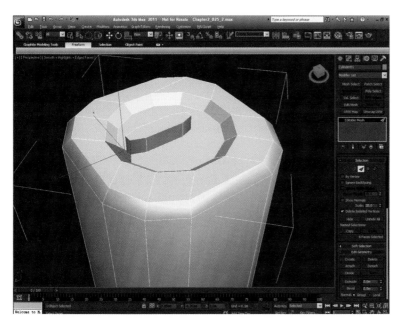

FIG 2.43

Next, we need to fill the gap by target-welding the vertices. Hit 1 to go to Vertex selection and select Target from the Weld menu. Select the vertices on the open edge of the handle and drag them onto the vertices of the edge of the barrel.

If the vertices seem to be sliding on a single axis, press F8 and then try again. You should now be able to move the vertices on multiple axes. Even without clicking F8, if you were to drag the cursor onto the correct vertex to weld, it would still have done it correctly. If you rotate the barrel around, enabling you to see the back of the handle to complete the weld accurately, you should end up with a shape as shown in Fig. 2.44.

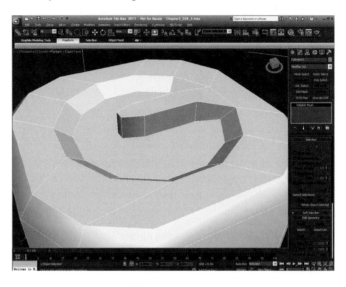

FIG 2.44

Now that we have the basic form of the top of the barrel, we need to compare it with the reference photo again and manipulate the top vertices so that they match the photo. Type T for Top viewport, and then press Alt + B to load up the background image. Select **Img_0301.jpg \Chapter2\CH002_Textures** and select Lock/Zoom Pan and Display Background, and click OK.

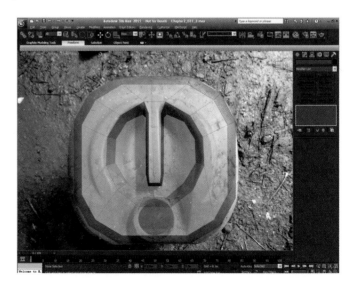

FIG 2.45

There are a couple of different ways in which we can manipulate the model and still see the reference photo. One is by pressing F3 to toggle wireframes, and the other is to set the image so that it is see-through.

With the object selected, right-click on it to open up the Options fly-out. In Transform (bottom right), select Object Properties, select See-Through from the Display Properties, and click OK.

This option changes the look of the object, enabling you to see both the polygons, as well as the reference photo behind it. Now we just need to match up the vertices with the photo using Select and Move and also Select and Uniform Scale. To accurately select the lower vertices to taper the handle, jump into Perspective view and select them individually before returning to the Top viewport to spread them out.

The last part of modeling that we need to complete before we start texture-mapping is the flattened area around the spout. In the Front viewport (shortcut F), make sure that the top of the handle is flush with the top of the barrel and that the vertices are laid out similar to Fig. 2.45.

Press F3 and rotate the barrel slightly forward. Select the two edges on the top of the barrel nearest to you and move them down so that they are level with the indent on the top of the barrel. Once we've selected the edges, we need to jump back to the Front view (shortcut F) so that we can see how far we need to move them down. Hit F3 to make this easier. Moving these edges down has highlighted how a few of the edges need to be turned so that the curves on the barrel look more realistic.

Press F2 and then Ctrl + A to display all the edges. Have a look to see whether you can improve some of the curves by turning edges. This isn't important; it just improves the form of the model when viewed from some acute angles.

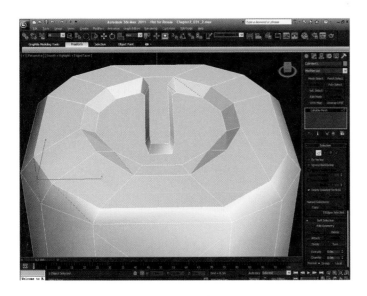

FIG 2.46

Creating the Texture for the Barrel

There are a few different ways to create texture maps for models like this, but I'll show you the method that I think is most appropriate for this exercise.

First of all, we need to think about how the barrel texture can be laid out or unwrapped. We want to represent the key components of the photos, and we want the barrel to look as realistic as possible when we finish.

For this model, I think that there should be three main parts to the texture map: the top, the bottom, and the sides.

To make the model look realistic when it is mapped, we want as few joins on the texture map as possible, as all of the edges on this model are rounded. If we were modeling an asset like the cardboard box again, this issue wouldn't matter, as the joins on each of the sides are hidden by the corners and also by the smoothing groups. But for this model, we'll need to treat the edges differently.

Although the barrel shape has flat sides, its corners are rounded, so in this instance, we should consider mapping the sides with cylindrical mapping. This means that the texture for this part of the model needs to "tile" (that is, to wrap seamlessly around the model).

With this in mind, we will dedicate most of the texture page to the sides, but we'll also make sure that it covers the top area of the texture completely (from left to right) so that we can use the Offset tool in Photoshop. This approach will enable us to tile the texture and thus to seamlessly map all the sides on the barrel.

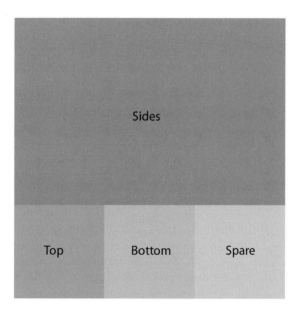

Sides

Top   Bottom   Spare

FIG 2.47

To keep the texture resolution roughly even across the model, allow the top and bottom of the barrel around 30% of the height of the texture page as shown in Fig. 2.47.

Dividing up the texture map in this way should give us plenty of room for the top and bottom details and also enable us to tile the side's part of the map easily in Photoshop. It does, however, leave us a small area spare. We can use this for any extra details that we haven't thought of yet, or maybe a label or some other feature not on the source photo. Dividing up the texture page, in this way, will mean that we will not be using each side of the barrel directly from the photograph.

As texture pages need to be either square (512×512) or divisible by two (1024×512), we would have to cram and stretch the four sides of the barrel into this area, which wouldn't really work, as it would cause distortions.

A texture that is divisible by two could be used, which would give us plenty of room for the four sides and the top and bottom, but again we would still be stretching the photo reference to use the texture page efficiently, so we will opt for the first layout, as it is closer to the reference.

Obviously, if you never intend to put your texture maps into a game engine, you could make them any size or shape you like. The best way to do this is to model your barrel, then take screen grabs or wireframe renders of the front, sides, top, and bottom, and use them as a guide for your map. There are also other plug-ins and tools that help, but these are the simplest methods to get you started.

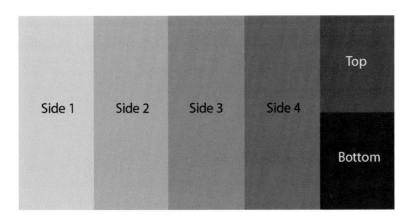

FIG 2.48

Let's get started with the texture map creation. First, open up the reference photos from the project files **Chapter2\CH002_Textures** and paste the components that you'd like to see on your texture map into a new Photoshop file. Once you have the main components for the sides, crop the image and save it out. Next, flatten the image by going to Layer > Flatten Image. This step should give you with a nice canvas to start to work on.

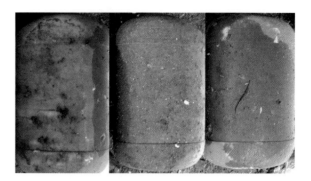

FIG 2.49

Next, use a combination of the Clone Stamp tool (shortcut S) and the Healing Brush tool (J) to cover up the parts of the texture map that we don't want. Start with the really dark areas and the lines that don't line up by replacing them with the more generic parts that we do want. If you have an older version of Photoshop, you'll probably just have the Clone Stamp tool. Don't worry—you'll do just fine using that.

If you haven't used these tools before, here are some basic instructions. Start by holding down Alt and left-clicking the area of the texture map that you want to clone from, then just left-click and hold to paint over the area that you want to change. Experiment with the opacity settings of the tools for varied effects.

One thing to watch out for when creating texture maps with these tools is not to repeat obvious areas of the texture. This sort of repetition really stands out and ruins the illusion of your model being real. Any bright spots or dark creases should only exist once or be completely removed. The horizontal lines around the barrel should be removed too, as we'll add these back in later.

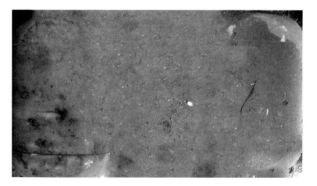

FIG 2.50

As you can see from this image, after only a few minutes of cloning and healing, the texture map is starting to take shape.

Continue this process until you have eliminated all the areas of the texture map that we don't need, and you have a fairly generic barrel texture. If the

Healing tool is taking a long time to calculate, just resize the image so that it is smaller and use slightly shorter brushstrokes; this should improve the update speed.

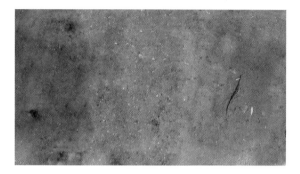

FIG 2.51

Let's next make sure that the image tiles. To do this, we use the Offset tool in Photoshop: Filter > Other > Offset and select an offset so that the join mark is roughly in the center of the image.

Use the same Heal and Clone tools to remove the join line down the center of the texture map. Once the join is removed, we can either leave the texture map as it is or offset it back to its original position. I always like to offset it back, but there's no need, as this texture map now tiles on the horizontal axis. Once finished, you should end up with something like Fig. 2.53.

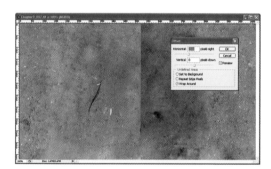

FIG 2.52

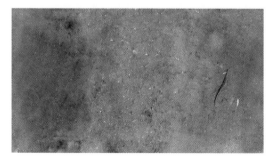

FIG 2.53

Now we need to add the other details of the texture map.

As we didn't create the first part of the texture page with any size considerations, let's do that next. We need to start to lay out the texture map so that the new components will be in the right place and at the right scale. We need to create a new image to lay out our map, so create a new file measuring 1024 × 1024 pixels.

Go to Edit > Preferences and set the rulers to measure in pixels, and then press Ctrl + R to show the rulers, if they are not already displayed. We next need to create a few guidelines to help us with the proportions of the rest of the texture. To do this, click on the ruler on the left-hand side of the image and drag a guide out to 341 pixels. Just drag it out to approximately 341 pixels and use the Move tool (V) along with the Zoom tool (Z) to make it accurate. Do this again from the left margin to 682 pixels and again from the top margin to 682 pixels. This should give you perfectly measured guidelines to fit the top and bottom of the barrel on the texture map.

Next, cut out the top and bottom of the barrel from the photo reference and lay them out in the gaps on the texture map.

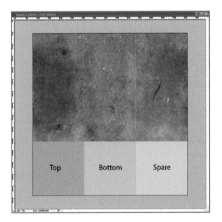

FIG 2.54

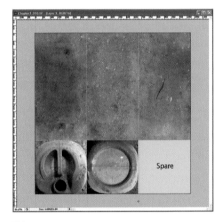

FIG 2.55

Then clone and heal the areas around the top and bottom of the barrel so that they blend into the surrounding area. You can adjust these joins once you have the texture mapped onto the model. We might make these areas slightly lighter or darker, depending on their corresponding edge on the model. We then fill in the blank space on the map with base texture or we can choose to leave it blank, so that we know there is some spare room on the texture map, should we come back to this model in the future to make changes or add details.

Finally, create a new layer and draw the dark and light lines across the sides to suggest that there is extra detail where there isn't—and our texture page is complete.

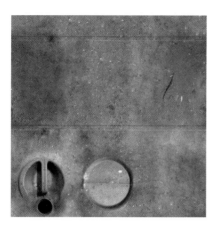

FIG 2.56

Texture-Mapping the Barrel

Now we need to move on to texture-mapping the barrel. First of all, let's get rid of the background image and return the barrel to solid shading (Alt + B, uncheck Display Background Image, click OK. Then right-click on the barrel, select Object Properties, uncheck See-Through, and click OK).

Next, we need to open up the Material Editor (on the top toolbar or click M). Then click the map button next to Diffuse in Blinn Basic Parameters. In Blinn Basic Parameters, click on the box next to Bitmap to load the texture and select Drum001_004.tif (Chapter2\CH002_Textures\), and click Open.

Next, click Assign Material to Selection; you should see the texture map applied to the barrel object.

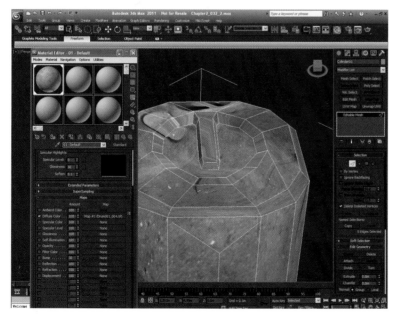

FIG 2.57

You can now close the Material Editor. At this point, although we have applied the texture map to the object, the only mapping co-ordinates on the barrel are from when you initially created it, so we need to apply new ones. We'll map the sides of the barrel first, and then we'll map the top and bottom.

Go to the Front viewport (F) and Zoom Extents so that you can see the whole barrel. If the top of the handle is sticking out above the barrel, select the vertices and drag them down so that they are level with the top of the barrel.

Select Editable Mesh if it isn't selected already, and then select Edit Polygon (shortcut 4). Drag-select all of the barrel's side faces, including the small bevels on the top and bottom. Take care not to select the extra polygons that make up the handle detail on the top.

Next, click UVW Map from the Modifier List, and check Cylindrical in Parameters > Mapping. On this model, we will try to wrap the top mapping over smoothly from the sides, so we also need to check Flip in the V Tile Mapping parameters. Press F3 and go to Perspective view to see what you have.

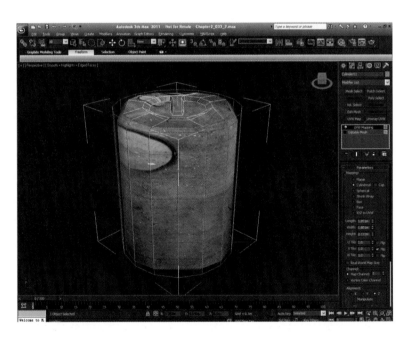

FIG 2.58

Although the mapping looks really rough and there seem to be parts of the barrel map everywhere, we should at least see the texture map wrapping continually around the sides of the cylinder.

Next, we're going to slightly rotate the mapping on the sides of the barrel so that the top and the sides line up. Rotate your view around the barrel so that the handle is pointing away from you, and then click on UVW Mapping in the modifier stack to select the sub-tree (which will turn yellow to indicate the mode change). Then choose Select and Rotate and rotate the mapping (not the model), until the handle on the map roughly lines up with the handle on the model (even though it is below it).

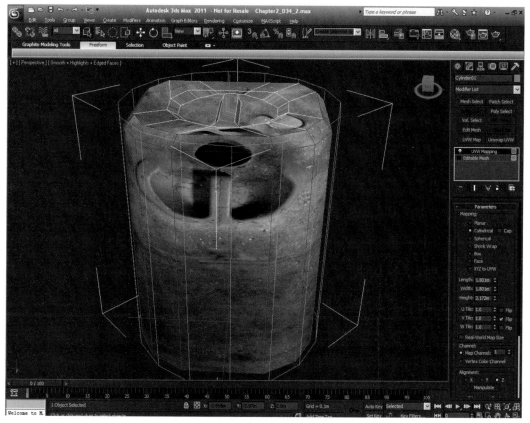

FIG 2.59

Next, we'll adjust the UVW co-ordinates so that the top and bottom details on the texture map are no longer seen on the sides of the barrel. Select Unwrap UVW from the Modifier List and then select Edit from the Parameters rollout. The Edit UVW box should appear on screen.

Now go to the top right-hand corner, open up the drop-down menu, and select the texture map, which is map #1 in the list. This step shows the texture map and also how the polygons are laid out on it.

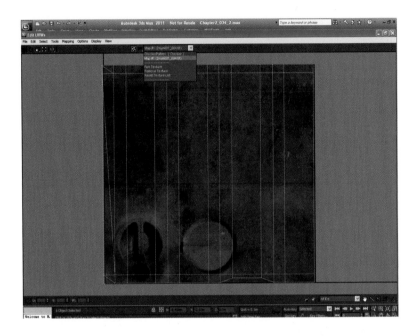

FIG 2.60

We now need to move some of the vertices around in the Edit UVW window so that the texture map fits our barrel model a little better. First select the bottom two rows of vertices in the window and move them vertically up just past the top details on the texture map. If you hold Shift down while you move them, they will move in a straight line up or across.

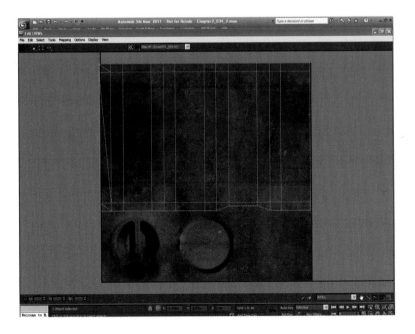

FIG 2.61

You can close the Edit UVW window now and have a look around your barrel. You should now see that the sides of the model are mapped. All we have to do is map the top and bottom, and we're pretty much done.

As the top and bottom mapping will be pretty much the same, we can use one planar map to apply mapping co-ordinates to both the top and bottom. We will then unwrap them separately, as we have just done.

Now we will add Edit Mesh to the stack from the Modifier List. Then press 4 to edit polygons and from the top menu choose Edit > Select Invert (Ctrl + I) to select all the remaining polygons to map. You should now have all the polygons on the top and bottom of the barrel selected.

We now need to go to Top viewport (shortcut T) and click UVW Map and make sure that Planar is selected in the Mapping Parameters.

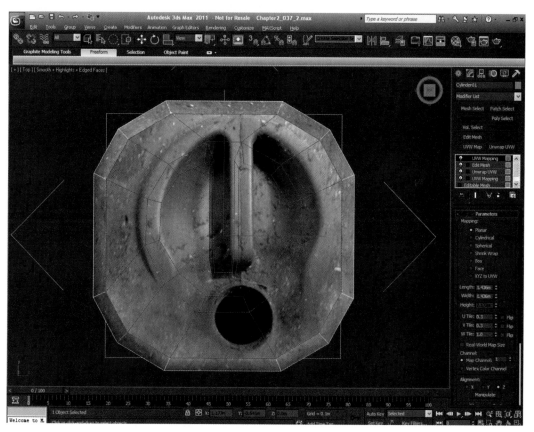

FIG 2.62

Scroll down the right-hand side to Alignment and select View Align. The texture map will be aligned to the Top viewport, not the model's transform. Select Fit (still in Alignment) so that the texture fits to the selected polygons only, with no overlap.

Finally, in mapping, as we know that the top and bottom only take a small amount of the texture page, we can set the U Tile to 0.3 and the V Tile to 0.3. This step makes unwrapping the UVs a bit easier, as they are now closer to their final position. You should now see the texture map for the top of the barrel almost aligned.

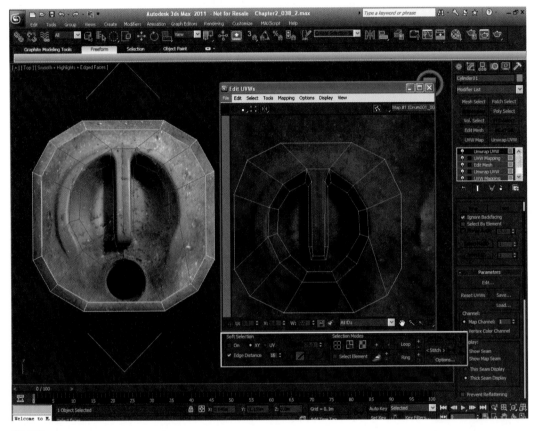

FIG 2.63

Select Unwrap UVW (from the Modifier List), and then select Edit and pick Map #1 from the drop-down menu in the Edit UVW window that appears. Using Zoom Region, we need to get in close to the vertices so that we can adjust the UVs accurately.

Click Ctrl + A to select all the vertices. Now we can scale them up so that they fit the rough shape of the barrel a little better. Don't worry too much about getting them pixel-perfect at this point; we can always fine tune them later.

We can now close the Edit UVW window and have a look at what we have so far. To really see what we've got, we need to add another Edit Mesh to the Modifier stack and press F4 so that we can see the joins in the mapping between the top of the barrel and the sides.

Without using programs like Maxon's BodyPaint 3D (www.maxon.net), it is extremely difficult to create textures that wrap seamlessly around 3D models; so don't worry too much if you can see a slight edge. Most imperfections like this will never be seen in a game, so we don't dwell on them. If however, you are working at a studio and this problem arises … well, you know what to put on your purchase request.

Now we're on the home stretch. All we need to do is adjust the UVs on the bottom of the model and we're done—or almost done.

Jump into the Front viewport and deselect all the polygons on the top of the barrel (hit F and then Ctrl + Alt + Z), and deselect the polygons on the top of the barrel (click Select Object and while holding Alt, drag and deselect the top polygons). Click P for Perspective view, rotate the barrel so that you can see the bottom polygons, and we'll map the last part.

Once again, select Unwrap UVW from the Modifier List, select Edit (from parameters), and select Map #1 from the drop-down menu in the Edit UVW window that appears. All we need to do now is to slide the vertices along to the right to match up with the bottom of the barrel, and we're almost done. Now click Ctrl + A to select all the vertices and move them into place using the Move tool.

FIG 2.64

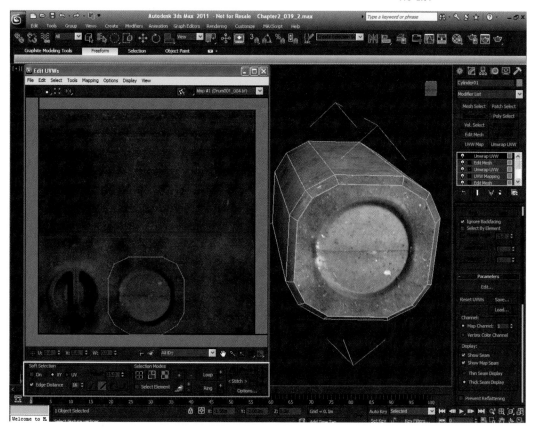

Once again, close the Edit UVW window, apply an Edit Mesh to the model, and press F4 so that you can see the model fully mapped. If there are any areas that look stretched, select the polygons and edit the UVW unwrapping until you are happy. Render the model in the same way that you rendered the cardboard box from part 1, print it, and add it to your portfolio.

Congratulations! You've completed the second chapter, and I hope that you learned a few new techniques. With the skills that you've learned so far, you should be able to make almost any low-poly object. So well done—you're well on your way.

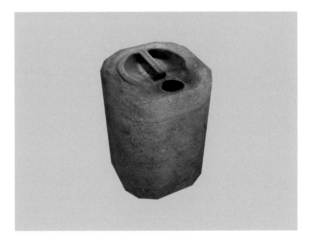

FIG 2.65

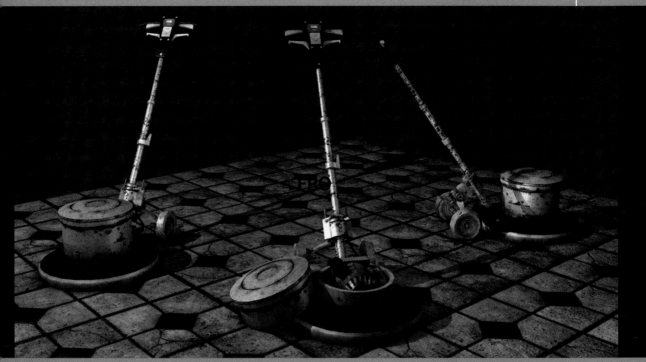

CHAPTER 3

Creating Complex Objects from Primitives

In this chapter, we are going to go through the process of creating a more complex model using only standard primitives and standard modeling tools in 3ds Max.

The model I've chosen for this exercise is a floor buffer which was photographed at the same location as everything else in the book. The reference shoot took place at an old abandoned mental hospital in the North of England. A lot of photos from the reference shoot are available to download from the Web site that supports this book. Check the introduction for dull instructions. Here is a selection of these photos from the shoot.

As you can see from the reference, the floor buffer is mainly a collection of cylinders all placed together in a specific way. The motor and possibly wheel brackets and breaking pedal will require additional modeling as they are not simple shapes.

In Fig. 3.2, I have created paint over of the main section of the floor buffer showing the simpler form of each individual component. I'm not considering any fine details, just the main shapes. This technique of breaking down a complex shape into simpler geometric shapes can really help you to model it.

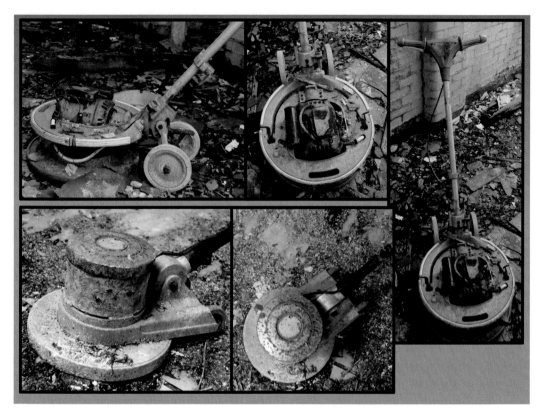

FIG 3.1

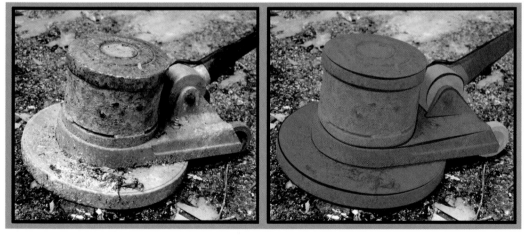

FIG 3.2

Also, the reference does not give us all the details. There are two different floor
buffers with only a few shots of each. I'll be taking elements from both buffers
to create one final design.

In this situation, you could fill in the blanks yourself for missing details with concept art or as I have done for this model with extra research found online to assist me in figuring out a design.

We will start off with a quick blockout to work out any design concerns which will help us to settle on a final shape. We will then build around this blockout to create the final model.

This stage of the process shouldn't take too long. The idea is to quickly throw together a rough representation of the object. It is likely that the final model will differ from the blockout as it is only intended as a guide.

The rough budget I have given myself for this object is 2000 triangles for the mesh with a 512×512 diffuse texture and 256×256 specular map.

2000 triangles is a lot for an object of this size, but most of the polygons will be spent making the object as smooth as possible as it is mainly made up from cylinders.

You could expect a 2000-triangles object to be used in an FPS game. For a third-person game or a racing game, it would probably be more like 600–900 and probably less for an RTS or similar game.

Now, let's move into 3ds Max and get started.

I start by creating a cylinder for the base. I'm not too concerned with the number of sides at this point as this is only a blockout guide.

Creating the Blockout

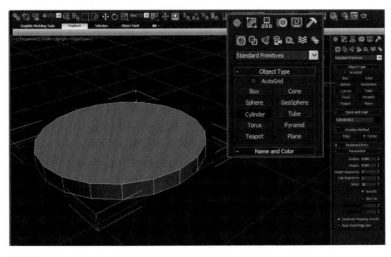

FIG 3.3

Holding Shift, I move the cylinder up in the Z-axis to create a copy. The copy is then scaled to block out the section where the motor is contained.

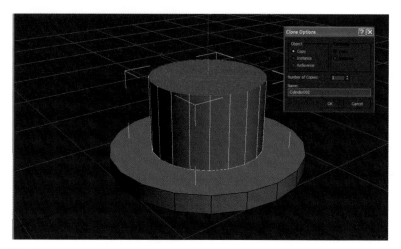

FIG 3.4

The cylinder is duplicated three more times and moved into position. It's then rotated and scaled to represent the wheels and the handle. I often change the coordinate system to local when rotating shapes like the handle as it makes objects easier to work with as the gizmo goes with the object's position in 3D space. This can be done by selecting local from the drop down.

FIG 3.5

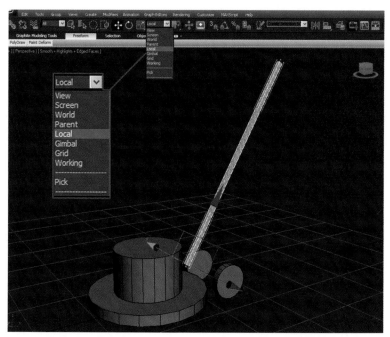

Next, some boxes are created, adjusted, and placed to block out the shapes around the base of the handle. I'm always referring to the reference as I add new elements to ensure the position and scale look right.

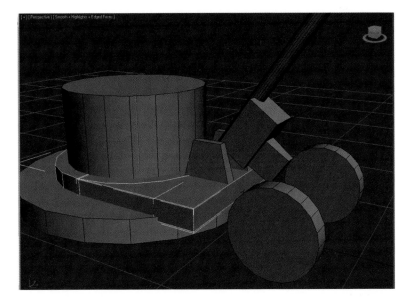

FIG 3.6

The blockout is almost complete after adding a couple of more boxes to help figure out how the wheels are attached to the base of the handle. The handles on top are also added. They are currently angled as in the reference images but I may change this later.

At this stage, I am trying to figure out design issues like this and see if these solutions will work.

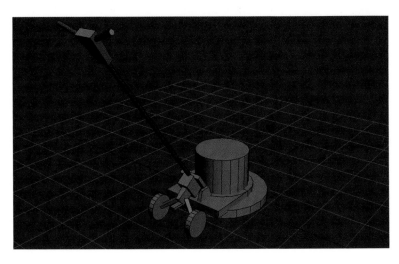

FIG 3.7

A few additional details were added, most notably, the edge loop showing the division between the lid and the motor encasing. A rim was also added to the lid. The intention will be to have the lid as a separate mesh and removable, so we can see the motor beneath.

The statistics are displayed in the top left corner of the viewport. The triangle count currently sits at 924 triangles, so almost half of the intended budget.

To display these statistics, click on the plus "+" symbol in the top left corner and select Configure. This will open a new window which is displayed in Fig. 3.8. You can tick or untick the information you wish to see. I prefer to at least always have the Triangle Count and Total + Selection ticked. These statistics will be of more importance as we get to the final stages of the model. It's always good to keep an eye on the numbers, so you don't go too far over the intended budget.

FIG 3.8

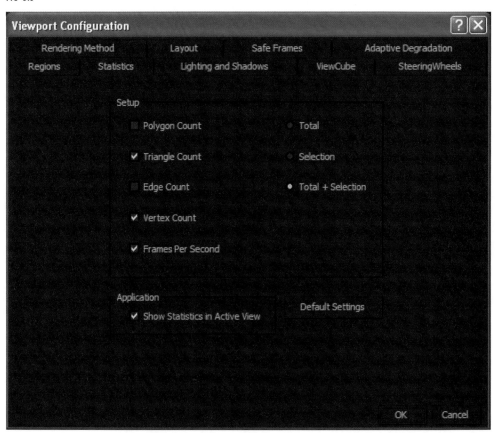

70

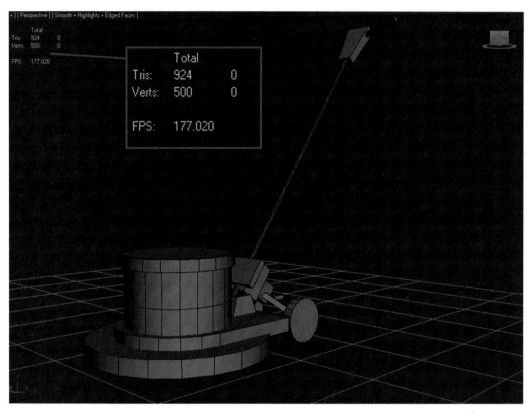

FIG 3.9

Creating the Final Model

Scene Setup

The first thing I do is to assign a different color to the blockout mesh, so it can be distinguished from the final model as this will be built over. I have assigned a standard material and changed the diffuse color. The blockout model was then placed on a layer using the layer manager. This can be accessed by clicking on the manage layers icon on the menu toolbar, and the location is displayed in Fig. 3.10.

Using layers for scene management is really useful as you can hide or freeze multiple objects with just one click. All you need to do is click on the relevant column for the particular layer in the layer manager. In Fig. 3.10, the active layer is the blockout layer as there is a check to the right of the layer name. In this state, any new meshes created in this scene will automatically go into this layer.

This is a good point to create a final mesh layer, so all new meshes will go into that instead as we do not want to be adding anything else to the blockout layer.

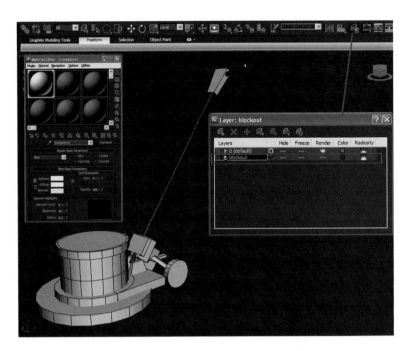

FIG 3.10

After freezing the blockout layer, we can start to create the final model. Frozen objects turn gray by default while they are frozen. If you wish to adjust this, go to Layer Manager and select all the objects in that layer. Then, right-click and choose Object Properties. A pop-up window will appear. Then, uncheck the Show Frozen in Gray option.

You can also access these options by selecting an object and going to Edit Menu > Object Properties > Object Properties dialog > General panel.

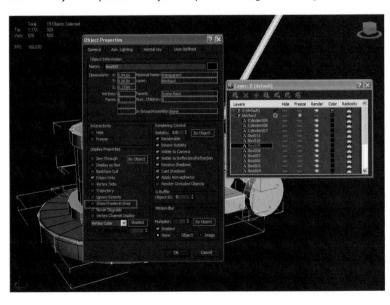

FIG 3.11

I then create a cylinder with 25 sides, one cap segment, and three height segments to start the model. It was then converted to an Editable Poly. The two height segments were moved and scaled to create two beveled edges around the edges of the cylinder.

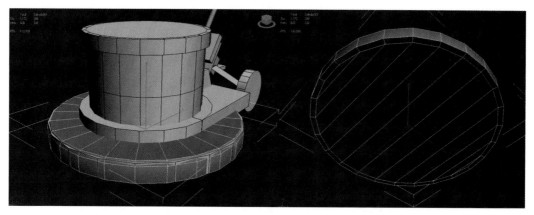

FIG 3.12

The top faces were left with the cap segments with all the edges converging into one vertex. The bottom was remodeled to be more efficient as shown in Fig. 3.13.

First, select the edges highlighted in the middle shape and use the Remove option from the Edit Edges tab on the modify panel to delete the edges. In this instance, it should also remove the vertices as there are no edges left on the surface. Sometimes you may need to go into vertex mode and manually delete the vertices off edges left running across the face.

The third step is to connect up all the vertices around the edge of the face with straight lines as in the third shape on the right.

This can be done by using the Cut tool under the Edit Geometry tab to manually connect one vertex to another by left-clicking on the vertex or edge where you want to start and then clicking on where you want the cut to go. Right-click to finish.

The other method is to use the Connect option in the Edit Vertices tab also found on the modify panel. I find this cleaner as you just select two vertices (it works with more also) and then hit Connect. This will connect them with an edge.

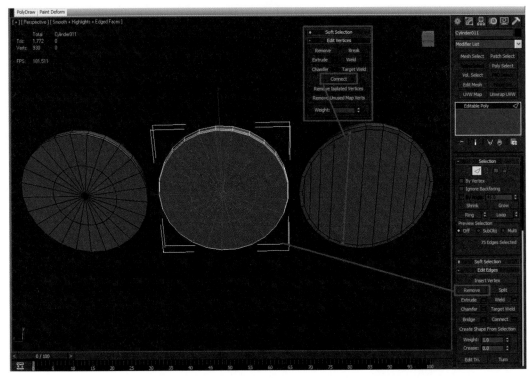

FIG 3.13

When this section is complete, duplicate it and delete the faces on the bottom as in the left image of Fig. 3.14. Then, delete half of the remaining cylinder and perform the same optimization task as before, cutting edges across the top surface of the half cylinder. Then, position this mesh on top of the buffers pad section.

FIG 3.14

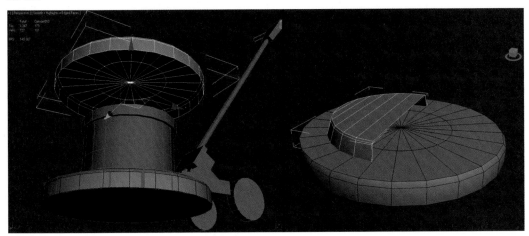

The central faces on the top surface of the pad section are now deleted as they will not be seen as we are about to build over them. The border around the hole was selected and scaled, so the edge lines up with the new half cylinder. Select the back edges of the half cylinder and extrude them backwards to roughly line up with the blockout as shown in the right image of Fig. 3.15.

The Extrude tool was used to do this. It is located under the Edit Edges tab on the modify panel. You can click on the button Extrude and control the outcome manually in the viewport, or you can select the icon to the right of this button which will bring up a small options box. You can input the settings you want into this and select the green tick to confirm. I personally set all the values to zero, confirm, and then manually adjust the edges with the Move, Rotate, and Scale tools.

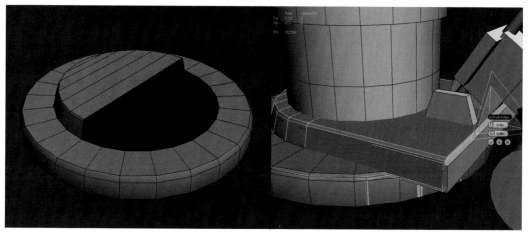

FIG 3.15

The faces at the back were created by using the Bridge tool to connect the four corner edges beforehand.

The first and failed attempt at the beveled recess consisted of using the Slice Plane tool and Cut tool to add geometry to be modified and modeled into this shape. I was not happy with the results.

At this stage, I did delete half of the mesh after using the Cut tool to create an edge running down the center of the mesh. I then applied a *symmetry* modifier to the remaining half so I would only have to create one of these edges.

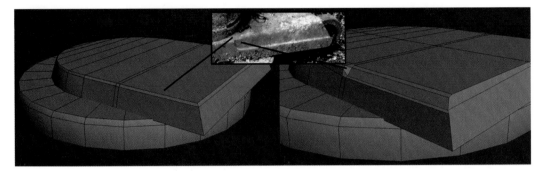

FIG 3.16

The problem was creating the curved surface leading into the beveled recess from the existing mesh. The solution was to start by creating a cylinder and deleting most of the sides. The remaining section of the cylinder would then form this curve. It is pictured in the top left image of Fig. 3.17.

The surface normals then had to be flipped so they were facing the right way. This option is found under the Edit Polygons tab. It's called Flip. This will change the direction of selected polygons face.

The curved section needs to be combined to and worked back into the existing model as described in the following four steps which are displayed in Fig. 3.17.

Step 1 Delete the surrounding polygons in this area to accommodate the cylinder section. Then, model the curve to suit the existing mesh by moving the vertices.

Step 2 Use the Cut tool to add extra edges and vertices to the outer faces adjoining the cylinder section so it matches up. To snap the new vertices onto the curves, use the Move tool with snap turned on. To toggle snap on and off, press "S."

Step 3 Once all the shared vertices are matched up to the curved cylinder section, combine it with the main mesh using the Attach option found under the Edit Geometry tab. Select the main shape and then attach. Next, click on the mesh you wish to combine to the main shape. When this is done, move into vertex mode and drag select around the vertices which are shared, one at a time. The statistic counter should show two vertices selected. To weld them, select the Weld option under Edit Vertices. If the weld is successful, the statistics counter should show one vertex selected. Do this to all the vertices we snapped on top of each other. It's wise to double check all vertices in the area at this time.

Step 4 The final step consist of reducing the amount of edges in the curved section using Weld as I decided at this point there were too many. The missing side faces were replaced by extruding the top edge down and welding the vertices to close the mesh. Any remaining floating vertices or unconnected edges were fixed by using the Connect or Cut tools. The bevel running along the outer edge was also extended up along the curve in step 4 in comparison with the version in step 3 to get a nicer result.

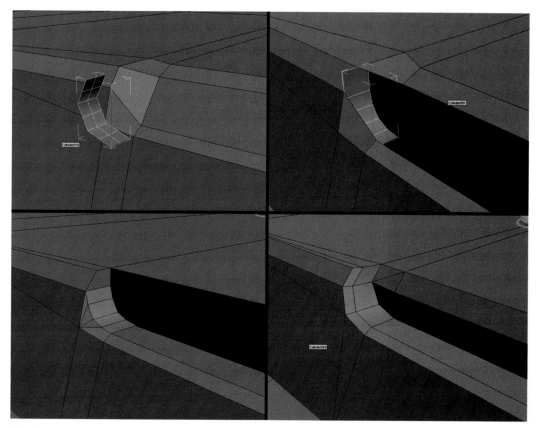

FIG 3.17

The mesh should be missing the bottom face which hangs out over the buffer pad section. Create this by extruding the bottom edge of the back face as shown in the left image in Fig. 3.18.

When you are satisfied with the results of one half of this mesh you can collapse the stack so the symmetry modifier creates the other half of the model. To do this, right-click on the *symmetry* modifier in the modifier list on the modifier panel and select Collapse All. This will reduce the modifier stack back to Editable Poly.

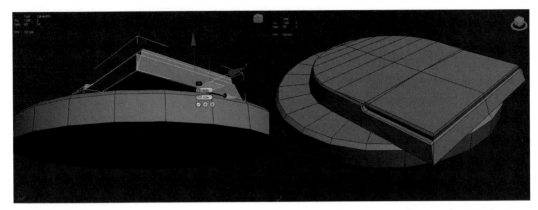

FIG 3.18

The shared vertices running down the center of the model will need to be welded using the same method as before to seal the mesh.

After welding all the vertices along the central edge, the central edge is also removed as it is no longer needed.

The motor casing and lid sections are next. These meshes can be duplicated from the blockout model to use as a starting point. The motor casing or bottom section was first to be worked on as in the left image in Fig. 3.19.

Delete the top polygon. Then, select the edge border and extrude it inwards to give thickness to the cylinder. At this stage, I did add a raised edge loop on the surface by making two separate extrusions. As I deleted it, later you can just do one extrusion.

Then, use the Extrude tool again, downwards this time to create the inner sides of the casing.

Selecting the border edge, which should now be at the base of the inner sides, use the Cap tool to fill this empty area with a polygon to create a bottom to the casing.

After this, the vertices need connecting up as before with straight lines running across the bottom surface.

You should end up with a shape similar to the version on the right in Fig. 3.19.

The only difference is I carried out a small optimization. As we do not need the inner cylinder to be as round and smooth as the outer section, I selected pairs of adjacent vertices and welded them together resulting in the final version as shown in Fig. 3.19.

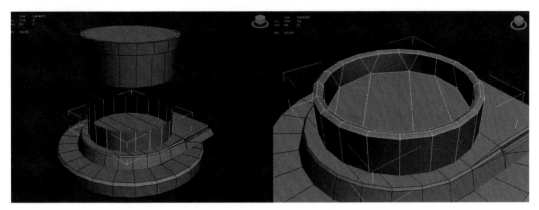

FIG 3.19

The lid is next; I start on the top surface. First, delete the current top polygon and select the new border edge and extrude it inwards part way. This is to start creating the small groove visible on the top of the buffer lid in the reference photos.

Continue to extrude, move, and scale to get a result similar to the right image in Fig. 3.20. The groove consists of three edge loops in the end which together formed a *V* shape.

Finish the lid by capping the final border edge just before the center to create a flat poly to define the plastic area in the center of the lid top visible in the reference image.

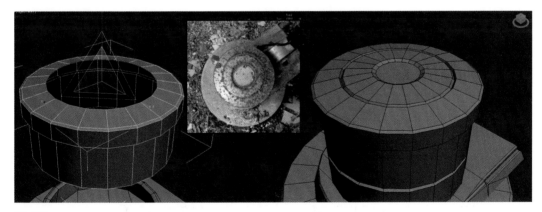

FIG 3.20

To finish the lid, connect all the vertices around the plastic area as shown in the left image of Fig. 3.21.

Then, create the inner surfaces of the lid using the same method as before. Remember to optimize it at the end by welding the adjacent vertices. The final result is shown in the right image in Fig. 3.21.

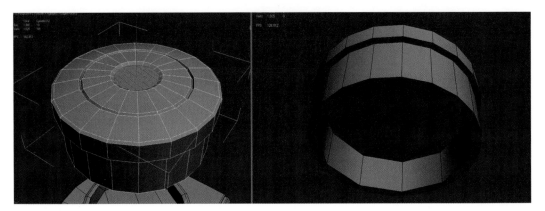

FIG 3.21

After positioning the lid back on top of the motor casing, I moved on to the wheels. Again, I duplicated the wheels from the blockout to use as a starting point.

As before, delete the large-side polygon on the front of the wheel, and then select the border edge left behind. Extrude this once to create an angled surface to form the rim of the wheel. Then, extrude inwards again, this time all the way in to merge all the edges into one point. Then, weld this group of vertices before moving the vertex inwards to create a dipped surface for the wheel.

The back of the wheel was created in a similar fashion, except instead of going with the dipped surface, create a flat surface and make horizontal cuts across it to connect the vertices.

Next, duplicate the final wheel and rotate it 180° to make the wheel for the other side.

FIG 3.22

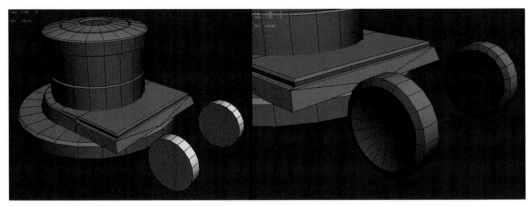

The next few steps required a bit of trial and error as I worked out the design for the wheel brackets and how it is connected to the box at the back of the pole. I wanted to try out a curved bracket instead of a straight one like the blockout mesh. At this point, I also created two cylinders for the wheel axles so that the brackets connect.

In Fig. 3.23, I had started by creating a cylinder. I then applied a *bend* modifier from the modifier list. I only used the angle setting to bend the cylinder. You may need to adjust the axis the modifier bends in depending which way your model faces in the scene.

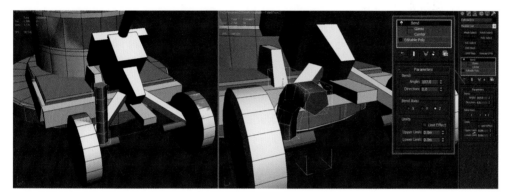

FIG 3.23

After collapsing the stack when I was happy with the bend result, the bracket was rotated and moved into place. I tried scaling it in the *X*-axis to reduce the roundness as I decided it did not suit the model. It was then duplicated and mirrored to create the right bracket. An extra cylinder was also created to be a bolt where the bracket and box meet. The left image in Fig. 3.24 shows the model at this stage.

I still did not like the roundness. Looking at the reference again, I preferred what was there, a flatter but bent bracket which is slightly tapered. I created a box with four height subdivisions and applied the bend modifier again to start the new shape.

FIG 3.24

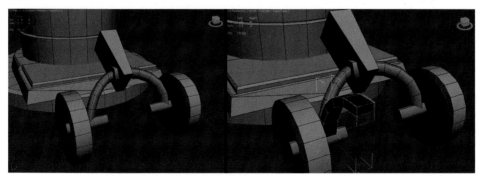

Figure 3.24 shows the final version of this new bracket. I kept this version closer to the reference while being mindful of the polygon budget. To taper the bracket as it nears the axle, select the edge loops or relevant vertices in vertex mode and scale them in the correct axis to get a result similar to the center image in Fig. 3.25. In my case, it was the X-axis.

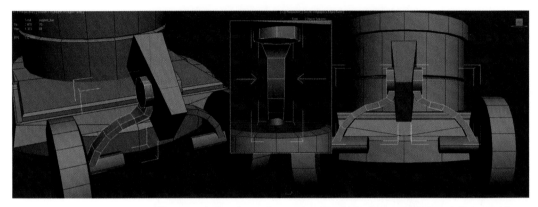

FIG 3.25

After completing the earlier section, I had a look around the model to re-evaluate the polygon distribution. In doing so, I came to the conclusion that the wheels for their size use too many polygons. I decided to remedy this now rather than later on, and I made cheaper versions using the same method as before.

The original mesh was 198 tri's. The two new meshes were 94 tri's and 78 tri's. To play it safe, I went with the 78 tri option. I swapped out both wheels for the new lower resolution versions.

You may find yourself bouncing between different sections of a model a lot as you create it. I find this useful, always keeping an eye on the bigger picture and not getting sucked into small areas of detail until the end of the build. Work with broad strokes and get a consistent level of detail all around the mesh before adding really fine details.

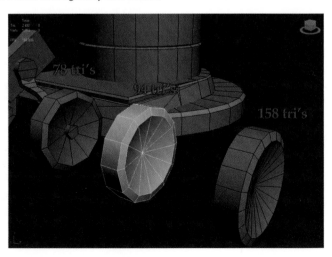

FIG 3.26

After resolving the wheel issues, I moved on to the base of the handle, to the shapes that connect the stem, buffer, and wheel brackets. I only loosely followed the reference to create this section, since if we were to follow the reference exactly, it would be rather expensive. You can interpret this area as you like. I found a solution which I feel looks good but it is also cheap and follows the idea of the reference.

First, delete the face on the box facing the buffer that the wheel brackets are connected to. This can be seen in the left image of Fig. 3.27. We will build the new pieces over this area as intersecting geometry.

To get a result similar to the middle and right images of Fig. 3.37, create a cylinder with two height segments. The top segment is moved up slightly, and the top face was scaled in to create the beveled edge.

Next, just rotate the cylinder into position, sitting it over the face we deleted earlier.

Then, select to opposite side faces on the cylinder and extrude them outwards creating "wings." After extruding them, I scaled the faces horizontally using the local axis, and then moved them back to create the tapered and angled "wings" on the side of the cylinder.

Two rivets created from a five-sided cylinder were placed as intersecting geometry on the front of the cylinder. All unseen geometry was deleted. Two more cylinders were used to represent the pins protruding out of the top of the "wings." A modified cylinder was placed on one side to create a little asymmetry. In my mind, I thought this piece once held the electrical cable feeding the buffer.

Select the bottom face of the cylinder and use extrude with 0 settings. Then manually scale the new face so it sits well inside the original face. This will then be extruded down to act as a continuation of the pole and connect the cylinder to the buffer. Before extruding down, you could weld pairs of vertices together to optimize the mesh before extruding the pole segment.

FIG 3.27

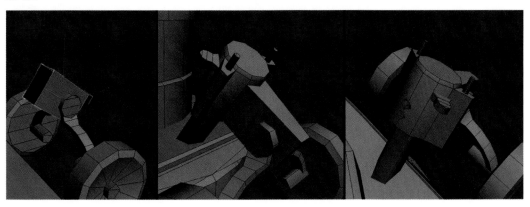

As described earlier for the bottom face, use a similar technique to extrude the main pole section up from the top face of the cylinder.

Select the top face and extrude it inwards making sure the new face stays flush with the original. I adjusted the position slightly, so it was not central before extruding it upwards using the local axis to move the new extrusion. When you are happy, delete the top face of the pole as this won't be needed.

FIG 3.28

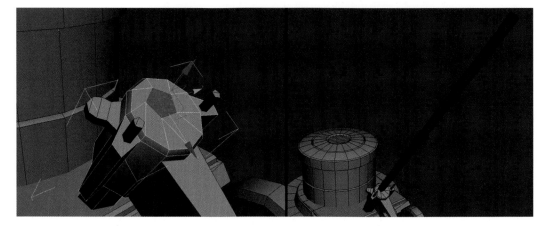

Where the pole touches the buffer I decided to put in an extra mesh to make both meshes sit better. This can be seen in the left image of Fig. 3.29a. To create this shape, start with a cylinder and delete the underside faces along with half of the remaining faces. Select the back edges facing away from the buffer and extrude them back. Use extrude again to create a back face. Then, use bridge to create a bottom face just where this shape hangs over the buffer pad.

In the right image of Fig. 3.29a, I highlighted the two rivets created from a couple of five-sided cylinders. Again, all unseen geometries such as downward facing faces have been deleted.

FIG 3.29a

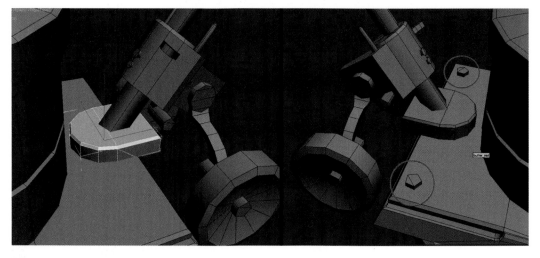

Some extra attention can now be focused on the pole. To break it up, a few extrusions were added to give the impression it is telescopic/adjustable. Using the Slice Plane tool, make four slices similar to the left image in Fig. 3.29b. Then, select the faces between the inner edge loops and scale them outwards first of all, then scale them towards each other to create a beveled surface. This will help to show off the detail more.

The same process was followed for the extruded section lower down the pole. This can be seen in Fig. 3.29b and also Fig. 3.30. The only difference is that one of the faces on the side of the cylinder was extruded outwards, and then the top face of this extrusion was extruded upwards.

These new faces were then modeled to resemble the example in the image using the Weld, Scale, and Move tools.

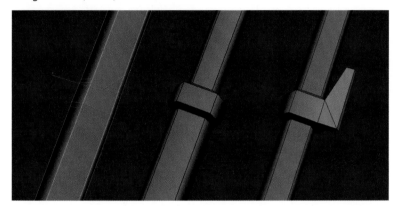

FIG 3.29b

The handle and brakes were started from a standard box. The Slice Plane and Scale tools were used on the box to add a few edge loops, matching the shape to the reference images. Once I was happy with the shape, I used the Chamfer tool to bevel the handles and then cleaned up the extra edges using the Weld tool.

As mentioned before, feel free to do some research and create something unique if you find a more interesting design for the handle. I went for a

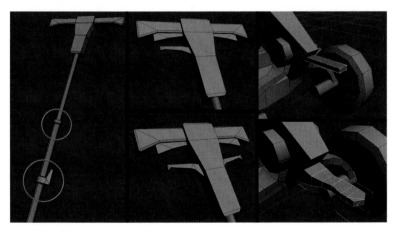

FIG 3.30

simple more box-like form, so it would use less of the triangle/polygon budget.

As seen on the right of Fig. 3.30, the brake pedal was created from a box, which was then sliced up and modeled into shape. The Slice Plane and Scale tools were used for this.

The piece connecting the brake pedal to the box was then created using a similar modeling technique starting from a box. The only extra tools used were the Rotate and Move tools to create the slightly curved shape seen on the left of Fig. 3.31.

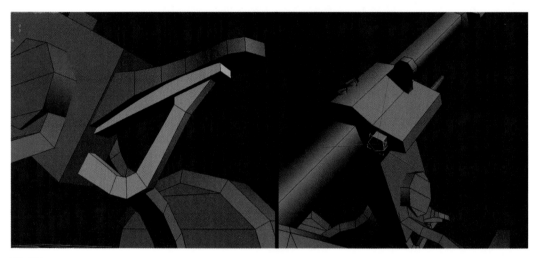

FIG 3.31

Next are the two bolts and some cable to connect them. This concept was loosely lifted from the reference. To start, one of the five-sided bolts created earlier was duplicated and placed on the under side of the cylinder. Select the front face of the "bolt" and delete it. Then, select the border edges and extrude them inwards.

There is no need to have the cable a five-sided mesh, so weld two vertices together to make the border edge four sided. As seen on the left example of Fig. 3.32, the shape is not quite right. So, to fix this, I created a four-sided cylinder as a guide and positioned it up against the bolts surface.

You could use the Auto Grid option located on the *create panel* to create the cylinder directly on the bolts surface. This can be turned on by going to the top of the *object type* list and ticking the box beside Auto Grid.

Then, select the four vertices defining the cables shape and snap them to the cylinders vertices, so it creates a better shape as highlighted on the right of Fig. 3.32.

Once one bolt was complete, it was duplicated and then positioned on the side of the mesh connecting the pole and buffer pad.

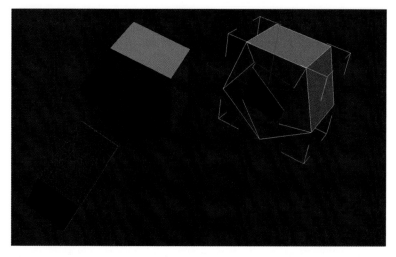

FIG 3.32

A curve was then created and modified to be the cable hanging down connecting the two bolts.

Go back to the first bolt, and select the internal border edges and start extruding them down. Follow the curve all the way to join up and meet with the bottom bolt. Rotate the extrusions as you go. I did have to do some remodeling of the cable at the end to get a smoother result.

Another way to do this is to use Extrude along Spline found under Edit Polygons in polygon mode as we have all the elements to do so. You will need to select the border edge and cap it first as you need a polygon to carry out this operation. I personally preferred to do this manually. Either method will require some extra modeling to clean it up.

When you are satisfied with the cable then combine this and the two bolts together and weld all the shared vertices to close up the mesh.

FIG 3.33

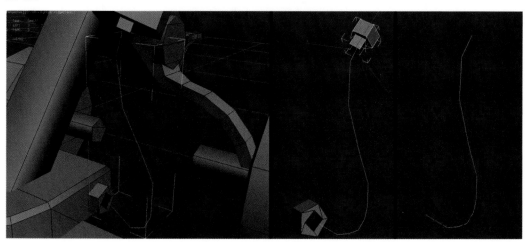

The motor is next. First, move the lid to the side for now. Start with creating a cylinder as shown in Fig. 3.34. Then, delete the bottom half and move it into position. Use the height segments to create curved ends on the cylinder.

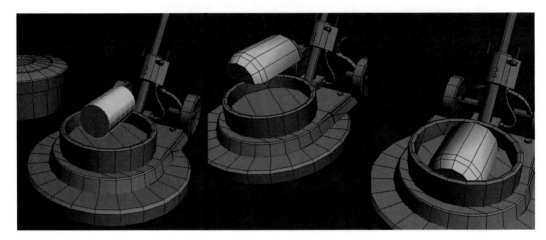

FIG 3.34

Keeping the motor simple, finish it by following the reference and building it up with boxes and cylinders.

You can leave these primitives all intersecting each other as the amount of overdraw is very small. All unseen geometry were then deleted. When I was happy with the result, I combined all the meshes using Attach and then reset the Xform of the new mesh.

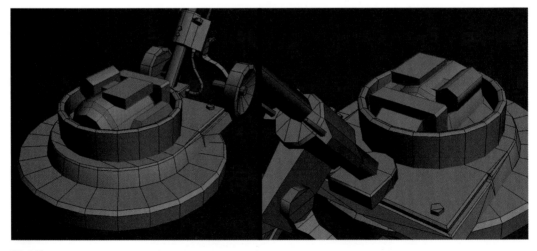

FIG 3.35

At this point, the model is pretty much complete, so all that is left before unwrapping and texturing the model is a pass on optimizing the mesh and tweaks of the smoothing groups.

The triangle count at this moment is 2300, and the polygon count is 1401. As I was aiming for 2000 triangles, some details will need to be removed. Figure 3.36 shows some of the areas where edges or details were removed. I usually get rid of excessive bevels first and then reduce the smoothness of cylinders. After that, I look at completely removing small details like rivets, if necessary. Geometry that either does not contribute to the overall silhouette or has a purpose relating to smoothing groups or unwrapping can also be removed.

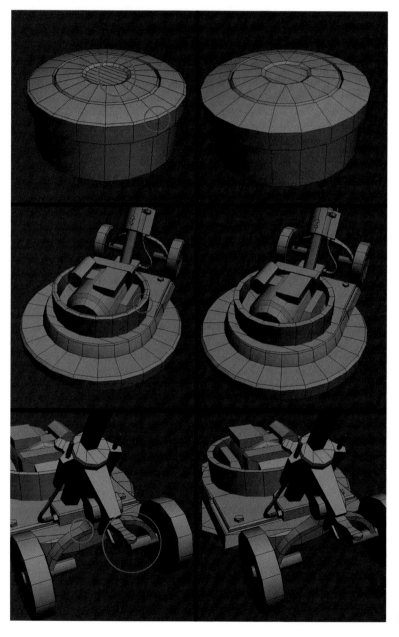

FIG 3.36

After optimizing the mesh, it ended up as 2138 triangles or 1153 polygons. This is still not the estimated budget of 2000 but it's close enough as I'm happy with the model at this detail. It could be possible to reduce the model more to 2000 triangles if you want the challenge.

Smoothing Groups

The last step I always carry out on a model is to go through the Smoothing Groups. This process ensures that I get the shading that I want across all the surfaces. I have been doing this as I went along throughout the build which is a habit I'd encourage you to pick up.

If you are not familiar with Smoothing Groups, these control the shading of the edges between faces over the surface of a mesh. I'll use the top of the buffer lid as an example to demonstrate how they work.

The model on the left of Fig. 3.37 has only one smoothing group, so the shading is averaged across the whole of the mesh. The example on the right has multiple smoothing groups to define some of the edges better. This is extremely important when doing hard surface modeling.

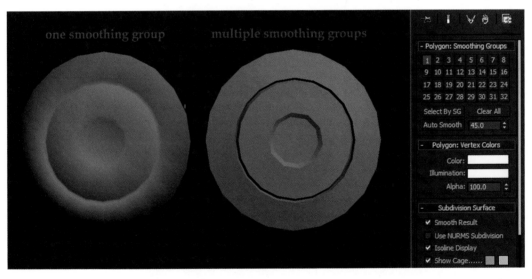

FIG 3.37

The smoothing group options are only available on the modify panel under the polygon or element modes.

A good approach to applying them is to first select all the faces of a mesh and then apply smoothing group 1 by clicking on "1" from the number table pictured in Fig. 3.37. After this, select faces you wish to be shaded differently and assign group 2 to them. If you need to have two faces adjacent to each other but shaded separately from each other as well as group 1, just assign group 2 to one face and group 3 to the other.

Figure 3.38 of the lid highlights the different smoothing groups applied to the mesh. Go around the entire mesh adjusting these groups accordingly to get the desired look.

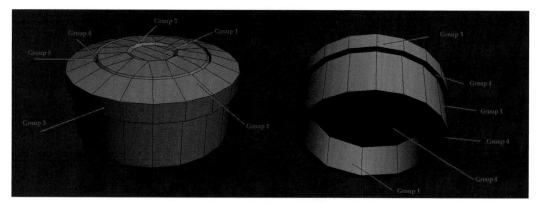

FIG 3.38

When the smoothing groups were complete, I used Attach to combine all the meshes together so they could all be unwrapped together in the UV texture editor.

Figure 3.39 shows the original blockout in comparison with the final model. As you can see, I had made a few design changes and scale modifications as I modeled the final version. This is very common when creating assets for games.

Never be too precious about your work and always be willing to improve and change it as you go. The blockout served its purpose as a quick initial first step, but it was only a rough guide.

FIG 3.39

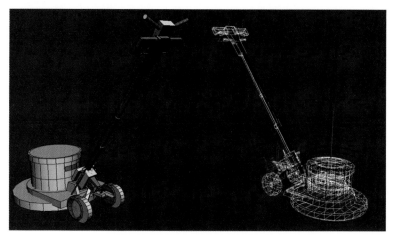

Unwrapping and Texturing the Floor Buffer

Before even starting the unwrapping and texturing process, I first put together an image showing what type of textures I'd like to have on the model, and where they would be placed.

I find this useful as it helps me to keep a clear picture of where I want to take the model. The texture samples were taken from various sources including personal photos and online texture libraries.

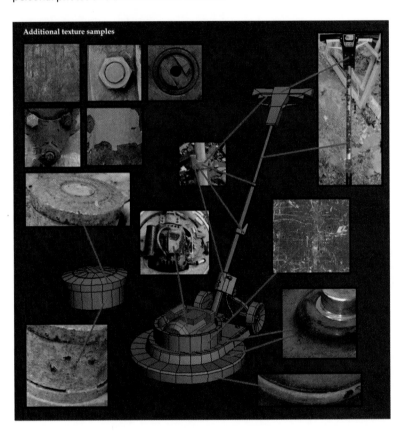

FIG 3.40

Now it's time to look at unwrapping the model.

The first step is to apply an Unwrap UVW modifier from the modifier list. At this stage, we need to figure out the object's size and make a decision on the texture size—whether it should be a 512 × 512, 1024 × 1024, or 2048 × 2048 texture map.

As I have already started the scene that this object is designed for, I can import some reference meshes to compare it against. The general rule for the scene is that a 5 m² will use a 1024 × 1024 texture.

Figure 3.41 shows the pavement mesh I have imported and the original buffer on the left. I ended up scaling the buffer by 17% in the end.

I decided that a 512 × 512 texture would be sufficient for the buffer model as the pavement was using a 1024 × 1024 texture. The buffer's texture will in fact be a slightly higher resolution than other elements in the scene. I decided that being a prop I'll allow it to go over a little. It can always be reduced to a 256 × 256 later if it looks out of place within the environment.

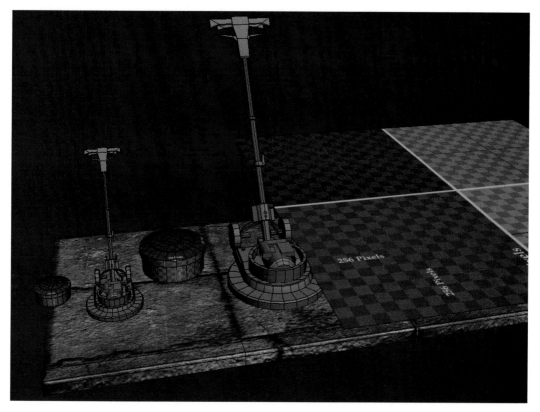

FIG 3.41

With all these questions answered, we are ready to look at the process of unwrapping the model and creating the texture in Photoshop.

To start the unwrapping process, I created a custom UV map template. This is used to initially unwrap the model using the checker pattern to ensure the various UV shells get a consistent amount of space on the texture sheet. The different color quadrants are useful to know where each UV shell sits within the 0–1 range in UV space. Figure 3.42 shows the UV template which is in the project files and the lid unwrapped using it.

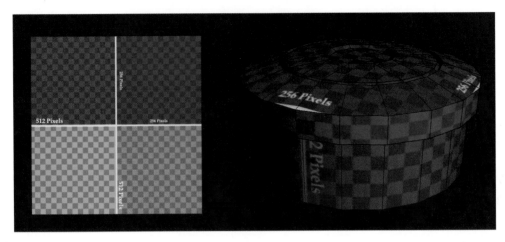

FIG 3.42

The actual process of unwrapping this model was quite simple as I only used the planar mapping, box mapping, and cylindrical mapping options available with the Unwrap UVW modifier.

Some tweaking had to be done to the UV shells/clusters using the Move, Rotate, and Scale tools in the Edit UVWs window.

The intention at this stage is to work out the layout of the texture and unwrap the most visible sections that require a different texture. Which sections to choose and what textures to apply have already been decided in Fig. 3.40.

I knew a strip of metal would be needed for the sides of the lid, so I started here using cylindrical mapping and then also planar mapped the lid top. Figure 3.43 shows these UV shells moved to one side. Each section was scaled to get a consistent resolution similar to the lid shown in Fig. 3.42.

FIG 3.43

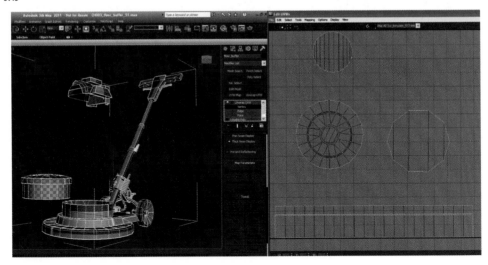

I am trying to group all horizontally tiling strips for the bottom half of the texture sheet. The next obvious choice is the orange plastic rim highlighted to go around the buffers pad section. The UVs were placed above the metal strip of the lid. The buffers pad was also planar mapped. It was scaled to a small size as it will rarely be seen it does not require as much texture space as other elements.

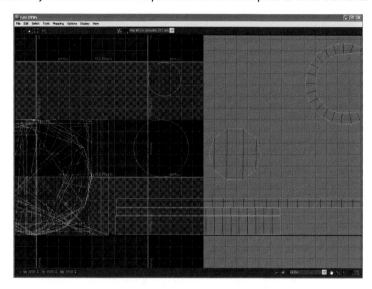

FIG 3.44

Continuing to use the unwrapping, tools, the rest of the buffers pad was unwrapped and also the interior sections of the lid and casing. These areas will be either covered by other meshes or rarely seen, so were given half the texture space than they would normally get. In Fig. 3.45, you can see that the casing interior's checkered pattern is larger than the outer faces.

The wheels were unwrapped next using a planar mapping for the sides and back and cylindrical mapping for the rim and tyre.

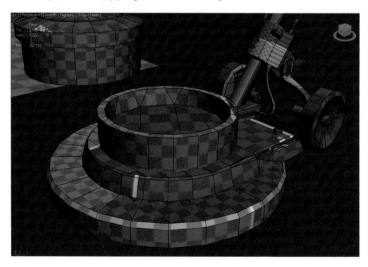

FIG 3.45

95

Figure 3.46 shows the UV layout at this stage. All unwrapped UVs have been moved outside of the 0–1 range. I then placed the strips running along the bottom half of the texture (the green and yellow quadrants). Some uniquely unwrapped assets like the lid top and wheel's elements were placed in the blue quadrant.

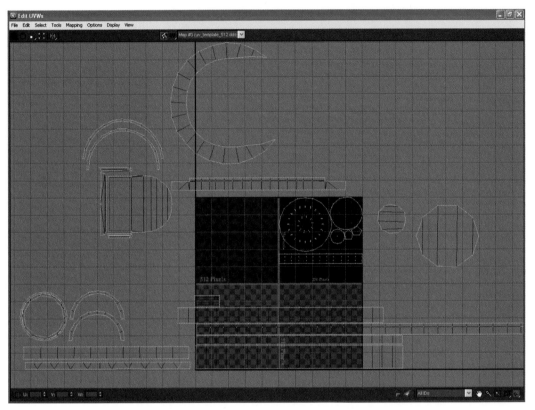

FIG 3.46

You may notice that the interior faces of the casing and the UV shells for the black plastic areas are outside of the 0–1 range. The interior pieces will just use whatever texture elements are on the sheet so I'm not including them as unique elements. Looking at the texture sheet, I have decided that the black plastic on the pad section will use a 256 × 256 tiling texture as this will work more efficiently for this section.

The unwrapping of the pole and handle section was next. These elements were placed in the orange quadrant. The UV layout of the blue quadrant in Fig. 3.47 has already been modified. Until all the shapes are mapped, I tend to constantly modify the layout.

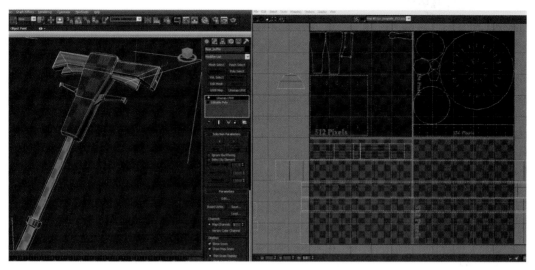

FIG 3.47

At this stage, I felt I had enough information to begin texturing. Figure 3.48 shows the final texture with the texture layout highlighted. If you compare this with the layout in Fig. 3.47, you can see how the texture sticks closely to this layout.

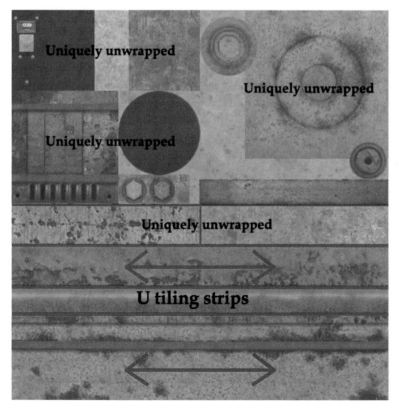

FIG 3.48

To get a render of the UV layout that we can bring into Photoshop, go to the menu along the top of the Edit UVWs window and select, Tools > Render UVW Template. This will open a pop-up window that will contain the settings to save this image out.

I set the size to 512 × 512. To save the file out, click on Render UVW Template at the bottom. This will save it out as a specified image file.

This image file seen on the left of Fig. 3.50 was brought into Photoshop and set to lighten over a flat gray background. This is then saved and forms the basis of our texture map.

I find texturing is a very subjective part of the 3D process. Each artist has their own opinions on what works best. The rest of the tutorial shows how I would typically do this. At any stage feel free to try your own things. Remember you'll learn more by experimenting than following these tutorials to the letter.

FIG 3.49

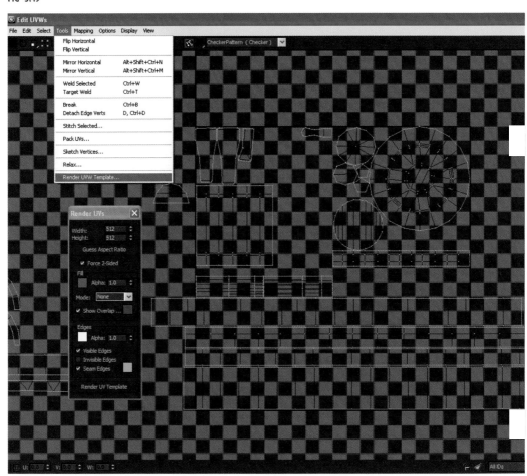

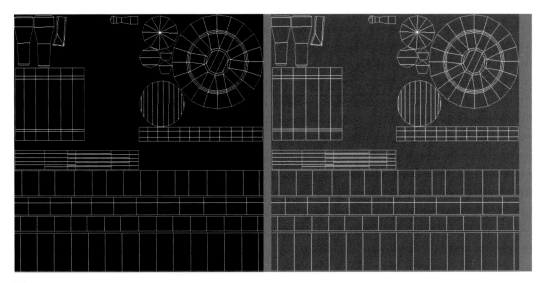

FIG 3.50

Using the UV layout as a guide, paint flat color with the standard brush onto the map. Use different colors to define the various materials in the texture. I choose to paint orange for the rubber strip, black for the handle, different shades of gray for metals, and brown for rust. The result can be seen on the left image of Fig. 3.51.

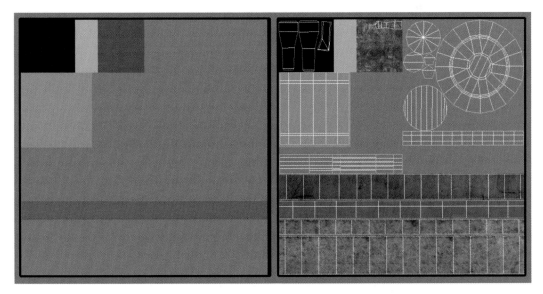

FIG 3.51

The next step is to start bringing in sections of the photo and texture reference to create the first pass of the diffuse map. This can be seen in the right Fig. 3.51.

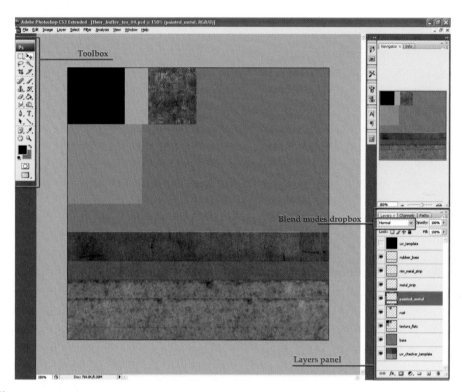

FIG 3.52

Figure 3.52 shows Photoshop's workspace. The toolbox is highlighted on the left. This is where you will find the Brush and Crop tools. On the right is the layers panel. This is where all these images will appear once brought into the file. The blend modes dropbox is a list of different blend modes which change how the selected layer affects the layers beneath it. We'll be using these various blend modes a lot.

Figure 3.53 shows a slightly later version of the texture with all the different elements in place. To bring the image sections into the texture file, open the source image. Then, use the Crop tool to define the section you want to use by dragging around this area. Then, click on the Crop tool again to bring up the option to crop the image and select it. This will leave you with only the section you defined.

Then, using the Move tool drag and drop this into the texture file. You may need to adjust the order of the layers and use the Move tool to position the image section into the right place.

Most of the layers at this stage are using the blend mode *normal*. The only one that is not is the noise/grunge over the orange rubber strip. This is a gray scale image set to *overlay*, so it picks up the color beneath it. You can open the texture wip file **floor_buffer_tex_05.psd** to see the order of the layers and blend modes used in Fig. 3.53.

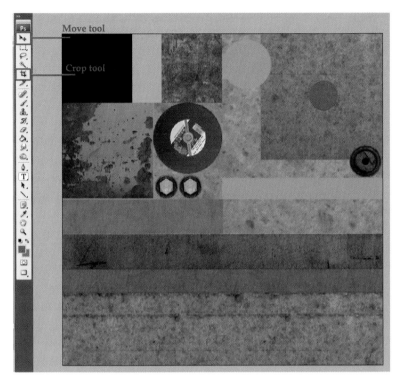

FIG 3.53

Figure 3.54 deals with the buffer lid top. A different rusted metal image was placed above the metal shown in the left image. The new image is very similar but has larger patches of rust. I used a layer mask to blend the two images together. This is a technique I use very often when I want to have two textures uniquely blended together such as metal and rust or mud and grass.

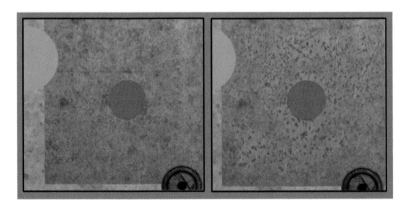

FIG 3.54

To create a layer mask on the new metal images layer, select the Add layer mask button at the bottom of the layers tab. It's highlighted in Fig. 3.55.

This will add a thumbnail to the right of the layer's default thumbnail. A Layer mask is a gray scale image that works like an alpha map. Areas you paint white will be visible, and areas you paint black will be invisible. All gray values in between will have the relevant amount of transparency. I usually start with flooding the mask black and then manually paint white with a brush at a medium to high opacity building up the new layer over the original gradually. The final result can be seen on the right of Fig. 3.54.

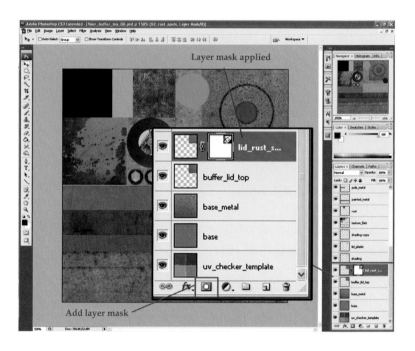

FIG 3.55

Next, I wanted to create a build up of dirt in the circular groove on top of the lid. The UV template was used as a guide. Select the Elliptical Marquee Tool and draw a circle precisely over the grooves UVs.

When you are happy that the Marquee tool sits right on top of the correct area, go to Menu > Edit > Stroke. The stroke options window will appear. Stroking the Marquee tool will draw a line of pixels that follow the marquee shape. The color, blend mode, and thickness of the line can be set in the stroke options.

To finalize the action, click on "ok." I used a dark gray color for the line, and then set the blend mode to overlay so it will darken the texture beneath it but still allow some details below to come through.

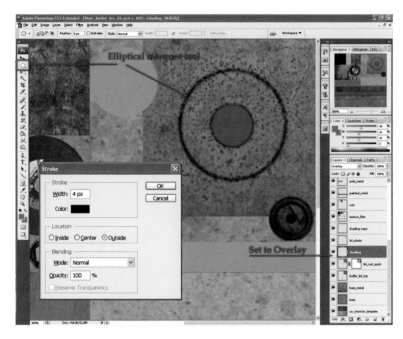

FIG 3.56

Using the layer mask technique again, additional rust was then painted on the lid and also along the metal strip running along the bottom of the texture.

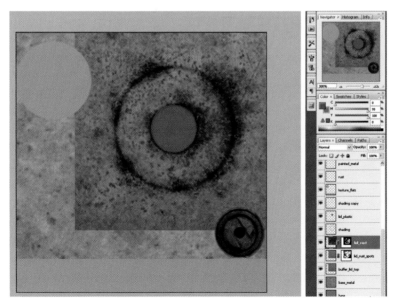

FIG 3.57

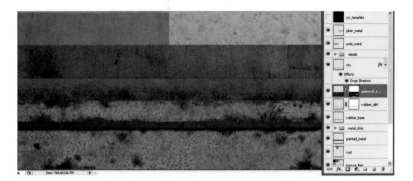

FIG 3.58

This technique was also over the orange rubber strip, used but with a dirt texture. A thin metal trim was also added over the metal strip as seen in Fig. 3.58. A layer style called Drop Shadow was applied to the metal trim to create a sense of lighting and depth in the texture. You can assign this by going to the Menu > Layer > Layer Style > Drop Shadow. Then just play with the settings until you are happy with the result.

You can always go back to the settings later if you don't flatten the image by double clicking on Drop Shadow which will appear on the bottom of the layer in the layers panel.

At this stage, if I felt the texture had enough detail I could go back and apply it to the model and continue with the unwrapping process. Before moving back to 3ds Max, a small 256 × 256 tiling texture needs to be created for the black plastic areas of the model. This is a simple texture to create consisting of three layers.

The base layer is a flat dark gray color. Use the paint bucket tool to fill the background layer with a color.

The middle layer was extracted from a photo of metal and desaturated (Shift + Ctrl + U). The blend mode is set to overlay at 59% opacity. The purpose of this layer is to add some noise and color variation to the flat gray layer.

The final layer was taken from a photo of concrete and also desaturated. The blend mode was set to soft light at 51% opacity.

The final task is to make sure this texture can tile in the *U*- and *V*-axes. When you are happy with how the texture looks, flatten the image.

To tile a texture in Photoshop, use the Offset tool found on the Main Menu > Filter > Other > Offset. This will bring up a window with options to offset the selected layer or image horizontally or vertically. As this is a 256 × 256 texture, it's best to offset it in both axes by 128 pixels. This will make sure the texture edges end up in the center of the screen. Sometimes seams can be harsh and very noticeable.

To paint out the seams, pick the Clone Stamp tool from the toolbox. Then, define an area of the texture to clone that's away from the seams by holding ALT and left-clicking in the selected area. Now, when you start painting over the seam you will clone the earlier selected area where you paint.

When the two seams are finally gone, apply the same amount of offset using the offset filter to return the texture to its normal position, this time without seams. Now, it is ready to be saved out and tiled over the plastic areas of the floor buffer.

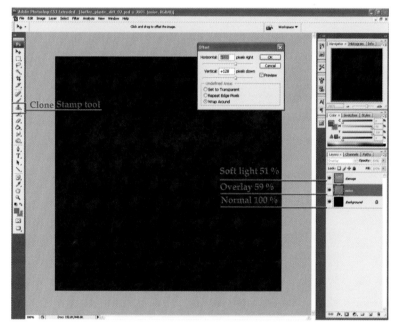

FIG 3.59

Moving back to 3ds Max, open up the Material Editor (M).

As the floor buffer will need two different textures assigned to the model, we'll need to use a multi/sub-object material.

Select a blank material and click on the Standard button (Fig. 3.60). From the Material Map Browser, select Multi/Sub-Object to change the material type from being a standard material to a multi/sub-object material instead.

The left side of Fig. 3.61 shows the default multi/sub-object material which contains 10 slots for submaterials. As we only need two, delete the excess slots and rename the two remaining slots accordingly. You should end up with a shade similar to the right of Fig. 3.61.

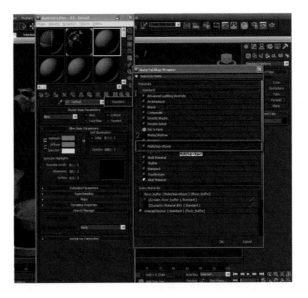

FIG 3.60

Submaterials are in fact standard materials except there can be lots of them assigned to a single model. Which material is assigned to which face is determined by each polygons material ID number, which we covered whilst mapping the box earlier in the book. As there are only two submaterials, this model only needs two material ID's. The primary ID is the main buffer texture. The secondary is the tiling plastic texture.

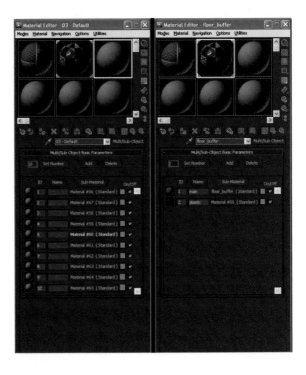

FIG 3.61

We need to collapse the stack of the model and go back into polygon mode, and then select all the faces and set the material ID to 1.

Next, select only the faces that will use the plastic texture and set the material ID to 2. Then, assign the shader to the model if you have not already done so. You should have a similar result to Fig. 3.62.

When this is complete, we can reapply an unwrap UVW modifier and continue to unwrap the model.

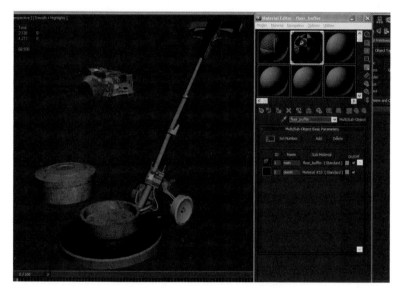

FIG 3.62

After spending more time in unwrapping the model and getting a feel for how I want to continue with the texture, I moved back into Photoshop. I tend to bounce in between texturing and unwrapping a lot as I prefer to see both tasks progressing together. You could easily stay with the unwrapping process and completely finish it as there is enough information in the texture.

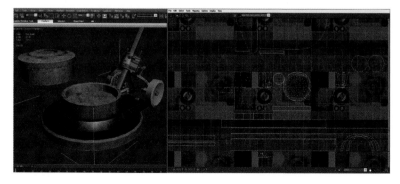

FIG 3.63

Looking back over the texture reference, I decided to add rust patches to the red metal and the pole. One of the rivets below the buffer pad was placed over a section of rust then desaturated and set to overlay. Work on the motor texture has started by taking part of the reference image and placing it using the UV template as a guide.

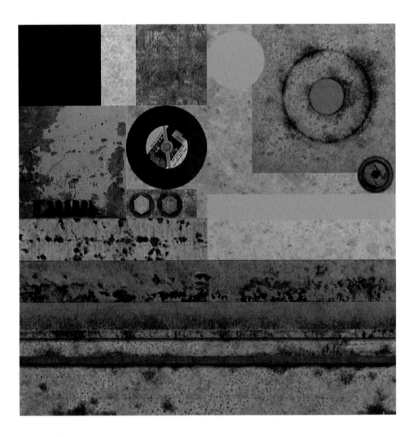

FIG 3.64

Figure 3.65 shows the results of a technique I use when creating diffuse textures. The top example in the image is a painted, rusted metal layer masked out over the red metal texture. On its own, I think it looks ok but it's a little flat if there is no intention to use a normal map. As a general rule, it's not advisable to have any sort of lighting in a diffuse map, but in the second image, I have used the nvidia normal map plug-in to create some subtle ambient lighting to make the flaking away paint "pop."

I personally prefer this look over the top image.

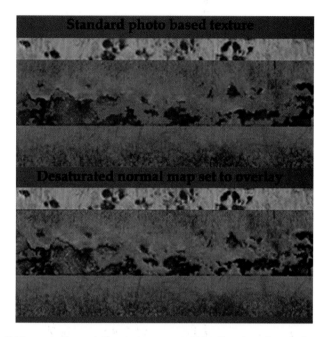

FIG 3.65

In Fig. 3.66, we go through the steps to create this effect. I tend to use it mainly for surfaces that have different layers or details such as rivets or grooves.

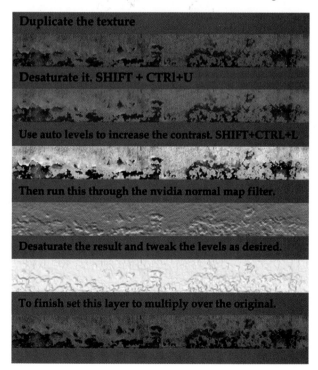

FIG 3.66

In Fig. 3.67, we show some more progression on the texture map. Various metal and mechanical elements were taken from photos I found online and used to give the motor some detail similar to the reference. Each element had to have the hue and saturation tweaked to make them sit together better.

More sections of metal images were imported and placed over the wheels tyre and surface and then set to overlay. The levels were manually tweaked to create a bit of contrast.

A new layer was created over the orange rubber layer. Using the standard brush tool and using the UV template as a guide, a white highlight was painted along the edge to pick it out on the model. This layer was then set to soft light, duplicated, sharpened and both layers had the opacity reduced until the result looked natural.

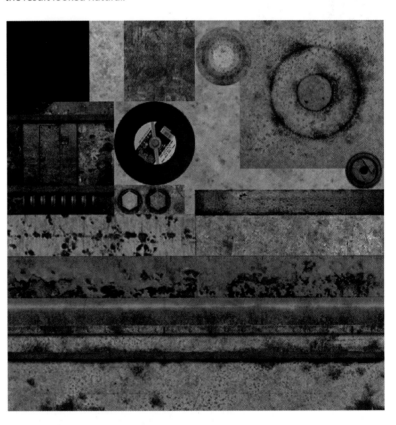

FIG 3.67

Jumping back into 3ds Max, a little more unwrapping was done to see how the new texture elements were working. Luckily no major changes needed to be made. If you take a look at the Edit UVWs window in Fig. 3.68, I have placed many of the UV shells outside of the main 0–1 range square. This is ok to do as I will not be baking any textures, and it helps to keep the workspace clean and easy to manage instead of having all the UV shells piled on top of one another.

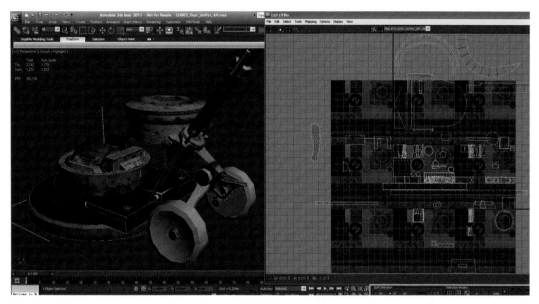

FIG 3.68

The last steps in adding polish to the texture included changing the buffer pad texture, as I found a better example online. A label and rivets have also been added to the handle in the top left corner of the texture.

At this point, once you are happy with the texture, it is advisable to flatten the image and save it as a different file. Once this is done, use the offset filter to offset the texture horizontally by 50% its width in pixels.

This is just to give the texture one final check to ensure all the U tiling strips at the bottom of the image do not have any seams. If there are any noticeable scenes, use the Clone Stamp tool to sample other areas of the texture and paint over the seam. Once it is seamless, use the offset filter to return the texture back to its original position.

To create the specular map, save the diffuse .PSD as a new specular .PSD file. Then, create new hue/saturation and levels adjustment layers. Reduce the saturation with the hue/saturation layer to 0 to desaturate all the layers at once. The levels layer can be used to adjust the overall lightness and contrast of the image, but before tweaking this, we need to use brighten and contrast on each individual layer to separate what will be shiny and what will be matte. Darker areas of the image will have no specularity, and the lighter values will have a relevant level of shininess.

Figure 3.69 shows the final textures. We should have a 512 × 512 diffuse for the floor buffer with a complimentary specular map to match.

The other two textures are the 256 × 256 diffuse black plastic texture with a 128 × 128 specular map.

I have halved the specular map for an optimization as it's just to add a little noise and interest to the material. If the floor buffers specular map is halved (which it could be), the contrast in shiny and matte surfaces would not be as sharp.

Once all the textures are final, you may need to go back into the Material Editor and tweak the specular level and glossiness to get the most use out of the textures.

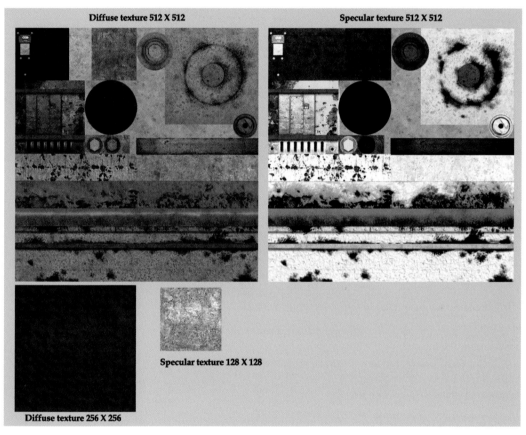

FIG 3.69

That's it. The model should now be ready for preparation to be used in an environment. If it was to go into a game engine, it would need LODs and a collision shape first. We'll be looking at lodding this mesh in Chapter 6.

Figure 3.70 is the final render to display the asset in all its glory on a dirty floor.

Presenting your work well is as important as creating it, so it's always worth going that extra mile to show off your work.

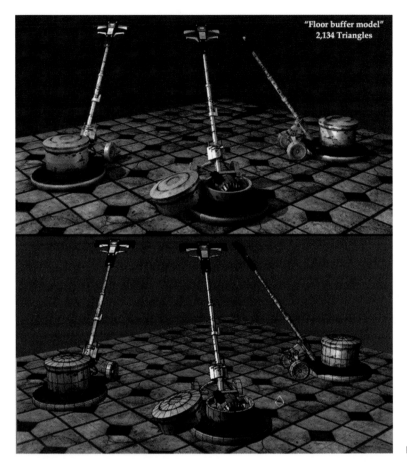

"Floor buffer model"
2,134 Triangles

FIG 3.70

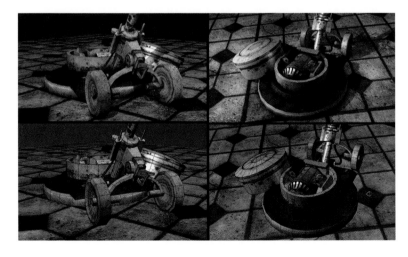

FIG 3.71

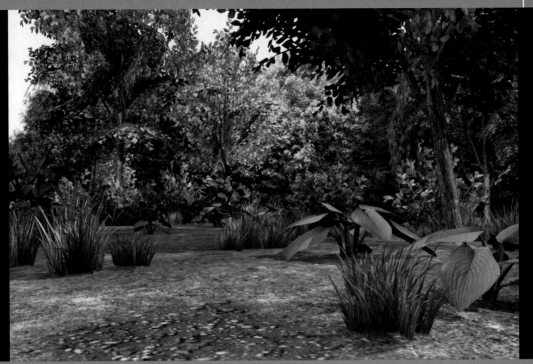

CHAPTER 4

Vegetation and Alpha Maps

Creating and Using Alpha Maps/Channels

In this chapter, we are going to look at the most common methods of creating various forms of vegetation used in the games industry.

As creating foliage and leaves still relies heavily on alpha maps or a texture with an alpha channel, I'll start off with a brief explanation.

An alpha map is a black-and-white or grayscale image, which controls the transparency of a surface when it's applied to a mesh using a shader. In the example pictured in Fig. 4.1, the alpha map is on the left, the diffuse texture is in the middle, and the final result applied to the mesh is on the right.

Alpha Map   **Diffuse Map**   **Both on model**

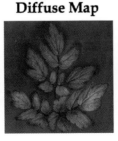
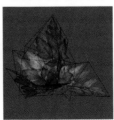

FIG 4.1

This works because the shader is interpreting values of 100% white as being fully opaque, and values of 100% black as being fully transparent. Any gray tones between 100% black and 100% white will be transparent.

Now that we know what an alpha map is, let's look at how we go about creating them.

The first step is always the source image for the diffuse. Whether it is hand painted or taken from a photo, you'll need to have this first before you create the alpha map. I'll use the previous example to demonstrate.

This was initially taken from a photo and then modified using a mixture of Photoshop's blending modes hand painting.

Initially, I "extracted" the leaves I wanted from the original photo and then used them to create the alpha channel.

Source photo   **Background removed**   **Alpha Channel**

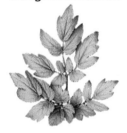
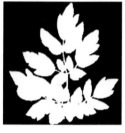

FIG 4.2

There are a few ways to do this.

I could simply create an alpha channel and start painting white around the leaves I want visible using the standard brush tool, but this takes time and also means the background will remain. I wanted to remove this.

I started by creating a 512 × 512 image file. I then copied the source image into this file and scaled it to fit into the square texture page (Ctrl + T). I then used the Lasso tool to create a selection around the area I wanted to keep.

I then inverted the selection by going to Select > Inverse on the menu bar. I then deleted the highlighted pixels. In a few key strokes, a large chunk of the unwanted image has been removed.

For the remaining pixels around the leaves, you could either use the eraser or manually paint the pixels out or you could use the magic wand tool to make pixel selections and delete them. The magic wand works best when the background is a different colour to the leaves, for example, a blue sky.

In this instance, it also works as there is a decent level of contrast in the image, but the tolerance needs to be kept low as the image is mainly green.

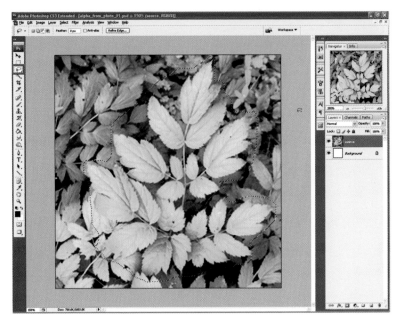

FIG 4.3

I decided to use the magic wand to quickly remove chunks of the image. I then finished up by using the eraser to manually tidy up the final few stray pixels.

I also adjusted the levels and hue and saturation on the final version before starting work on the diffuse texture.

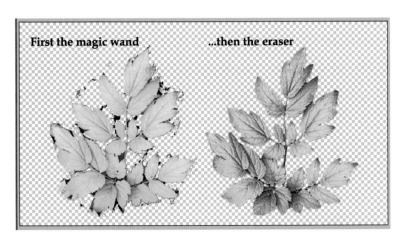

FIG 4.4

Now, we have separated out the piece of vegetation. We can quickly use this to create the alpha channel or at least a good starting point.

With the layer that the leaves are on selected, hold Ctrl + A and then select the small thumbnail image on the left of the layers name. This will select all pixels on the currently selected layer.

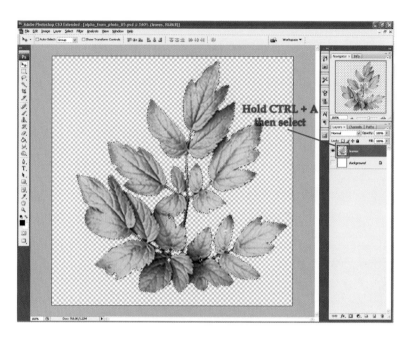

FIG 4.5

With this selection active, click on the channels tab. Go to the bottom right and click on the new layer icon highlighted in Fig. 4.6.

This will create a new alpha channel in the texture file. Next, select the standard brush tool at 100% opacity and paint the selected area. The result is fairly good, but there are a few gray and white pixels around that will need painting over with 100% black (RGB 0,0,0).

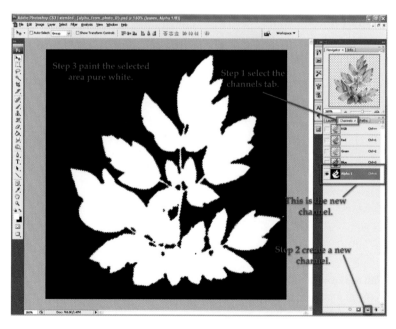

FIG 4.6

When the alpha channel has been cleaned up, we can preview the results in Photoshop over the RGB image.

Do this by turning on the RGB channels by clicking on the box to the left of the RGB channel at the top of the channels list. This will show or hide these channels. The same applies to the alpha channel.

When the alpha channel is displayed over the RGB channels, it will only show pixels under the white pixels of the alpha channel. In the next image, all the purple area represents the black values of the alpha channel.

You can change the color and opacity of the alpha channels appearance by double-clicking on the alpha channel.

It's worth noting that you can still paint and edit the alpha channel while viewing all the channels at once.

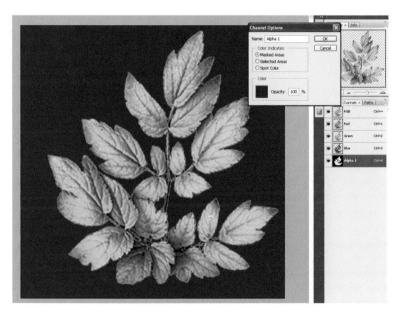

FIG 4.7

The last step would be to save out the final texture (once the diffuse map is complete) with the alpha channel, so it can be used in 3ds Max. There are two ways to get the alpha channel or map displaying in real time in the viewport.

The diffuse texture can be saved with the alpha channel in the same file with a format that stores the alpha information. Some formats are BMP, PNG, TIFF, TGA, and .DDS.

This texture, which will contain the diffuse and alpha channel, will need to be assigned to both the diffuse and opacity slot in a material. When it is assigned to the opacity slot, the bitmap parameters will need adjusting. By default, the Mono Channel Output is set to RGB Intensity. It needs to be changed to Alpha.

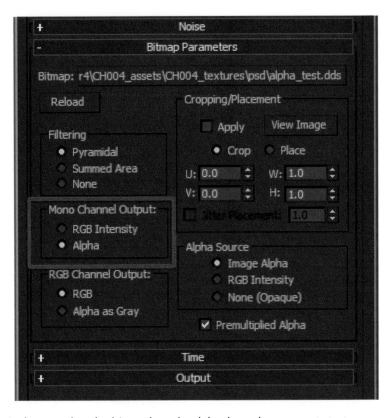

FIG 4.8

In the second method, I saved out the alpha channel as a separate texture. This can be done by pressing Ctrl + A over the selected alpha channel to highlight it, Ctrl + C to copy the selection, and then Ctrl + V in the RGB channels in the layers tab to paste it as a new layer. Then save the file as a separate texture after flattening the image.

Then just assign it to the opacity slot in the 3ds Max material and assign the diffuse texture into the diffuse slot.

Both methods should display the diffuse map working with the alpha map in the viewport once Show Standard Map in Viewport is turned on in the material and the following display mode selected main menu > Views > Show Materials in Viewport as > Standard Display with Maps is also on.

That concludes alpha maps—next we'll take a look at diffuse maps.

Creating the Diffuse Textures for Vegetation

In this section, I'll demonstrate how I created all the diffuse texture maps in Fig. 4.9.

The first thing to look at is the layout of the textures. The bushes in the first two images take up the entire texture sheet. This was intentional as I intend

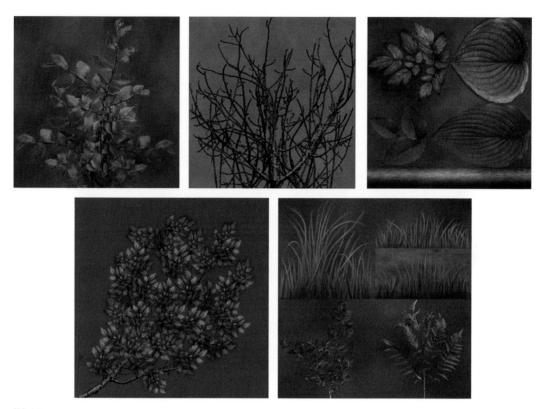

FIG 4.9

for the bushes to range from a medium to large size, so giving them more texture space will result in a higher resolution. All the textures are 512 × 512 pixels.

The texture sheet in the top right consists of four different types of leaves that will be used to create a variety of plants. This includes a horizontally tiling stalk section at the bottom, which will be shared between the various plants. Each leaf gets about 256 pixels square of texture space. These leaves are intended for small- to medium-sized plants.

The benefit of sharing many elements on a single texture sheet will mean that there are less individual texture files to deal with. In terms of real-time rendering in a game engine, the engine will also only have to call upon one texture and not four.

I also followed this concept of sharing through on smaller models on the bottom right image. This consists of a variety of grass and small plants, which will be used as a cheap solution to filling an environment full of vegetation.

The texture on the bottom left will be used as foliage for a tree. The leaves run diagonally across the texture sheet so that the space is used more efficiently.

121

If we were to have it vertical like the bushes, this would result in a top-heavy texture with a lot of wasted empty space at the bottom.

Let's move on to the actual texture creation.

The texture layout is the only real difference between all of these textures. The technique for creating the diffuse texture is largely the same for all of them.

I'm going to take the leaves used in the alpha map section to demonstrate this technique.

In the previous section, we extracted the leaves from the photo similar to the Fig. 4.10.

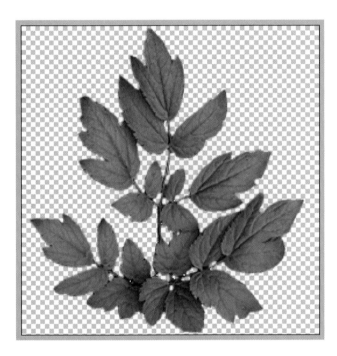

FIG 4.10

The first step is creating a background. Use the colour picker to select two different green colors, one for each swatch. Make sure there is enough contrast between the values, so we get a good result.

Then create a new layer (Shift + Ctrl + N). We're going to use the clouds filter to create a random blotchy background. Go to the main menu > Filter > Render > Clouds.

You may need to try adjusting the two colours a few times to get a good result. You should now have an image similar to the one in Fig. 4.12.

The layer the leaves are on has the blend mode set to normal. You could easily play around with all the different modes to see the results. The one technique may not work every time. It all depends on the initial photo reference.

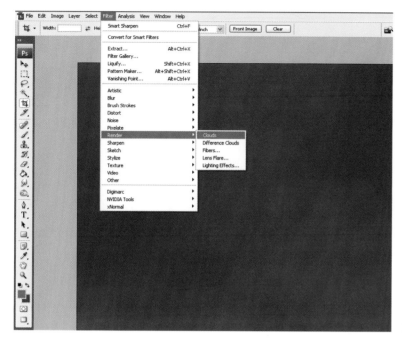

FIG 4.11

The issue I have with the leaves as they are now is that I don't like the varying colours and lighting from the photograph. In this instance, the color dodge blend mode worked really well to reduce these issues.

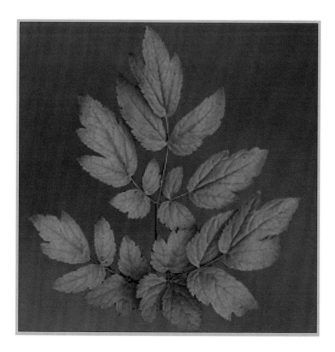

FIG 4.12

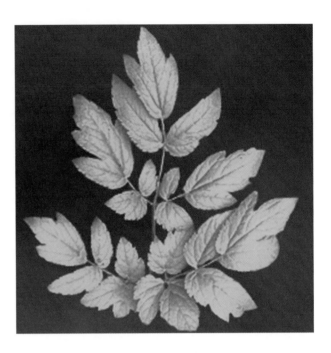

FIG 4.13

Obviously, now it is oversaturated, so use Image > Adjustments > Hue/
Saturation to rectify this. Move the slider to the left to reduce the strength of
the saturation. Even after this, I reduced the brightness and contrast on this
layer to reduce the details further. The results are shown in Fig. 4.14.

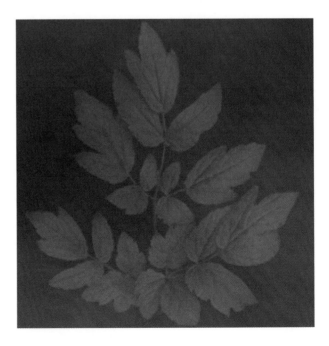

FIG 4.14

Now, copy the leaves layer (Ctrl + J). Then set the blend mode to normal. Press Shift + Ctrl + U to desaturate the image. Then press Shift + Ctrl + L to apply auto levels. This will increase the contrast of the values in the layer as in Fig. 4.15.

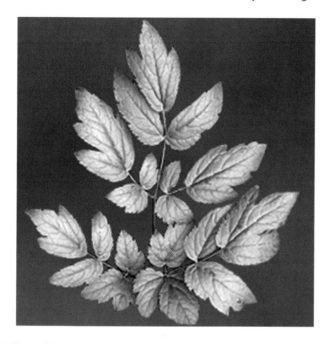

FIG 4.15

Set this layers blend mode to overlay. I also reduced the opacity to 46%. This will create contrast in the image. It is true that the previous steps removed the contrast and here we are putting it back in.

So I don't appear crazy, have a look at both textures compared side by side with each other in Fig. 4.16.

As you can see, my preferred texture on the right is softer with less color variation and contrast. As the grayscale layer set to overlay can have its opacity adjusted, we can control the contrast easily.

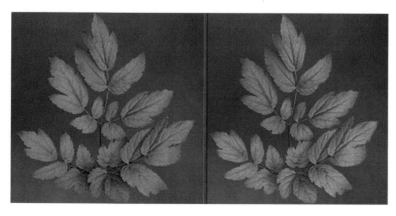

FIG 4.16

Create two new layers and place them below the original leaves layer and set to color dodge. We will use these to paint color variation back into the texture. I want to take this a lot further than the original image.

For the first layer, I painted the stalks of the foliage brown and used a darker green with a touch more blue to paint some shadows. A lighter green was used to paint highlights. I used the standard Photoshop brush with a medium opacity. In Fig. 4.17, the new layer is on the left over the background, and on the right, all the layers are displayed.

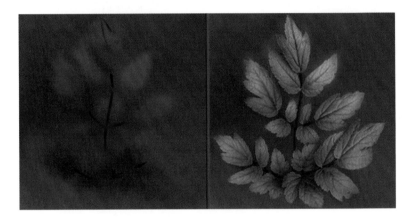

FIG 4.17

At this point, we could easily leave this texture as complete.

For the environment tutorial later in the book, I really wanted more color in the foliage. More specifically, I wanted autumn colors. Using the second layer that we created, I gradually built up a range of yellows and browns around the ends and edges of the leaves. At this point, I was satisfied with the result. Figure 4.18 shows the second paint layer on the left over the background and the final result on the right.

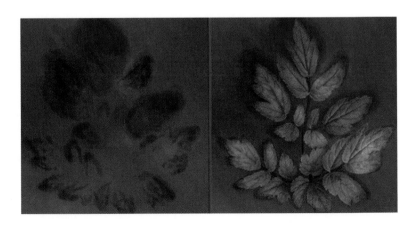

FIG 4.18

126

I created the other three sets of leaves on the texture sheet in exactly the same way, using reference from different photos. The horizontally tiling stalk element running along the bottom of the texture sheet was created by using the Rectangular Marquee Tool (M) to create a selection.

I then created a new layer and used the gradient tool set to reflected gradient. This applied a cylindrical style shading to define the stalk.

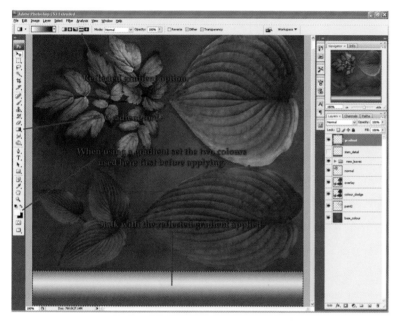

FIG 4.19

I then set this gradient layer to overlay. As it then looked too smooth, I copied a section from another image and stretched it out horizontally over the stem and set it to soft light. This was just to add a bit of noise and variety to the stem. This layer was also tiled horizontally using the offset tool.

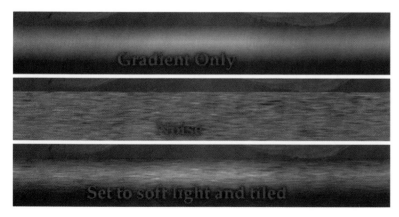

FIG 4.20

The other textures were created in the exact same way. For the dry bush, I extracted the section of tree branches from a photo. I then duplicated some elements and moved them around to fill out the texture sheet more. After this, the background was created. The texture was then adjusted afterwards to blend in with the other textures within the scene.

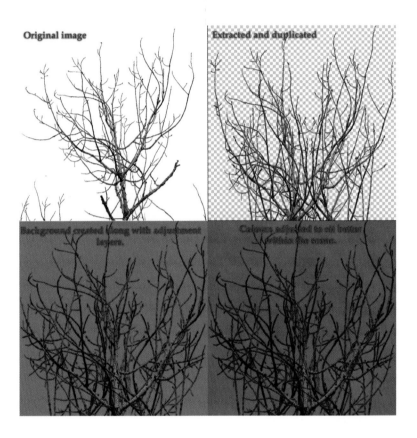

Original image

Extracted and duplicated

Background created along with adjustment layers.

Colours adjusted to sit better within the scene.

FIG 4.21

The tree branch and foliage were created by using the leaves from the earlier section and taking a section of the bush from the previous texture. Figure 4.22 shows the steps in creating this texture.

First, the branch was rotated, so it starts in the bottom left corner. I then started to duplicate and move, rotate, and scale the sets of leaves and place them all over the branch.

I tried to get as much variety as possible by tweaking the lightness, hue, and saturation of some copies as I went along.

After I was happy with the result, I dropped in a background. This time the foliages blend mode is set to normal, so I did not use the cloud filter on the background.

The final steps were to duplicate the leaves and desaturate the image. Then I set it to multiply to get some shading and contrast into the foliage. Another common thing I do with foliage is to duplicate the final version and place this layer beneath the original. Then blur the copy. The reason for this is that if you use a file type or game engine that uses mip-maps, it will prevent the alpha and diffuse maps having issues such as a "halo" effect on the textures.

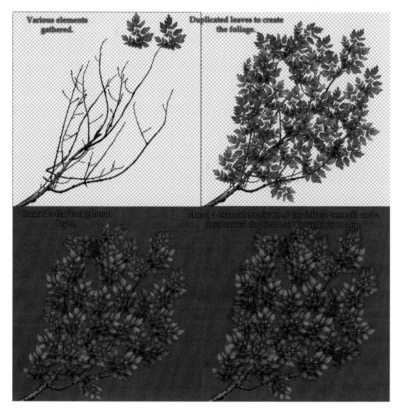

FIG 4.22

Finally, there is a slightly different technique I use for creating grass.

The two bottom sections of the grass texture were created by using photographs as a base as in the previous examples. The other types of grass were created entirely in Photoshop.

First, create a new file with the dimensions of 512 × 512 pixels. Go to the main menu > Edit > Preferences > Guides, Grid, Slices & Count. Under the Grid option, set the Gridline every to 256 and pixels. You can also change the color if you wish. I have set mine to red.

If the grid is not appearing, you can toggle it under View > Show > Grid or by pressing Ctrl + H.

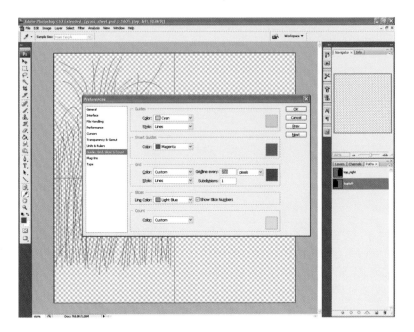

FIG 4.23

The grid should now be displayed over your texture, dividing it up into four sections of 256 pixels square. This tool is very useful when creating texture sheets as you can ensure all the elements are the correct resolution. I intend for most of the grass to fit inside a 256 pixels square.

Then using the *pen tool* lay out some curved paths that will be used later as the grass, I tried to emulate the way grass grows with the flow of the paths. To use the pen tool, simply left-click on the image to start a path. Left-click and hold elsewhere to create a new point. You can then adjust the curve of the line by moving the mouse. Then keep repeating this process until you are happy with the amount of paths. You can adjust the path's anchor points after they are created using the direct selection tool. This is in the same area as the path selection tool. Hold the LMB to access it.

In Fig. 4.24, you will notice I started the paths near the base of the bottom left quadrant. This was because when stroking the path, the Simulate Pen Pressure will be checked. This option will create a tapered line for the grass from bottom to top. The blades of grass should be thickest at the bottom and taper to a fine tip, so by starting the paths below the area we want to have the thickest will give the desired result.

To do this, select the paths with the path selection tool. Then right-click and choose stroke path or go to Edit > Stroke… This tool takes the options from any tool in the drop-down list. For this, I used the brush tool. Make sure Simulate Pen Pressure is ticked and then press OK. Figure 4.25 shows these options.

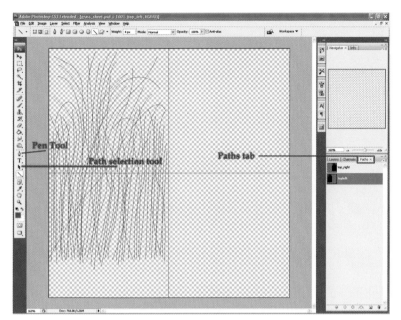

FIG 4.24

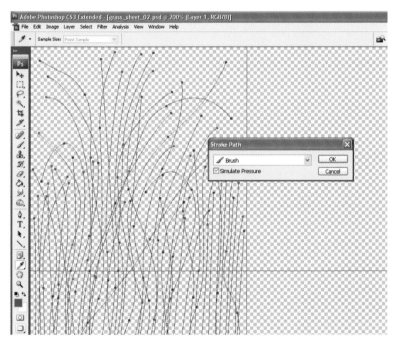

FIG 4.25

The end result should be similar to the grass on the left on Fig. 4.26. To finish off the grass, I used a soft airbrush with a low opacity to build up a gradient on the bottom of the grass. Then with a standard brush on a medium opacity, I manually painted some highlights onto the blades of grass.

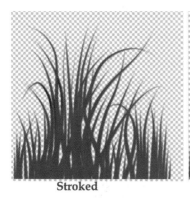
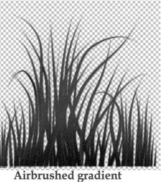
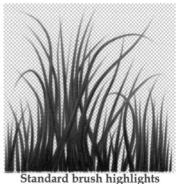

Stroked   **Airbrushed gradient**   **Standard brush highlights**

FIG 4.26

This concludes the work on our diffuse textures.

Always experiment using different methods, blend modes, and photographic reference.

Next, we'll have a look at modeling vegetation.

Modeling Vegetation

Creating vegetation for games using alpha maps usually means the geometry can remain quite simple. You only need a group of planes with some simple modeling, letting the textures do all the work.

A good approach to creating vegetation models is to look at the "flow" of the plant or how a plant or tree grows. Also pay attention to the overall silhouette. This will determine the form of the mesh and how components will be placed together to create the overall shape to achieve a realistic natural look.

In Fig. 4.27, I did a quick paint over of a variety of trees to show how they differ in the way they grow. The blue lines represent the "flow" of the foliage or how it grows on the branches. The red lines are the growth patterns of the trunks and branches. I use this approach to breakdown the shapes into simpler forms before I begin modeling the tree.

FIG 4.27

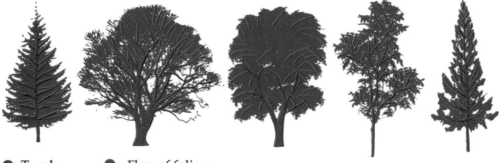

● **Trunk**   ● **Flow of foliage**

This approach of breaking a complex object down into simpler parts also works well for plants. In Fig. 4.28, I demonstrate this. On the left is the reference. In the middle are quick sketch attempts at breaking down the shape of the leaves and growing pattern of the plants. Finally, silhouetted images of the final models are on the right to show how this technique has been applied.

Plant silhouettes

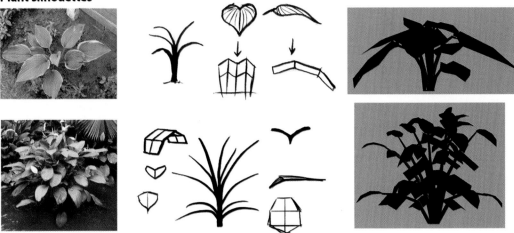

FIG 4.28

We'll start with the grass models.

Create a square plane and apply the grass texture sheet to it and planar map it. Then using the slice plane tool, divide up the different grass elements as shown in Fig. 4.29. Then duplicate the plane four more times. The idea is to delete all except one grass element on each plane. The end result will be each mesh consisting of only one type of grass. You should end up with five types.

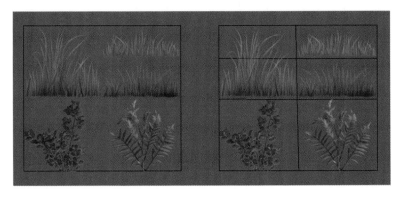

FIG 4.29

In Fig. 4.30, on the top two grass meshes, I duplicated the polygon and rotated it 90° to create crossed planes. Then the two planes were combined into one mesh. This is the most common and basic grass model used in games. It is very cheap and can be duplicated a lot within a scene to quickly create dense areas of grass.

This model was taken a step further in the bottom two examples on Fig. 4.30. Slice Plane was used to add in some additional edges to the plane. These new edges were then used to add some bends on the polygons. The example on the right is a combination of this method and the crossed plane method to create a really dense patch of grass.

You can make the grass models as complex or detailed as you like, by using a few different textures or adding extra edges to create smoother more detailed shapes. In current games, the methods shown here are usually enough.

The more detail you add, the less efficient the models will be when they are placed thousands of times in a scene.

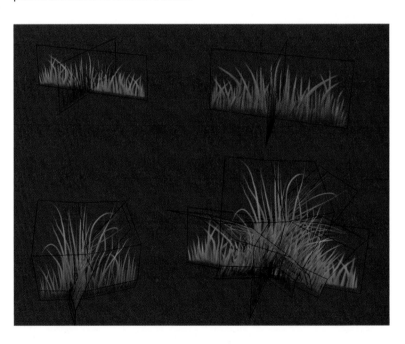

FIG 4.30

In Fig. 4.30, I have cut around the texture to reduce the amount of unused transparency on the mesh.

This is a widely used optimization as unused transparency on the surface of the mesh will still be calculated when rendering even if it is not visible.

In Fig. 4.31, the area highlighted in red is the area I have removed. This makes the mesh more efficient to render, especially when there are a lot of instances of the model in the scene.

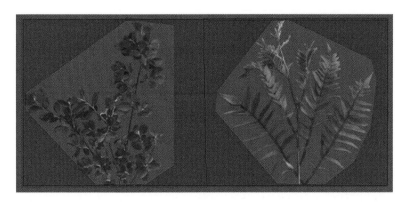

FIG 4.31

I then used these extra vertices to add depth to the model by pulling them back.
The meshes were then duplicated and positioned to act like crossed planes.

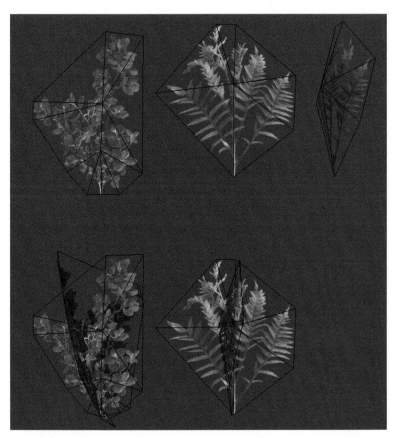

FIG 4.32

The next models are the selection of smaller plants. They are very simple
models and designed to be cheap and used numerous times. These models
were created in the same way as the grass. Three of them also have stems.

These were created by moving, rotating, and scaling the vertices of a three-sided cylinder. You could start with a cylinder with a few height segments or use slice plane to add in some edge loops as you need them.

The leaves on the far right plant have more modeling detail on them. The cut tool was used to add extra geometry. The vertices were then adjusted to create a central crease in the leaf.

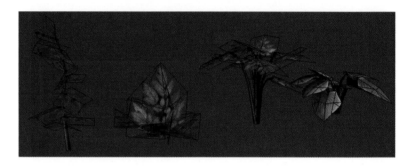

FIG 4.33

The next models created were the bushes. The starting point was a square flat plane. Another was added with some extra edges, and the central vertices moved out to create some depth.

I then built the bush out from a central point on the ground using duplicates of these two meshes. The model on the right is much cheaper and intended for use on the edges of the scene.

I could have cut around the bush as an optimization from the initial state before I duplicated them as mentioned earlier to reduce the surface area of unused transparency.

FIG 4.34

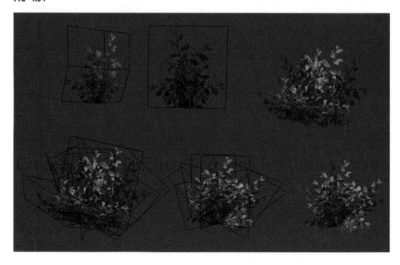

As an example to how flexible vegetation meshes are, I assigned the dry bush texture to this model. It looks a lot different even though it's the same mesh. This is easy to do as a texture swap as long as the texture layout is similar; this will mean you won't need to remap anything.

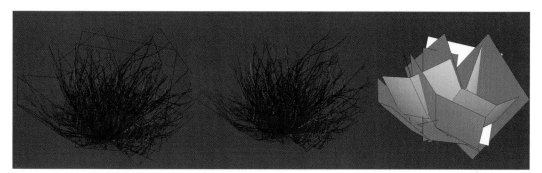

The final model we will look at is the tree.

FIG 4.35

Start with a cylinder and delete the polygons on the top and bottom. Then using the slice plane tool, add some edge loops.

Next, use these to model the bottom of the trunk. Duplicate the mesh, scale it, and position it high up on the original mesh. This will form the basic shape of a branch. These steps are shown in Fig. 4.36.

FIG 4.36

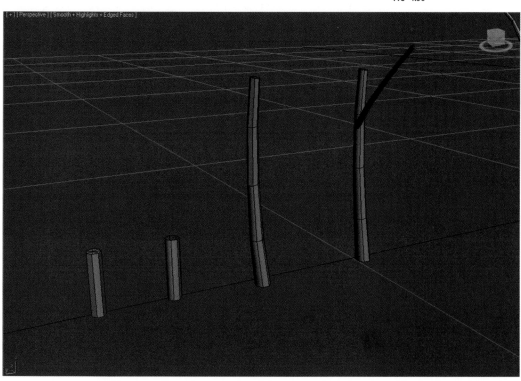

Duplicate the trunk and branch meshes a few more times and use them to create the tree. Figure 4.37 shows the final version of the first-pass tree model.

After placing all the branches, I spent a few minutes modeling more to create some variety in the model.

The next step was to combine all the meshes together using attach and then to stitch the branches into the main trunk mesh. Use the cut tool to create the edges on the trunk to match the branches. Delete the faces on the trunk where the branch will connect. Then use weld or target weld to stitch the vertices of the trunk and branches together.

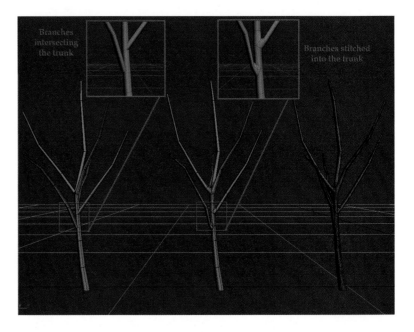

FIG 4.37

Attaching the branches to the trunk is a personal preference of mine as I prefer to have the branches and trunk as one solid mesh. It is ok to leave the branches intersecting the trunk as in the version on the left of Fig. 4.37. I just prefer the look of the lighting and shading on the stitched version in the center.

When you are satisfied with the tree model, next we need to unwrap it.

Cylindrical mapping was the main technique used, paying close attention to keeping the seams facing inwards into the tree, so they'll be hidden by foliage later.

Figure 4.38 shows the final unwrap of the trunk and branches. I tried to have as few UV shells as possible. There is one for the trunk and one for each branch.

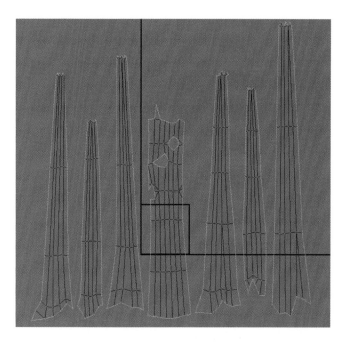

FIG 4.38

Now that the tree itself is complete, it's time to look at the foliage. Just as we did before, I created a flat plane and one with some extra detail. I then used many duplicates of these to fill out the foliage on the tree placing them around the branches. Moving, rotating, and scaling them as I went. Figure 4.39 shows the two foliage meshes used on the left and the final tree on the right.

When the foliage was complete, it was attached to the trunk to create one mesh. The pivot point was then centered to the object and snapped to the bottom vertices at the base of the trunk. This will allow for easier placement of the tree in the environment later.

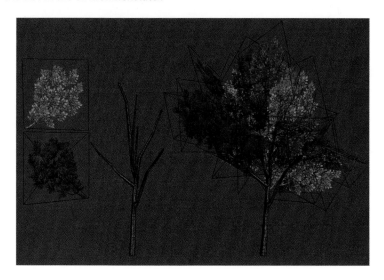

FIG 4.39

As it is still not possible to build current game environments full of thousands of trees, many cheaper solutions are used to make environments seem fuller than they actually are. One of these methods is the use of tree walls.

Tree walls are flat planes or simple meshes used on the edges of an environment. They usually consist of one texture that may tile. Figure 4.40 shows a flat plane with the texture applied.

FIG 4.40

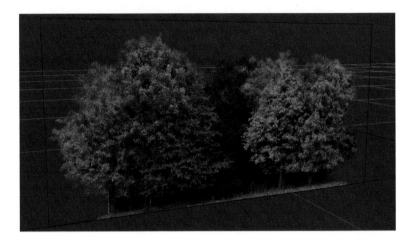

Figure 4.41 shows a similar mesh, but a section of a cylinder has been used to give the model more form.

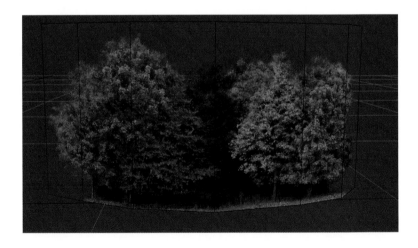

FIG 4.41

As always, this concept can be taken one step further. I would personally use the previous tree wall methods if they were to be placed a good distance away from the game play area. They are great background fillers, but they don't hold up well to close inspection if a player is beside them.

One solution is to fill out the tree wall with other meshes and create a more expensive version that will sit well just off to the side of the game play area behind other assets. Figure 4.42 shows a good example of this.

It was created from most of the meshes created in this tutorial.

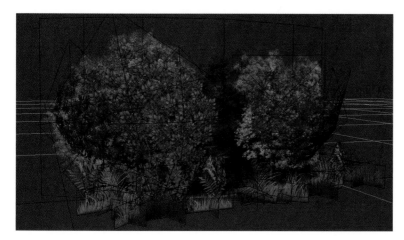

FIG 4.42

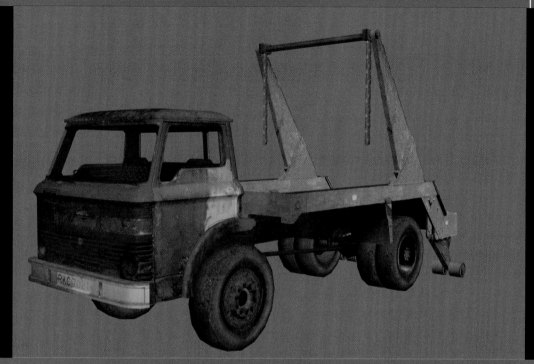

CHAPTER 5

Low-Poly Vehicle

David Griffiths

Note from this book's author: David has taken a step-by-step approach for this tutorial. If you get stuck at any point, feel free to grab the 3ds Max file from the Web site and move on. Remember that you'll really benefit only if you do the whole build yourself, so try to solve your own problems instead of jumping ahead. You will improve quicker and will be a stronger artist at the end with the ability to troubleshoot future problems.

Some of the original (consecutive) build files have been removed in the text to speed up the build process for you (Files 23, 24, or 77, for example); please follow directly to the next instruction in the text.

Create a plane for each view of the vehicle. A front, back, side, and top, so four in total. A good tip to get accurate proportions and avoid distortion is to create a plane the same size as the image. Ensure you are using the same measuring system throughout the project—for example, the metric system.

Once created, freeze the planes by going to the Display panel > Freeze > Freeze Selected and make sure to uncheck "Show frozen in grey" in the Display Properties, which is under the Freeze menu. Turn on the Poly Statistics in the viewport to keep a tab of the polygon budget (by typing 7 on the keyboard).

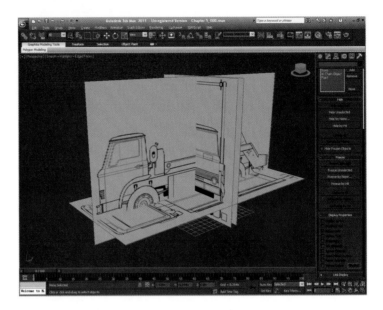

FIG 5.1

Create a new layer using the layer manager, by clicking on the Manage Layers button on the main toolbar.

Then click on the top-left button on the layers pop-up window, Create New Layer. You can rename this layer to whatever you like, but I have just left it as the Max default name. Make sure there is a black tick to the right of the layer name to show it's the current layer. If not, click on the white box to make it the current layer. Every newly created layer will by default be the current layer.

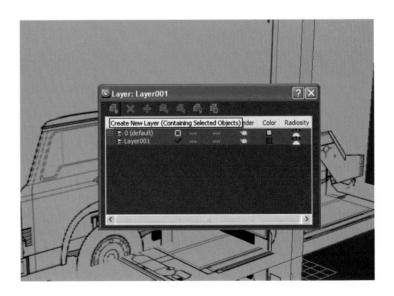

FIG 5.2

In the Top viewport, create a box that will automatically be assigned to this layer.

In the materials, give the box a color and set the opacity to something like 70% so that you can see the blueprint planes through the box. Turn on edge faces and give the wireframe a color different from the material color. I have chosen black.

I created the box in the Top viewport and positioned it roughly around the cab.

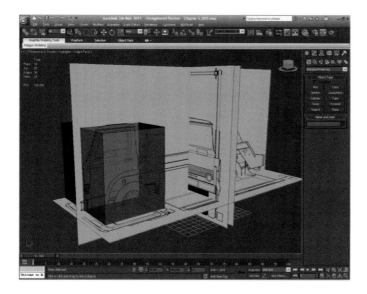

FIG 5.3

Right-click on the box to bring up the Max menu and convert the box to an editable poly. Scale the box, moving the vertices, so it fits approximately around the truck cab.

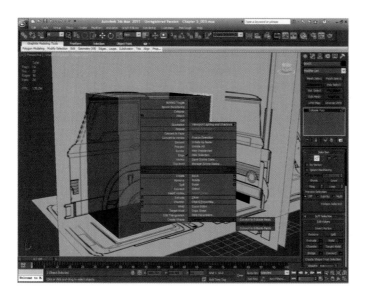

FIG 5.4

Using the Slice Plane tool, start splitting up the box along the z-axis with subdivisions at key intervals and then follow the details of the cab in the pictures. If you can't see the splits that you are making and you want to see all the edges, then make sure that you have the edges unchecked only in the Object Properties menu. Sometimes it is good to toggle edges on and off.

You should end up with something like Fig. 5.5:

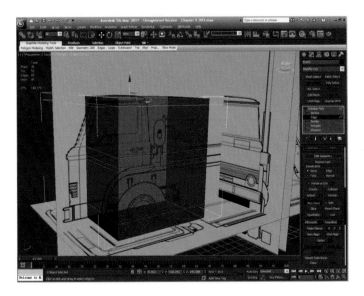

FIG 5.5

Split the cab directly down the center and delete one half of it. Now, start moving the new vertices of the remaining half that you have made to fit the shape of the cab more accurately.

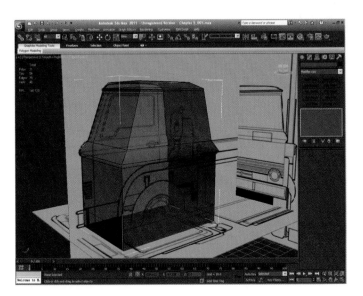

FIG 5.6

Now, we need to make it more rounded by using the chamfer tool. As you can see, I have chamfered the outer edges once to make it more rounded, but it still needs much more work to make it rounded, and we need to tidy up the new edges that 3ds Max has given us.

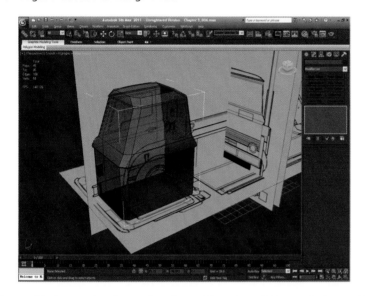

FIG 5.7

I have added more chamfers to the edges of the cab, and I have tidied up and moved the vertices to better interpret the roundedness of the shape. The edges can't be rounded too much because that would give us too many polygons, so look for something that is fairly smooth, but still low enough on detail.

Here you can see that I have used the same principle to round the center section of the cab in the same way, keeping the detail low while maintaining the curves.

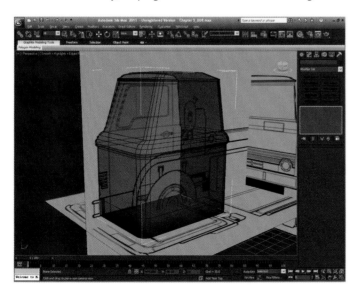

FIG 5.8

Now, split the roof to create the same amount of detail in the form of the curve.

When adjusting the splits in the roof, you will need to move the vertices around to fit the shape of the cab. You can do this a number of ways: by moving the vertices by hand or scaling them. If you scale them, you might want to consider mirroring your cab model to make the scaling easier, as 3ds Max will by default scale from the center.

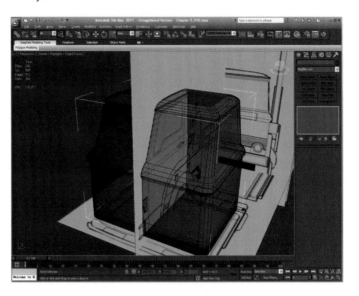

FIG 5.9

The cab needs a few subdivisions along the world x-axis so that we can add more curvature to the roof and the rest of the body in general. I have deleted the other half of the cab again, as this is the way I like to work, although you could use the mirror instance so the other half is modeled at the same time.

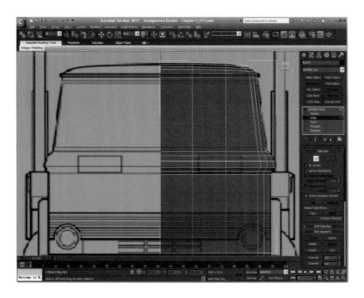

FIG 5.10

With the subdivisions added, move the points to fit the curve of the roof more precisely. I recommend that you keep going through your entire cab model and keep refining it because this is very important in 3D modeling. Adding new vertices, edges, and polygons can get out of hand if you don't watch what is happening.

Next, let's move the vertices in the new divisions we have made on the world *y*-axis to curve the front and the back ever so slightly.

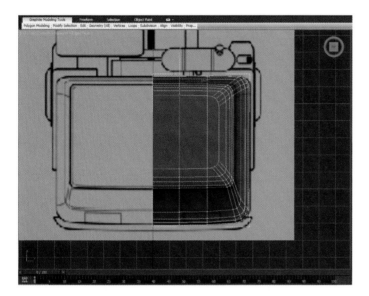

FIG 5.11

We need to add some more divisions along the world *y*-axis so that we can create more detail in the side of the cab.

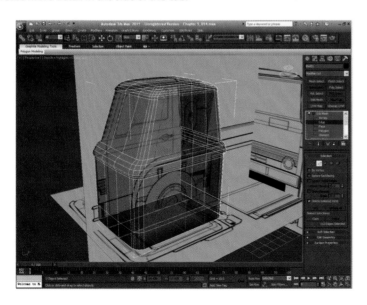

FIG 5.12

The cab has a lip just underside the roof, which needs to be modeled, and we can extrude that from the preparations we made earlier.

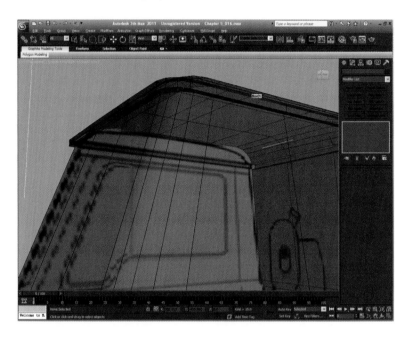

FIG 5.13

Let's look at creating some of the other features of the cab such as the wheel arches. We need to create a shape that we can use as a Boolean to give us the shape. Create a cylinder. I have created one with 28 sides.

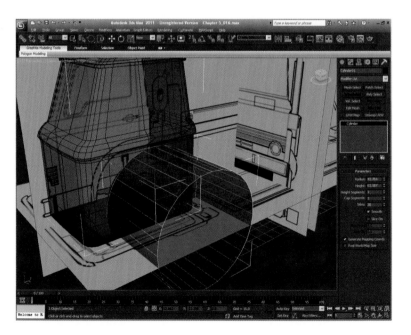

FIG 5.14

Delete 3/4 of the cylinder so that you leave the quarter of the shape that will make up the wheel arch.

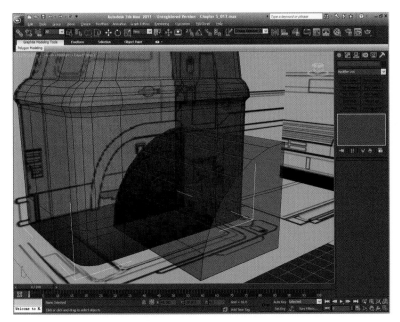

FIG 5.15

Extrude the outermost edges of the new wheel arch so that they extend past the bottom of the cab and out of the back of the cab. It is important that the edges go beyond the boundaries of the cab for the next Boolean.

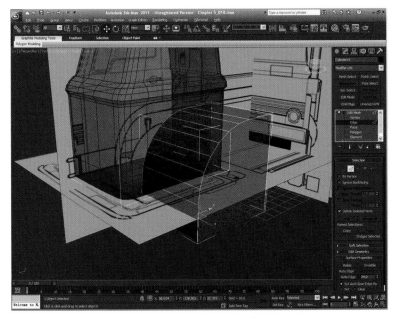

FIG 5.16

To begin to make the shape of the start of the wheel arch, we need to create a Boolean with the cut/refine function. First, select the cab, go to Create > Compound Object > Boolean, and then select Cut > Refine from the Parameters menu. Then, click on "pick Operand B" and select the 3/4 cylinder. It will disappear leaving the cuts we need behind.

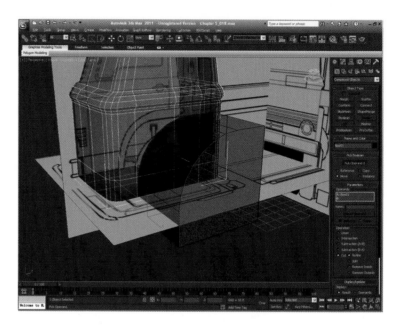

FIG 5.17

Now, we can delete the polygons left in the Boolean function to create a hole, which will become the wheel arch.

FIG 5.18

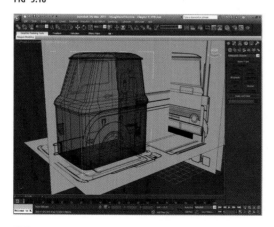
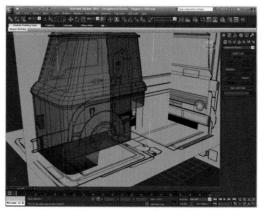

Select all of the edges from the curve of the Boolean that we just created and extrude them to create a lip, which will form the protruding lip of the wheel arch.

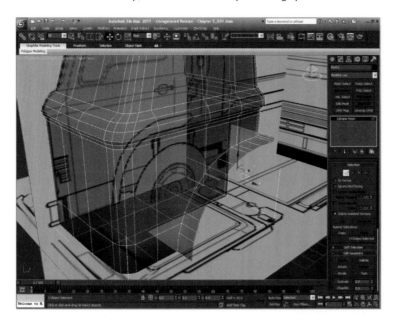

FIG 5.19

Some of the extra lines and vertices that we created when performing the Boolean will have to be cleaned up. It is important to keep the model as neat and tidy as possible. We need to look for the extra vertices and edges and decide which ones can be deleted or welded. Obviously, if you delete vertices, you will create holes, so use something like Target Weld and Move instead.

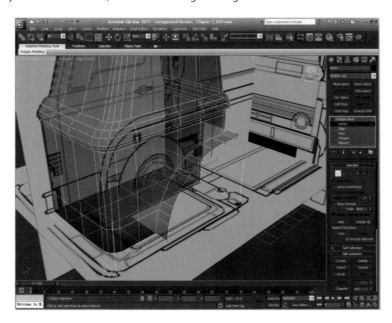

FIG 5.20

We also need to create a few new edges to the wheel arch so that we can preserve the curve and keep it regular.

The wheel arch needs to be extended further out from the cab body. Select the edges at the back of the cab for the wheel arch and extrude them.

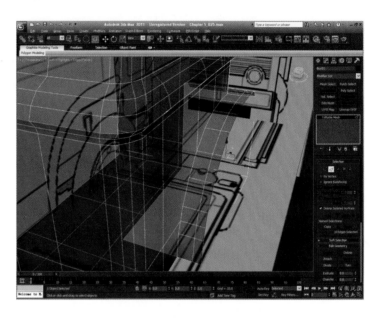

FIG 5.21

The edges of the wheel arch need to be curved around. This is done by scaling the outer vertices. The form of the arch needs to be altered slightly, so a little refinement is required.

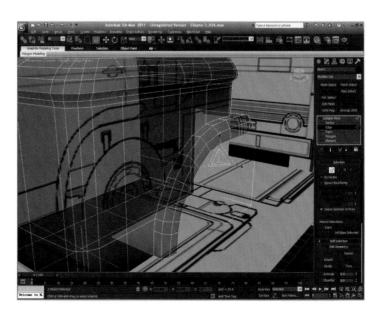

FIG 5.22

154

We now need to start looking at the detailing on the doors and windows. I create these by using the Divide Edge function, but you could select polygons and use Slice if you prefer. We could Boolean these details, but most of the information for the door and front window could be put in manually; feel free to use the Boolean function for them if you're more comfortable with that tool or whichever method you're most comfortable with. Remember to remove any unwanted detail after each Boolean transformation to keep your model neat and efficient. You should now have the seam of the door detailed as shown in Fig. 5.23.

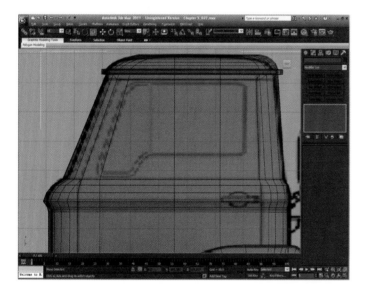

FIG 5.23

Select the edges of the door and add a chamfer modifier to them.

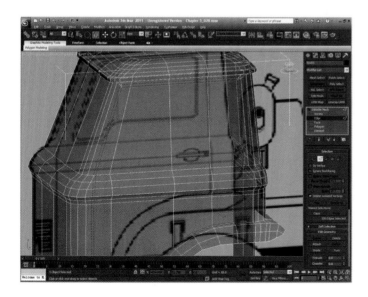

FIG 5.24

Clean up the undesired vertices that the chamfer function has given you. Some of the edges also need to be tidied up slightly to keep all the lines and edges flowing across the model. Try to keep a neat topology when creating any new faces or edges, and try to make sure that any new details are constructed from edges that neatly loop around the object

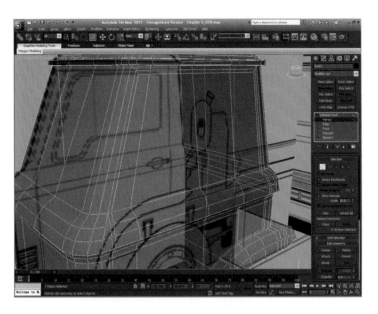

FIG 5.25

Select the polygons that were created by the chamfer command and extrude them inwards by approximately 0.8. These polygons will be used to create the start of the door seam.

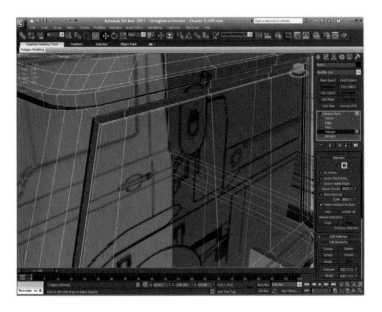

FIG 5.26

Now weld all the inner vertices of the seam together to create an inner groove. Your door seam is now complete.

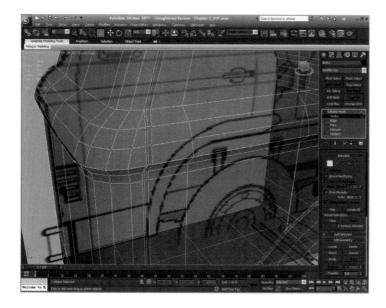

FIG 5.27

Detail the seam of the front window, using Divide Edge (or Slice or whatever you prefer) as before. To do this accurately, you will need to jump into the Front viewport and outline the edges of the glass.

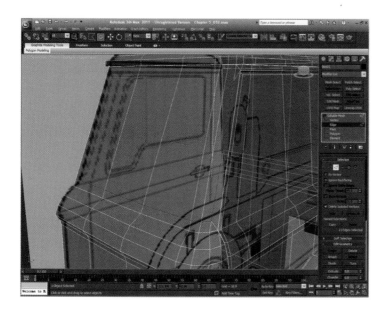

FIG 5.28

Chamfer the window edges and clean up the result.

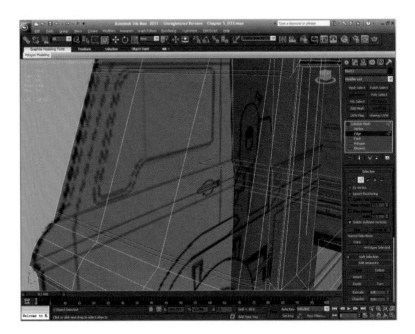

FIG 5.29

As with the door, we need to extrude the polygons that the chamfer has given us. This time, instead of extruding polygons inwards, we extrude them out and then weld the outer vertices. This step will give us the raised edge required.

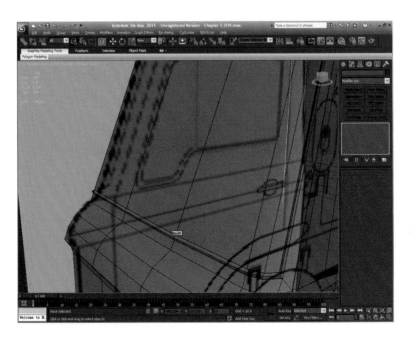

FIG 5.30

Next, we need to create the door window with the help of a Boolean shape. First, create a box in the Side viewport with a couple of subdivisions. Manipulate it until it fits the window shape as shown.

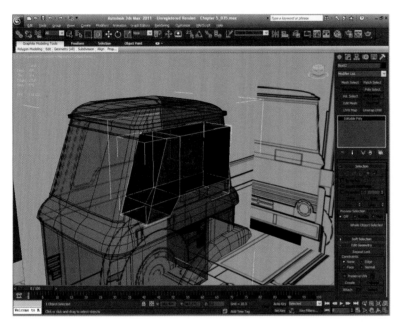

FIG 5.31

Now, we need to create the Boolean using cut or refine and clean up the result edges, vertices, or polygons.

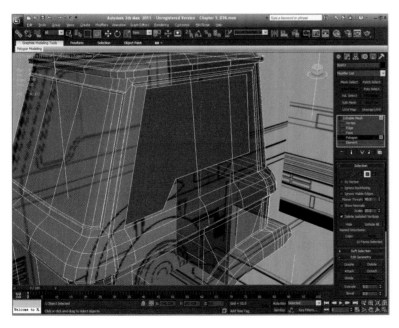

FIG 5.32

We need to create a recess or lip similar to that in the real photograph or blueprints of the cab door. To do this, extrude the selected window polygons and then scale them to create the required indentation.

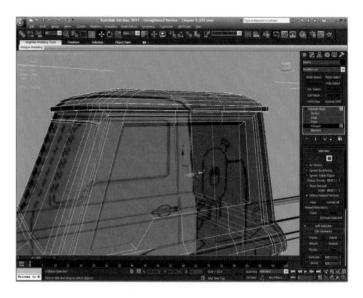

FIG 5.33

We will now create another edge in the door window all round the sill that we just created. To do this, divide all of the polygons right through the middle. To make sure that 3ds Max splits them in the center, turn on 3D snap with "midpoint" checked. Once created, the new midpoint vertices need to be scaled slightly outwards. You can use the scale tool or move the points manually. I've gone through and selected all the edges so that you can see clearly what I have created.

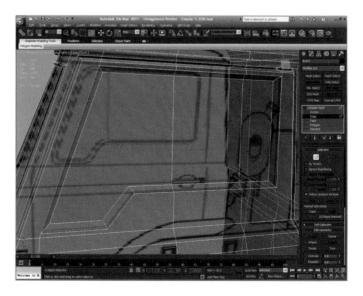

FIG 5.34

Now we need to repeat the same process for the rear windows. These will be created exactly like the door window, so just follow the steps again. You should end up with something like Fig. 5.35. Don't worry too much if yours doesn't match my example exactly—it doesn't have to be perfect.

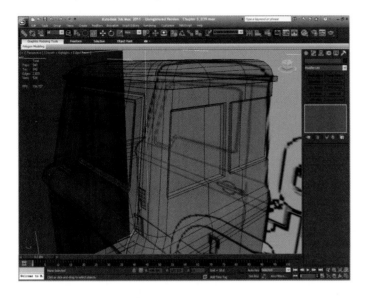

FIG 5.35

Looking at our progress so far, the side windows we created look a little too square, making the truck look slightly fake or a bit too low poly. It would be a good idea to round them off slightly by chamfering the corner edges. We should probably only do this once to keep the polygon count down on the truck. Feel free to make the curves more complex than I have if you want a better-looking vehicle, but remember that this is a low-poly vehicle.

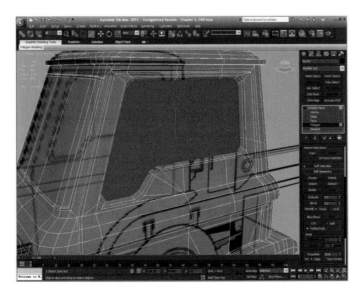

FIG 5.36

As before, we need to clean up any extra vertices created and make sure that all the edges are clean and run round the object smoothly. I have chosen to make some of the edges visible, although this isn't strictly necessary. Unchecking "Edges only" in the Object Properties helps you see all the edges that define an object and therefore to see clearly what edges, if any, are causing problems.

Repeat the same chamfer process on the rest of the windows to make the windows look a bit more smooth and realistic.

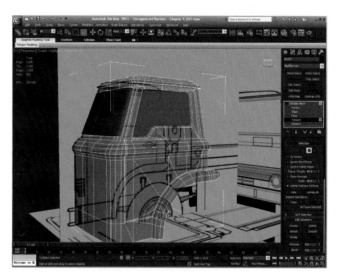

FIG 5.37

We need to do the same recess-type structure around the front wind screen. This usually wouldn't be modeled, but because the final model won't have windows, we must show it to keep continuity. This recess lip is created the same way as for the other windows. I have selected the polygons here so that you can see what I've done.

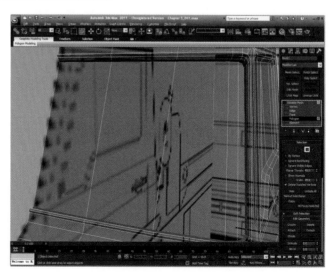

FIG 5.38

Now, we can start to look at the front lights. We need to Boolean a cylinder into the cab. The cylinder should be approximately of 12 sides (I wouldn't use fewer than twelve sides, but if you would like more fidelity and a smoother look to the light, use more sides; but always go up in twos).

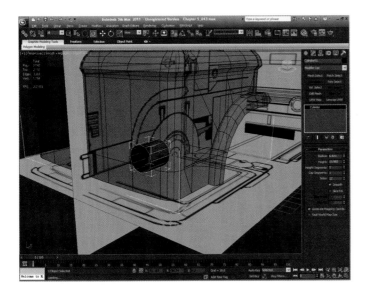

FIG 5.39

The cylinder has now been Boolean'd from the cab. The Boolean was again set with the cut/refine option. As always, you have to clean the mesh. This is a common task to perform after every Boolean transform you perform.

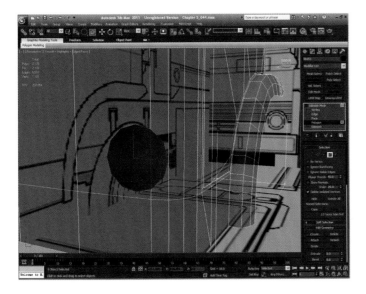

FIG 5.40

The new polygons that have been made for the light can now be extruded inwards so that we can start making the concave form of the headlight.

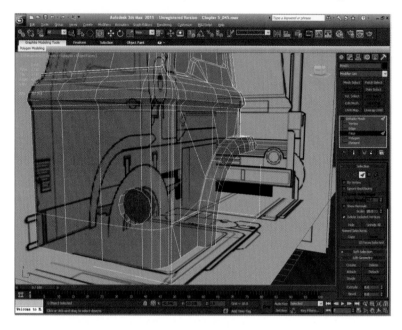

FIG 5.41

Once the polygons have been extruded, they must be made planar. An easy way to do this is to convert your model into an editable poly (if it isn't one already) and use the Make Planar function located in the Modify panel when a polygon is selected. In this instance, I used Make Planar on the y-axis.

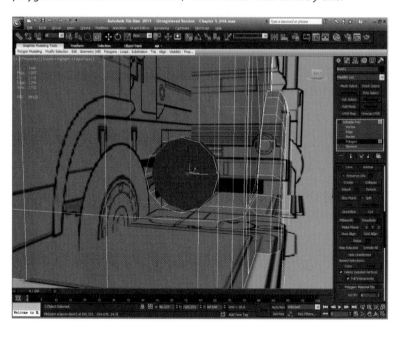

FIG 5.42

164

We need to scale these inner faces and extrude them again. Once the new sets of polygons have been extruded, we need to scale those, too.

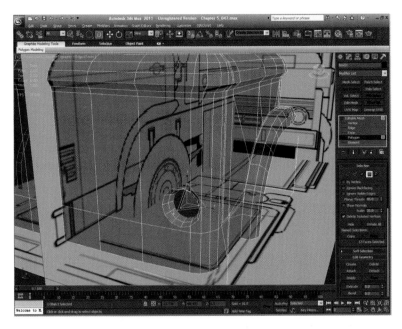

FIG 5.43

Extrude another set of faces, but instead of scaling them, select all of the vertices and collapse them into one using Collapse.

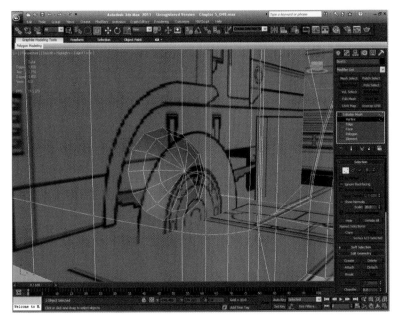

FIG 5.44

Let's take a break for a moment and see how our truck is progressing.

It's important to stop every now and again when you are modeling, to get a drink or move around, or just to take a look at your progress. It's so easy to select one or two vertices too many when collapsing and take out a few that you didn't mean to. If you notice the mistake quick enough, it won't do much harm, but if you fail to spot it because you're so busy detailing specific areas, it can cause you a bit of pain and some lost time. Remember to drink plenty of water when you are trying to learn something new and take a 10-minute break every hour or so—it really does make all the difference.

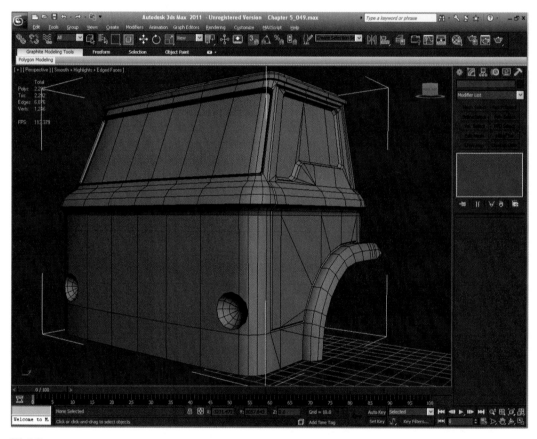

FIG 5.45

Let's take a look at the back of the cab where the engine would be. On the photographs, we can see that the cab appears to have been cut out to give the engine and gear box more space. The cab on this particular truck also has a cover over the engine, so it can't really be seen. Some of the engine details from this part of the truck need to be guessed or researched further, as we don't have accurate blueprint information for this area. Make the cuts to accommodate the engine as shown.

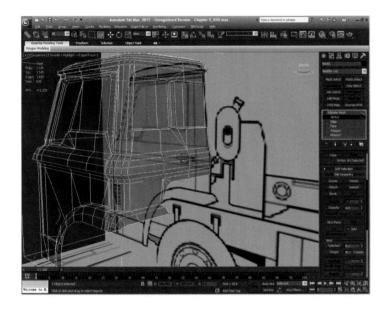

FIG 5.46

Even though the engine cover is a separate object on the real truck, we will make it a part of the cab, as we don't want to spend the polygons to make areas like this separately. You may have noticed at this point that the blueprints don't completely match the original photographs; this is because the blueprints incorporate some of the other details of the other skip truck (from the photos) including the fuel tank and generator on the back. Next, we need to extrude these edges to build this form using scale on the vertical axis to get the edges or vertices level along the bottom edge.

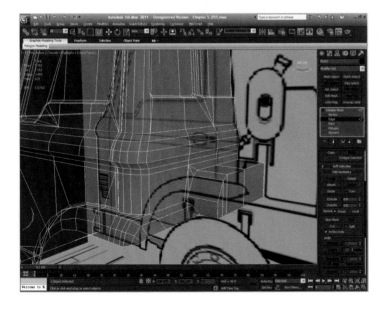

FIG 5.47

167

Let's move onto the truck's front bumper. Once we have done this, we'll move on to the back of the truck. Obviously, the truck still needs lots of work, including an interior, but if we complete the back of the truck before the interior, we will get a better impression of how many polygons we have left to use for the interior. What may happen is that we go over budget anyway, even if we try to be conservative. If we do, we just have to trim polygons at the end of the build—this is quite common. If this does happen, always keep a copy of your higher polygon model for future use.

Let's get on with the bumper. To start, extrude the polygons that we made at the very start of the truck build to form the rough bumper shape.

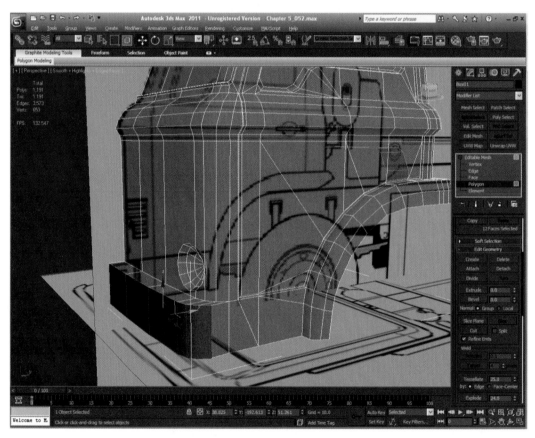

FIG 5.48

Move the vertices of the extruded polygons to match the bumper on the blueprints a little more closely. We can do this most effectively in the Top viewport.

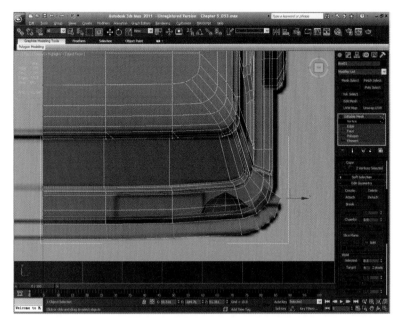

FIG 5.49

We need to improve how the bumper attaches to the cab. Show edges and turn the edges on the ends of the bumper. Make sure that you also make them visible to help you to do this.

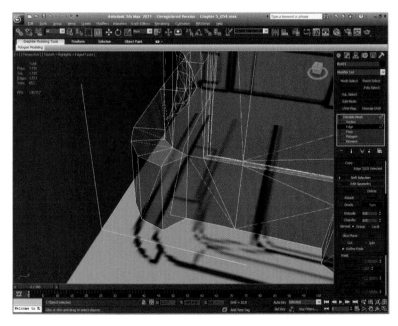

FIG 5.50

Next, we will delete the end polygons and create some new ends that are much closer to the blueprints.

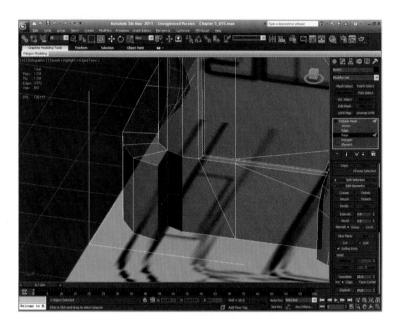

FIG 5.51

We need to build the bumper ridge that runs along the top and bottom of the bumper. Select the polygons along the front of the bumper.

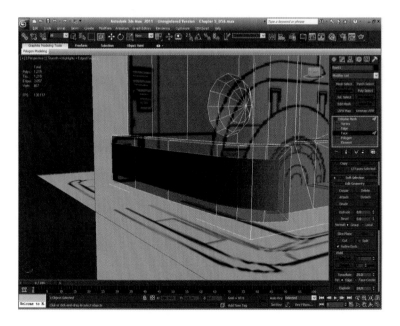

FIG 5.52

Now, extrude and scale them so that you end up with a depression. We will leave the truck's cab there for the moment and move onto working on the back. Remember to take a break, grab a drink of water, and have a look at what you've done so far.

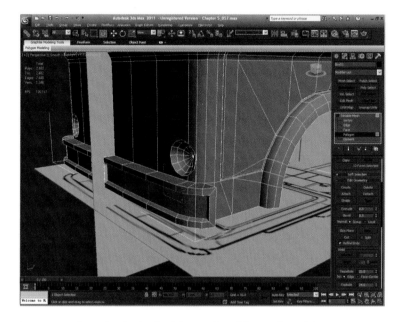

FIG 5.53

Create a new layer for the back of the truck and freeze the cab layer or turn it off for now. Next, create a box and scale it to resemble the main bed of the back of the truck and taper the back.

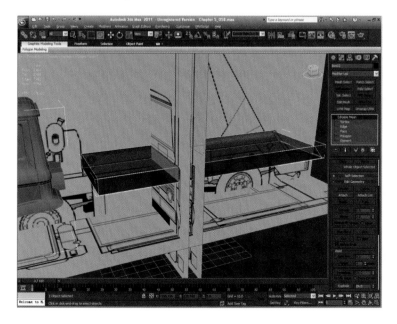

FIG 5.54

Start to split the back up into the component parts like we did for the front cab, adding all the cross sections that we will need.

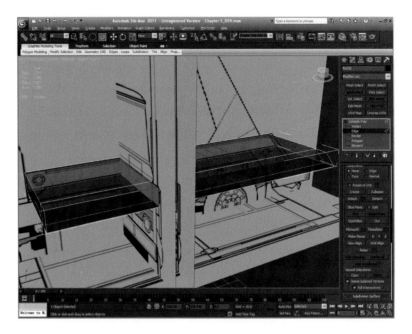

FIG 5.55

Now, we will extrude and shape the trailer arms that come up from out of the trailer base. Again, we are using only Extrude, Scale, Move, and a little Rotate, just as we have before.

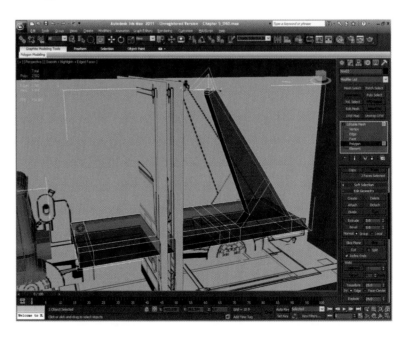

FIG 5.56

172

As you can see, the top of the arm is too thick, so detach this, make it thinner, and then reattach it.

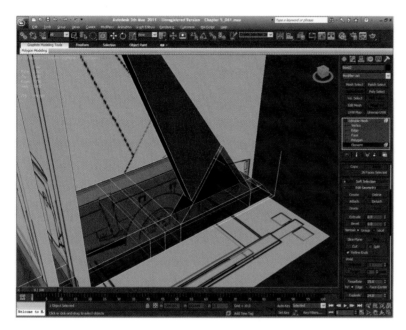

FIG 5.57

We need to fuse the model together properly, so divide edges and weld the vertices. Create new polygons to fill in the holes we just created.

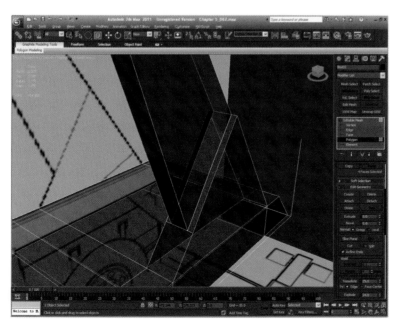

FIG 5.58

The back of the trailer needs the rest of the structure building. To do this, make some more divisions at the bottom so that you can extrude the necessary face.

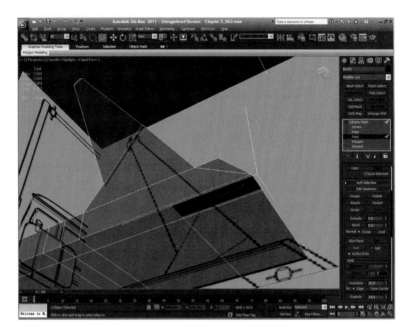

FIG 5.59

Now, the faces can be extruded and shaped to make the back structure and that will ultimately house the rear lights.

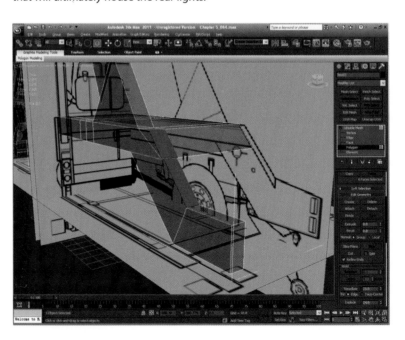

FIG 5.60

The end of the rear lights arm needs to be capped as shown in the blueprints. We can do this by extruding the sloped faces out and then extruding the side faces as well. This will need cleaning up and welding when completed to make it neat and tidy.

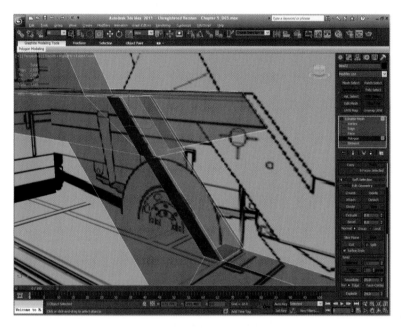

FIG 5.61

The capped end has now been cleaned up.

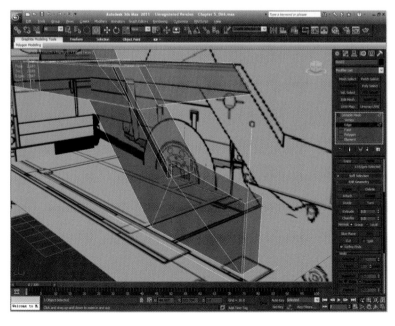

FIG 5.62

Now, we will start adding more detail to the trailer back. First, make an inner edge to lower the height in the middle by extruding the interior faces downwards.

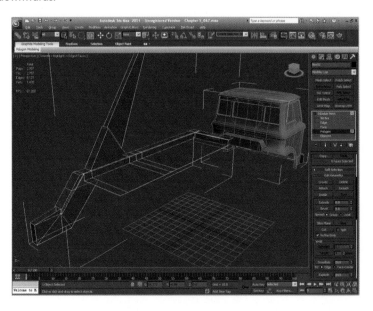

FIG 5.63

As with the inner lip that we just created, we need to add more detail to the arm, as it has to have a thickness for the hydraulic system. Detach the arm and alter the width so that you can build an outer lip. Leave the arm detached because this will be refined later on.

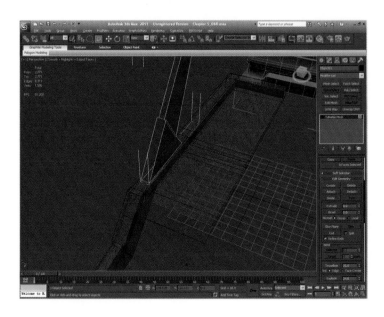

FIG 5.64

Refine the edge for the inner lip down the back of the rear light arm, as this will eventually make the gap for the arm to move in. Tidy up the vertices and edges and alter the lip widths so that they match the thickness of each other. Make sure that the model still lines up with the blueprints. You may find that you need to move some of the vertices to realign your model again.

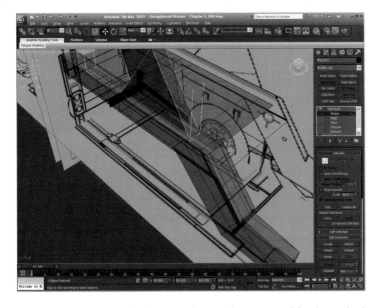

FIG 5.65

Once you are happy with the divisions that you have created for the trailer lip, select the inner faces that need to be copied and moved downwards to create the recess. When you have selected the faces, move the faces down with the Move tool while pressing the Shift key. This step creates duplicate faces.

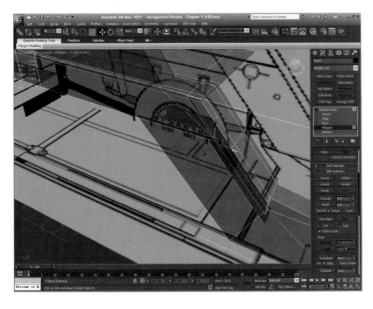

FIG 5.66

You can now delete the original faces. Once deleted, create the faces that make up the sides of the inner recess.

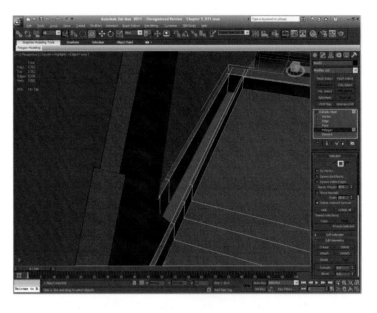

FIG 5.67

Your trailer should now be starting to take shape.

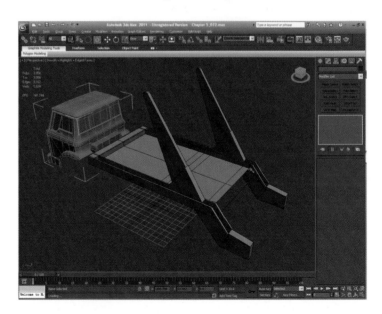

FIG 5.68

The trailer back now needs to be closed up so that it looks like the back of the real skip truck. Make sure that the truck bed is roughly the same height as in the blueprint. Extrude the back edge down to create a vertical step, extrude it again to create an angled step, and then make a final extrude to create the last step down.

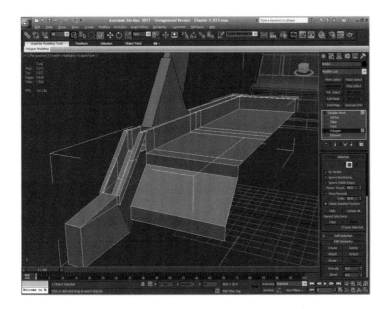

FIG 5.69

Now, the new back can be integrated properly with the rest of the back. You need to fill holes to make the rear of the truck solid. Because this is difficult to see in orthographic blueprints, I suggest that you use your artistic eye in conjunction with the photographs and interpret the back the best you can. Take a look at this file to see how I tackled the problem. Note that I have tidied up stray and unwelded vertices. I have also deleted the faces underside and reduced the polygons by welding vertices that I no longer needed.

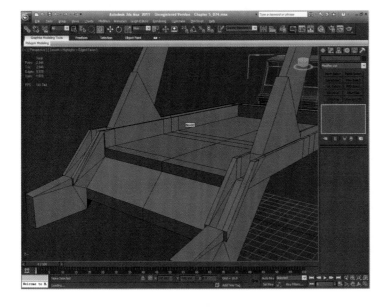

FIG 5.70

To make the back more realistic, I have added a slight recessed section where the rear light arm flows into the back. This was easily created by extruding the inner face inwards and then deleting the polygons at the top and creating new polygons, which were welded together.

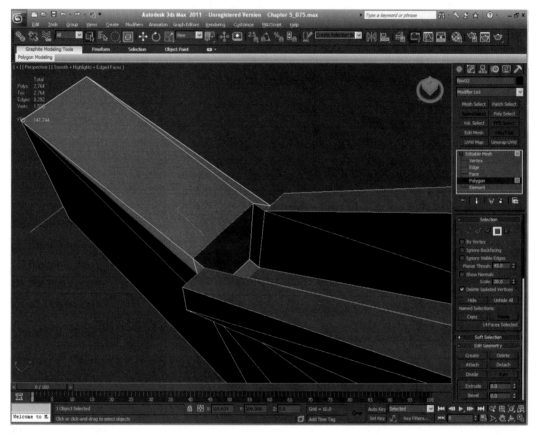

FIG 5.71

Now, we can start to look at the underside of the truck. It must be created from imagination because we don't have much information for this area from the reference photos. This bottom will be fairly simple. It is created by extruding edges vertically and horizontally so that we can enclose the gap at the bottom. Look at Fig. 5.72 to see how I finished off the bottom area. Make sure that whatever you create is tidy and that all vertices are welded. Don't worry about the underside too much. There is no plan for the truck to be flipped over, so it doesn't have to be perfect; just keep it clean and simple. Here's my interpretation of what the underside of the trailer might look like.

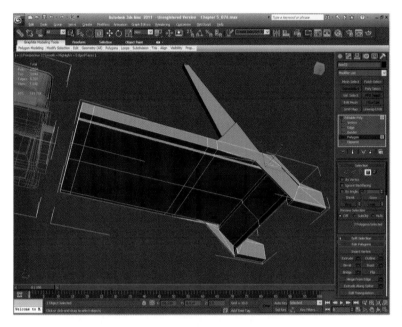

FIG 5.72

Now, we can start modeling the trailer details. Start with the mudguard. First, move the two edge loops in the model to where the mudguard should be placed. On the underside between the two splits, create another division.

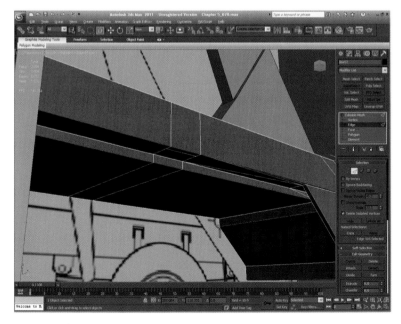

FIG 5.73

Extrude the face downwards to create the outer edge of the mudguard. Once extruded, shape the faces to resemble the mudguard shape. Split the mudguard in half on the inner face.

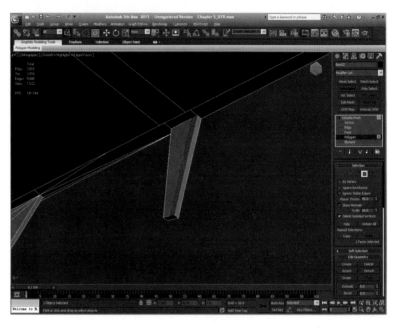

FIG 5.74

Pick the polygon that has been split on the outer back edge and extrude it until it reaches the first lip. Delete the inner poly and weld the mudguard inner faces to the inner lip. Tidy up remaining polygons that are no longer needed.

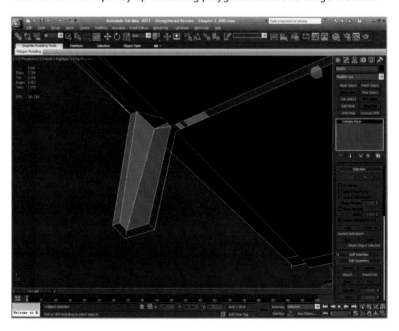

FIG 5.75

182

Select the inner open edges and extrude them roughly halfway to the middle of the trailer. Close the holes and weld all vertices.

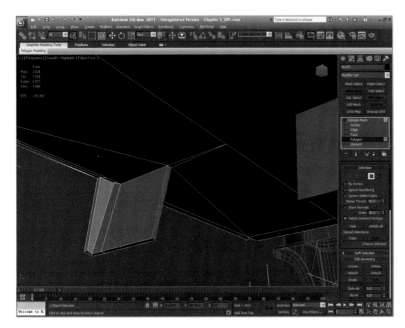

FIG 5.76

Select the back face where the rear lights will eventually be. Extrude and scale the face to create an edge all the way around and then extrude the face once inwards to create the rear light recess.

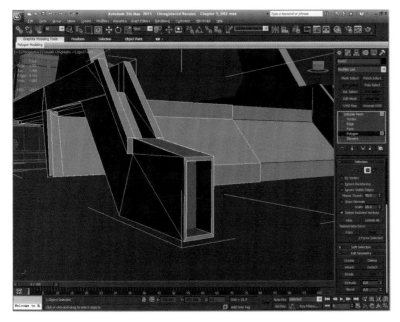

FIG 5.77

Create a cylinder with 12 sides and no divisions and place it where the stabilizer arm is going to be attached to the main trailer. Make it the same thickness as the trailer frame.

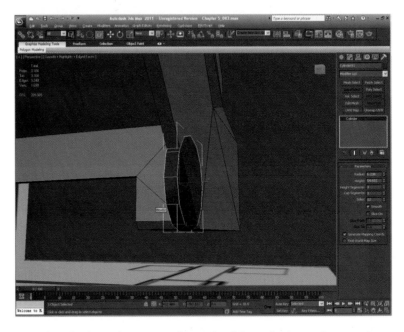

FIG 5.78

Copy the cylinder and move it to the inside of the trailer frame. Once you have both cylinders placed, join them to the trailer. For this step, I am going to use the Boolean union operation and then clean up the results.

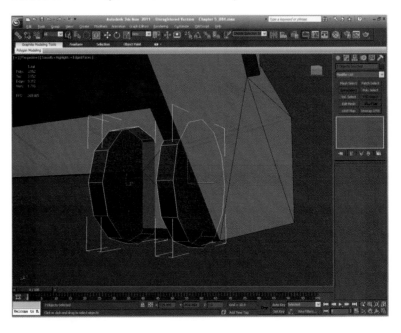

FIG 5.79

The finished brackets have now been merged onto the trailer to make one object. I extended the inner bracket with the inner top faces so that it looks a little stronger.

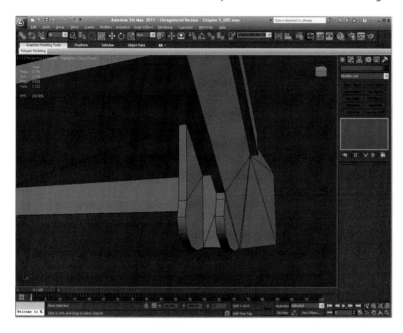

FIG 5.80

We will now make the stabilizers. Create a new layer and create three circles using the Spline menu on that layer.

Convert one of the splines into an editable spline and attach all of them together.

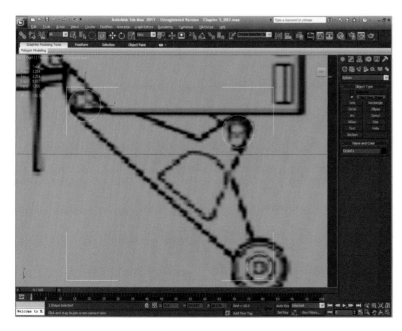

FIG 5.81

Click on the vertex function in the Spline Menu and use the Refine button to add vertices to the circles at points where they will need to intersect with each other.

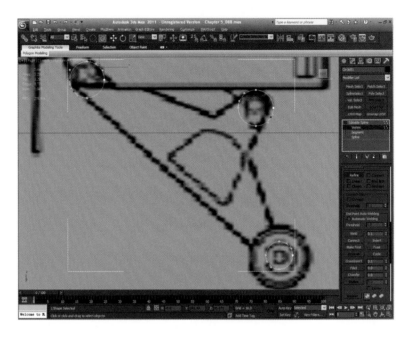

FIG 5.82

Delete the curves that are inside the points of intersection.

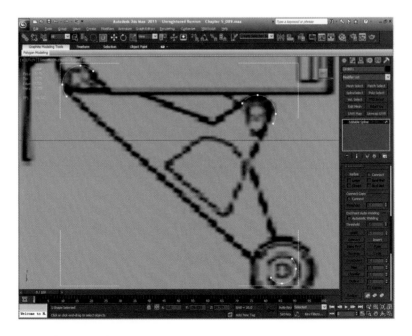

FIG 5.83

186

Use Create Line to attach the shapes together. Make sure the 2.5 snap is turned on and vertices are checked.

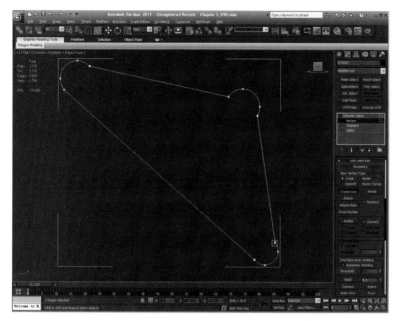

FIG 5.84

Use the Refine button again to add points to create the right-angle shapes. If the vertices are curved, make them a corner point by right-clicking on the vertex and selecting Corner. Weld all the points together.

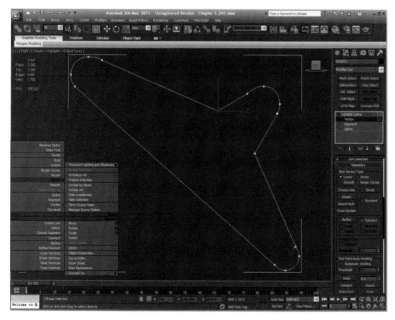

FIG 5.85

Extrude the shape using Modify > Modify list > Extrude. Make sure that Cap
Ends is checked. Move the extruded shape into the right position. It will be
easier to see what you're doing if you switch to the Perspective view for this.

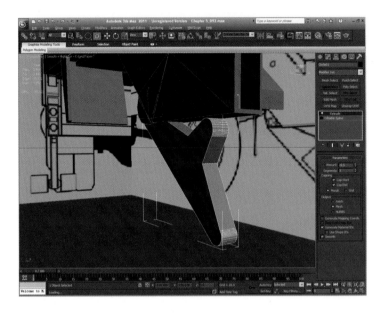

FIG 5.86

Reduce the poly count on the stabilizer by cutting polygons from the curves
of the semicircles in the model. Use any method you like to do this—Editable
Poly or Editable Mesh work equally well.

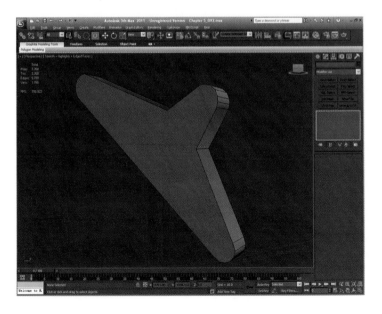

FIG 5.87

Create a box and Boolean it from the stabilizer. You need to Boolean the box from the arm that sticks out, so you can add the hydraulic arm. The hydraulic arm is simply two cylinders. You can probably get away with using six segments in the hydraulic arms for a low-poly object, but again, if you want the model to look a little better for your portfolio, feel free to use a little more. Remember that you probably won't see this detail on the finished model, so don't get too carried away with it.

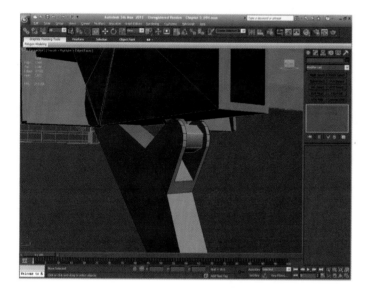

FIG 5.88

Make sure that the inner faces on the hydraulic arm are deleted, as you will never see these in the render.

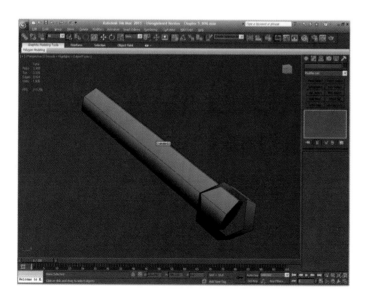

FIG 5.89

Attach this arm to the stabilizer. Create the little stabilizer wheels for the truck using cylinders of no more than 12 sides. Attach the wheels to the stabilizer arms.

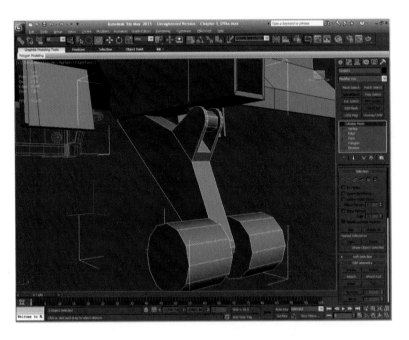

FIG 5.90

You may have noticed that the stabilizer arm really needs a hole or channel built into the trailer to allow it to move, but because this will never be seen, I have omitted this detail. Feel free to model it if you feel that you need to or if you plan on being able to see underside the truck. This detail can be added in the texture to make it at least look like it has a channel built into it.

Now, we can move back to the main trailer arm. Unfreeze the trailer layer, select the bottom edges of the arm, and extrude them. Divide the edges in the center and shape the vertices to where they would hinge on the trailer.

Divide the edges once more to give the bottom edge an L shape. Clean up the edge and the polygons that are not required. Fill in the bottom of the arm.

At this stage, move some of the vertices in the channel we made, where the arm can move. The bottom of the channel underside the trailer must be slightly adapted to allow the arm to hinge in the hole, but if the arm never moves, it's not terribly important.

At this point, I think it is a good idea to go through the trailer model again and make sure that the file is nice and clean and that all the vertices that should be welded are welded. It is a good idea to remove polygons that you consider to be no longer relevant to the model and just generally tidy it up after a mini-critique.

On the trailer arm, the ends of the struts that we created need to be rounded off slightly. This can be done manually by dividing the edge and moving the

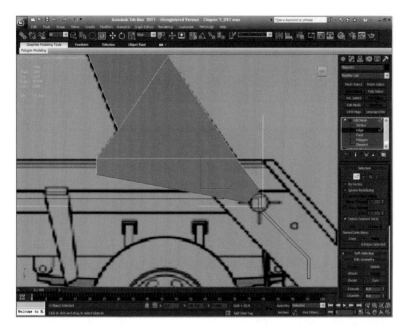

FIG 5.91

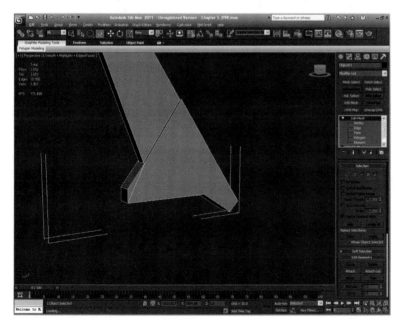

FIG 5.92

vertices to make it appear smoother. Also, the arm still needs to be modified
slightly to resemble the trailer arm at the bottom, where it is hinged. The
bottom needs to be lifted, and we have to create a lip that is present at
the bottom. We can do this by dividing the top edge of the arm and then
detaching the arm hinge at the bottom.

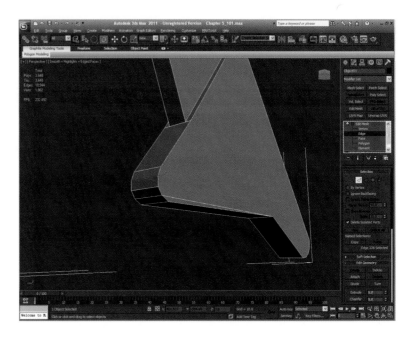

FIG 5.93

Reattach the bottom hinge part of the arm, then Boolean the part of the arm that is attached to the hydraulic arm. This is exactly the same process we used on the stabilizer.

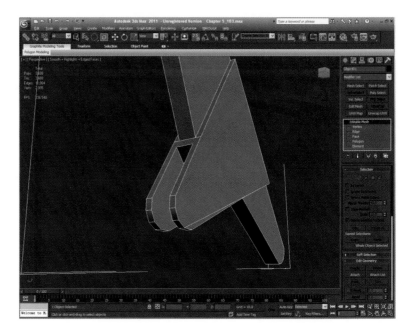

FIG 5.94

Let's build the main hydraulic arm. This again is simply a 12-sided cylinder. Before we create the cylinder, we must pull the top edges down to make the inner lip thinner.

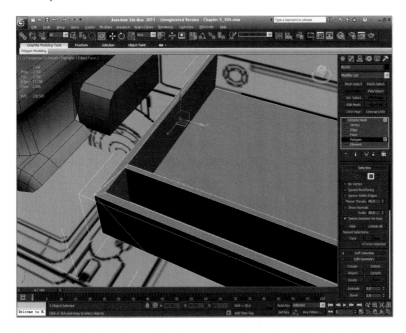

FIG 5.95

Create the cylinder with 12 sides. Once created, extrude and scale the faces nearest the trailer arm and extrude them again to make the end piece of the hydraulic arm.

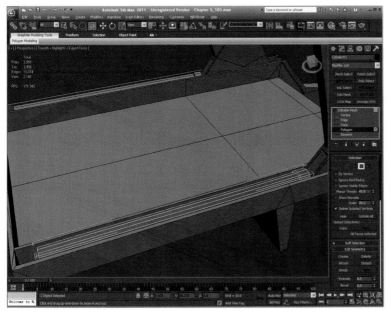

FIG 5.96

At the top ends of the trailer, extrude the faces and make the shape conform to the blueprints. The extruded polygons also need to be refined slightly and welded.

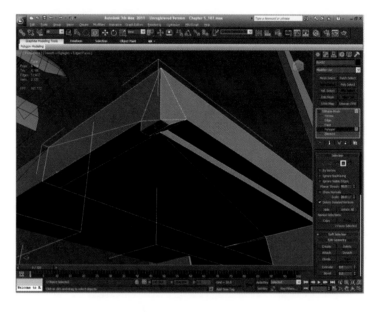

FIG 5.97

The bottom of the trailer needs an extra detail ledge that will rest on the truck chassis. This is done by creating an edge that runs from the front to the back; then the face can be extruded.

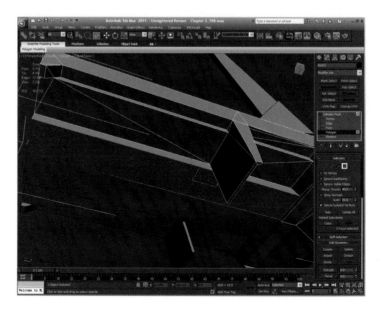

FIG 5.98

Create a new layer so that you can start a basic model for the truck chassis. This should be fairly simple, as we really don't have the polygons to spare for it. First, start with a box that will make up one side of the chassis and mirror it to create the other side.

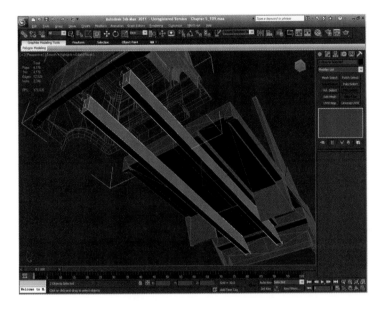

FIG 5.99

Now, we will create a wheel from a cylinder. The cylinder should be set with 16 sides with height segments of 5. This setup makes the wheel fairly smooth when rendered but keeps the poly count reasonable and manageable. Move the wheel into position.

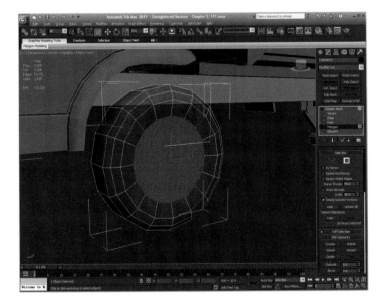

FIG 5.100

Delete the back face of the wheel, select the other side of the wheel, and scale the face to give the tire part of the wheel a more inflated look. You can (if you wish) set the smoothing groups so that you can see the tire section more easily to distinguish it from the wheel hub.

Select and scale the center polygons again to start creating the wheel hub. When you have made the rim, scale and extrude the already-selected polygons again continuously until you have created the hub. Use the photographs and the blueprints as the guide.

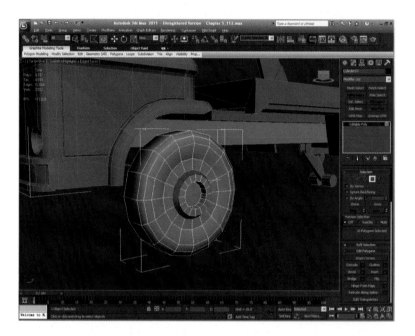

FIG 5.101

Select the hub part of the wheel and detach it. Then select the outer edges of the hub and extrude them backwards toward the inside of the tire.

Select the extruded polygons created from the outer hub and then flip the normals to create the inner rim.

Reattach the hub to the tire and then fill in the whole left in back of the wheel. You can do this by either manually creating new polygons or selecting the hub outer edge and extruding it to make a set of polygons, which you could weld to the tire's open inner edge. The front wheel now is complete. At this point, you can mirror the wheel to complete the set.

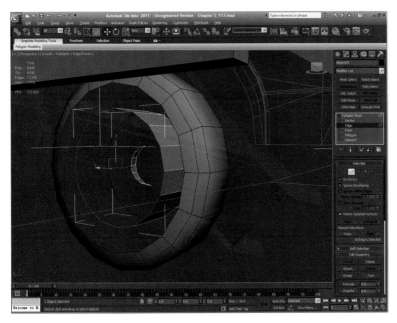

FIG 5.102

FIG 5.103

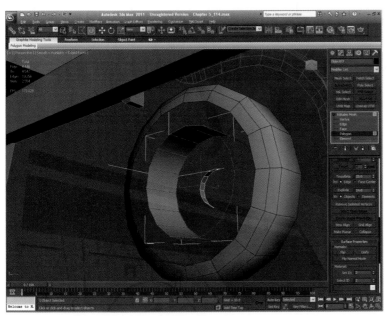

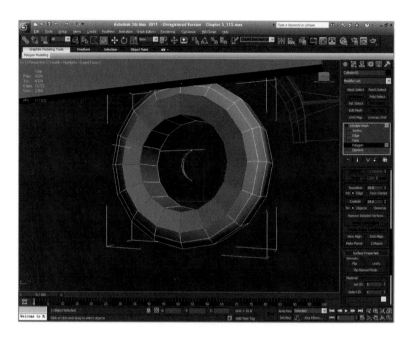

FIG 5.104

Next, we will move on to the rear wheels. We can modify the front wheels to make the rear wheels. The only real difference on the rear wheels are the hubs, so we won't have to make too many alterations. One thing to note is that the rear wheels are in sets of two. Select the front wheel, clone it, and move it into position by using Select > Shift-drag.

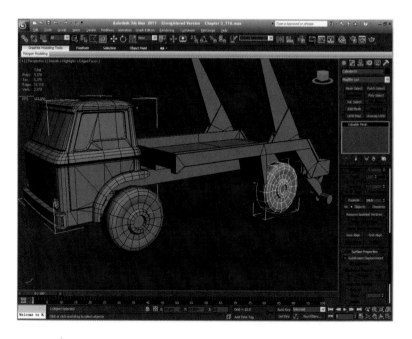

FIG 5.105

198

Select the innermost ring of faces on the hub and pull the polygons back.

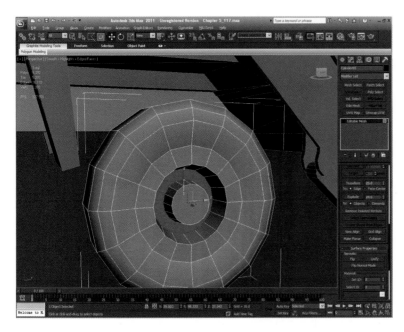

FIG 5.106

Select the inner edge of the hub and scale it outwards to make it wider than it currently is. Do the same with the next edge, continuing inside the hub.

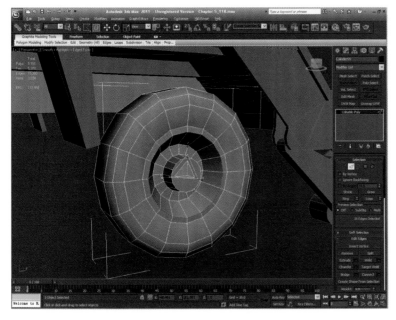

FIG 5.107

Copy the new rear wheel and move it inwards to make the rear wheel a double wheel. At this point, you could keep the wheel separate, but for this model, it will be connected in order to save polygons.

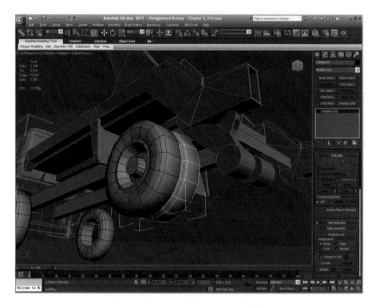

FIG 5.108

To keep the polygon count down, delete all the extra polygons from the hub facing outwards and the inner ring.

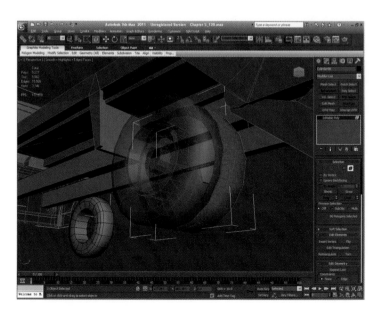

FIG 5.109

Now, delete the opposite face on the outer wheel, but keep the inner hub faces.

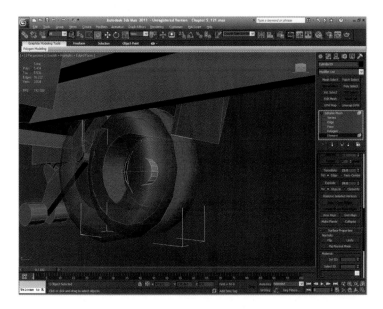

FIG 5.110

Now, we can attach both wheels together to make one double wheel. Weld the inner hub faces to the back of the outer wheel edge. Once this is done, mirror the wheel to complete the set. It would be wise to look over all the wheels that you have created and make sure that they are cleanly built and that all the vertices are welded. Ensure that all of the polygons and normals all look okay. You can also sort out the smoothing groups, if you wish; an autosmooth would be fine for the wheels.

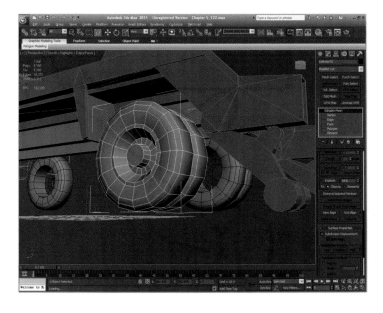

FIG 5.111

Now, we can start to model the suspension. To start this process, create a cylinder with six sides and a height segment setting of 5 to create the rear axle.

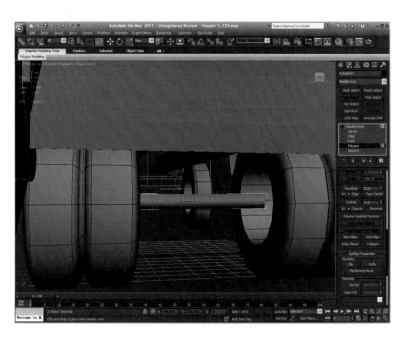

FIG 5.112

Scale the middle of the cylinder slightly to make the starting shape of the rear differential. Scale last two edges in to make the shape slightly rounded.

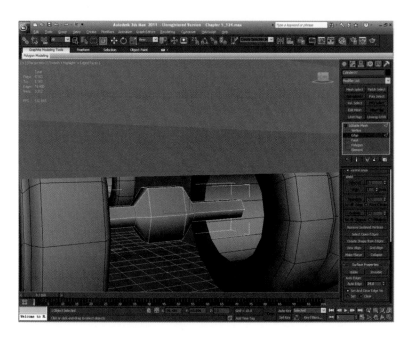

FIG 5.113

Split the center of the differential and scale it slightly to round off the shape again.

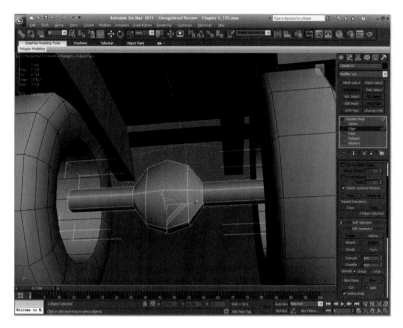

FIG 5.114

Select the inner faces of the differential and extrude them to pull them out. Scale the faces so that they are planar (that is, flat). Scale them again to taper the faces to more of a point.

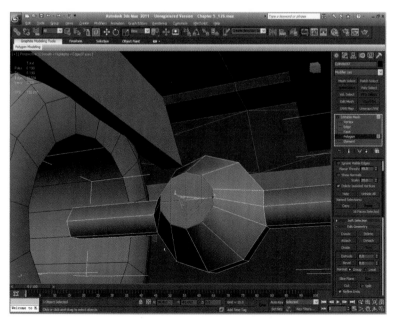

FIG 5.115

Clean up unnecessary polygons from the axle by removing them.

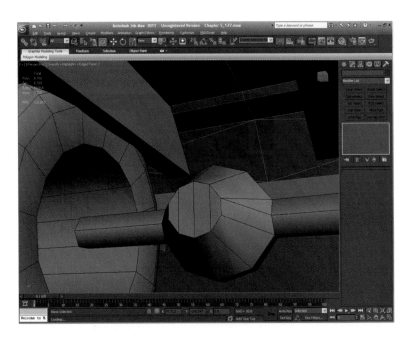

FIG 5.116

Create another cylinder; this time with eight sides, but set the height segment to 0. Move this cylinder to the outer edge of the axle. This is now the brake drum, so it now needs to be mirrored and attached to the axle.

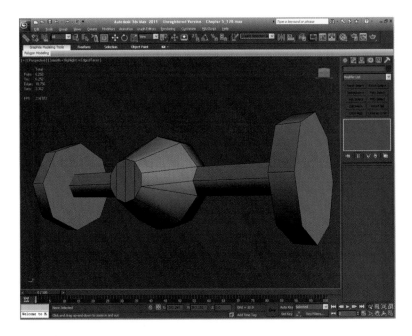

FIG 5.117

204

Copy the rear axle to the front. Delete the differential (the round chunky bit in the middle of the axle), as the truck is rear-wheel drive. Scale the width of the axle so that the brake drums fit within the front wheels hubs. To do this, move the hubs and the axle at the subobject vertex level.

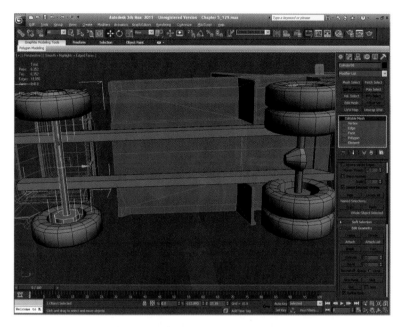

FIG 5.118

Create a box below the rear axle, between the differential and the brake drum. Create it by setting width sections to 5; this will form the leaf springs.

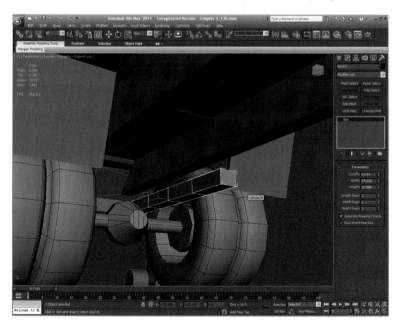

FIG 5.119

Convert the box to an editable mesh and move the outer bottom vertices to make it curved at the bottom.

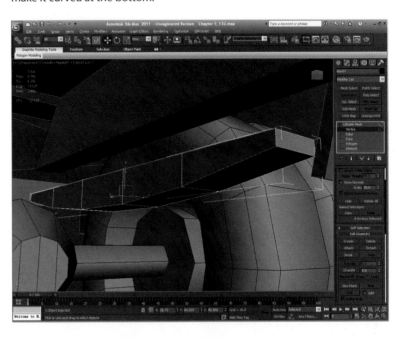

FIG 5.120

Now, with the Bend Modify, bend the leaf spring slightly.

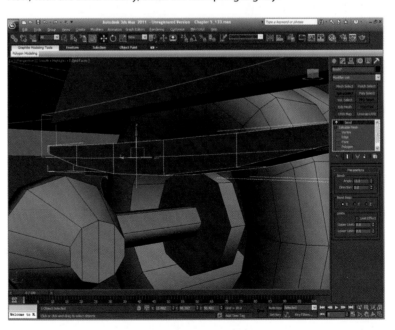

FIG 5.121

Select the center section of the leaf spring, scale the width, and then select and extrude the face on the bottom. Select and chamfer the extruded face's edges.

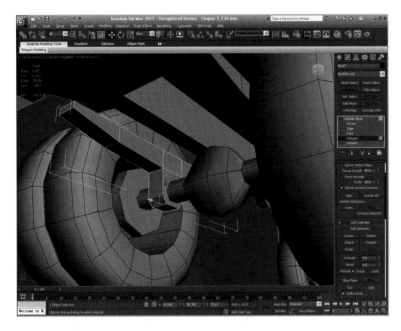

FIG 5.122

Because we altered the underside of the trailer at the rear, we need to make some alterations to the main chassis. We need to add a new division to the edge so that we can move the edge of the chassis up to the rear of the trailer to fill the gap. You can now make the leaf spring larger or smaller to match the blueprints if you didn't create it at the correct size in the first place.

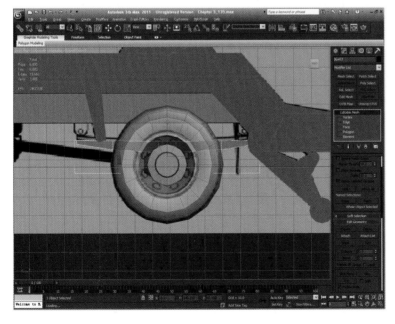

FIG 5.123

The leaf springs need to be fixed onto the chassis with brackets. These will be created using boxes with chamfered ends. You may need to scale the thickness of the leaf spring to fit in the brackets you have created. Attach the bracket to the leaf springs, copy the leaf spring, and then move it to the front. Attach both leaf springs to the chassis, copy them, and then mirror the whole chassis.

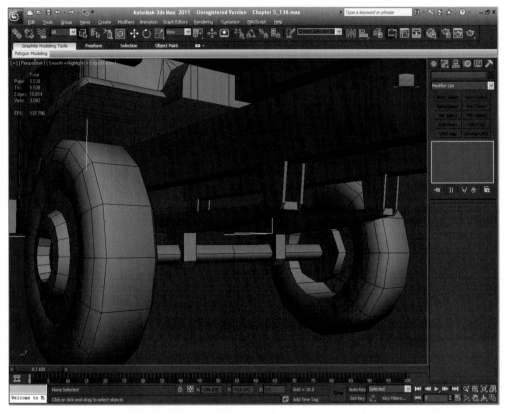

FIG 5.124

Now, we shall look at finishing off the cab. Fill in the bottom of the cab and delete some unnecessary polygons from it. Delete the windows, as the truck in the photos doesn't have any.

Welding the center loops in the headlights and reducing the polygons around the back end of the mudguards is a good place to start. The roof can also be cut down a little.

Keep removing the polygons that don't add anything to the overall shape or form of the cab. Often, divisions that we make as we perform specific tasks to make the modeling process easier will need to be removed at some point. If you build one side of an object and then mirror it to complete the build, quite often the center line is a good candidate for this. Have a look through your model to see whether you can spot any others.

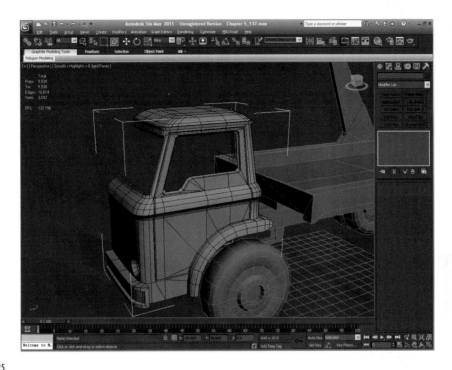

FIG 5.125

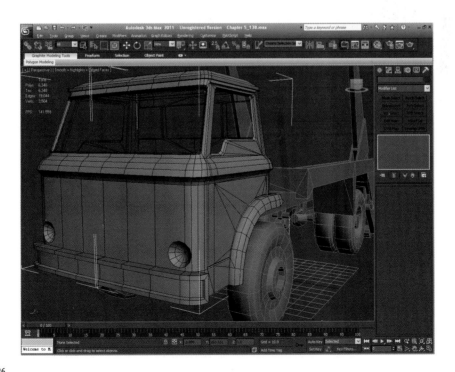

FIG 5.126

Now, we need to fill in the bottom of the cab. Select the edges of the mud-guards and extrude them until they meet the thickness of the mudguard.

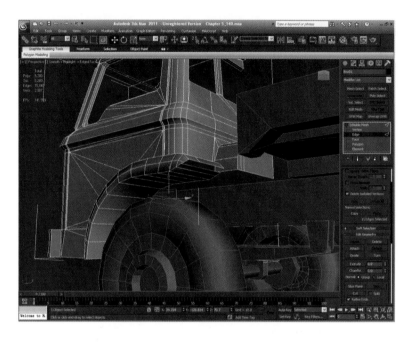

FIG 5.127

Cap the mudguard and then delete the unnecessary edges that were left from the creation of the mudguard.

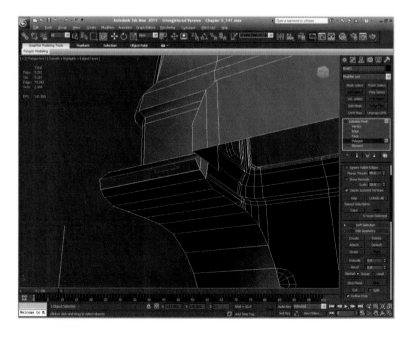

FIG 5.128

210

Do the same with the mudguard at the bottom. Also, pull the edges down on the engine cover at the back of the cab. Next, pull the edges down to the top of the chassis.

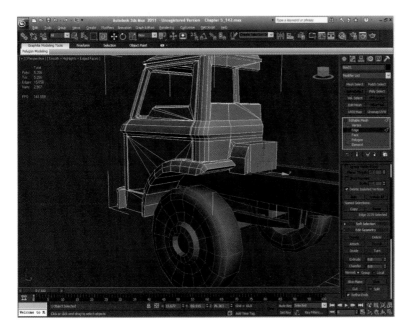

FIG 5.129

Start to fill in the whole underside of the cab. Extrude the outer cab edges and weld the vertices to make a solid closed shape.

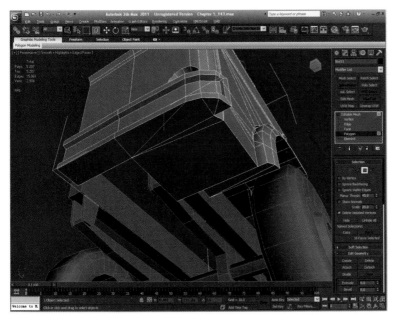

FIG 5.130

You need to incorporate the chassis in the underside construction of your cab model. Take a look at Fig. 5.131 to see how I have closed the bottom of the cab fully. You will notice that I have reduced the polygons slightly and cleaned up some of the faces to make it a neater model.

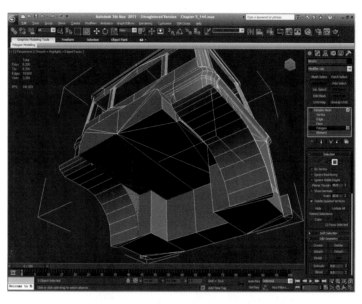

FIG 5.131

So, all we have to complete to finish the cab is a basic interior. We could start the interior off by using the shell modifier; however, I find that for this model, it gives us a very complex interior to clean up, so the alternative is to create it manually. Start by selecting the open edges of the front window and extruding them in, and then extruding again and scaling them larger.

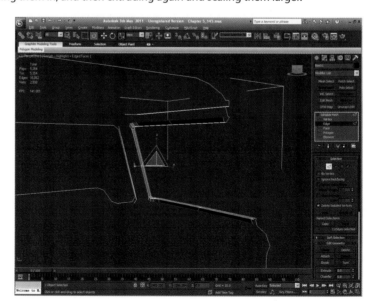

FIG 5.132

We will do the previous step with all of the open edges on all the windows to create an inner shell.

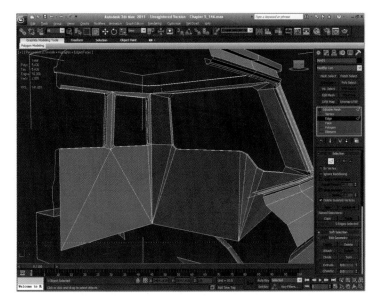

FIG 5.133

Now, we can start to weld and create new polygons from these starting points to fill in the interior. Remember that it should be pretty basic, though.

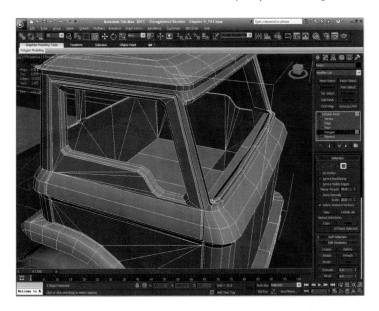

FIG 5.134

We need to build two chairs and a steering wheel and the steering column. These will also be very basic. In fact, they are pretty much made from single polygons. To make them look more detailed, they will be textured, but with alpha maps applied, so that you can see the frame of the chairs and the steering wheel.

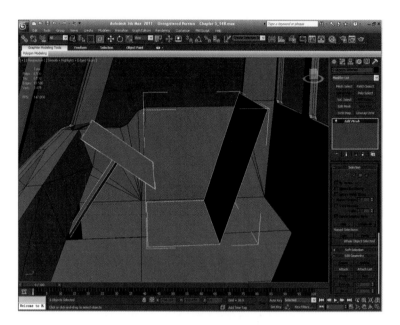

FIG 5.135

With the model nearly complete, we just need to finish off a few remaining details. Create a box-type shape underside the cab to act as an engine and gearbox. We can map this shape with an engine-type texture to make it look more detailed. Once we have modeled the engine/gearbox, we can link up the prop shaft to the rear differential.

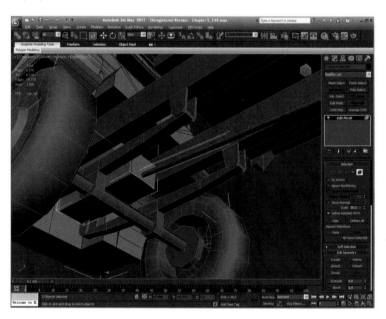

FIG 5.136

We can now add the final touches. Create a six-sided cylinder to make the bar that connects both the hydraulic arms at the top. Create a low-poly bracket box and a cross-section set of polygons hanging down from the bar so that you can map a chain texture to make it look more detailed without using lots of extra polygons. Feel free to add the extra fuel tank and the control box at this point, but try to keep the poly count as low as you can.

The basic model is now complete.

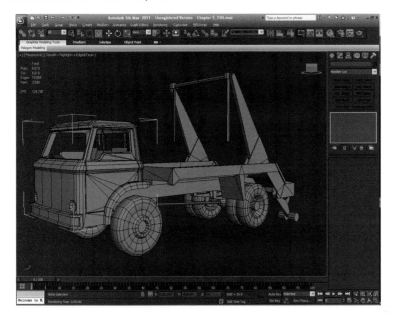

FIG 5.137

Create a new material and load TextureGrid.jpg into the Diffuse slot. You can find this texture in the downloadable scene files \Chapter 5\CH005.Textures

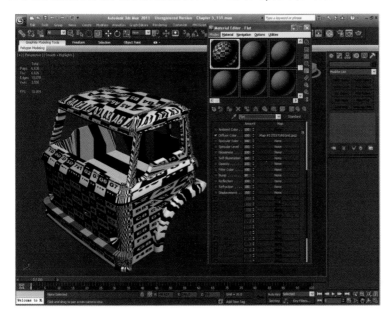

FIG 5.138

Under Modify in the modifier list, choose UVW Mapping and select the box-mapping method.

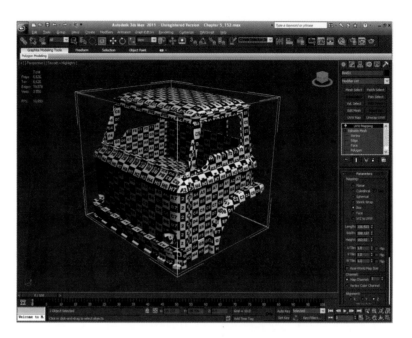

FIG 5.139

Under Modify, choose Unwrap UVW. Open the modifier stack and click Face. Select most of the front faces on the cab and select Planar in the map preferences. If the mapping is from the wrong angle, you can choose Align; for example, if you view the cab directly from the front view, you can select Align from View. If you use the Align using the axis method, use your axis guide in the bottom left-hand corner of the window to help you choose the correct one. This method will be repeated pretty much for the whole of the unwrapping of the truck. So, the rest of the instructions for the unwrapping will be a little less detailed.

Once you have planar-mapped the front faces, open up the Unwrap window by clicking on the Edit button under the Parameters heading and move the new mapped faces away from all the faces in the model. You're doing this so that you can organize all of the polygons in the model on the texture page in the future.

One important thing is to try to keep the mapping of the faces consistent in size (which includes their aspect ratio). This effort is where the texture grid comes in very useful. Use the grid to make sure that the mapping is equal all over the whole model. There are some circumstances in which you can alter the aspect ratio and size, but as a basic rule, try to keep it consistent.

To actually make the making process a little quicker, convert the cab to an editable mesh or editable polygon and delete half of the model. Now, reapply

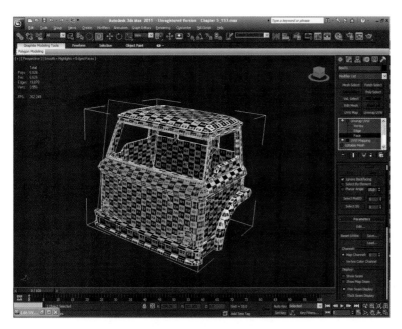

FIG 5.140

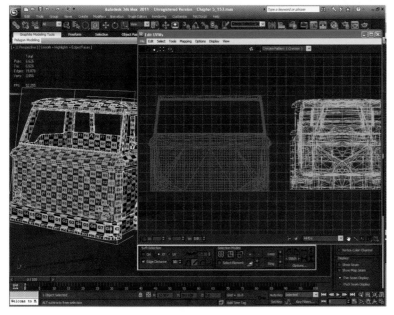

FIG 5.141

the Unwrap UVW to the cab and continue with the mapping process. Using the same method that we did for the front of the cab, select the side polygons and move the new faces away from all of the other faces in the Unwrap window. You may have noticed that there are some areas that look stretched. This issue will be rectified when we lay out the maps in a more organized fashion.

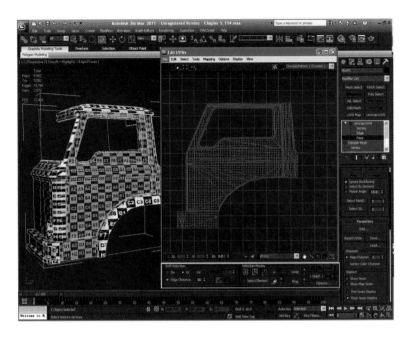

FIG 5.142

Using the same method as before, continue to unwrap the back of the cab and the roof. When working on the lip of the roof, you might want to include the relevant sides that correspond to the front side and back view or you can unwrap the roof as one whole piece to hide as many of the texture seams as possible. Choose whichever method you prefer; for this model, I am going to keep the roof as one whole object.

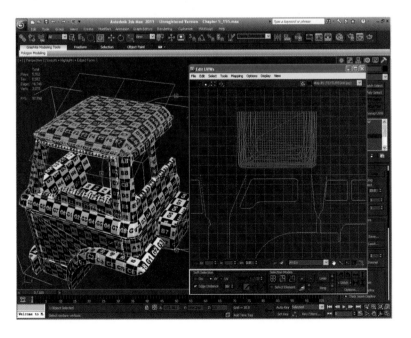

FIG 5.143

You should now be left with the underside of the cab to be unwrapped (excluding the wheel arch, bumper, rear engine cover, and interior at this point). Because we used a box-mapping technique from the outset, you can select the faces of the different parts of the underside and move them out individually in the Unwrap viewport. You may find that some pieces are separate from each other that should be connected, but if you go to the menu at the top and then into Display and turn on Show Vertex Connections, you can see where the faces should be linked. All that remains is for you to flip the faces using the mirror function.

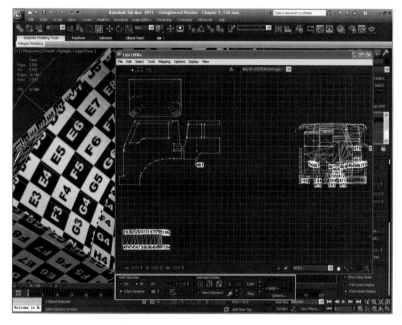

FIG 5.144

Remember that you can mirror both horizontally and vertically or even use the Flip Vertical or Horizontal functions. As you can see from this figure, I have moved the underside of the wheel arch. It was in two parts, but using the previous method, I have put it back together again. I will use this method for the rest of the underside of the cab.

All the underside components have been organized and connected to the relevant parts. You should have only the wheel arch, front bumper, rear engine cover, and interior now remaining to do. Notice that the underside cannot physically be unwrapped as one whole piece, so some of the faces must remain separate. Although this limitation can be annoying, it can also be used to your advantage when placing all the unwrapped faces on the texture page—but this is really done only at the very end of the whole unwrapping process.

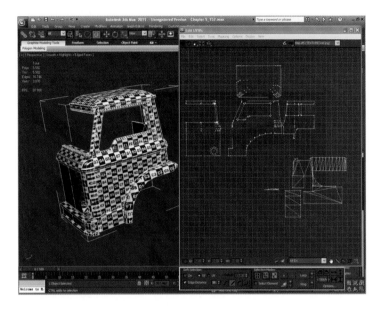

FIG 5.145

Now, we can finish the front bumper and rear engine cover, like we did with the underside of the truck.

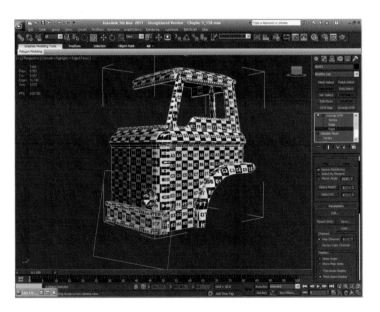

FIG 5.146

And we can now finish the exterior mapping of the cab with the wheel arch. Map this using the cylindrical mapping method. You will no doubt have to alter the texture gizmo. Use the cylindrical mapping modifier from the Unwrapping menu. Remember that you can put the polygons back together if the cylindrical mapping doesn't work like you want it to.

I have manually straightened some of the vertices on the wheel arch as you can see. Also, notice that I have altered some of the colors for the background and the mesh itself. You can do this by using Options > Preferences. I have turned off Display Seams and Show Grid. I have also performed a mass weld on all the cab polygons in the UVW Unwrap Editor to get rid of unnecessary texture seams. If you do this step, make sure that you don't weld the wrong vertices. You may have to adjust the weld threshold in the bottom right-hand corner of the Unwrap window higher or lower to achieve the overall weld.

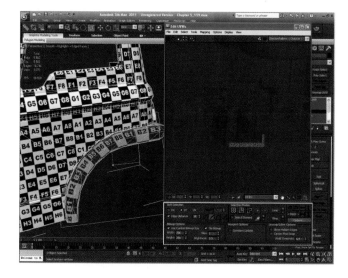

FIG 5.147

We can now adjust vertices around the front corner of the cab to minimize as much of the stretching as possible. It is virtually impossible to eliminate all stretching, but it can be improved or hidden with natural seams or natural shapes in the model.

The interior UV unwrapping should be the only thing left on the cab model. It is a good idea to double-check your model at this point to make sure that you haven't missed any faces that need mapping; this is a common mistake that is very easily made. If you have rogue faces, I suggest that you fix them now before you go on with the texturing, as they may be harder to find later.

As we have already done with the underside of the cab and the other various parts of the model, our aim here is to organize the interior into as close to a one-piece unit as the model and faces will allow. If you look at Fig. 5.149, you will see that all of the faces for the interior are now laid out by the same methods we've used earlier.

It is now time to mirror your cab model. Be sure that when you have mirrored the side, you move the copied model's texture coordinates away from the original cab. This step makes things easier to stitch together when you put the two sides together. If you look at Fig. 6.153, you'll see that I have mirrored the

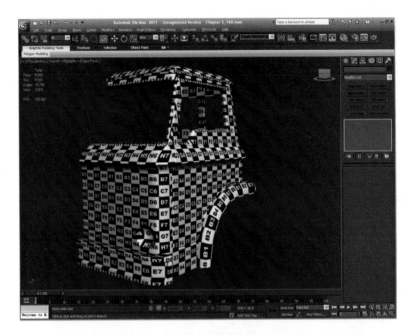

FIG 5.148

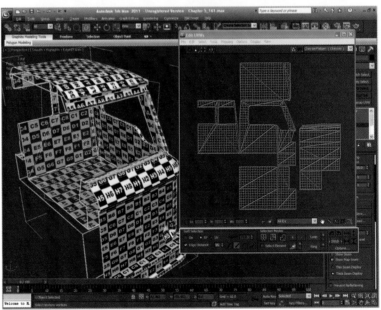

FIG 5.149

cab so that it is now complete again, and the texture coordinates have been reorganized. I am still keeping the cab texture coordinates away from the center of the UV Unwrap window so that they are easy to select once more of the model has been textured. Next, I have changed the background color in the Edit UVW window (from Options > Background Color) just to show you this step a little more clearly.

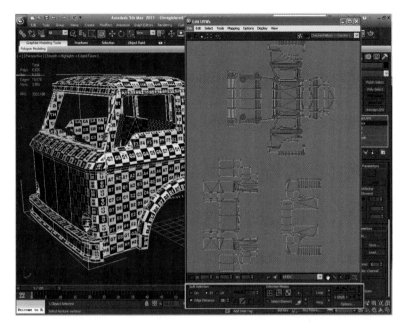

FIG 5.150

Let's move on to the trailer section of the model. The process is the same as it was for the cab. Start with a cube-mapping method and then sort out all the faces of the trailer by hand.

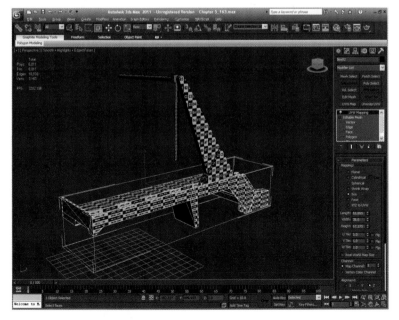

FIG 5.151

Next, I apply the Unwrap UVW modifier to the trailer and start to organize the different faces of the trailer. I have used the exact same methods as for the cab. The trailer in this image has its faces unwrapped.

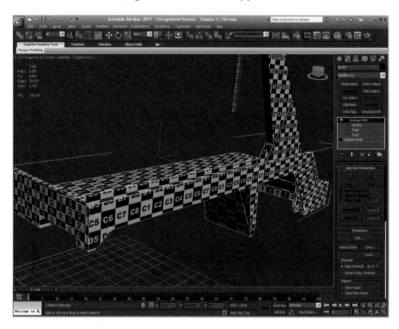

FIG 5.152

Once the trailer polygons have been unwrapped, mirror the model and stitch up the mirrored trailer UV coordinates to the original as in the cab model. Take a look at this image to see the end result.

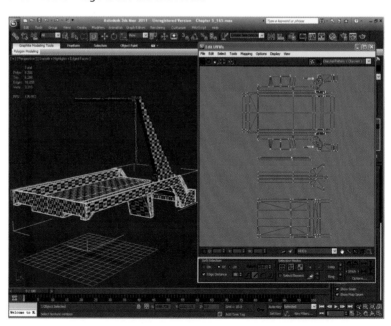

FIG 5.153

Now, we can move on to texturing the trailer arm and the hydraulic arm. Again, the method is the same. The only slight variation is the use of a cylindrical mapping technique for the hydraulic arm. (You may find that some of the cylinders already have cylinder mapping applied to them; these are usually created when you create the cylinder with "Generate mapping coordinates" checked. If this is the case, it just makes your life a little easier!) To map the hydraulic arm, move the end cylinder faces away from the main central cylinder, which makes it easier to select the middle so that you can apply cylindrical mapping to it. Also, move the two boxes and the end cap polygons away from the main cylinder. Once you have mapped the main cylinder, use the same technique on the end cylinders.

A good tip when using the cylindrical mapping technique is to try to hide the seam. For this example, the seam on the hydraulic arm is on the bottom of the model. The final step is to layout the polygons for the hydraulic arm.

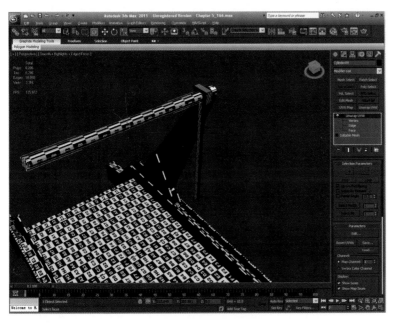

FIG 5.154

Now, we can mirror the objects like we have done with the previous models. Once you have mirrored the models and sorted the unwrapped faces, attach the models together to make one whole model—be sure to include the trailer.

Next, hide the trailer and unhide the stabilizers. We will map these in the same way as the trailer arms. Once you've finished, they should look something like Fig. 5.156.

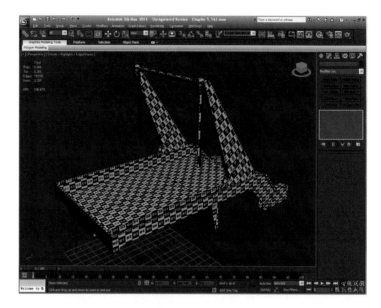

FIG 5.155

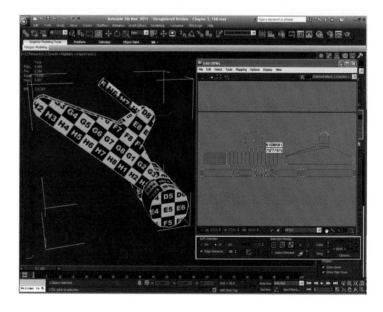

FIG 5.156

Mirror the stabilizer and attach it to the rest of the trailer. Your unwrapped trailer should look something like Fig. 5.157.

Let's start unwrapping the wheels. Unhide and unfreeze the chassis layer (or layer 04 if you have not named your layers). We have only one front and one back to do, as they will obviously be mirrored. Apply cylindrical mapping to the wheel in the UVW Unwrap window (if one wasn't assigned on creation).

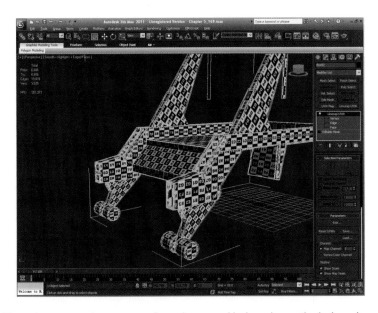

FIG 5.157

Move the outer polygons away from the central hub and map the hub and side wall of the wheel with a planar map. The inner hub cylinder should be cylindrically mapped, just like the outer faces of the wheel. The outer polygons will be mapped with a tread texture; this will be the same on all of the wheels, so the faces should occupy the same UV space on the texture page. In fact, only the hub front and back faces are unique on the front and rear wheels. After you have finished, you should have something that looks like Fig. 5.158.

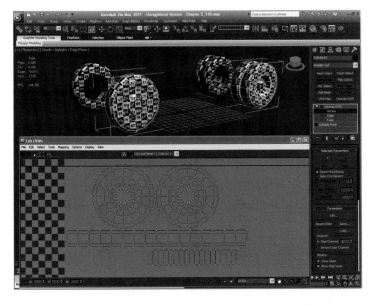

FIG 5.158

Now, we can follow the wheels with the rest of the chassis UV mapping. Again, you should see that there are some parts of the model that can occupy the same UV space, such as the main chassis girders, brake drums, leaf springs, and leaf spring brackets. When you have unwrapped all of the chassis, attach together all of the pieces, just as we did for the trailer.

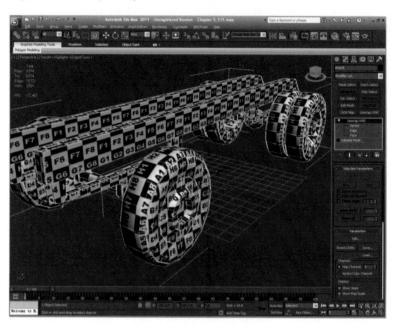

FIG 5.159

Unhide and unfreeze the cab layer again, as we just need to unwrap the engine block, prop shaft, seats, and steering wheel and column. Now, it's time to attach the entire truck model.

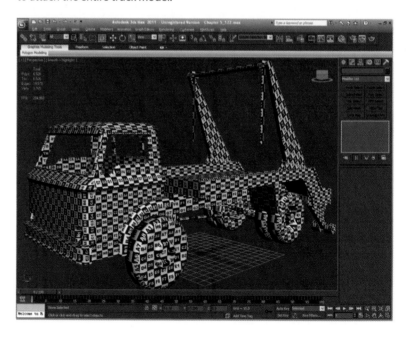

FIG 5.160

Now comes a tricky part. Once you have the entire model unwrapped, it needs to fit into a square. What I mean by a square is a texture page that is basically of a resolution to the power of 2. In this case, we are going to make the entire unwrapped model fit in a texture page with a resolution of 1024 × 1024 pixels. You might want to create the texture slightly larger—2048 × 2048, for example—so that you have a higher resolution map for renders or your portfolio. When you are finally organizing your texture page, keep in mind the priority of the model. For example, I suggest that you make the interior, the underside parts, and the objects that are obscured or seldom seen a little bit smaller on the texture page. This method allows you to assign more of the texture page to the most visible parts of the truck.

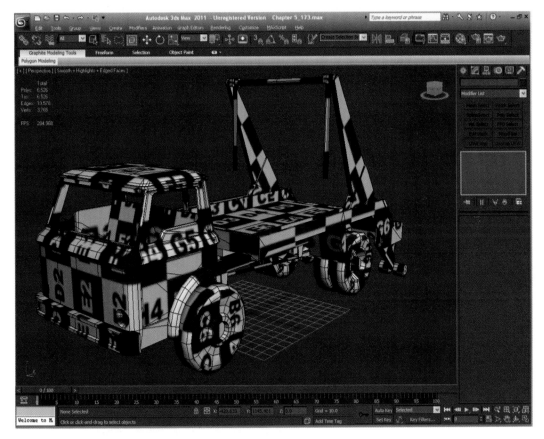

FIG 5.161

It is time to experiment and see what you consider to be the best compromise. Once you have all of the faces into the square, you can either take a screenshot and paste that into Photoshop or in the UVW Unwrap Editor under Tools or use the Render UVW template. Make sure that the resolution is set to 2048 × 2048 for the original map.

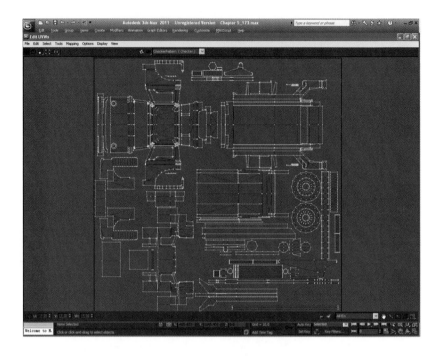

FIG 5.162

Creating the Texture Map for the Truck

Open the texture template in Adobe Photoshop. I suggest that you use the layer functions in Photoshop and even the layer folders to keep the collection of your textures together. What we need first is base rust texture template. To get that, I

FIG 5.163

am going to use what images I can find in the reference photos and seamlessly stitch them together using the Clone Stamp and Healing Brush tools.

Grab as many of the truck parts as you can from the reference images and line them up with our model UVs. Don't worry if they look a bit odd and the perspective is a bit off; you will probably need to do a lot of editing to line everything up and make them seamless. Tidy up parts of the textures as you go, just to make things clear on the page. Actions like trimming the images as you are placing them into the file will make your blending job that much easier when it needs to be done.

FIG 5.164

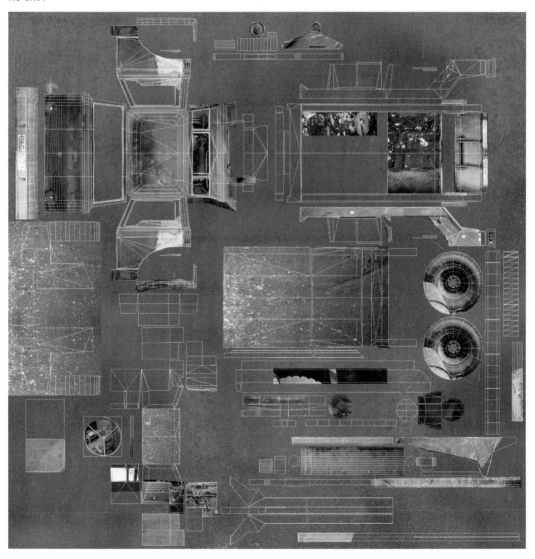

Use Photoshop to blend, copy, clone, color-correct, and generally fix all the photograph parts of the truck for the parts of the images that we have copied into our texture file. Feel free to use the other photographs or references for the tire tread and front wheels. If you find that there is a reference missing or if you don't think that there is enough information in some of the texture parts, use an Internet image search to complete your texture map.

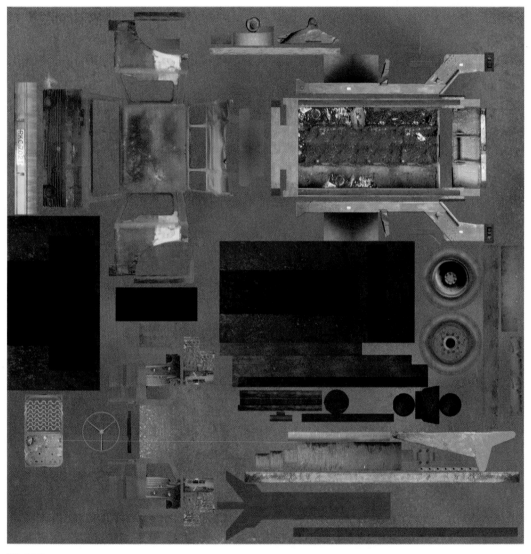

FIG 5.165

You should now have something that looks like Fig. 5.166 when you have finished the texture corrections:

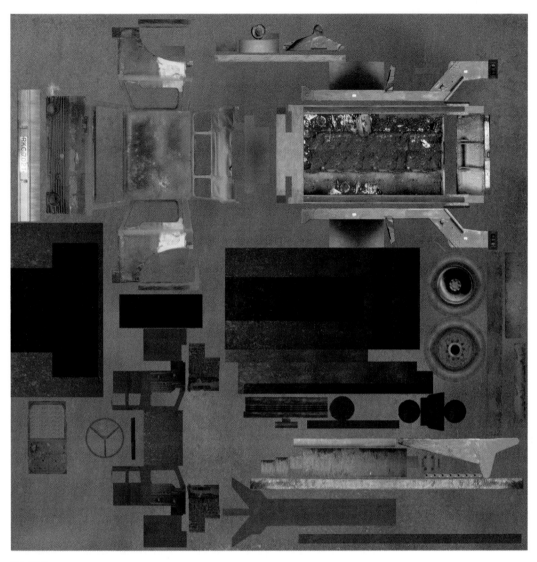

FIG 5.166

The only remaining tasks are creating the alphas for the seat, steering wheel, and chain by making an opacity map in Photoshop. Keep the original alpha in channels within Photoshop or create a new layer set and keep a layer as an alpha, but save a copy of your alpha map as a JPEG to be used in 3ds Max. If you intend to do any close-up render shots of the truck, you might want to create a higher resolution chain texture on your main texture page. This process is easy—and you should have plenty of space on your texture page.

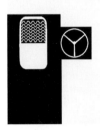

FIG 5.167

The Finished Truck

In 3d Max, apply the texture map to the truck.

Congratulations! You should now have a fully modeled and textured truck.

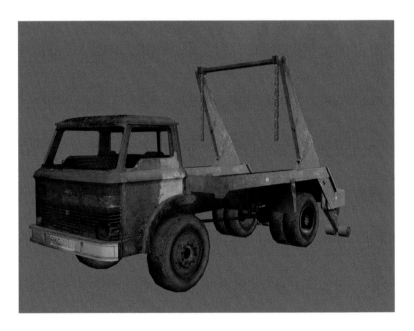

FIG 5.168

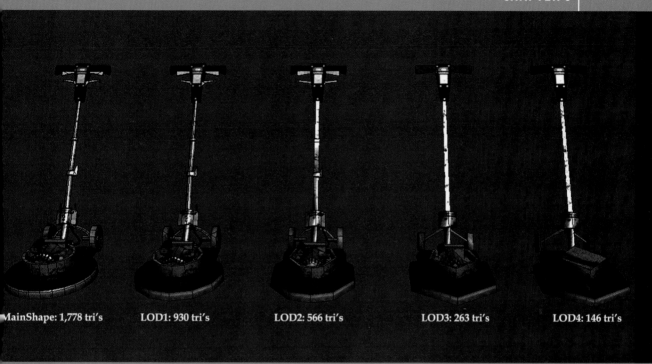

MainShape: 1,778 tri's   LOD1: 930 tri's   LOD2: 566 tri's   LOD3: 263 tri's   LOD4: 146 tri's

Creating LODs

The first question to answer is what is a LOD in a video game?

This is an acronym for Level of Detail.

If you have played a game recently, you will have seen LODs in action. When you see models "popping" as you get closer to them, this is the game engine swapping between LOD versions from the lowest to highest detailed version of the mesh. A good LOD is not noticeable.

LODs are a required optimization to ensure that a game's framerate stays optimal when drawing large expansive scenes full of objects. The principle is simple. Objects further away from the player will render at a lower LOD level meaning less geometry is drawn. Objects closer to the player will be the detailed versions as originally built.

This is probably considered one of the most boring areas of creating art assets for a game and as such is rarely covered. This task is probably what you will end up doing the most when you enter the industry as nearly every asset needs LODs. I feel dedicating this short chapter to the subject is a must.

An example of a LOD chain (a LOD chain is a name used for the group consisting of a main shape and all of its LODs) seen earlier in the book is displayed in Fig. 6.1. The model on the left with a triangle count of 953 is the main shape/final mesh. The model in the middle is LOD 1 with a triangle count of 390 and finally the LOD 2 consisting of 240 triangles. There could easily be a LOD 3 as 240 triangles can still be reduced further.

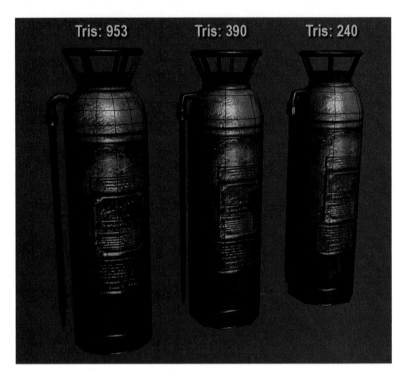

FIG 6.1

A LOD chain can consist of two to four LODs or maybe more depending on the complexity of the object and also the number of LODs a game engine can handle per object.

I'll be using the model from Chapter 3, the floor buffer to demonstrate the lodding process. Feel free to use your own model as the method, and workflow should be similar.

The first thing to do is to set out the triangle count goals for each LOD. Starting with the initial triangle count which is 2134, reduce the amount each time to calculate each LOD's triangle count.

Usually for LODs, each step down reduces the previous count by 50–75%, more if possible. The tables below show the estimations for the floor buffer model consisting of three LODs with a reduction of 50% each time. The main shape consists of the entire mesh. There is also a guide for the lid only and buffer only.

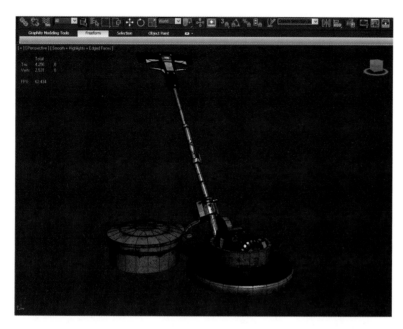

FIG. 6.2

Entire Model: 2134	Just the Buffer Lid: 356	The Rest of the Model: 1778
Lod 1: 1067	Lod 1: 178	Lod 1: 889
Lod 2: 534	Lod 2: 89	Lod 2: 445
Lod 3: 267	Lod 3: 45	Lod 3: 223

With the numbers calculated, we can get started. The actual process of lodding is fairly straightforward. The Weld, Target Weld, and Remove tools along with the delete button are the main tools of the trade.

A few things to be aware of when lodding are as follows:

Be careful of changing the silhouette of a model too drastically too quickly. Try not to remove any major details until LOD 3 onwards.

Take care with UV seams; don't delete edges or faces which separate two or more material types.

I'll start by showing the completed LOD chain for the buffer lid. I won't go through this process step by step as it really is just removing geometry with the earlier mentioned tools.

Working from left to right you can see the model's triangle count decrease. With the model being cylindrical, I was careful not to reduce the circular form on LOD 1 too much on top as this is very noticeable.

The recess and beveled edge on the top of the lid were removed straightaway. These kinds of details are always the best to remove first as they have the smallest visual impact.

The bottom section of Fig. 6.3 shows an example of how this set of LODs may work as they get further away from the camera. By LOD 3, you barely notice the fact it is now only a 48-tri, five-sided shape.

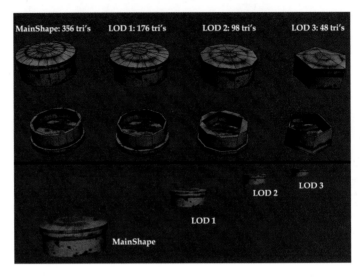

FIG 6.3

The final LOD's triangle counts for the lid are pretty much inline with the initial estimations.

As pictured in Fig. 6.4, the main part of the floor buffer has worked out in a similar way. The final LOD triangle counts are not exact but close enough to the first estimate. I have also created a LOD 4 in this example to show how far you can go with reducing a mesh. Chances are at this point, the mesh will cull (disappear) before a LOD 5 is drawn in game. To see these LODs as displayed in Fig. 6.4, open the file **CH006_fb_lod.7** in the chapter folder.

FIG 6.4

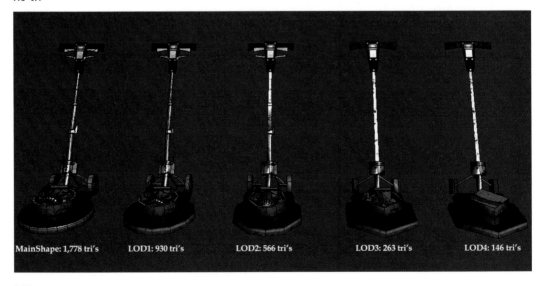

I'm going to run through the details removed at each stage while creating these LODs.

LOD 1

For this LOD, I stuck to only reducing the roundness of the casing around the motor and the casing around the buffer pad. The backs of the wheels had the geometry reduced. The front of the wheels was left alone as these would have popped badly.

All beveled edges were welded. Some welding was carried out on the motor also. The pole and other cylindrical areas not already optimized were reduced from five-sided to four-sided cylinders or from four-sided to three-sided cylinders.

The modeled bolts and pipe/cable were also reduced. No large reductions are carried out at this stage. A LOD 1 should still closely resemble the original mesh.

Figure 6.5 shows some close ups of LOD 1. Don't forget you can have a look in the 3ds Max file to properly inspect the model.

FIG. 6.5

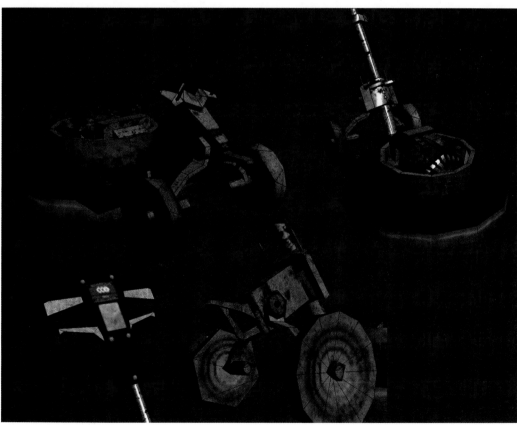

LOD 2

For LOD 2, we can stop being precious about the look of the model and remove more geometry. The fronts of the wheels were reduced to match the backs from LOD 1. The motor was reduced a little more.

The modeled bolts were all deleted as you are not likely to see them. The rusted metal pins were also deleted for the same reason. The overall roundness of the model was reduced in the same areas as before. Any remaining bevels or small details were welded.

Figure 6.6 displays a few shots of the model at this stage. As we progress through the LOD levels working our way towards the final LOD, the amount of work decreases as there are less and less polys to remove.

It's likely that during the lodding process you may need to remap areas of the model or adjust the geometry to maintain the same size and detail as the original model. When in doubt, move the LOD back over the main shape and use it as reference.

FIG 6.6

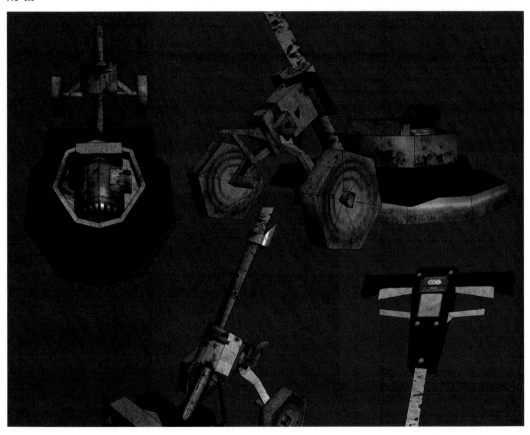

LOD 3

This is the LOD where you can start going all out and deleting sections of the model where needed and changing the silhouette a bit. The first thing to remove was the triggers and the brakes.

Again, the roundness has been reduced by some more welding; this also includes the wheels.

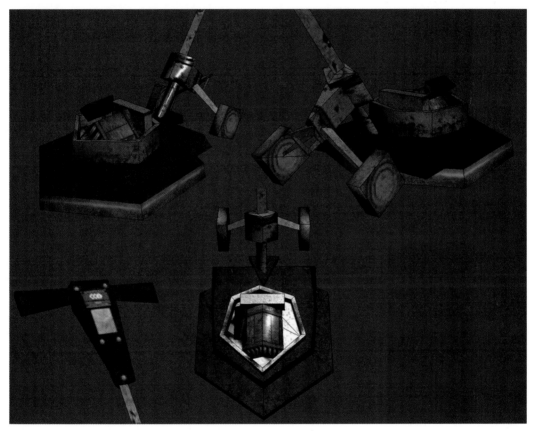

FIG 6.7

LOD 4

LOD 4 was created to show you how far it is possible to go with a LOD at this stage. All that matters by now is how low you can get the poly count before it looks too strange. Fig. 6.8 shows a few angles of LOD 4.

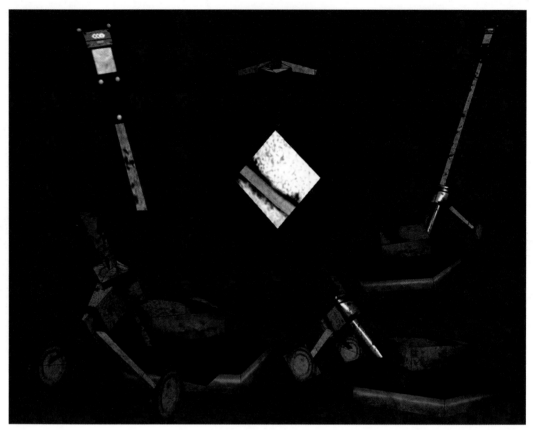

FIG 6.8

As a general rule, LODs should occupy the same space as the original mesh, and the pivot points will also need to match up. The LODs are then parented beneath the main shape.

I hope this brief introduction into lodding will help you in creating your own. It's good for practice to LOD some models you create, so you will gain an understanding of the process and get experience in dealing with different types of models.

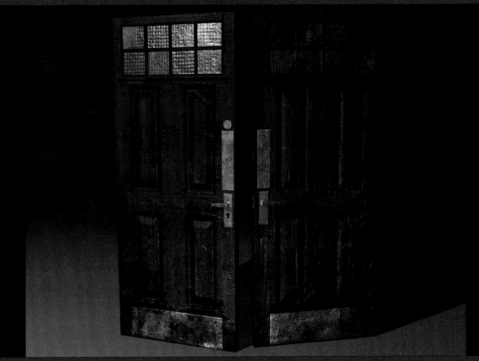

CHAPTER 7

Normal Maps

Normal maps have become a commonly used technique that has helped define the look of the current generation of video games. The purpose of a normal map is to make a low poly model look like a high poly model.

Usually, this means two different models need to be created to "transfer" the information from the high-resolution mesh to the low-resolution mesh.

Below are examples of a tangent space normal map baked from a high poly model and applied to a low poly version.

Each surface on a model has a normal direction. The surface normal is like a perpendicular line protruding outwards from the surface of the polygon. Normal maps work by storing a model's surface normal direction information in the RGB channels of a texture. Figure 7.2 shows some surface normals of a sphere.

The red and green channels of a normal map use a range of gray scale values ranging from black to white to represent the normal direction along the X- and Y-axes. The Z-axis represents depth; in a tangent space normal map the blue channel can only be a positive value, so the gray scale values range from 50% gray to white. The following image shows the three RGB channels first separately and then combined.

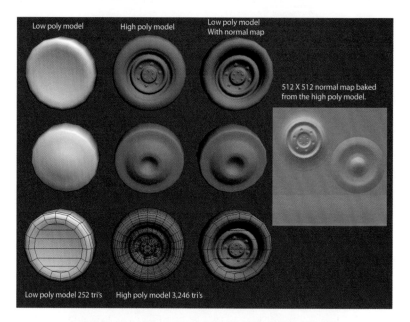

FIG 7.1

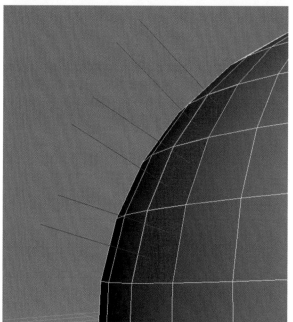

FIG 7.2

When a normal map is applied to a model with the correct shader, the information stored in the RGB channel is used to describe the normal direction of each pixel on an object's surface. These details react to lighting in real time as if they are actually modeled into the surface. The amount and crispness of details from the high-resolution model that will be captured by the normal map is limited by the texture's resolution.

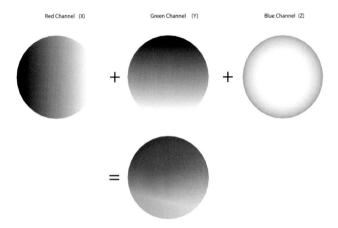

Red Channel (X)　　　　Green Channel (Y)　　　　Blue Channel (Z)

FIG 7.3

There are three main types of normal maps. Figure 7.4 shows a normal mapped head model. The example on the left is a tangent space normal map, and the one on the right is an object space normal map.

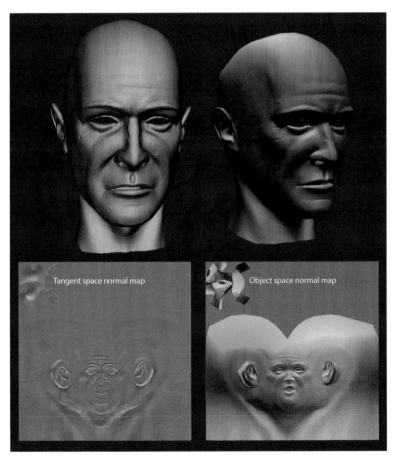

Tangent space normal map

Object space normal map

FIG 7.4

World Space and Object Space Normal Maps

These normal maps are visually different from tangent space normal maps as they use a wider spectrum of colours to define the different values for the normal direction of each pixel in relation to world space co-ordinates used in a 3D program. From a performance standpoint, world space normal maps are the most efficient. Object space normal maps are second. These techniques do come with certain limitations though.

One limitation of world space and object space normal mapping is that they must have their own distinct UV coordinates. Therefore, you can't reuse parts of the texture for more than one part of the model.

Models assigned world space normal maps cannot be rotated from their original position that they were created from, and the vertices of the model cannot be deformed as this will result in the surface normals' directional values being incorrect for their position and the surface being lit wrong.

Object space normal maps can be moved but cannot be deformed. Consider these restrictions when deciding which method to use. World space normal maps are best for unique static objects that will not move, such as a building. Object space normal maps are good for objects that move but do not deform—for example a door, window, or barrel.

Tangent Space Normal Map

Tangent space normal maps are easily recognized by their mostly blue appearance. Tangent space normals almost always look bluish because normals in tangent space are always considered "up" (coordinates 0, 0, 1), even if in world space this is not true. The normals mapped on this triangle are thus encoded, and that's the key point, relatively to (0, 0, 1). Because most normals are pointing "up," and since the vector (0, 0, 1) is colorized as blue-purple-ish, the result is a blue-purple-ish normal map. The benefits of tangent space maps are the removal of the restrictions imposed by world space and object space normal maps. Tangent space normal maps can rotate and deform; therefore, they are ideal for characters or objects that need to have vertex deformation, such as water or tree limbs.

In dealing with 3ds Max, the red channel is lit from the right, the green from below, and the blue represents depth.

The Process of Creating a Normal Map

Now that we have a better understanding of what a normal map is, let's go through the steps of baking a normal map from a high poly model in 3ds Max. You can use any model you wish to as long as you have a high poly model and a low poly version with UV coordinates before starting.

For this example, I have chosen to create a door. The high poly was modeled using the standard tools. A lot of the geometry is floating or intersecting geometry. When it comes to creating high-resolution models for generating normal maps, there is less need to worry about the amount of polygons or how clean the mesh is.

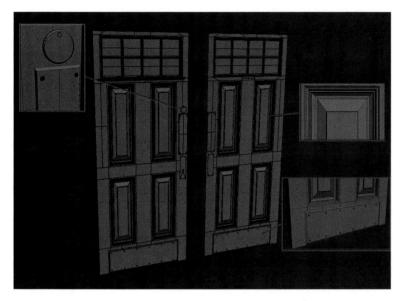

FIG 7.5

When creating high poly models for generating normal maps, try to avoid creating faces parallel to the surface normals. These details do not come out well because of how a 3D program gathers this information. It's better to chamfer edges or at least scale in any faces to ensure there are no faces at 90° angles to each other.

Figure 7.6 shows two diagrams to explain this. The one on the left shows a low poly surface in blue and a high poly shape with a raised cube on the surface. When a 3D program is baking, texture "rays" are cast perpendicular to the low poly surface in the direction of the surface normal. When these rays hit the high poly mesh, it gathers the information.

In the left image, as the sides of the extrusion are perpendicular to the low poly surface, this results in the surface normal direction appearing totally flat as the rays don't pick up a face parallel to them.

The example on the right has two corner edges chamfered or beveled. This creates new faces with a surface normal direction different to the low poly surface. As the rays hit these new faces, the data is converted to values in the RGB channels of the normal map.

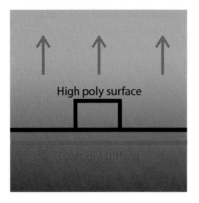 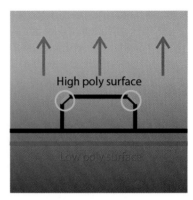

FIG 7.6

A simple way to check models before you bake the maps is to use one of the orthographic viewports such as the front or left ones to view the high poly model. If you can see all the intended details clearly, the normal map should turn out similar.

Figure 7.7 shows this quick test. The horizontal chamfered box appears clearly in the normal map and screen grab of the front viewport, whereas the vertical box with sides perpendicular to the surface of the low poly mesh appears nonexistent in all images.

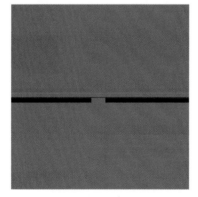 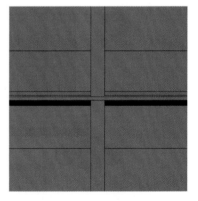

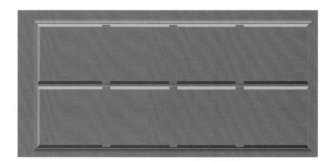

FIG 7.7

Since all we need is the surface normal information of this model, we can just create planes of the same size to bake the information on to before applying the final normal map to a fully modeled door. If you already have an existing low poly model, you can use that.

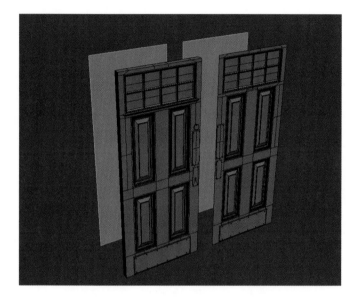

FIG 7.8

I have also created two different sides for the door to show the locking mechanism for both doors. Simple planes of a relative size have also been created for these in preparation to bake the normal map.

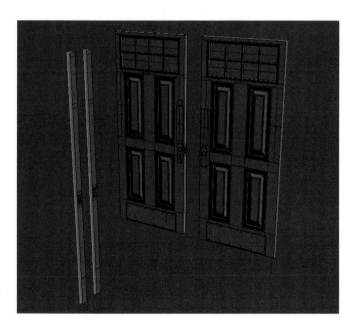

FIG 7.9

All meshes have been spaced out, so when the rays are cast from the low poly surfaces, they won't pick up any of the other meshes in the scene. Attach all the low poly planes together, so they can be unwrapped to one texture sheet. These planes need to have UV coordinates, so apply an Unwrap UVW modifier and planar map the low poly meshes. The UV layout is displayed in Fig. 7.10.

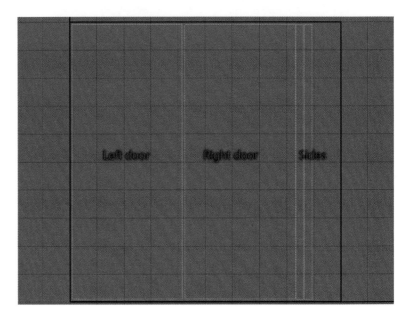

FIG 7.10

The final scene setup was displayed in Fig. 7.9. This file can be found in the chapter files here if you wish to jump straight into baking a normal map. **Chapter7\CH007_assets\ door_scene_for_baking**

We are now ready to bake the normal map. I'll be baking a tangent space normal map as I wish to reuse the texture on the front and back of the door. This is not possible with object or world space normal maps as they require unique UV space for every polygon.

Select the low poly mesh and press 0 to bring up the Render To Texture dialog or go to the main menu > Rendering > Render To Texture.

Select the low poly model as this will need to be selected from the beginning. It will appear in the list in the "objects to bake" section.

First up are the general settings; we will change the render settings. Open the drop down list and select the top option. Default scanline renderer. You can also chose the output path of where to save the files from the general settings also.

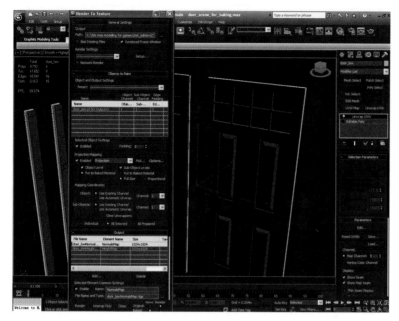

FIG 7.11

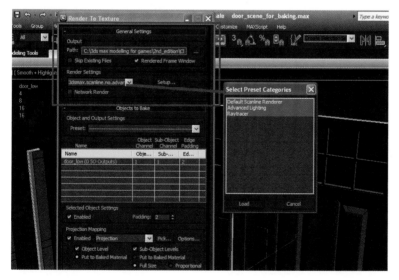

FIG 7.12

Under Projection Mapping in Objects to Bake, select Pick; a new window Add Targets will pop up. Choose the high poly mesh by its name, in this case door_high. You may have noticed a new modifier called Projection has appeared in the low poly models modifier stack. We'll be using this soon.

251

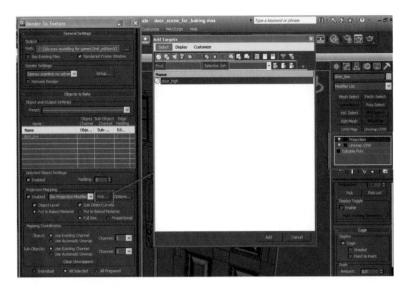

FIG 7.13

Now click on Options beside the Pick button to bring up a new window titled Projection Options.

The default settings should be ok, but just make sure the following is selected.

> Method > Raytrace > Use Cage
> Resolve Hit is at Furthest and that Ray miss is checked.
> Normal Map Space is set to Tangent. The orientation is Right, Green.

If you wish to bake a world space normal map or an object space one, you could choose the World or Local XYZ options instead of Tangent.

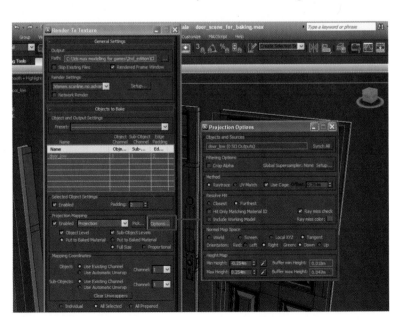

FIG 7.14

252

Under Mapping Coordinates, select Use Existing Channel as the object has been unwrapped.

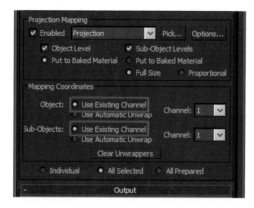

FIG 7.15

Add a normal map to the Output section by clicking Add and choosing NormalsMap from the list.

The Selected Elements Common Settings will appear. This is where we name the output texture and input its location to save it by selecting the icon to the right of file name and browsing to the desired location. You can also pick the texture's size by selecting from the options. I'll go for a 1024 × 1024 this time. It's useful to bake the maps at a smaller size than needed at first to iron out any problems that come up before committing a long time baking a really large map.

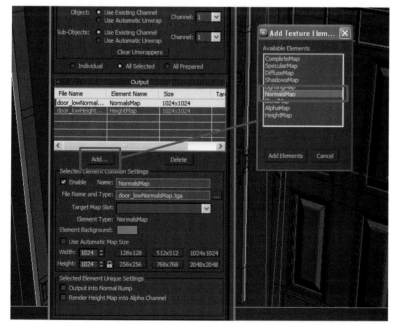

FIG 7.16

Going to the projection modifier and selecting the cage mode adjust the Cage to ensure it is covering the high poly mesh closely and that no areas are overlapping. The cage is represented as a blue wireframe.

This can be done manually just like editing a mesh. It may be easier to Reset the cage and adjust the Push values if the automatic cage has exploded too much. These settings are found in the modify panel. Figure 7.17 highlights these.

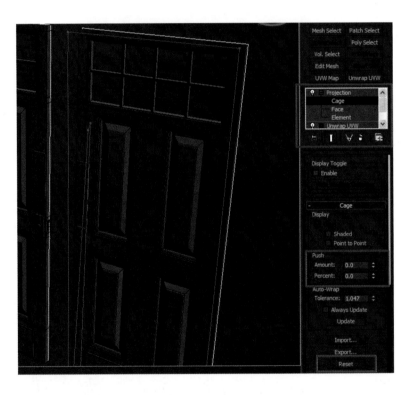

These are the only settings we'll need to deal with to get a tangent space normal map baked out. Once you are happy that the cage is sitting away from the high poly model, it's time to render the texture.

Go to the bottom and press Render; this will then bake the map for you and save it in the specified location as the chosen file type. A warning window will appear as we have not specified a target map slot in a shader. This is ok to ignore; press Continue.

The texture will render as a gray scale map. Open the Output file or reload it into the scene to see it as a tangent space normal map.

Now that we have a normal map, it needs to be applied to the model. I created a simple door double model with fronts and backs. The total triangle

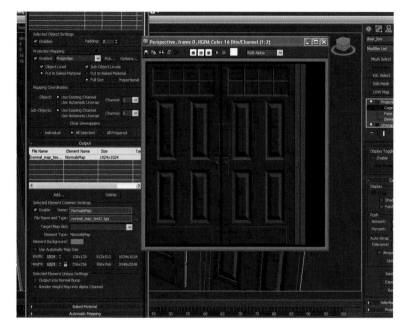

FIG 7.18

count was 542. This also included four handles and a modeled rim to sit below the glass panels.

As a normal map does not affect the silhouette of a model, I left these few elements as geometry to add depth to the model. The rest of the details such as the recessed panels and keyholes were left up to the normal map. Figure 7.19 shows the tangent space normal map baked from the high poly and the unwrapped low poly model.

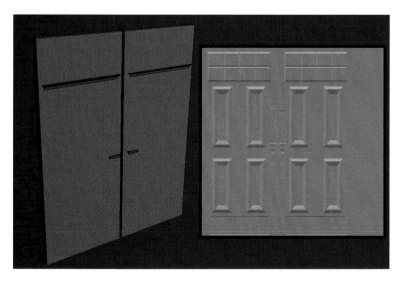

FIG 7.19

To apply the normal map to a model press M to bring up the *material editor*.

Select a shader to use. Under the maps list, tick the box to the left of the *bump* slot to activate it.

Increase the value from 30 to 100. Now click on the button None to the right and select *normal bump* from the list.

Click on the new None button that appears beside Normal: and select bitmap from the list.

Browse to the location of the output tangent map and select it. The map will now be loaded.

Press Go to Parent twice to go back to the main material editor screen.

Now left click and drag from the shader image to the mesh you want to assign the texture to. If the normal map does not appear in the view port go to the main menu > views > Show Materials in Viewport as > Hardware Display with Maps to display the normal map in the view port.

Figure 7.20 shows the high poly model on the left, the low poly model in the centre, and then the low poly model with the normal map applied to the right.

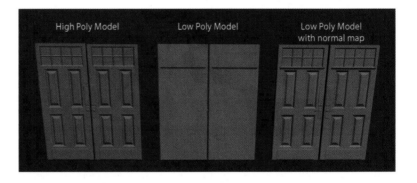

FIG 7.20

The door as it is now is looking reasonable, but it is missing the finer details such as wood grain to really push it further. It is possible to create these details in a sculpting package such as Z-Brush or Mudbox, but it's quicker to create these details in Photoshop from a modified gray scale version of the diffuse map.

Figure 7.21 shows the diffuse, specular, and normal maps that combine to give the final look to the doors surface. To create the specular map, the diffuse texture PSD was copied and renamed to be the specular PSD. All layers were desaturated and then had their levels adjusted to create contrast in the doors materials. Metal and glass elements were lightened to be shiny, and the wooden surfaces were darkened so they'd almost be a matte surface.

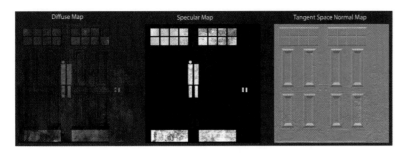

FIG 7.21

Figure 7.22 shows the original normal map created in 3ds Max on the left and the final normal map on the right that had the finer details added in Photoshop. These new details were created by duplicating the diffuse texture PSD and desaturating all the layers similar to the creation of the specular PSD.

I then went through the layers adjusting the levels until I was satisfied. Figure 7.23 shows the two different sets of details I was working on. The wood grain is on the right and was kept separate, so I could control how strong it would be in the final normal map.

The rest of the details such as dirt build up and damage can be seen on the left. When creating gray scale images to be converted into a normal map, remember that lighter values will be raised from the surface and darker values will recede into the surface.

When I was happy with the two images, I ran them through the nvidia normal map plugin available to download for Photoshop. These new layers were then placed over the original normal map from 3ds Max and set to overlay. The opacity was adjusted until all the details sat well together.

When the image was ready, I flattened the texture and normalized the normal map using the nvidia plugin. This is important as the values in a normal map can only range from 0 to 1, black to white. By normalizing the normal map, it adjusts any values outside of this range.

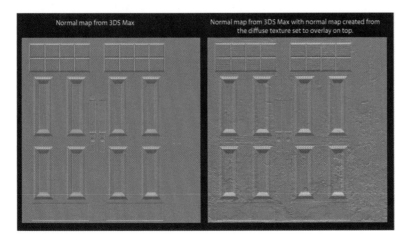

FIG 7.22

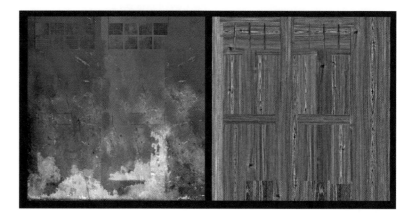

FIG 7.23

Figure 7.24 is a render of the low poly door with all the final textures applied to the model.

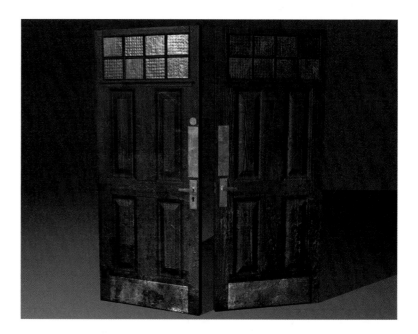

FIG 7.24

Tips for Creating Normal Maps

- Normal maps create more work for the artist. Always consider whether you actually need one.
- A tangent space normal map is the type most commonly used in games.
- Spending time in preparing a UV layout saves you time in the long run.
- Do not flip UVs; doing so will make your normal map display incorrectly.

- Building individual details and combining them in image manipulation software is a quick way of developing complex detail, without long build and render times.
- Normal-mapped elements can be moved and scaled but not rotated in image manipulation software.
- Avoid sharp angles, which can create strange artifacts in the normal map. This also applies to hard edges from smoothing groups. Unless you want a hard-edged look to your final model with the normal map applied, ensure the low poly model has all the smoothing groups set to 1 before you bake a normal map as hard edges may result in missed details and artifacts in the final texture.
- The quality of the normal map is dependent on its resolution and compression.
- Normal maps cannot be edited like normal textures. If you do need to edit one, make sure you use a plug-in to "normalize" the normal map when you are finished, so the values sit back within the 0–1 range.
- Normal maps can display differently depending on the software and hardware used. If you notice your normal map not lighting correctly, invert the green channel as this is usually the cause.
- It's best not to create any lighting information in the diffuse texture when using normal maps as they will take care of how the surface is lit.

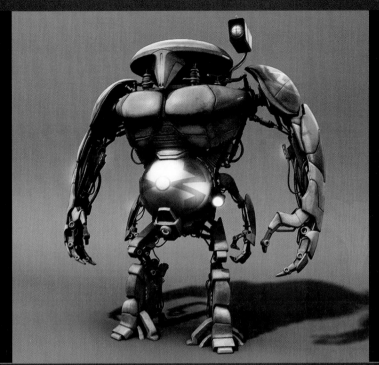

Gallery

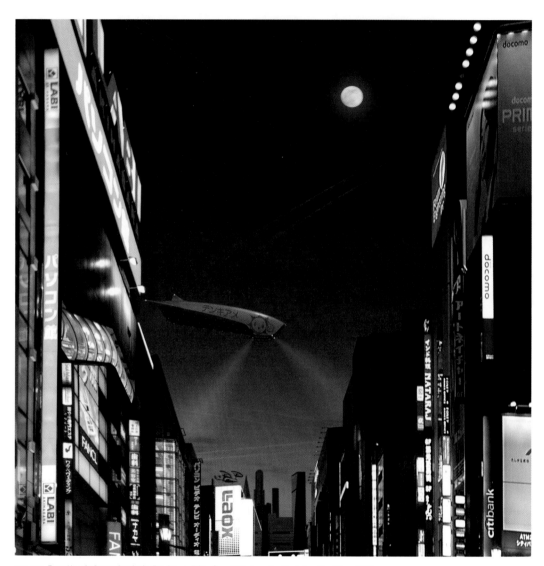

FIG 8.1 Team Hizashi Racing Render by Tim Brown. Taken from 3D Automotive Modeling, Focal Press 2011.

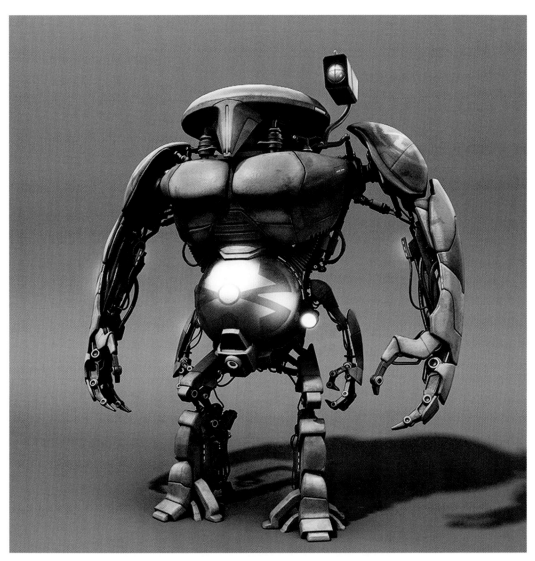

FIG 8.2 Mobile Suit 3D Render by Andrew Gahan. Taken from 3D Automotive Modeling, Focal Press 2011.

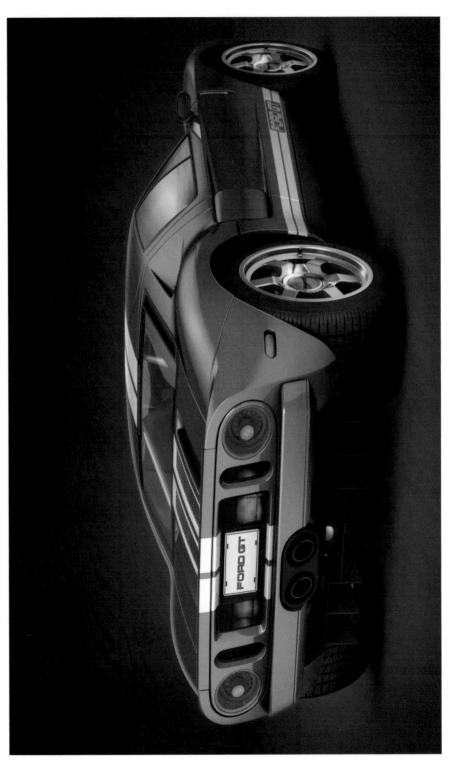

FIG 8.3 Ford GT 40 by Johal Gow.

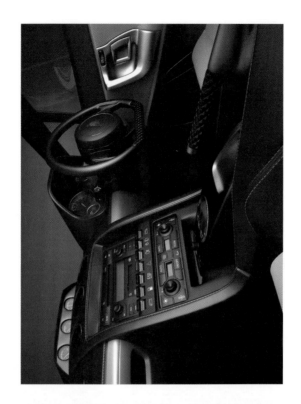

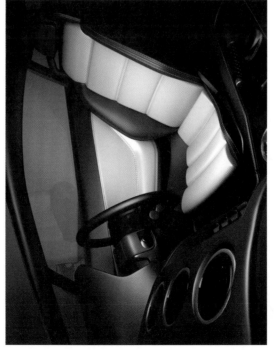

FIG 8.4 (a and b) Lamborghini interior by Simon Nuttall (www.iconized.com).

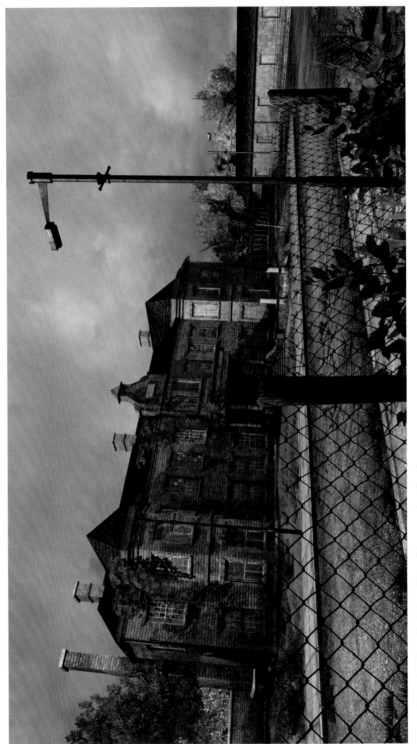

FIG 8.5 Whittingham Hospital by Anthony O'Donnell (www.antodonnell.com).

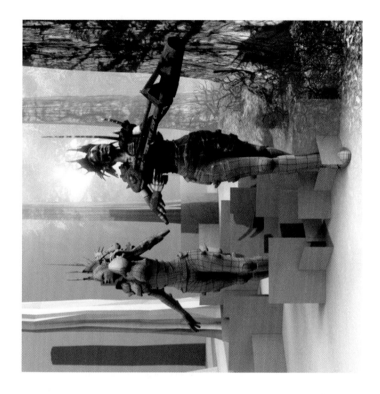

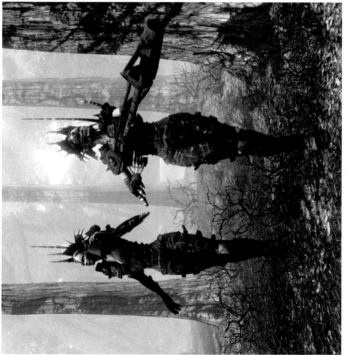

FIG 8.6 (a and b) Elf Scout by Mike Engstrom (www.engy.cgsociety.org).

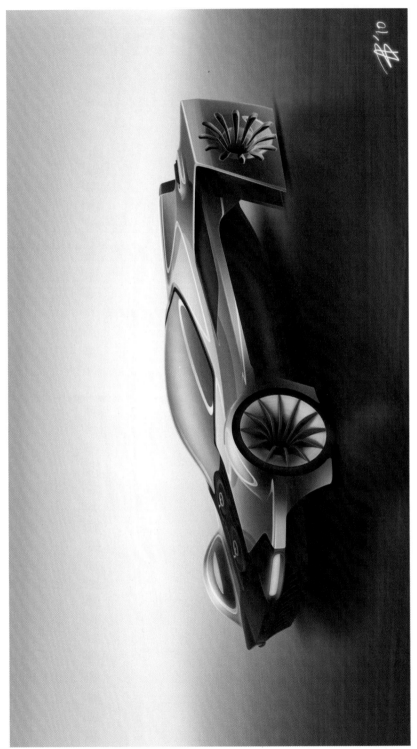

FIG 8.7 Team Hizashi Racing Concept by Tim Brown. Taken from 3D Automotive Modeling, Focal Press 2011.

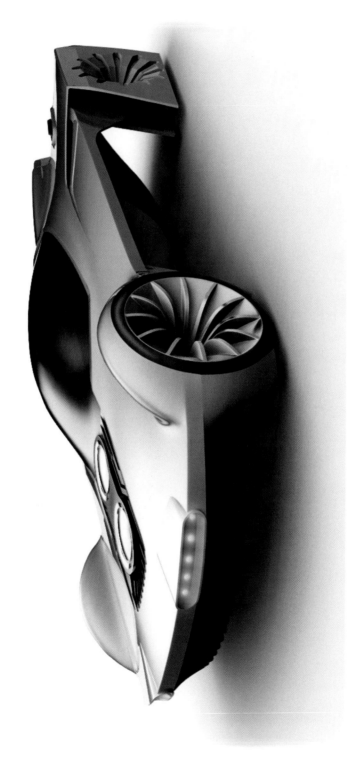

FIG 8.8 Team Hizashi 3D Render by Johal Gow. Taken from 3D Automotive Modeling, Focal Press 2011.

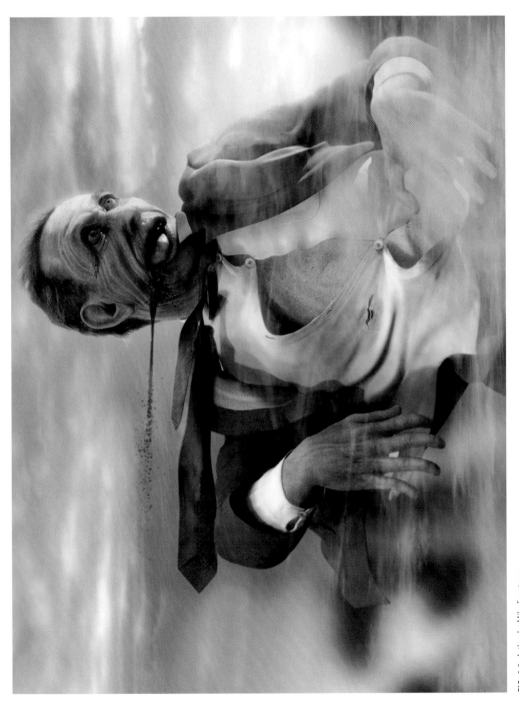

FIG 8.9 Arthur by Mike Engstrom.

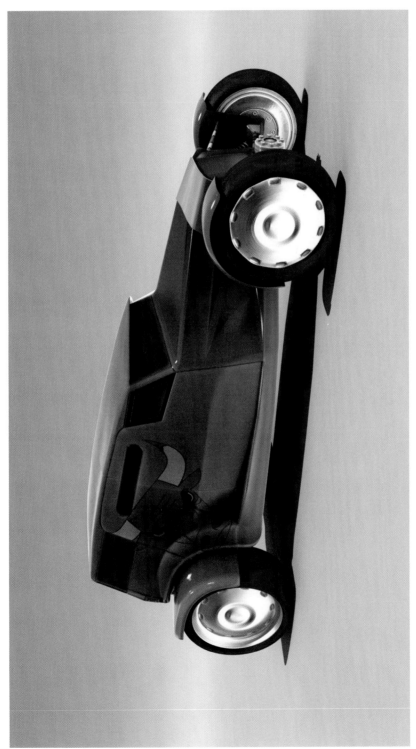

FIG 8.10 Chicago Styled Hot Rod by Andrew Gahan. Taken from 3D Automotive Modeling, Focal Press 2011.

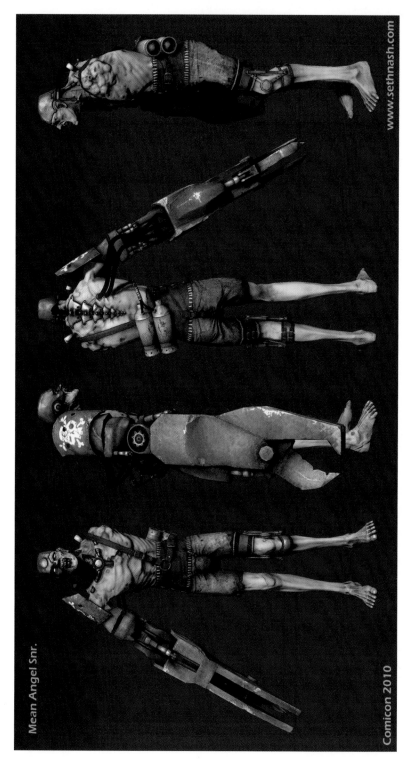

FIG 8.11 Mean Angel Snr. by Seth Nash (www.sethnash.com).

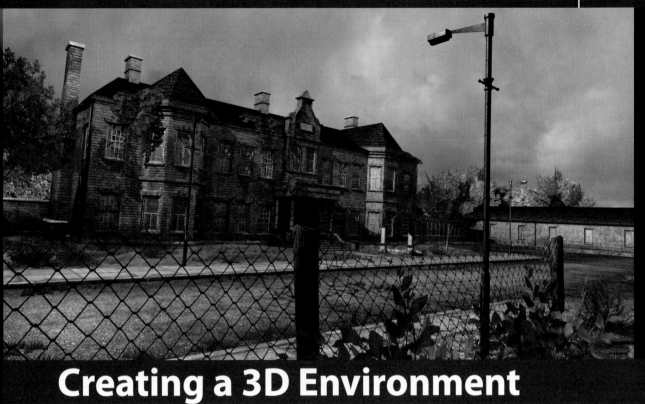

CHAPTER 9

Creating a 3D Environment

The purpose of this chapter is to utilize all the skills you have learned so far to produce an environment. While we do this we will be introducing you to a workflow for creating an environment and dealing with elements such as budgets and deadlines. We will not cover every single step in this chapter as a lot of the modeling and texturing techniques used have already been covered. Any new techniques will be explained as we go along.

Are You Ready? OK, Let's Go!

The environment creation process is usually an iterative one. In a development studio, we will constantly move back and forth between designers and artists as the environment is created. This is to facilitate both game play changes and of course esthetic appeal, with both being refined in stages. This tutorial will follow a linear workflow, but in reality, you will probably move in and out of all stages a few times during a production cycle.

The environment in this chapter uses the reference provided with the first edition of the book and that is also included in the Chapter 9 reference folder available to download from http://www.3d-for-games.com. Take a look at the introduction in this book for more detailed instructions on the download.

The photo reference is of an abandoned mental hospital in the North of England. Some example images are featured in Fig. 9.1. The goal is to create a section of the hospital grounds that includes exterior and interior sections of buildings.

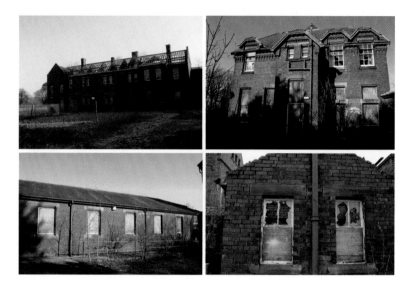

FIG 9.1

For this scene, I stuck to set a deadline much as you would in the games industry.

Here is a quick overview of the workflow that I'll be following including some tasks that will be completed during each phase. This workflow can still apply even if you decide to create a different environment.

Reference and planning

- Gather as much reference as possible to add to the existing set.
- Layout a rough 2D plan of the scene.
- Get an idea for the amount of items the environment will consist of.

Blockout

- Using the 2D plan quickly block out a basic version of the entire scene.
- Add blockout model for any objects or items that maybe needed.
- Aim to get a strong composition of objects at this early stage.

Concept

- Use the blockout to create a concept to define a final look for the scene including a pass on lighting and a first pass on composition.
- Draw up an asset list using the blockout and concept art to identify what needs to be built to define the workload involved.
- Create a texture list based on surfaces to be used in the scene.

Asset Creation

- Create the texture sets to be used in the scene.
- Identify and create any modular assets.
- Produce all 3D assets required for the scene such as buildings.
- Populate the scene with other assets like vegetation or lamposts.

Lighting and rendering

- Set up lights in the scene to simulate and overcast day.
- Find a solution to render high-quality images quickly.

The 2D Plan

This is a step you could possibly skip if you prefer to move straight on to the blockout. Try not to jump straight into modeling without some sort of sketch though, as this step can save you a lot of time later on.

I found the creation of a 2D plan was useful to quickly set the footprints of the buildings and to organize the overall layout of the scene. Remember this step is just the first version and not necessarily the final layout, so don't feel as if you need to stick to this 100%.

Figure 9.2 shows the final version of the 2D plan after spending about 90 minutes in Photoshop moving elements around. This could also have been done traditionally on paper. I find Photoshop quicker as you can freely move, rotate, and scale elements in the image easily to allow for quick iteration.

The plan was created by first using flat values of gray on individual layers to create the buildings, pavement, and road. The Line tool was used to define the edges of buildings.

Once this stage was complete, some photographic samples were placed beneath the flat colors to clarify the different surface types intended to be used.

Flat colors were then used as selections to cut out the shape from photo reference. For example, asphalt was copied from a photo by selecting the flat asphalt color layers icon while holding Ctrl + A.

You can then select the photo of the road and use Ctrl + J to copy the selection to a new layer. This technique makes the process of adding photo elements to the 2D plan very easy and fast.

If you wish to see how the PSD was arranged, the file is in the Chapter 9 folder available to download **Chapter9\CH009_concepts\environment_layout_final.psd**.

I put a scale reference bar in the image measuring 8 m. This will help me to match it up in 3ds Max later.

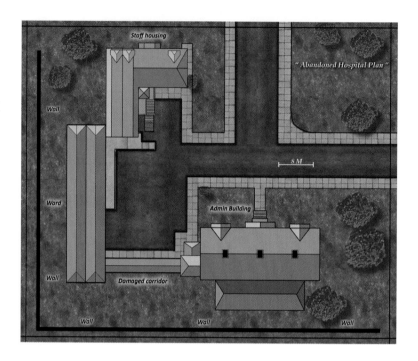

Staff housing

" Abandoned Hospital Plan "

Wall

8 M

Ward

Admin Building

Wall

Damaged corridor

Wall

Wall

Wall

FIG 9.2

Blockout

The process of blocking out an environment before jumping straight to making final assets is extremely important. I really can't stress this enough as it can really help you to understand just how much work you'll be getting yourself into. A lot of environments and scenes are never finished because the artist completely underestimates the amount of work involved. It's a very easy trap to fall into!

At an early stage you can solve a lot of issues that may arise and fix them early on with less effort by understanding what you need to do from your blockout. Issues that you could encounter are scale issues, game play problems, and poor composition.

Blockouts provide a lot of information depending on how far you take it. It can range from a group of basic primitives to a low poly version of a final scene with all the assets blocked out.

It's important to not get sucked into modeling details or accurate forms at this stage. The goal is to create a rough broad stroke of the entire scene. Get as many details blocked in as possible. If you have time, you can then create an accurate manageable asset list moving into the production phase.

The chapter folder contains 15 blockout files which we'll go through now. **Chapter9\CH009_assets\ blockout_1-15**.

The first step is to create a ground plane with the same dimensions as the 2D plan in 3ds Max, so the plan can be mapped onto it and used as a guide. The dimensions in Photoshop are in centimeters and in max are in meters.

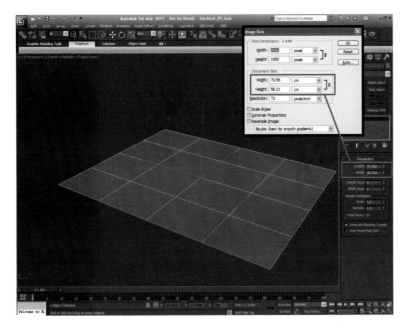

FIG 9.3

The 2D plan was then mapped onto the plane using planar mapping.

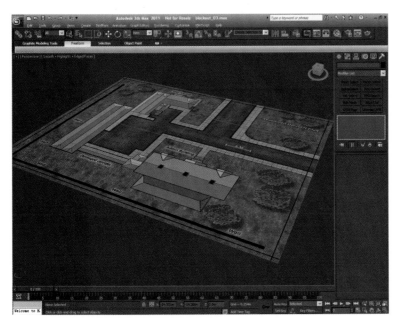

FIG 9.4

277

A rectangle 8 m in length was created using the units in 3ds Max. The 2D plan was scaled up matching the scale bar on the plan to the 8 m rectangle.

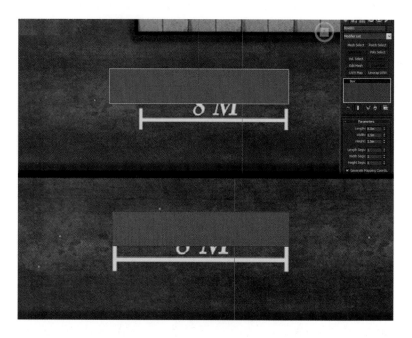

FIG 9.5

Using the plan as a guide, start blocking out the buildings using slightly modified primitives. Remember, don't add any fine details at this stage; keep to rough shapes to define height, weight, and depth.

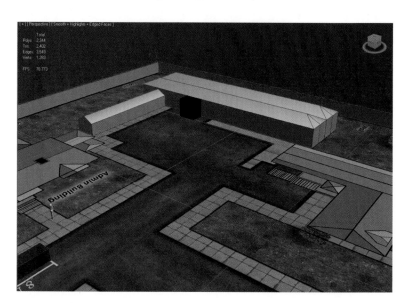

FIG 9.6

Continue to block out the rest of the buildings. At this stage, I am referring to the photo reference to work out the rough shape of the buildings. In Fig. 9.7, you can see a rectangle with two edge loops. This was used as a measuring tool to define three storeys or floors. So, for each division, it's one floor.

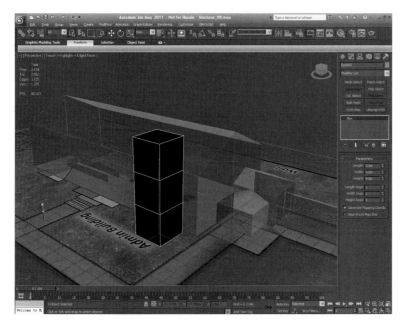

FIG 9.7

Continuing to use standard modeling techniques, the pavement has been created, and also, boxes have been placed as floating geometry over the facade of the building. This is so that I can get an idea of how many will be in the scene.

The window sizes were estimated from some of the photo reference. Depending on the style of building you are creating, I'd advise that you have a quick search online for standard or popular window sizes for the architectural style you are creating.

Even if you don't create a 1:1 scale replica, it's good to create something as close as you can get it. The more information you have, the more accurate the final production model will be. This can apply to any object you create.

It's at this stage if this environment was to be used for game play, you could assess the scale of objects such as windows and doors in relation to the players perspective. You may be surprised to find that real-world scale items may not always work well in a game. I tend to scale everything slightly to "feel" right.

In Fig. 9.9, the main elements of the blockout are coming together. Some more details such as the columns and entrance area on the main building have been added.

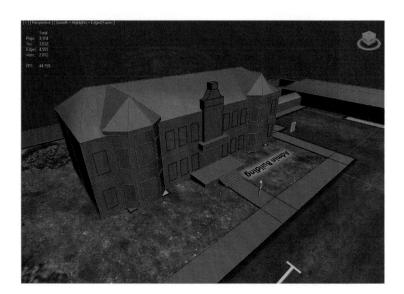

FIG 9.8

By Fig. 9.10, the blockout has all sides of all the buildings populated with basic details to give me an overall feel for the scene. At this stage, I'm starting to think that I may not be able to complete the entire environment that I have blocked out due to the deadline. It's a good idea for me to scale back my initial design at this point to ensure I can finish the scene.

This is an extremely important point and a very important part of this book. Even the most experienced professionals "get it wrong" sometimes. It's not important to do everything perfectly, every time—the important thing is how you plan and deal with issues as they come up.

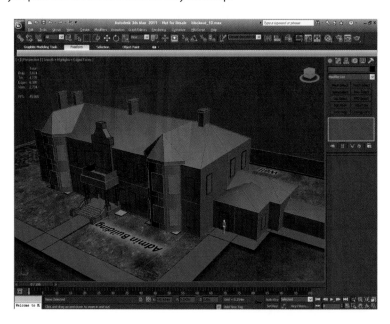

FIG 9.9

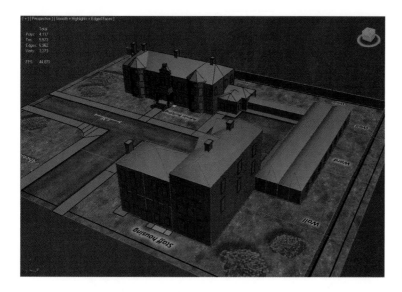

FIG 9.10

Standard blinn shaders with the ambient color changed were applied to the models to get some color variety into the blockout. This helps to separate all the surfaces and to identify materials that may be required, such as red bricks or the black slate roof.

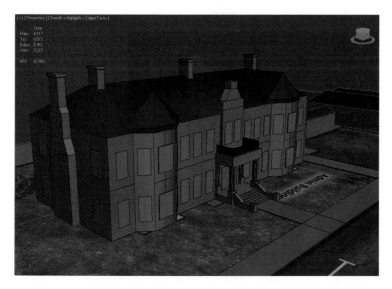

FIG 9.11

The last round of changes to the blockout included adding in some assets such as lamposts and a barrier on the road. Also, some roof damage was blocked into the corridor roof. The ward building had a side wall damaged and a basic interior blocked out. These adjustments can be seen in Fig. 9.12.

You could easily continue at this point and add more assets such as signs, abandoned cars, vegetation, rocks, or debris piles. What you add will be down to the type of environment you create.

The more refined the blockout is, the more it can help in making the production process easier. It will help you to identify the number of assets to create, and from this, you can jot down rough estimates on time and resources to get the scene completed.

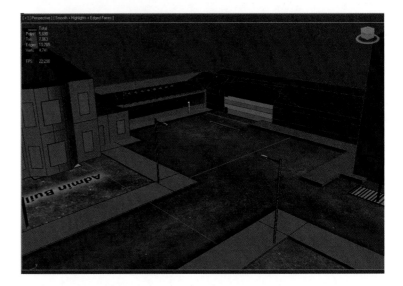

FIG 9.12

The reason I have not gone into more detail with the blockout is that for the next stage I have decided to create a concept image using the blockout as a base. Figure 9.13 shows the camera angle I set up to paint over to create the concept.

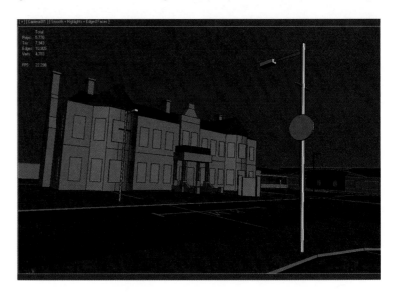

FIG 9.13

Concept

The concept sketch was completed in around six or seven hours in two sittings. It involved using photo elements and painting. Painter and Photoshop were both used. The goal of this stage is to create a "final" image to visualize the end result. Assets will be added, and the lighting within the scene will be worked out.

Concept art is very beneficial and is a great aid for artists to guide them through the production of an environment. Even though most companies will have a concept art team, it is worth gaining some experience in this area to be able to visually communicate clearly to others. After all a picture does speak a thousand words.

Starting with the blockout render in Painter, I used the artist oil brush for some colors and loose shading on a new layer on top of the render. The sky was painted on a layer beneath the render after the flat grey background was removed.

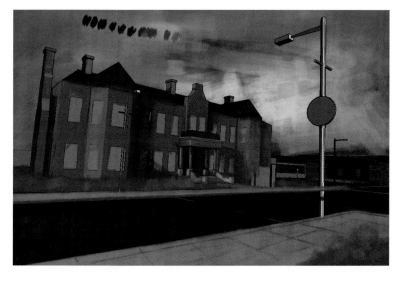

FIG 9.14

Figure 9.15 shows more painting over the render slowly tightening up the details. At this stage, I have moved back to Photoshop to take two photos of windows that were duplicated many times and manipulated into position with the Move tool and the transform mode perspective.

Although I was still in Photoshop, other photo elements were added to the image to speed up the process. These included the vegetation, bricks, fencing and rubble. Each image was passed through the Smart blur filter. Smart blur simplifies the details and gives it a more painterly look, blending everything in nicely for when I move back into painter. The results can be seen in Fig. 9.16.

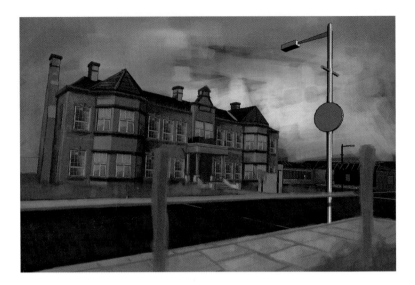

FIG 9.15

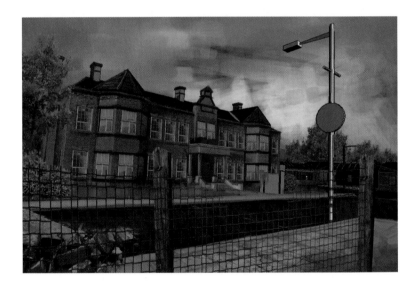

FIG 9.16

Figure 9.17 shows the image after spending some more time in painter. I worked into the photo sections to ensure they sit better within the image. A pass on shadows and lighting were also added.

The grass areas and bricks were refined and tightened up by using precise strokes and opaque brushes. The sign in front of the administration building was also rendered.

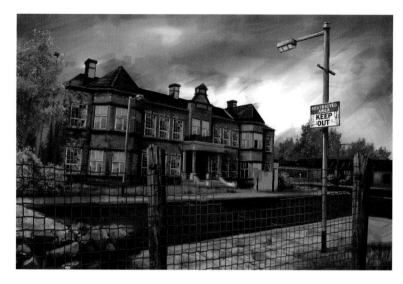

FIG 9.17

Figure 9.18 is the final concept image. Once I was happy with the level of detailing in Painter, I moved back into Photoshop to adjust the levels and colors of the image. Finally, some ivy was painted in using a brush.

A final pass on the lighting was also worked on. I choose to go with an overcast sky in the background with a break in the clouds outside of the image on the left allowing the sun to shine on the building. This will be my main light source in 3ds Max later once we get to the lighting stage.

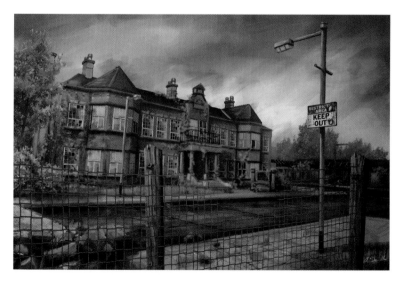

FIG 9.18

Production

After all that preparation we are now ready to enter the production phase and start to create the environment. The first thing I recommend doing at this stage is to draw up a work list based on all the steps we have taken so far. There will be two lists, an asset list to show all objects needed to be created and a list of all textures required for the scene.

A good thing to do at this point is to identify any textures that can be shared, or models that could be reused or created using a modular approach.

The following are the samples from the two lists used:

Asset list

- 1 x lampost
- A modular pavement set
- A modular brick wall
- A selection of windows
- A modular set of guttering
- The main building entrance
- Administration building
- Damaged corridor
- A door model
- The sign in front of the admin building
- The ward building
- Staff housing
- Reuse vegetation from Chapter 4.

Texture list

- 2 x road textures. One plain and one damaged for variety. Include normal maps.
- 1 x tiling concrete texture to be used on the concrete platforms and possibly pillars and steps.
- 1 x tiling grass texture.
- 1 x tiling dirt texture to blend with the grass texture. Include normal map.
- 1 x texture sheet containing a variety of windows possibly four types. Include normal and spec maps.
- 1 x tiling slate roof texture. Include normal map.
- 2 x pavement textures. One plain and one damaged for variety. Include normal maps
- 1 x tiling wooden post texture.
- 1 x tiling texture of a variety of wooden beams.

These sample lists are useful as work lists to keep you focused when creating an environment. They also help you to estimate the time it's all going to take and can stop new elements creeping in later on in the production phase. Each item on these lists should be estimated so that you have a good idea of how long each task will take you.

This kind of information and organization is crucial if you have set a deadline. At any point, you will know how far off the goal you are, and how much work you need to do to achieve it. Again, this is a good point to look at whether you think you can produce all the work, or whether you need to work on a smaller, less complex scene.

All the work files can be downloaded from **Chapter9\CH009_assets\ environment**.

You don't have to create all assets in the same order as I have, feel free to complete the environment in any order you like.

As mentioned earlier, considering the amount of details to go through, I won't be repeating any techniques covered previously, so if you are unsure of anything, flick back through the book and continue once you're happy.

Starting with the pavement, the blockout mesh was used as a base to create a new model. The model is simple. It's a plane with a chamfer to round off what will be the kerb, with an edge to the left to show the start of the kerb.

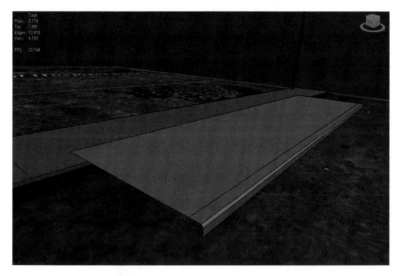

FIG 9.19

At this stage, I was intending to create a 2048 × 512 texture for the pavement. The pavement section was created to match this ration to bake the normal map from a high poly model.

Work continued with creating a simple modular set for the pavements. So, to go with the straight section, the next step was to add a corner section. This was created from a quadrant of a cylinder. It was built to match up to two straight sections including the chamfered edge. The model is shown in Fig. 9.20.

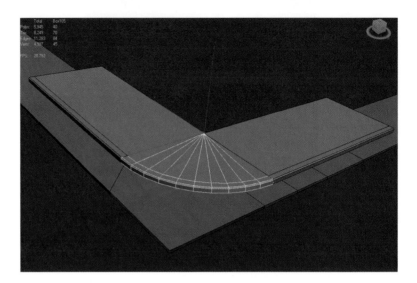

FIG 9.20

After the low poly corner and straight sections were complete, a high-resolution version of each was created to bake normal maps from. The high-resolution models were created with floating geometry and made up of a series of boxes with chamfered edges to give a rounder look to the kerbs and pavement slab edges. Both models can be seen in Fig. 9.21.

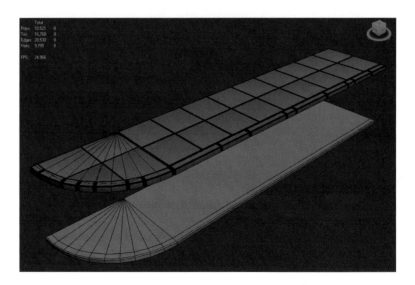

FIG 9.21

We have now come to a question that needs an answer. So far, we have not created any textures for the environment, so the texture resolution per square meter needs to be defined now before we proceed. This is to ensure that we have a consistent texture resolution throughout the scene.

To do this, I have created a texture template that will allow us to judge what size texture to use and to what scale. This template is found in **Chapter9\ CH009_assets\ uv_template_1024.**

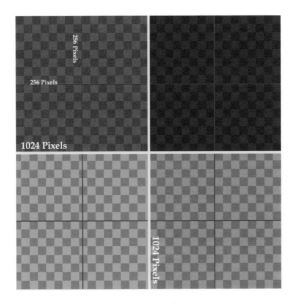

FIG 9.22

The template is made up of four different colored quarters, each consisting of 512 × 512 pixels. The red lines mark out the 256 × 256 sections. The overall texture is a 1024 × 1024 map. I use this template by placing it on a square plane the size of the chosen square meter area per 1024 pixels.

I then move this template around the scene and place it against assets to determine how big the texture needs to be compared with the template based on how much surface the asset takes up.

In this instance, I have chosen to use the 8 m scale bar from the 2D plan as my guide. That means an 8 m^2 area will use a 1024 × 1024 texture. This is now the set resolution for the environment. You can make this whatever you want. 512 × 512 per 4 m^2 or 2048 × 2048 per 10 m^2—it's up to you what you deem to be an acceptable resolution.

With this in mind, I created an 8 m × 8 m^2 plane and mapped the template on to it in the scene. I can see straightaway that the road will be exactly 1024 × 1024. For now, we need to figure out the pavement. I have decided to drop the 2048 × 512 texture format as originally intended.

Now that the template is in the scene, I have decided to go with a 512 × 512 square tiling texture for the pavement. This will mean the texture will tile more, but that's fine. A blend will be used to break it up.

The low and high poly models needed to be readjusted to fit a square format. The new models with the template are shown in Fig. 9.23. You can see that the pavement section is just larger than a 256 section on the template. As the pavement is an important texture as it'll cover a large area of the scenes surface, I feel going with a 512 × 512 will be better. If it creates a noticeable inconsistency with the set texture resolution, it can be scaled to a 256 × 256 later on.

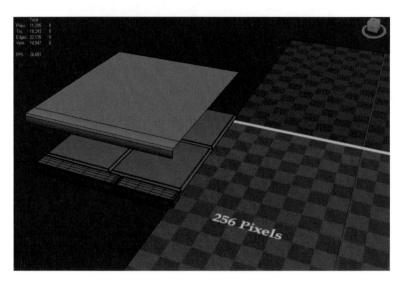

FIG 9.23

The low poly pavement section needs to be unwrapped and placed over the high poly mesh in preparation of baking the normal map. The process used to bake the map was the same as in Chapter 7, on the door model.

Jumping past this process and moving on to the final result, Fig. 9.24 shows six steps in the creation of the main pavement texture. I'll go through these briefly now. Don't forget you can load up any of the texture PSDs in Photoshop to have a more in depth look at how they were put together.

Step 1 This is the tangent space normal map that was baked from the high poly model. It was used as the guide for the diffuse texture.

Step 2 The diffuse map was created by sourcing photo reference of concrete online and using Photoshop's blend modes to achieve the desired result. Matching the grooves and kerb details to what was present in the normal map.

Step 3 This shows the addition of moss added to the gaps in the paving slabs. This was achieved by placing a tiling texture of moss over the diffuse map. A layer mask was applied to the moss layer and filled with black, so it was totally transparent/invisible. Then, using a brush with the color white set to approximately 60% opacity, I painted in the areas where I wanted moss. Don't forget to use the offset tool to tile the mask once you are finished to make sure the texture stays as a tiling one. For the pavement, we only need it to tile in the U-axis.

Step 4 This is a desaturated version of the diffuse texture with the levels adjusted to increase contrast. This is going to be put through the nvidia normal map filter plug-in.

Step 5 This is the texture after it has been converted to a tangent space normal map. This was then set to overlay above the texture in Step 1 and then flattened and normalized to create the final pavement normal map.

Step 6 This shows the final composited normal map.

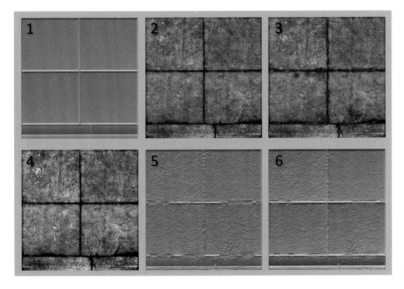

FIG 9.24

Figure 9.25 shows the regular and damaged variants of the straight and corner sections of pavement. These were all created using a similar method.

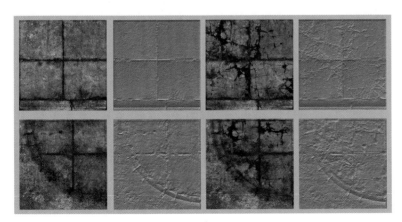

FIG 9.25

Once all the pavement textures were created, I moved back into 3ds Max and mapped the original rectangular straight section and the corner piece. Both these were then duplicated numerous times and placed around the scene following the blockout to create the final pavement.

The pivot point was moved using "affect pivot only" on the hierarchy panel to a corner of each model before duplicating them, making them easier to snap together.

The blockout pavement was then deleted. For now only the undamaged pavement texture was applied to the models as the damaged version will be painted later using vertex colors and a blend shader.

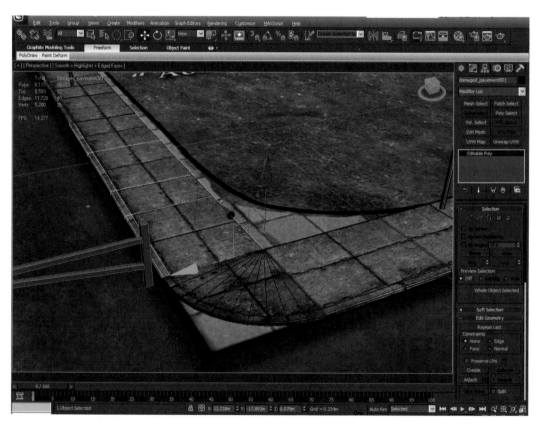

FIG 9.26

Next, I moved on to the road textures. Like the pavements, a plain version and a damaged version will be created for variety. There are 10 work in progress PSDs available in the chapter folder showing the progress of the road textures, but here are the main points.

As the roads are 8 m wide that means one 1024 texture is suitable. It only needs to tile in one direction but it never hurts to tile a texture in both directions just in case.

The texture was started with a simple asphalt base which was tiled in both the U- and V-axes. The Gradient tool was used to create darker sides for the road edges where there is less wear and tear. This layer was set to soft light at 47% opacity.

On a new layer, lighter vertical stripes were painted running along the texture in the center with the airbrush tool to create areas that have been worn down due to constant use. This layer was set to overlay at 32% and was placed over the other layers. The wip file for the texture at this stage can be downloaded from **Chapter9\CH009_assets\textures\texture_wips\ environment_road_01.**

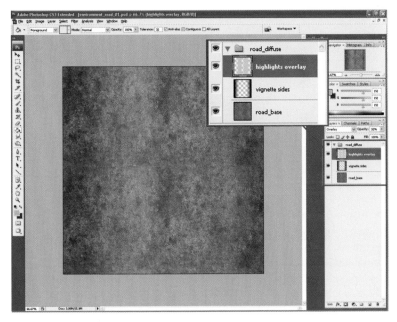

FIG 9.27

The next stage uses file **environment_road_02.psd**. It has a more detailed section of asphalt compared with the base that was used in step 1, which was brought in and tiled using the Offset tool. I choose this as I preferred the chunkier look of the asphalt rather than the smoother base asphalt texture. The final result is seen in Fig. 9.28.

This new layer was placed over the base layer but under the dark sides and highlights. It was set to hard light after being desaturated, so the color and detail of the base texture still comes through while keeping the chunky details.

In **environment_road_03.psd**, I imported the moss layer from the pavement textures. I had to duplicate it four times to fill the 1024 texture.

After checking it still tiled I moved onto **environment_road_04.psd**, where a layer mask was applied to the tiling moss layer. The mask was filled with black ready for painting the moss over the road by using white on the mask.

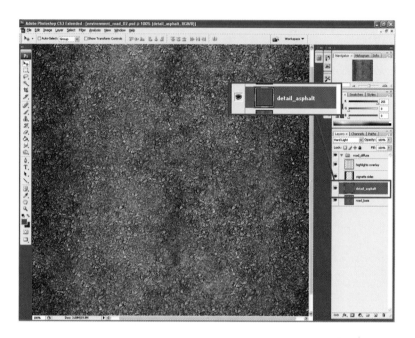

FIG 9.28

The results of the work carried out in the **environment_road_04.psd** can be seen in Fig. 9.29. It shows the effect of painting in the moss with the layer mask. I also started playing around with desaturated and highly contrasted crack textures. These were set to multiply to try and get a nice looking damaged surface. At the moment, this is looking weak so it needs more work.

Environment_road_05.psd to **environment_road_08.psd** were spent trying out different crack textures. I finally found one, I really liked and tiled it. I then set it to multiply over the base road textures. This texture is shown in Fig. 9.30.

At this point, I have created two groups in my layers to keep the file tidy. These were the base road group called road_diffuse, and the layers for creating the damaged version over the base called road_damage_ageing.

Environment_road_09.psd and **environment_road_10.psd** were spent finalizing the base and damaged diffuse textures. I then duplicated the groups and desaturated them in preparation for running them through the nvidia normal map filter to create the normal maps.

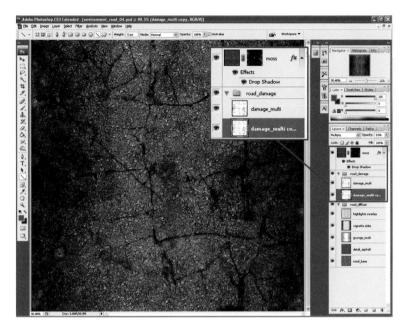

FIG 9.29

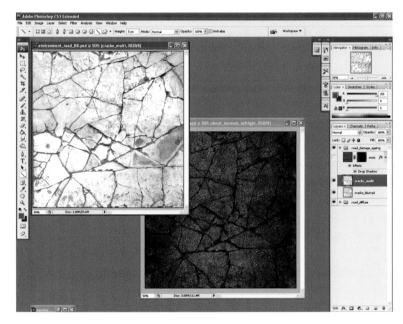

FIG 9.30

When desaturating all the layers before converting them to normal maps, remember to remove any lighting such as the dark sides and highlights. All you want in the normal map are the surface details.

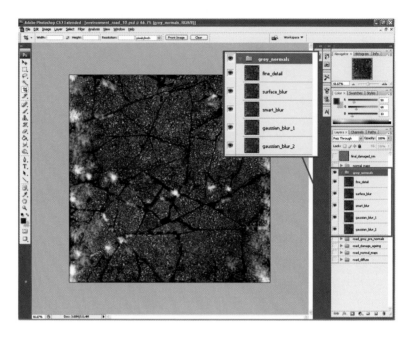

FIG 9.31

Figure 9.31 shows the desaturated layers of the damaged variant. The mask layer of the moss was copied to a layer of flat white. This means the moss will be raised off the surface by the normal map. The cracks have been darkened and pushed back to create recesses.

When I was happy with the values making the detailing raised or pushed back in the normal map, I made several duplicates and ran each one through different filters to get more interesting shapes and details for the normal map. This group of layers was then duplicated and renamed to normal_maps, so the originals can be kept for editing.

The filters are pictured in Fig. 9.31. Smart blur and surface blur are particularly good for simplifying a busy noisy texture like this.

Each of these layers was then converted to normal maps. Each layer was set to overlay except the bottom one which was set to normal. I then adjusted the opacity of each layer to reduce the "noise" of the normal map.

When the result was satisfactory, the group was duplicated and merged to one layer. This layer was then tiled using the smudge and Clone Stamp tool. I tried to edit a normal map as little as possible.

When the normal map tiled correctly, it was normalized using the nvidia plug-ins normalize only option. It is necessary to normalize a normal map after every time you modify it to ensure the values stay within the 0–1 range.

This process was carried out to create a normal map for the base and damaged version. After the diffuse and normal maps were created, copies of the diffuse textures were reduced to 256 × 256 and then desaturated. The levels tool was used to increase the contrast of the new texture. This was then used as a specular map placed in the specular level slot of a blinn shader.

All the textures created for the road are pictured in Fig. 9.32.

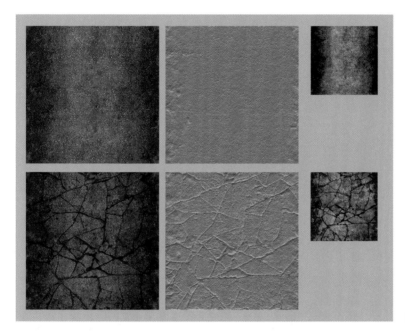

FIG 9.32

These textures will be used in a blend shader where the damaged version can be painted on the surface using vertex colors. This is a common technique used in games today to add variety to surfaces and break up tiling of textures across large areas.

Most game engines have shaders that can blend between multiple textures. The technique we are using at the moment can only blend between two shaders. It is limited but it's a good introduction to the concept. In 3ds Max, using the default shaders, we can only see the results when the scene is rendered. It is possible to find many CGFX shaders online that can be used that display the results in the viewport depending on your graphics card.

This blend shader technique was used for the pavement, brick, and grass/dirt textures. Let's go through setting up the shader for the road textures now. The same technique can then be used on the others.

Open up the material browser. Click on the Standard button to bring up the material/map browser. Change the shader type to "blend."

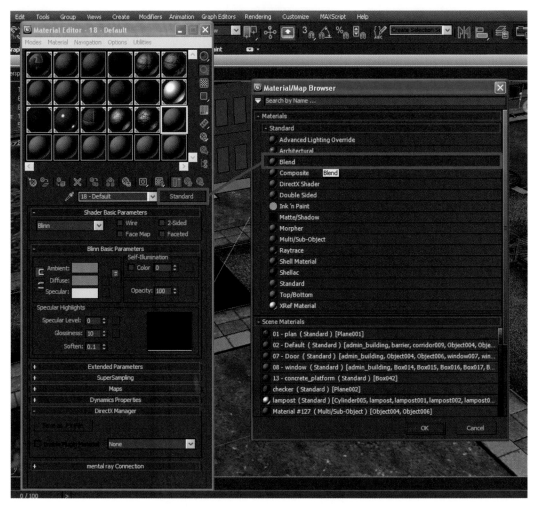

FIG 9.33

The default shader slots and options will now change to display the default blend shader options. This is shown on the left of Fig. 9.34. The three slots are material 1, material 2, and mask. The mix amount and curve settings can be adjusted to affect how the blend works based on the masking technique you use.

If you click on one of the material slots, you will be brought into a standard shader layout. This blend shader consists of two standard shaders and a mask for blending them.

Material 1 is where the primary texture will go. As you can see from the final road shader on the right of Fig. 9.34, I put the base road texture in this slot. As material 1 is a standard blinn shader, the diffuse, specular, and bump slots were used as normal with the three relevant textures.

Material 2 will be the material we paint on the surface over material 1.

I placed the damaged road textures in this material.

The mask can work a few different ways. Click on the slot to bring up the options. For the shaders in this scene, I have chosen vertex color near the bottom of the list as the mask. This gives the ability to use vertex colors painted onto the mesh to determine where material 1 and material 2 appear.

Another method you could use is to use a bitmap and place a black and white or grayscale image in the slot. This will then make the shader render both materials over each other. The greyscale image will then determine which layer is rendered on a per pixel basis. Darker pixels will be material 1 and lighter pixels will be material 2. The effects of this method are nice, but it will only place the textures over each other and not allow us to freely paint the location of the different materials.

It's possible to toggle which material is displayed in the viewport by selecting the interactive option to the right of each slot. The material in the slot highlighted will appear in the viewport.

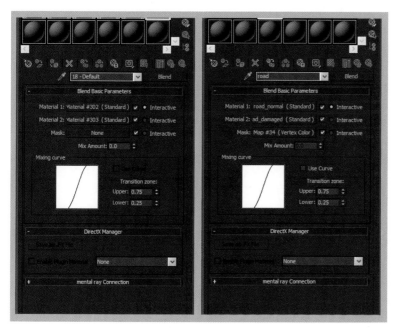

FIG 9.34

A mesh is now needed to try out the new blend shader, so create a plane between the pavement meshes to become the road.

Assign the road blend material to the new mesh. The road mesh will still need to be unwrapped before the vertex colors can be painted.

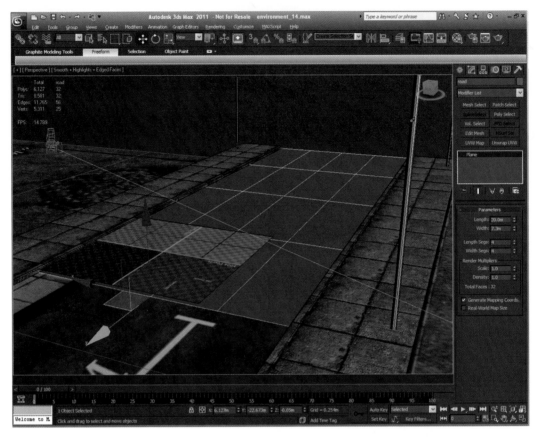

FIG 9.35

Once the road mesh is unwrapped, select the mesh and go to the utilities tab on the far right of the command panel. Click on "more" to bring up the utilities window and choose "assign vertex colors." These steps are pictured in Fig. 9.36.

A selection of options will appear in the utilities panel relating to vertex colors. We just need to click on "assign to selected," as all the default options will work fine.

Don't be afraid to read up and explore the other options as they can all be very useful. These options are displayed in Fig. 9.37.

We should now have a new item called VertexPaint on the meshes modifier stack. The mesh may also change color as a vertex color has been assigned to the meshes vertices.

The VertexPaint window will now also appear every time you select a mesh with an active VertexPaint modifier. Figure 9.38 highlights the options we'll need to use to paint material 2 onto the road surface.

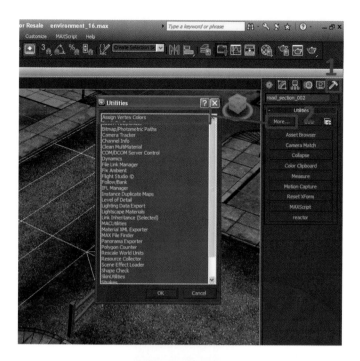

FIG 9.36

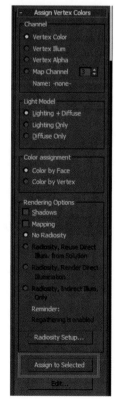

FIG 9.37

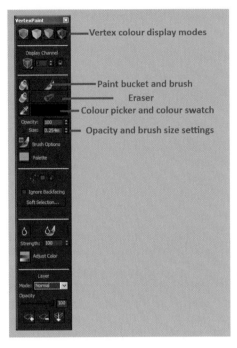

Vertex colour display modes

Paint bucket and brush

Eraser

Colour picker and colour swatch

Opacity and brush size settings

FIG 9.38

Start by using the Fill/Paint Bucket tool to flood the mesh with a 100% black. This will turn the mesh a solid black color.

Next, change the color to white and use the paint brush to paint white on some of the vertices in the viewport. Areas where you paint white will reveal the base texture in the viewport as seen in Fig. 9.39.

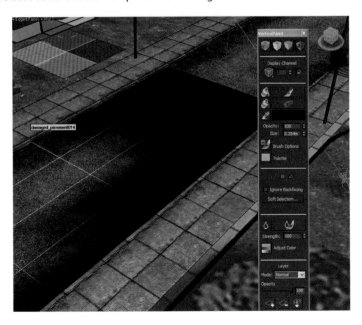

FIG 9.39

When this model is rendered, we can see the results of the blend shader. A test render is seen in Fig. 9.40.

As the mesh of the road is fairly low poly, the vertex colors painted will be large strokes that fade out across the mesh. If you want to paint more specific patches, you need to cut into the mesh or use tessellate to add extra edges/vertices. The more vertices you have to paint on, the more defined the results will be.

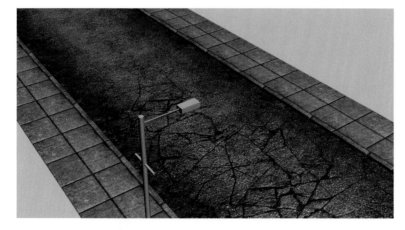

FIG 9.40

An example of a slightly more refined vertex painting can be seen in Fig. 9.41. It is a wall model that we'll build later on in this chapter. It has extra geometry cut in, to vary the amount of surface each stroke covers. You could also cut more irregular edges into the mesh to get different shapes. I'll be leaving this until the last polish stage on all the meshes.

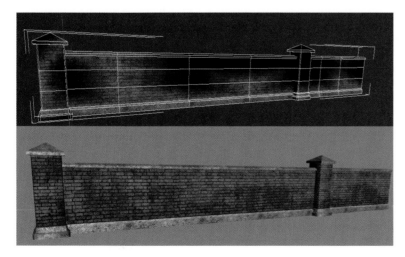

FIG 9.41

Next, more planes were created to be the grass areas of the scene. A blend shader was created and applied. Following the same procedure as before, I painted between both materials on the mesh. You can also repaint the meshes later easily if you change where you wish to have material 1 or material 2. The grass and dirt textures were created as tiling textures; they are seen in Fig. 9.42 along with the grass mesh and a small section rendered showing the blend.

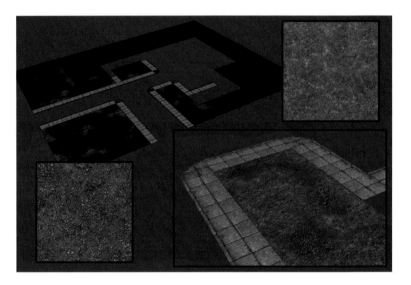

FIG 9.42

The perimeter walls and building facades are next on the list. I think it'll be wise to use the same red brick textures for the wall as the brickwork on all the buildings. The brick texture will be created as a 1024 × 1024 with a normal map. After searching online, I found a red brick texture that suited what I had in mind very well.

The creation of the texture was straightforward; it just required a lot of work as there were a few issues with the source image that made it unsuitable as a tiling texture.

Figure 9.43 has a 1024 × 1024 cropped section of the original source image on the left and an offset version of the same image on the right. It's hard to see in this image that in the offset version the bricks do not line up correctly along the edges leaving obvious seams in the texture. There's also a lot of contrasting value changes in the colors which will stand out when the image is repeated.

You'll be able to browse through the 11 wip texture files covering the production of this texture in the chapter download from here: **Chapter9\ CH009_assets\textures\texture_wips\ red_bricks_01-11**.

The tiling issue was the first problem tackled by copying and pasting sections of the texture over the areas with the seams so that the bricks would at least be in a straight line and match up better. The Clone Stamp tool was then used to clean up the pasted elements, so they blended seamlessly back into the original image.

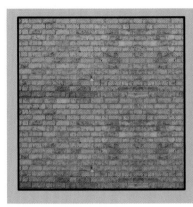

FIG 9.43

Again using the Clone Stamp tool, any bricks which stood out too much were stamped over to reduce any large jumps in value. The idea is to create a texture that is almost monotone as any contrasting details will stand out and show in the tiling.

The role of a generic tiling texture is to have no specific noticeable details that people will easily spot repeating over a surface. That is why I created another variant of this texture with a lot more visual interest to blend with this one to break up the bland surface.

After the base brick texture was sorted, another generic texture shown on the left of Fig. 9.44 was placed over the brick layer and set to overlay to add a little variety to the bricks coloring, but obviously not too much. It's a tough balance trying to get something that looks reasonably interesting without standing out. The combined version of both layers is on the right of Fig. 9.44.

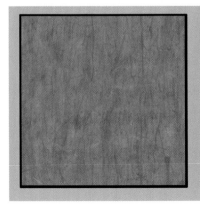

FIG 9.44

Now that the diffuse texture is out of the way a normal map will be needed. As always, the starting point will be a desaturated copy of the diffuse texture. This is on the left of Fig. 9.45. The levels were adjusted to lighten the image up to be almost white. The problem with this is, for bricks, they need to stick out from the cement between them, which will need to recede.

At the moment, the image will not work. The only solution is to darken the cement between the bricks so that it recedes in the normal map. The method I used was to create a new layer and paint the cement areas of the texture manually with the standard brush set to 100%. The finished version is on the right of Fig. 9.45.

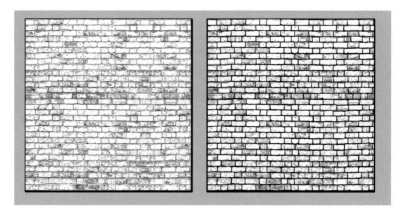

FIG 9.45

Just like the road texture, a few duplicates of this layer were made and passed through some of the Photoshop filters to get some variety to the details. These layers were than converted to normal maps and set to overlay over each other. The first pass I created of this normal map turned out too noisy and lumpy on the surface of each brick as there were still a lot of gray values in the texture.

As I only wanted the dark cement to recede, I had another go and used the levels tool to push the contrast further leaving the brick surfaces mainly pure white. This new texture was then converted to a normal map creating an improved result. Figure 9.46 has the improved grayscale map on the left and the normal map generated from it on the right.

As a final bit of polish on the texture, I have used a technique mentioned in Chapter 3. The first lumpy normal map was desaturated and placed over the diffuse texture and set to multiply to add some ambient lighting information to the diffuse texture. The levels were adjusted to control the level of contrast.

This is a very subtle touch, but one that makes a difference. The example on the left of Fig. 9.47 is the original diffuse texture, and the sample on the right is the same sample but with the desaturated normal map set to multiply over it.

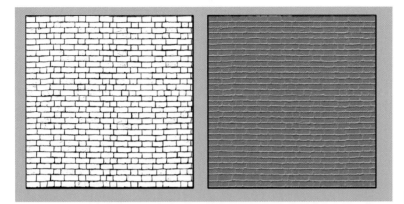

FIG 9.46

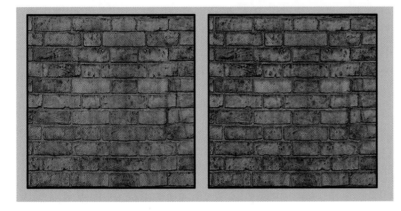

FIG 9.47

Figure 9.48 displays a move back into 3ds Max. Now that the default red brick textures have been created, the model for the perimeter wall can start. All I need to make is one pillar and one wall section. These models can then be copied and placed around the scene to create all the walls. Unique details can be added, where required later such as ivy growing on the wall or damaged sections.

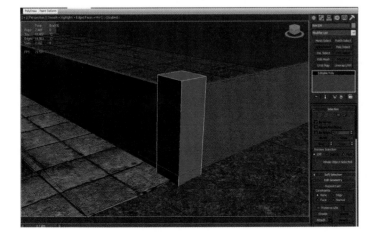

FIG 9.48

The pillar was built from a simple box with chamfered edges. The cap stone was created as floating geometry, and a new simple tiling concrete texture was applied. All unseen interior faces were deleted. The red brick texture was applied to the template plane so that all the assets in the scene will have consistent brick size by using the template as a guide.

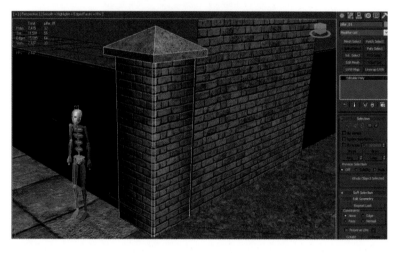

FIG 9.49

A base was created on the pillar by using the Slice Plane tool to add in some edge loops that were scaled outwards to create a stepped base. The concrete texture from the cap stone was also applied to the base.

After the pillar was completed, a box was created in between two pillars as seen in Fig. 9.50. A trim along the bottom of the wall and a cap stone on top were also added. The pillar and wall sections were then duplicated and placed around the scene. When this was done, all the blockout walls were deleted.

The wooden door from Chapter 7 was also imported at this stage and put into replace the blockout doors.

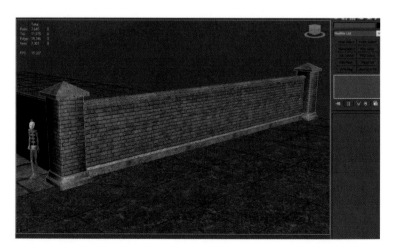

FIG 9.50

With the walls and doors in, I started the outer walls of the buildings. The process began with duplicating the chimney model from the blockout, Fig. 9.51.

This chimney stack then had the edges chamfered, and the red brick texture applied after it was unwrapped. I only used planar mapping to unwrap all the sides one at a time. Any unseen faces on the model were deleted to reduce any overdraw keeping the model efficient.

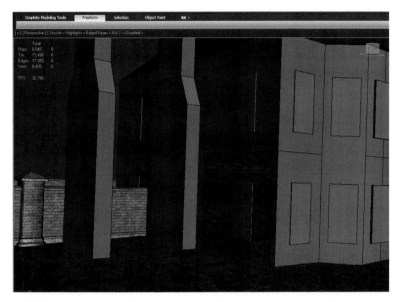

FIG 9.51

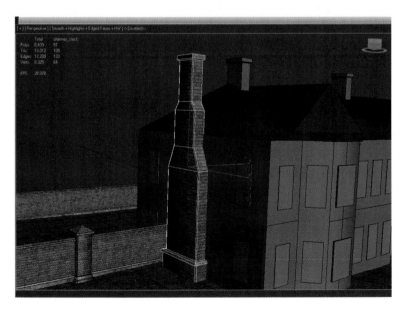

FIG 9.52

Figure 9.53 shows the first step in creating the facade of the main building. It started with a plane built over the left side of the blockout. Using the Extrude tool, the right edge of the plane was extruded around the front of the building following the contours of the blockout and continued around to the back edge on the right side.

After this was done, the Slice Plane tool was used to create four edge loops around the model. Each of these edge loops was snapped to the top and bottom of the two rows of windows on both floors of the building in the Z-axis. The shortcut for the snap tool is "S." With this switched on and a sub object selected, you can snap it to any other vertex in the scene.

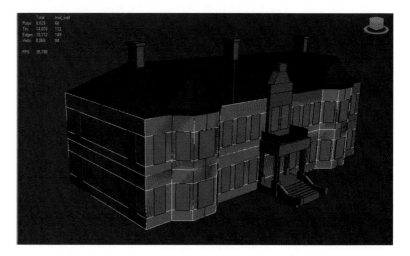

FIG 9.53

Continuing with the Slice Plane tool, vertical cuts were made to define the sides of each window in the blockout. Some extra horizontal cuts were added to the base of the building. These will be scaled out to form a plinth much like the base of the wall or pillars. You should end up with a mesh similar to Fig. 9.54.

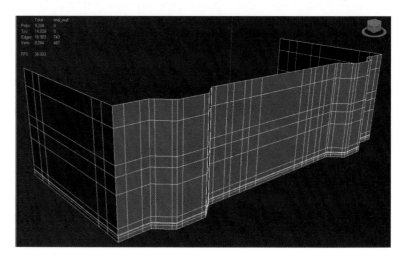

FIG 9.54

The faces where the windows will go have been deleted in Fig. 9.55. These new border edges were extruded inwards to create the recess the window models will be placed into. Before moving any further, the final windows have to be created, so the building model can be adjusted to accommodate them.

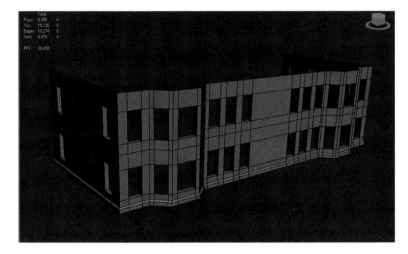

FIG 9.55

I decided to only make two types of windows at this stage as I was conscious of the time the scene was taking, but at least two varieties of each. Using the blockout windows as a guide, a simple high poly model was created for the frames of the window. This was to generate a normal map to base the rest of the texture off. This initial texture is shown in Fig. 9.56.

The texture is laid out in a way that there will be two typical windows on the right and four-paneled windows on the left. My goal is to be able to mix and match these panels in different combinations to get as much variety as possible. These paneled windows will be used the most in the scene.

The empty area on the right side and below the two normal windows will be used for space to map the window frames.

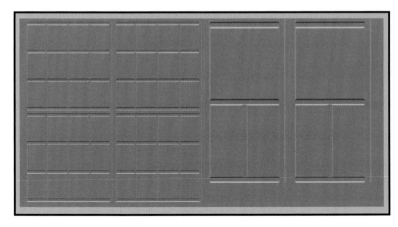

FIG 9.56

In Photoshop, the diffuse texture was created with a mixture of painting and the manipulation of photographic elements to match the layout set out by the normal map. The PSD is available in the chapter folder with the others.

The diffuse texture was desaturated as before and used to generate finer details to be set to overlay over the base normal map.

The real trick of these windows will be the use of the specular map seen in Fig. 9.58. This was created by saving off a different version of the .psd.

A hue/saturation adjustment layer was then placed on top of the layer stack. All the layers then had their brightness and contrast adjusted one by one until I got the desired look I was after.

The aim was to have the glass left in the window to be almost pure white whereas the holes in the broken panes were almost pure black. All the other elements such as dirt and rust were also adjusted to remain dark values. The cleaner areas of metal and painted wood were left somewhere near the lighter end of the scale. When all these textures are combined in max, the result should be decent.

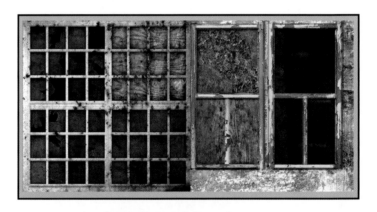

FIG 9.57

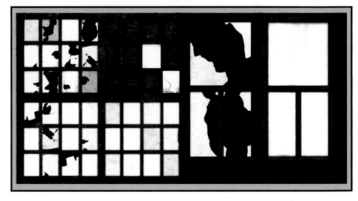

FIG 9.58

The final window models seen in Fig. 9.59 are quite simple, as most of the work is done by the textures and shader. In the end, I managed to get nine varieties of window out of the 1024 × 512 textures. I did this having two faces on each paneled window model, so I could map various combinations of the paneled windows on each one.

The window sills were textured using another generic tiling concrete texture. The UVs for each sill were placed on different areas of the texture so that there would be some variation with them also.

Now that the windows are ready they need to be placed into the recesses of the main building.

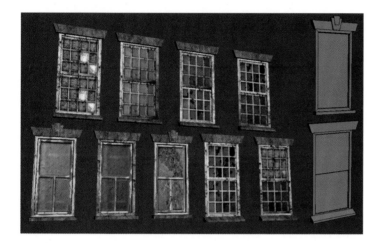

FIG 9.59

The building model had to be adjusted when the windows and sills were placed in as they did not match up exactly. In some cases, the sills had to be moved forward. The building model was also optimized by merging some vertices along the bottom of the plinth and also along the top of the model. As the sills covered the top and bottom of the recesses, all these faces were deleted.

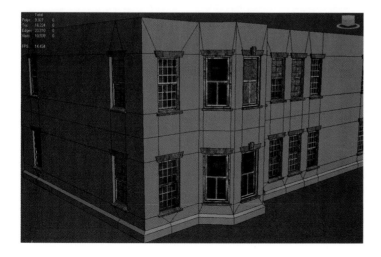

FIG 9.60

Now that the building model is complete, the brick and concrete textures have been applied, and the model unwrapped. The UVs were laid out in one continuous strip which was then stitched together to make it seamless.

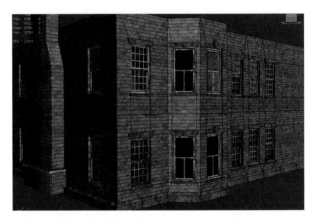

FIG 9.61

It's worth going through the environment WIP files found in the Chapter 9 folder to inspect exactly how the UVs were laid out for all the assets.

The chimney stacks and central section above the entrance were also modeled and unwrapped. These pieces were created from a duplicate of the blockout mesh that was worked into.

While unwrapping, I found the relax tool in the edit UVWs window helpful in keeping the UV shells at the correct ratio. Go to the Menu > Tools > Relax. From the drop down list, choose "relax by face angles" and hit Apply or Start Relax. This should gradually flatten out the selected UV shell and help reduce any stretching on the model.

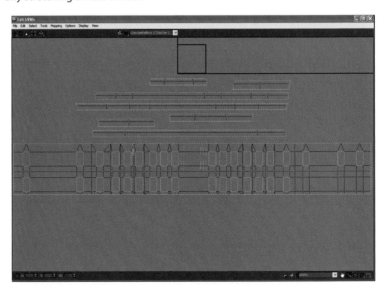

FIG 9.62

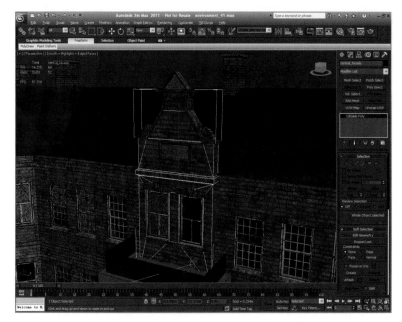

FIG 9.63

As you may have noticed, the number of buildings in the scene and how they are made up has been changed. This was as a result of adjusting the content to fit the time allocated. Quite often, this situation happens within the games industry and I wanted to make a point of it here so that you don't get into the habit of not finishing work through lack of preparation or reluctance to change a plan.

I made a choice to spend the remaining time finishing the scene and only making the corridor and ward buildings, rather than spending extra time on the staff housing building. This extra time can then be used to improve what sections have been created already. It's always better to reduce the scope of a scene if you are on a tight deadline, finish on time, and then polish, than to try to over-deliver and produce a rushed piece of work.

The ward building was built in exactly the same way as the administration building. A plane was extruded around the blockout shape. The Slice Plane tool was then used to add in edge loops where the windows will be. The faces representing the windows were deleted, and the vertical side edges were extruded inwards.

The windows were placed in the recesses, and the building walls were unwrapped. Figure 9.64 shows the production of the ward building. The door was already present from earlier, as was the concrete ramp in front of the building which can be wheelchair access.

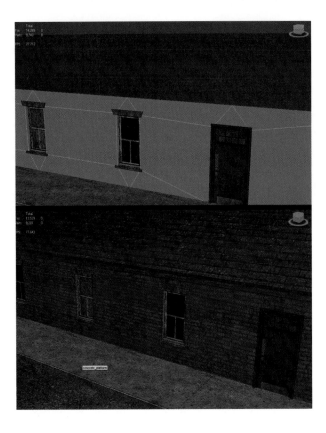

FIG 9.64

A simple roof slate texture 512 × 512 pixels was added to the scene and applied to all the roofs. The blockout model was used as a starting point for the roof models.

The corridor involved a little more work than the ward as the paneled windows are in one long row. These needed to be arranged and attached together. There was also a damaged roof which exposed the wooden frame beneath.

This was an element I really wanted to keep from the blockout. The final version was made by creating a cross-section of the frame and unwrapping it and then duplicating it across the corridor.

I intentionally left a gap in the middle as if the roof has caved in to break up the solid look in the blockout.

Some individual boxes with the slate texture applied were placed on the edges of the solid roof of the corridor and along the beams. This was to break up the rigid look of finishing the roof with a hard edge.

Some of these loose slates were also put on the pavement in front of the corridor to add some visual interest to this section of the environment.

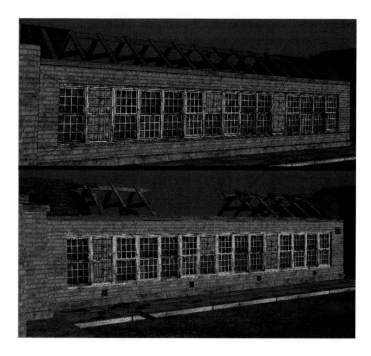

FIG 9.65

Figure 9.66 shows the tiling slate texture on the right which also has a normal map to accompany it. The texture on the left only tiles in the *U*-axis and was split into two halves. The bottom half was used for the exposed roof frame, and the top half was also used for beams. This time it was faded and aged painted red beams. This was applied to the exterior wooden beams running along the tops of all the buildings just below the roof.

These exterior beams were created by placing a box near the top of the building facade using Auto Grid to create it directly on the surface. The top, sides, and back faces were deleted leaving only the front and bottom faces. The ends of the beam were then moved to fit the building. For nonflat surfaces like the bay windows of the administration building, the ends were extruded around the top of the building following the wall surface.

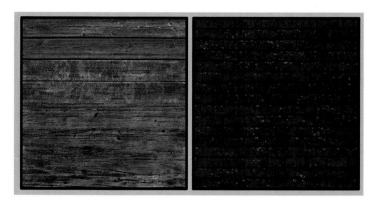

FIG 9.66

The last main modeling task is the entrance area for the admin building. I found a few reference images online which inspired this design. They were a lot more ornate, so I took the overall feel of stairs leading up to an entrance platform with a stone covering supported by columns but kept the design functional as it's not supposed to be a decorative building.

Figure 9.67 shows the production model being produced on the left and the final textured version on the right. The Slice Plane and Extrude tools were used to create these sections from boxes. The columns were straightforward cylinders with the no end faces.

One of the tiling concrete textures, along with a new cracked concrete texture, was used to texture the entrance area. The cracked concrete texture was also used on the steps and entrance platform to the ward building.

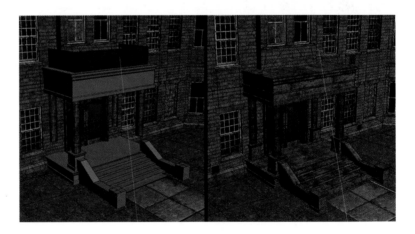

FIG 9.67

After the ground surfaces and main buildings were created, I then started looking at creating some smaller details to break up the tiling on areas of the buildings and also to add more variety to the scene.

These details included metal railings, guttering, air vents, lamposts, and a broken sign in front of the admin building.

A modular approach was taken for creating the guttering and metal railings. These both used the same texture which also had the vent textures on it.

A modular approach involves creating all the separate sections or modules of an asset once. These elements are then assembled together to make the final object. This is an efficient approach for creating repeatable objects such as the railings as it is a lot quicker than making and unwrapping every single bar.

The only downside to a modular approach is you may end up with some repetition. This can be reduced by later adding some more unique elements on top like dents in the railings.

Figure 9.68 shows the modules used to create the guttering and railings.

Figure 9.69 has a section of the final metal railing and an example of the finished guttering on the ward building. Both were created with the modular kit.

When you are happy with the results, all these modules can be combined to be one single model.

The vents were boxes with the backfaces deleted. The vent texture was mapped onto the boxes. The vents were then placed on the ground below the guttering as a drain or under windows for ventilation.

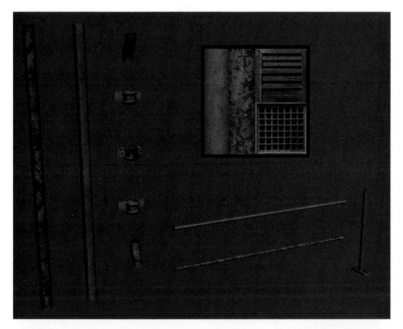

FIG 9.68

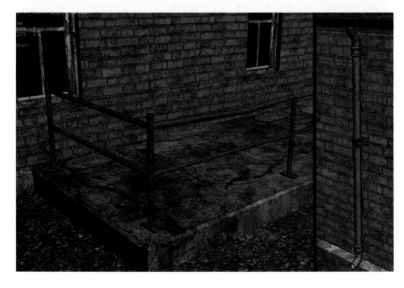

FIG 9.69

Figure 9.70 shows the current state of the scene. The core elements are all in place, and the blend shaders have been set up.

The next phase will be to import all the vegetation models created in Chapter 4 and to populate the scene with them. I just imported them directly and moved, rotated, and scaled them to get some variety.

While placing all the vegetation in the scene, I realized I still do not have any ivy models or textures. To solve this, I just popped outside and picked a few leaves of ivy and scanned them.

After these leaves were extracted from the white background, I built up the ivy texture by duplicating, rotating, and scaling the leaves.

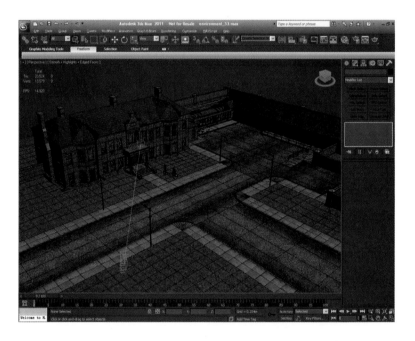

FIG 9.70

For the texture layout itself, a bunch of ivy was created for use on a plane, and then a vertical thin strip of ivy was created to use on a long plane which can be modeled into tendrils of ivy growing across the building or over a wall.

Figure 9.71 shows the original source image of the ivy leaves. The final diffuse texture and the texture were applied to two different meshes.

It would have also been an improvement to have a separate vine texture to place beneath these ivy leaves over the surface of the building.

For now, the bricks' secondary material which is a version of the bricks overgrown by moss will be painted underneath where the ivy will be placed. This should help it sit better over the red bricks.

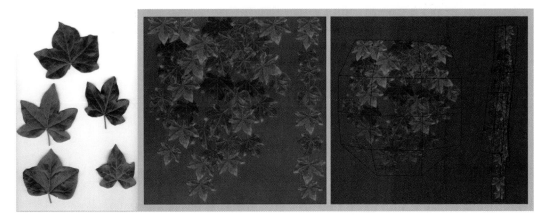

FIG 9.71

For the placement of the vegetation around the scene, this is down to your personal preference, and how detailed and overgrown you want to make this.

I stuck loosely to the concept and placed more vegetation where I felt they would look good.

I really recommend the use of reference when completing tasks like this. Have a good look online or go outside and have a look at how grass and other plants grow in built up areas. Good placement of these elements can really benefit the overall look of an environment. Never build what you "think" something looks like in a photo-real scene; always build what it actually looks like, with some artistic license of course.

The tree walls were placed at the back of the image to provide a backdrop for the scene. Figure 9.72 shows the **wip file environment_54**. At this stage, the environment is almost complete.

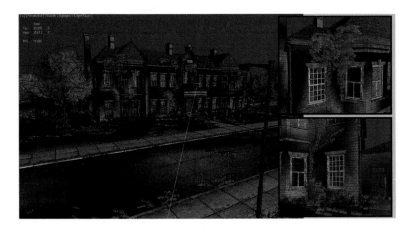

FIG 9.72

A few final touches are added to match the concept. A hemisphere with a sky texture applied is created around the scene to represent the sky, and some wooden posts and a wire mesh fence are created as they appeared in the foreground of the concept.

Six cameras were also set up to get some renders of the final scene. Some extra work was carried out to populate these areas more, making them appear fuller.

At this point, as cameras are set up, and lights are added to the scene, a lot of minor tweaks and changes are made to improve the final renders.

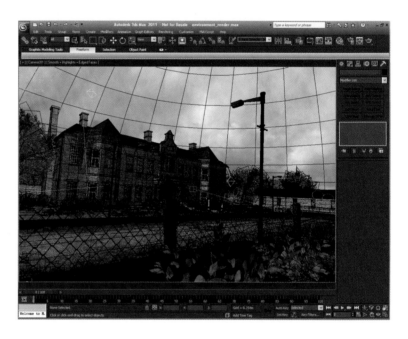

FIG 9.73

Lighting and Rendering the Final Scene

This part of the process was kept fairly simple. I used the default scanline renderer for the base image. An ambient occlusion pass was then rendered separately and set to multiply over the default render using Photoshop.

For the lighting itself, I used a number of omni lights to light the scene. One key light was placed in the sky over the left side of the building to match the direction of the light in the concept. This light being the main source was the only one set to cast shadows and had the highest intensity value.

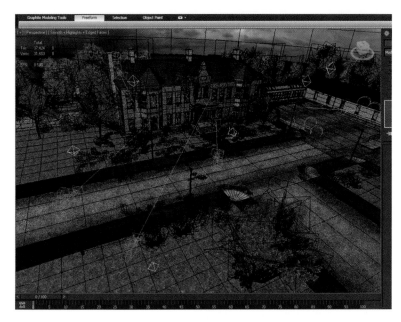

FIG 9.74

All the other lights intensity values were kept below .25. These lights were used to simulate bounce light and global illumination around the scene. Figure 9.74 shows the lights placement around the scene. This file can be downloaded from here: **Chapter9\CH009_assets\environment\ environment_render.**

Simply put, the ambient occlusion pass is a method of shading that calculates the reduction or absence of light when it is blocked by objects. For the ambient occlusion pass, I followed this method.

You'll first need to make mental ray the current renderer by opening the render setup options. Go to the common section and expand the assign renderer section. Click on the button to the right of production to open a pop-up window, where you need to select mental ray. This will now make mental ray the current renderer. Figure 9.75 shows these steps.

Open the material browser and select a blank material. Click on the "standard" button to open up the material browser and scroll down to find the mental ray shader.

Under the basic shaders option, open the surface option by clicking on "none." Now, add an ambient/reflective occlusion node from the mental ray section.

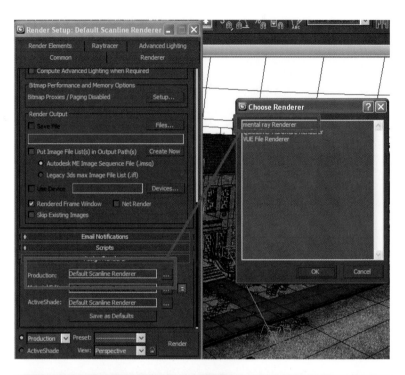

FIG 9.75

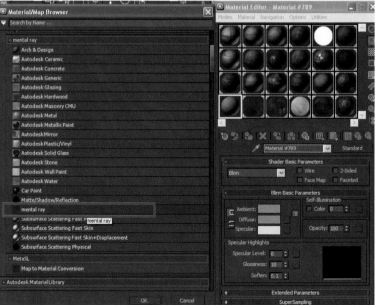

FIG 9.76

The shader options will now change to the ambient/reflective occlusion parameters. Input a value for the max distance—I have put in 50.0, but this can be adjusted later. The other settings such as samples can be increased to get smoother results from the AO pass. This will also increase render times.

The settings are pictured in Fig. 9.77. A good tip is to render the AO pass a little smaller than your main render and then use Photoshop to upscale the image before compositing it.

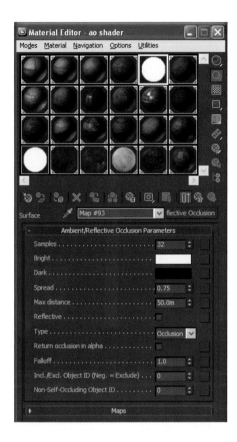

FIG 9.77

The shader values can always be adjusted later on. For now, open the render settings options. Under processing, enable the material override option. Then, drag and drop the newly created mental ray shader in the material slot. This will now override all the materials in the scene and use the AO shader when the material override option is enabled.

Before you render, turn off final gather, global illumination, and your exposure. If you don't do this, you will get a black rendering.

You can now hit render and see the results. The only problem with this method for this scene is that the alpha textures don't get taken into account when the AO pass is rendered resulting in the geometry being rendered instead.

When this AO render was composited over the default render, the results were less than desirable. The result can be seen in Fig. 9.79. You can clearly see all the geometry outlines of the vegetation.

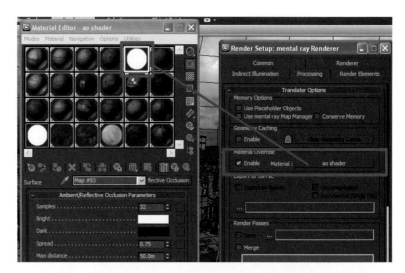

FIG 9.78

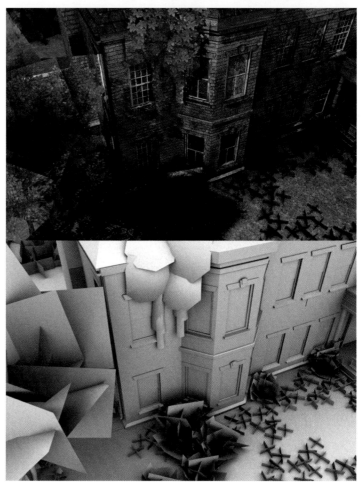

FIG 9.79

A suitable work around for this that I found useful was to use the layer manager to create a vegetation layer. I then selected and added all the vegetation to this layer. When it was time to render the AO passes for all the renders, I just used the layer to hide all the vegetation.

The results were a lot more successful as the AO pass did not include any vegetation. It did mean losing out on some occlusion from the vegetation, but I felt this was acceptable. I did have to paint out some areas of the AO pass that sat over the vegetation in Photoshop as the lines and contours of the building were being shown over the vegetation.

The final image in this chapter is the composited render of the environment from the same camera angle as the concept.

By the end of this chapter, the environment had taken more than 40 hours to get from the initial reference hunt to the final renders. The end result is heading in the right direction and is a solid base to build upon.

Feel free to continue to work into this scene by adding more assets to populate it such as abandoned vehicles or signs around the building giving more hints as to its purpose. Rubble and debris can litter the area around the buildings. Maybe some subtle sci-fi elements can be incorporated into the scene creating some mystery as to the hospital's true purpose.

The options are endless. So, see how far you can push the concept.

I will set up a thread on the forum at http://www.3D-For-Games.com/forum to show you what I did to complete the scene—I'd love to see your submissions too. We'll also be on hand to help you with this or any other part of this book or the others in the series.

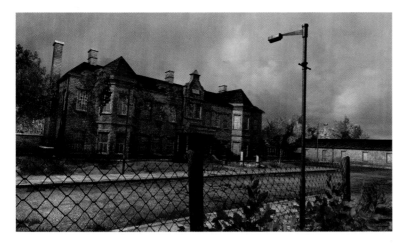

FIG 9.80 The Completed Scene.

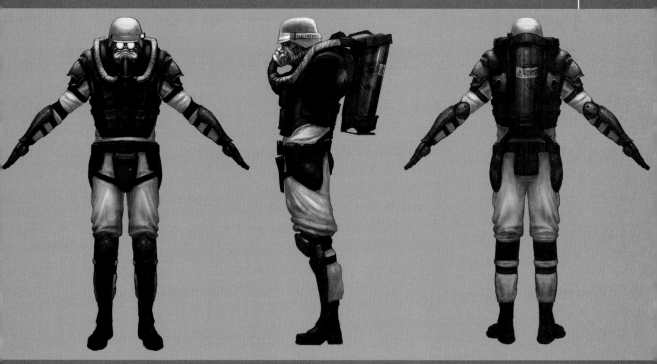

CHAPTER 10

High- and Low-Poly Characters

Introduction

Being a 3D character artist is an incredibly rewarding job—it's great fun to turn your raw ideas into living, breathing beings, and there is always a challenge around the corner. To create photorealistic and believable characters, you must balance your 3D technical expertise with a sound knowledge of human and animal anatomy. Without a doubt, your most important asset is your "eye"; you must objectively scrutinize your creations at each stage of their development.

It is beyond the scope of this chapter to guide you through each and every one of the thousands of operations required to build this character. Instead, I would like to guide you through my working process, my way of thinking, and the tools I use. You need a competent working knowledge of 3ds Max, and you need to solve your own problems from time to time. This tutorial starts off fairly basic and gets into some more advanced concepts as we move along. If you get stuck on a problem with any particular tool, your best friends are the help menu (press F1) and Internet search engines. This is how I advanced my knowledge of 3ds Max once I had absorbed everything that the entry-level tutorials had to offer. As long as you make regular incremental saves (i.e., man01.max, man02.max, and so on), it's pretty hard to break anything—so press all the buttons to see what they do!

Our "Pipeline"

The way we work, the tools we use, and the order in which we do things are known as our "pipeline." I have refined my pipeline over many years to get things running as smoothly as possible.

Before we start the 3D work, let's first plan out exactly what we will do. Once we know precisely what we will be creating, we will make a rough, low-polygon "proxy mesh" that will capture all the basic proportions and main shapes of the character. From this mesh, we will develop a high-polygon mesh that has all the little details that bring the character to life. We will apply UV co-ordinates to the high-resolution mesh and create realistic surfaces by applying a number of different textures to the surfaces of the character. We can use this high-polygon mesh for portfolios, advertising materials, in game cut scenes, and any other prerendered media.

Next, we will return to our low-polygon proxy mesh and optimize its level of detail so that it is suitable for real-time videogames. After we bake down all the details from our original high-polygon mesh onto this new low-polygon game mesh, you might be surprised how similar it looks to the high-polygon mesh. This mesh will be suitable for inclusion in any modern Sony Playstation 3, PC, or Microsoft Xbox 360 game, ready to be rigged and imported into the game engine.

Before You Start: The Concept

Perhaps the most common beginner's mistake is to rush headlong into modeling without sufficient planning. Modern video game characters can take more than five weeks of solid work to finish, so you don't want to get to the end only to find out that the basic design is flawed. The best approach is to have everything drawn out in color *before* you start. Most studios will have at least one concept artist for this job, often recruiting specialist character artists to do the job. If you draw out your idea and it doesn't work out, only hours or days are wasted—not weeks or months!

Often a good character starts with a simple thought, like "I'm going to make a tough-looking, futuristic commando," but it is the concept process that will prove whether your idea works visually. As you draw out a detailed character concept, you are visually solving problems that might not have been apparent when it was just a rough idea in your head.

It is usually much quicker to experiment with designs on paper than it is to make a series of changes to your 3D model. Early in the concept phase, many fast and loose pieces are produced to try out as many different ideas as possible in a short period of time. Once the concept artist is happy with a final look for the character, he or she drafts up detailed blueprints to be scanned and colored on a computer. Using paint packages such as Photoshop makes it fast and easy to experiment with alternative colors, hairstyles, costumes, accessories, and so on. After the art director approves these concept designs, they are sent to the character artist for production.

Many character artists use a two-monitor setup; typically, one monitor is used for working in 3D applications and the other is used to display reference and concept images. This two-monitor setup works well; however, I recommend that you print out your most-used images and hang them on the wall near your desk. For the weeks that you will work on this character, you will save lots of time browsing folders looking for your reference and you will free up your precious RAM and processor resources for those greedy multimillion polygon meshes!

An Extensive Knowledge of Anatomy

If you're serious about specializing as a concept artist or 3D character artist, you need an extensive knowledge of human anatomy. Even the most weird and wonderful alien characters will most likely have some similarities to us and your knowledge of human anatomy can add believability to your other-worldly creations.

The most intuitive way to learn anatomy is to spend a good amount of time in life-drawing classes studying direct from life, but it is essential to read up on your anatomy, too, unless you fancy cutting up some cadavers! Although there are many medical texts that will familiarize you with the inner workings of the human body, I've found it much easier to learn by reading artists' guides to anatomy. Artist-specific guides are more relevant, as they concern themselves only with representing the main forms and the surfaces of the body, without getting too bogged down in the details. You don't need to learn the names of each individual element, but it is essential to learn where all the major groups of muscles, tendons, bones, and areas of fat are in the body. It is quite common for beginners to focus on modeling all the muscles but forget about bony protrusions such as cheekbones, shoulder blades, and ankles. Your models will look formless and blobby without a good consideration of the bones that hold the body together.

The proportions of body parts in relationship to each other are of critical importance in character modeling; if you get the basic proportions wrong, your character will look terrible, even if you include loads of cool, small details. Small changes to proportions make a big difference in how people perceive your character—especially in the face, where tiny adjustments to the eyes can have a massive effect on the personality and mood of the character.

I heartily recommend the classic series of books about drawing the human figure by Andrew Loomis. The first editions are now out-of-print collector's items, but you can find the books freely available for download on the

Internet. *Drawing Comics the Marvel Way* by Stan Lee and John Buscema and the *How to Draw Anime & Game Characters* series by Tadashi Ozawa (Graphic-Sha) are also great, as they are very specific to the typical, idealized characters you often find in a contemporary game.

It may help to study classic artists such as Leonardo da Vinci. Leonardo shows in his art that there are many general proportional rules that loosely apply to almost everybody. Many of Leonardo's works (and those of many other artists) make extensive use of the "golden ratio," a number, known in mathematics as *phi*, that can be observed in many instances in nature. This number (approximately 1.6180339887) can be measured in the proportions of spirals in seashells, the length of bones in animals, and the distances between stems on plants. Look at the joints in your fingers; each successive joint is roughly 1.6 times longer than the last.

The ancient Greeks and Egyptians used the golden ratio in their classic architecture like the Parthenon and the pyramids. Modern studies have deemed these proportions to be esthetically pleasing and closely linked with our perceptions of beauty. You could even apply your knowledge of it to your own fantasy creature creations; it would be fair to hypothesize that if aliens do exist, they too might have evolved with "golden" proportions.

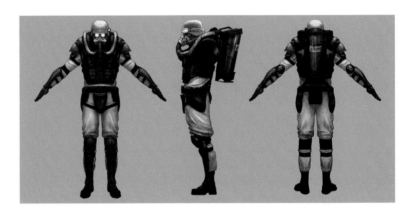

FIG 10.1

Ask Questions

Upon receiving the "future commando" concept, our first job is to get to know him. As we want our character to be realistic and believable, let's start by assuming that he *is* alive. Usually I ask the team and myself a number of questions, such as the following:

Q. Where does he live?

A. *The scene is based in the United Kingdom; the reference was taken in an abandoned mental hospital in the Northwest of England. It's not terribly important to tie the character to a location, but a Union Jack flag on his shoulder might be a nice detail.*

Q. What material is his suit made out of?

A. *He wears an NBC (Nuclear Biological Chemical) suit. The lightweight material is fairly tough, but flexible. The fabric has a charcoal layer in between the layers to protect him from nuclear fallout, gas, poison, or germ warfare. The fabric is unique: although it is flexible, it has a crisp quality and will hold creases. See if you can get your hands on an NBC suit in an army surplus store.*

Q. Has he had any previous battles and have they left him with any damage to his suit?

A. *Being on his hands and knees in various combat situations has left him with many surface scuffs and areas of ingrained dirt on his suit, but there is no real damage. His suit is his lifeline; it is replaced every six months, and if its function is compromised in any way, it is replaced immediately.*

Q. What sort of soldier is he?

A. *He is part of a specialist fighting unit, a real bad ass.*

Q. What kind of gloves is he wearing? It is unclear on the concept sketch.

A. *They are slash-resistant Kevlar gloves with lead lining. Perhaps it would be a good idea to extend the gloves to half-gauntlet size, to give better protection from his flamethrower.*

Q. How old is he?

A. *To become this tough, he must have been in various branches of the military for a number of years—he is in his early 30s.*

Q. How old is his gun? What type of gun is it?

A. *It is a flamethrower, maybe with a small shell launcher or other weapon on the bottom.*

Collecting References

Before we get into the modeling, it's mandatory to gather a wealth of reference material. You might think you know what things should look like, but reference photos always help you add that extra touch of authenticity. Detailed reference materials show you things about your subject material that you might have overlooked: the way it fades in the sun, the wear from children scratching their names into it, or the bits of chewing gum that get stuck to it. These observed details put your object into a real-world context and prevent it from looking unrealistically new or featureless. When it comes to the texturing stage, your reference will help you analyze the materials that make up your character—and you might be able to use a reference photo directly in your final textures.

For each object you research, it is advisable to get reference shots from as many different camera angles as possible. We need to know about every inch of the object's surfaces; within your range of images, there should be no blind spots where important details are hidden. Don't settle for just front, side, and back views. If you take the time to observe reference shots from the more obscure angles, such as the bottom, the back, and three-quarter views, it will add a professional level of depth to your models.

I use a Google image search for most of my research, set to "high-res images only" in the advanced settings. If this search is unsuccessful, I change the settings to medium- or small-size images. The Internet has a wealth of information, and there are many Web sites specific to whatever subjects you are researching. If you can't find what you are looking for, try using alternative key words; use a thesaurus to come up with as many different names as possible for the thing that you are researching.

One of my favorite sites is www.3d.sk. For a subscription fee, you can download very high-resolution professional photographs of *real* humans—no airbrushed skin tones here! The library includes all shapes and sizes of humans: fat, thin, young, old, black, white, Asian, bearded, armored—pretty much whatever you might need as reference for your modeling. The images are all shot in scattered white studio light with no harsh shadows, which is perfect for use in your textures. The average subjects are normal everyday people, so you end up with lots of acne, spots, skin diseases, blemishes, moles, and birthmarks—all the things that add character to your creations!

You should make sure to have folders full of images concerning every aspect of what you are about to model.

Getting Ready to Start—Setting Up Image Planes

Image planes are used so that you can trace over the concept artwork inside 3ds Max to ensure that your model remains true to the original vision. I strongly recommend that you do not trace photos directly in the viewport, but instead use your reference as a reference—not as the blueprint for your model.

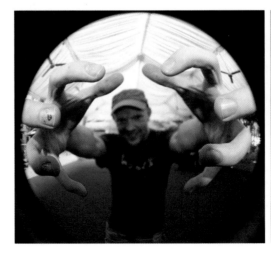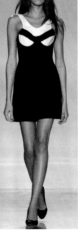

FIG 10.2

All photos are distorted by the camera's lens, which exaggerates and warps the image. Wide-angle or "fish-eye" lenses like the one used in this page are an extreme example of lens distortion. If you study some catwalk fashion photography, you will notice that models are often shot from afar with a strong zoom lens to minimize the lens distortion effect. Ideally it is this type of photograph, if any, on which you should base your dimensions—but be warned that directly tracing warped images will lead to warped models. It's better that you study proportions from life instead of relying on tracing.

To get a photograph with truly zero perspective distortion, you would have to be an infinite distance away from the object, with an infinitely powerful zoom lens just like the orthographic viewports in 3ds Max! Good concept artwork is drawn like this, with zero perspective, free from all lens distortion.

It is very important that the different views of the concept art are drawn out next to each other with ruled lines to ensure that the features match up accurately across the range of views. It can be very tricky to work from wonky and inaccurate concept art.

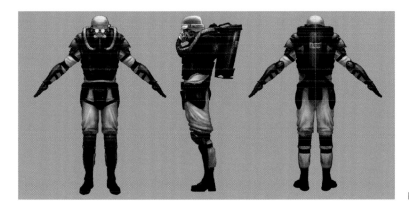

FIG 10.3

Starting to Build the Character

Let's open the concept art in Photoshop now to prepare it for use in 3ds Max as the blueprint for our character. We need three square images for front, side, and back that line up perfectly with each other.

Use the rectangle selection tool while holding down the Shift key to make a precise square selection around the front view, and then copy and paste it into its own image file. Go back to the original concept art image again and use the right arrow key to nudge your square selection over to the side view. Copy and paste the side view into its own image file, then repeat the process for the back view. Our use of a nudged selection to produce our three images ensures that they will line up perfectly in 3ds Max. Save each of these three views as a separate jpeg file.

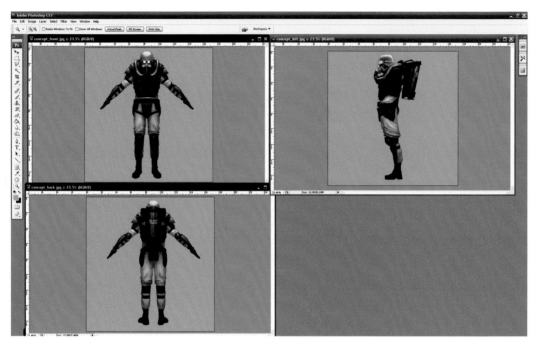

FIG 10.4

Rather than using 3ds Max's Viewport Background functionality, I prefer creating the image planes myself as geometry. I find it easier to manipulate the scale and position of the blueprints if I just map images onto planes. If I want to scale or transform the model, it's easy to include the image planes in the transformations and keep everything in sync.

Open up 3ds Max and create a square primitive plane (Create > Standard Primitives > Plane). It is important to hold Ctrl as you drag out the dimensions of the plane to ensure accurate square proportions like the images we prepared in Photoshop. Be sure that Generate Mapping Coords. is checked to save yourself the trouble of manually creating UV co-ordinates. Apply a Blinn material to this plane object, with 100% self-illumination and the ambient color set to white, and load the front concept image into the diffuse slot of the material. Now position the plane so that the character is centered on the origin (the center of the world co-ordinate system) with his feet directly above the origin.

Select the "front image plane" object that you have just created and rotate it 90°; my favorite way to do this is to hold Shift while rotating the object to copy and rotate the object in the same operation. Be sure to turn on the angle snap toggle button on the main toolbar to ensure an exact rotation of 90°.

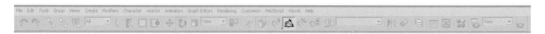

FIG 10.5

Apply a new material to this new copied object and map the side concept image onto it to create the "side image plane." Now copy/rotate the side image plane another 90° and apply another new material to it to create the "back image plane," translating it back slightly to move it away from the front concept plane. The use of square images on square planes ensures undistorted and perfectly aligned features: no more messing around with translate, scale, and rotate trying to get everything to match up correctly.

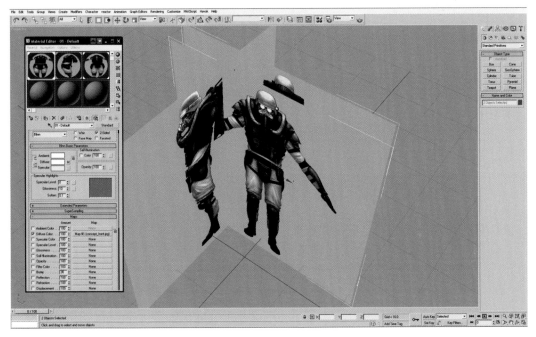

FIG 10.6

Expert Mode, Hotkeys, and Scripting

Most modeling work involves a heavy amount of repetition, so it is more than worth your time to learn all the hotkeys for the major tools. If hotkeys are not assigned to your favorite tools by default, you can do it yourself using the Customize > Customize User Interface options. Sometimes, I write a script that performs a series of commands that I repeat again and again—it's really not that hard to write basic scripts, so don't be afraid to try it out yourself. Over the years, I have customized my workflow quite extensively to save me hours of repetition per day. Once you have made a couple of characters and want to save some time and energy, you should look at using scripting and hotkeys as a way of saving lots of time.

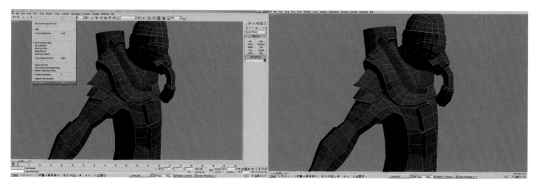

FIG 10.7

As I've been using 3ds Max for more than nine years, I'm very comfortable with the tools and my hotkeys for each modeling function that I use on a daily basis, so I don't often use the icons. I usually run 3ds Max in Expert Mode (Views > Expert Mode), which keeps my interface free of clutter, giving me more room for looking at my character. If you are just starting out, you probably won't want this, as it is good to explore the interface and each tool that is available, but it is a great option once you know exactly what you are doing.

As we are concerned with modeling, not animating, you can definitely turn off the track bar to save some room on your interface (Show UI ≥ Show Track Bar).

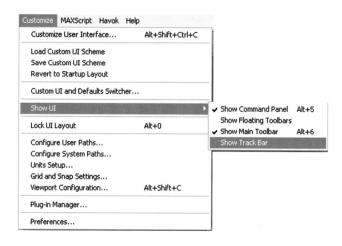

FIG 10.8

Viewport Preference Settings

By default, 3ds Max's viewports display rather low-resolution textures by today's standards. If you select Customize > Preferences > Viewports > Configure Driver, you can increase the maximum texture size. Select "1024" and check "Match Bitmap Size as Closely as Possible" for both "Background Texture Size" and the "Download Texture Size."

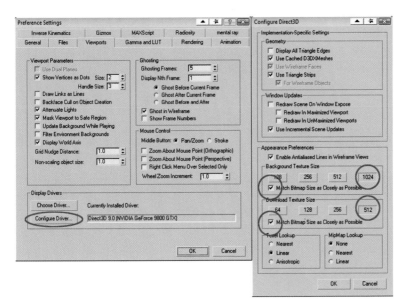

FIG 10.9

Getting the Basic Proportions Right

Let's start the modeling with the classic starting point: the "primitive cube,"
known in 3ds Max as the "box primitive." Right-click your cube to convert it
into an Editable Poly. We will make half the character initially. Press 4 to select
polygon mode and the top polygon to select it. Now use the Extrude tool to
extrude the polygon upward to make a chest, select the top poly on the left
side of the shape and extrude out to make an arm, and select the bottom poly
and extrude out to make a leg.

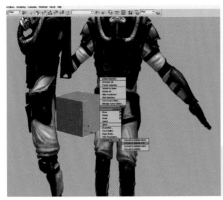 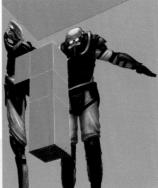

FIG 10.10

You might need to move the side image plane out of the way a little so that
you can see what you are doing as our character widens. Ensure that you
move it only by sliding the X transform handle; this way, we will not lose the

vertical "registration" with the front and back concepts. Press 1 for Vertex mode and move all the object's vertices into better positions to match the concept. It is easier to see what you're doing if you apply a new material to our object, with 30% opacity and a strong red color.

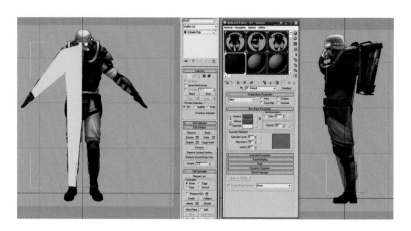

FIG 10.11

Next you should select the polys on the inside of the mesh, where the line of symmetry will go, and delete them. Press F4 to show the edged faces clearly.

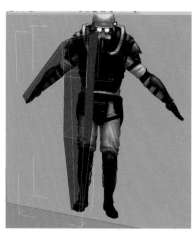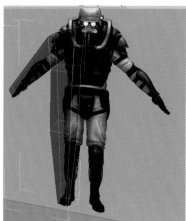

FIG 10.12

Let's mirror our mesh to make the full form—it would take twice as long to do everything if we didn't use symmetry to our advantage. Activate the Affect Pivot Only button in the Pivot panel and move the pivot to the origin; be sure to deactivate the button after you have finished. Next, apply a Symmetry modifier; you might need to check the Flip box and then adjust the threshold slider until the center vertices snap together. We now have a full figure.

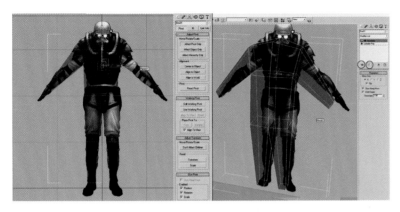

FIG 10.13

If you click on Editable Poly on the stack, the symmetry will disappear. You must press the "SHOW END RESULT ON/OFF TOGGLE" button (the little test tube under the stack); this will switch on all items further up the stack, which is invaluable for modeling with most modifiers. As we work, you can also switch on and off the light bulb icon next to the Symmetry modifier to turn its effect on and off.

Let's add some more geometry to refine the shape. Select one of the horizontal edges running down the leg and press the Ring button, which selects all the parallel edges running down the leg. When the mesh gets more complex, the Ring and Loop select functions become invaluable for making quick, accurate selections. Next, hit the rollout box to the side of the Connect button in Edit Poly to connect these edges with new polys and select two segments.

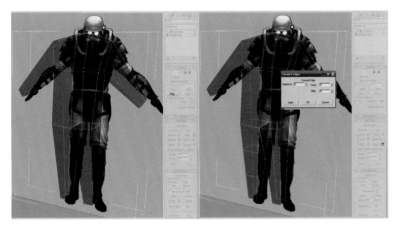

FIG 10.14

Repeat the select Edge, select Ring, and Connect process for the vertical edges running across the arm and the torso to increase the detail level further. Now spend some time moving these vertices around to fit the concept sketches.

The key to modeling fast is to add new geometry only as you need it. Before you add any new polys, make sure that the ones that are there already are well-placed; this reduces the amount of translating work you do substantially, as any new geometry you make will already be somewhat in the correct area. Create, refine, create, refine: our basic workflow.

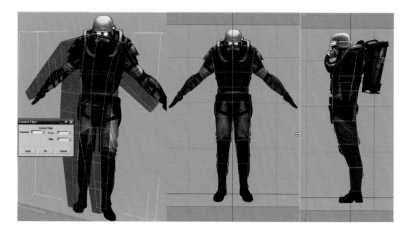

FIG 10.15

Click the poly at the end of the arm and extrude it out to make a hand. Do the same at the end of the leg to make a foot.

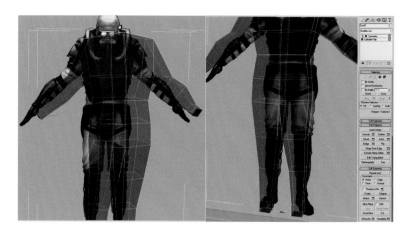

FIG 10.16

Extrude out the poly at the front of the foot to make it more natural-looking and refine all the vertices of the hand and foot into better positions.

Now let's add more geometry so that we can match the concept closer. Select Poly mode by pressing the 4 key, and then press Ctrl + A to select every poly on the model. We will turn every poly into four polys by pressing the Dialog Box button next to the Tessellate button in the Edit Poly rollout.

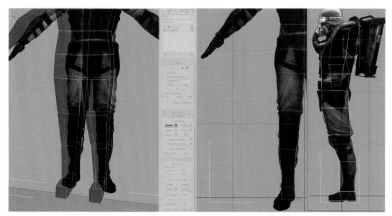

FIG 10.17

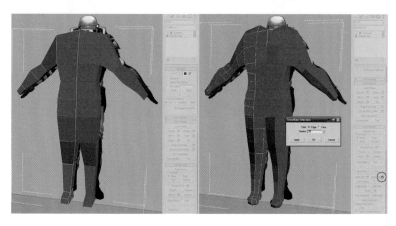

FIG 10.18

Now refine the vertices to match the concept shape better. If you like, you can change the opacity of the material a little to make it easier to see the concept underneath.

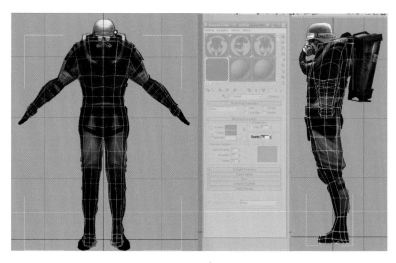

FIG 10.19

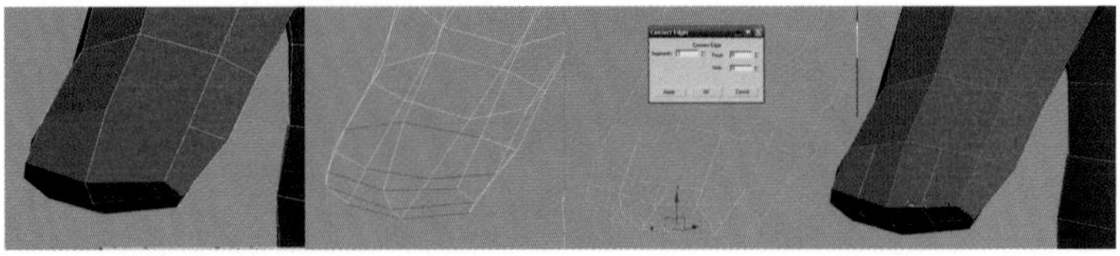

FIG 10.20

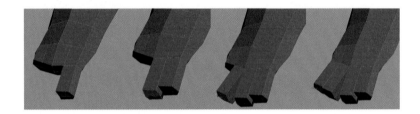

To make the fingers, connect the edges at the end of the hand to make four columns of polys.

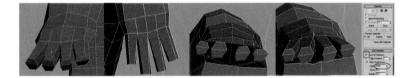

FIG 10.21

One by one, extrude each column of two polys to form each finger.

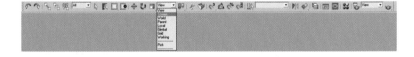

FIG 10.22

Refine the new vertices to make more natural finger shapes. I used Soft Selection with a larger Falloff setting to put a natural bend into the hand without having to move each point separately.

FIG 10.23

When moving vertices in the Perspective view, I find it useful to switch the co-ordinate system from View to Screen. Screen co-ordinates aren't locked to the world x-, y-, z-axes like the View co-ordinates are, making fine adjustments in a Perspective view much quicker and more intuitive.

It's important with nearly all models to keep a clean, quad-based topology. A pure quad mesh is much easier to "read," and you can work faster using the

Loop and Ring functions. It's hard to see what's going on if you use a lot of triangles in your mesh and they subdivide very unpredictably.

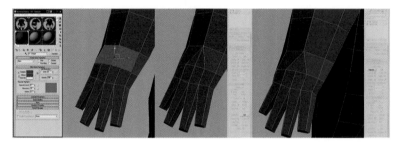

FIG 10.24

If you study the previous figure, you will notice that the two selected polygons have five vertices each; these faces with more than four vertices are called "Ngons." Ngons are just as bad as triangles when subdividing; during rendering they are triangulated unpredictably, so it's better that we turn them into quads. Use the Cut tool to cut some new edges as shown previously, and then select the center edge and use the Remove button to eradicate it. Do the same on the bottom of the hand, too, to rid our mesh of all the evil Ngons.

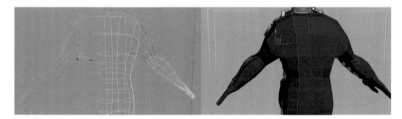

FIG 10.25

Let's add more detail to the upper arms. Select and connect the top two rings of edges.

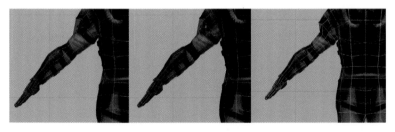

FIG 10.26

Work the forms into the mesh, adding new edge loops wherever you need more detail.

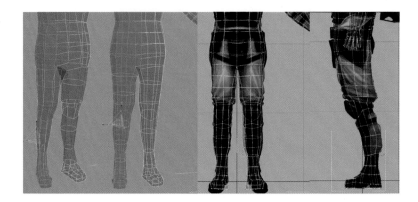

FIG 10.27

Add more edge loops to the legs and then shape the details. Try to model the edge loops along the main creases. Notice where I have angled the edge loops down to fit the shape of the kneepads.

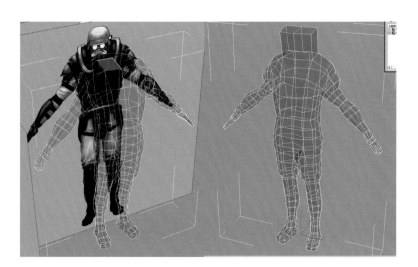

FIG 10.28

Extrude out a head from the top center polygon, making sure to delete the polygon that the extrusion creates on the line of symmetry, and then Tessellate the head to add more detail.

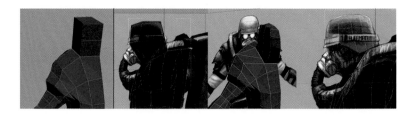

FIG 10.29

Cutting in More Detail

Now that we have the basic character shapes, let's cut in the medium-frequency details. These are the subshapes within each major shape, such as the main shape of each piece of armor, each strap, and the main flow of the fabrics. Add more geometry to the head, taking care to preserve a clean quad-based surface as you go. Try not to make tiny details in one area before you have cut in all the main shapes—keep the level of detail consistent across the mesh.

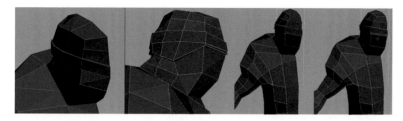

FIG 10.30

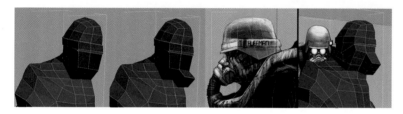

FIG 10.31

The flow of the edges is very important; our aim is to try to make all the edge loops join together in flowing and continuous lines. Good edge flow makes much smoother and more natural surfaces.

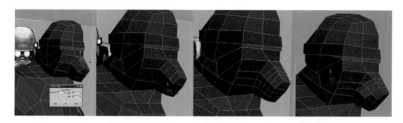

FIG 10.32

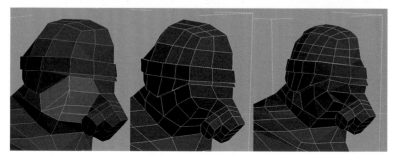

FIG 10.33

Notice the bad edge flow on the selected polygons in Fig. 10.33. There is a triangle in there, too, which isn't ideal. If we add edges and rework the topology, we can create a more organized surface. Don't expect the art of a perfect quad-based surface to come to you overnight, but with lots of practice, you will prevail. If you need some inspiration, visit some Internet forums and study other people's meshes to see how they are arranging their edge flow.

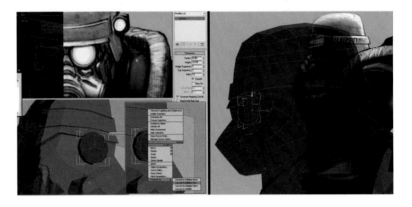

FIG 10.34

A primitive cylinder makes a great starting point for the eye, as it is perfectly round. We must make efficient use of our polygons, so play with the parameters until you get a good balance between a nice model and a reasonable amount of geometry. I chose 12 sides and only one height segment. Convert the primitive into an Editable Poly when you are done, and remember to delete the backfacing polygons. A classic beginner's mistake is to have loads of unnecessary polygons that are never seen because they are inside the mesh hidden by other polygons—don't do it!

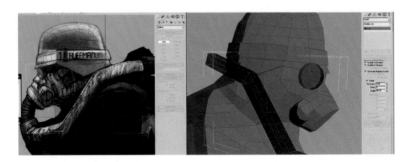

FIG 10.35

Another great starting point for your pipes, legs, and other twisty cylinders is the Line primitive in the Shapes section of the Create panel. First, draw out your line with a few simple vertices, and then in the Modify panel, enable the line in the renderer and viewport, generate Automatic Mapping Coords (saving you UVing time later), and play with many aspects of the topology on the fly. It's easy, fast, and versatile, but best of all is that it creates very accurate meshes.

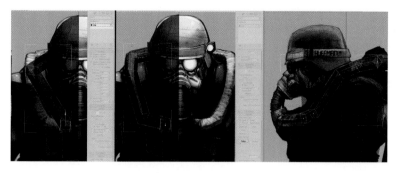

FIG 10.36

You can select and move the vertices in the Line, similar to how you would in Edit Poly by using the stack in the Modify panel. Once you get the vertices in the right place in each viewport, you can use the Refine tool to add more points to get the correct shape. Change the Sides parameter to give your line four sides and perhaps adjust the Angle setting, too. If you are happy with the shape, you can convert it into an Editable Poly. Before you do so, make a copy of the line and hide it—you can return to this hidden line if you want to make quick changes to the pipe topology later on.

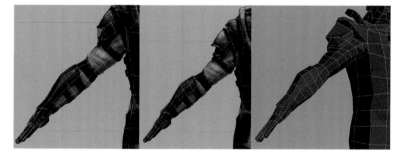

FIG 10.37

Once you have the main shapes and the edge flow working well on the arms, it's time to start extruding the pads and the straps to block out the detail. Be careful that your extrusions do not create hidden polygons inside the main geometry. The Hide/Unhide Polygon tools in Edit Poly are your best friends when things start to get a little more complex.

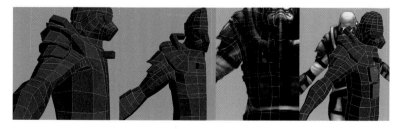

FIG 10.38

Remember to work on your model from as many angles as possible as you develop it. It will start to look flat if you use only the front and left views.

349

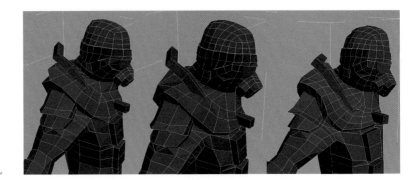

FIG 10.39

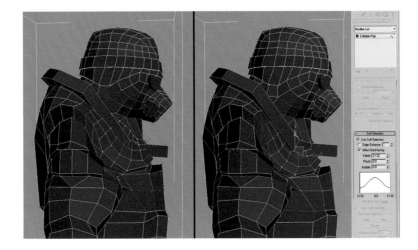

FIG 10.40

When meshes get more complex, it can be time consuming to make changes to the overall shape, so remember to use Soft Selection. Why move one vertex at a time when you can move hundreds together? Adjust the falloff and away you go.

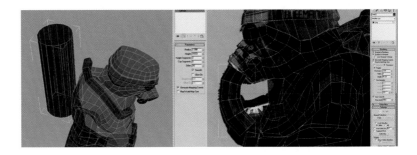

FIG 10.41

A primitive cylinder makes a good start for the oxygen tank; another Line primitive does a great job for the central pipe on the mask.

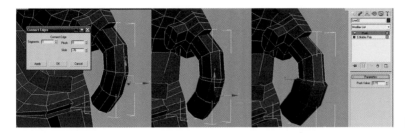

FIG 10.42

Select the line that makes the central pipe on the mask and convert it to an Editable Poly. Select the ring of edges where we want to increase the diameter of the pipe and connect the edges; use the Slide parameter to move it higher. Select the two lowest rings of edges below and apply a push modifier to flare out the pipe a little, and then collapse the stack back down to an Editable Poly.

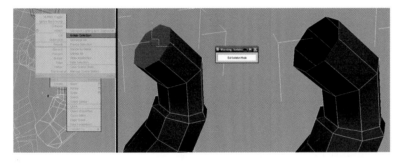

FIG 10.43

Right-click on your pipe object, and choose Isolate Selection. This command is very useful when you want to see all sides of the object without other objects getting in the way. Delete the hidden faces at the top, and click the Exit Isolation Mode button.

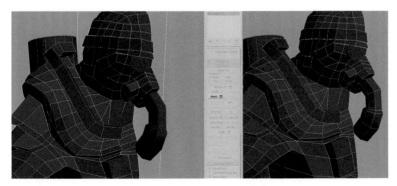

FIG 10.44

To add this pipe geometry to the main mesh, first delete the left-hand side of it so that it can be mirrored like the rest of the model. Select the main mesh, click the Attach button, and click the pipe.

Add some more geometry around the torso and under the arms. It's important to visualize the body underneath the clothes as you mold your character. Imagine where the major muscles are sitting and how they are pushing on the clothes. It's a good idea to look at the model from underneath quite often; if you make your model look correct from this often-overlooked view it helps make your model more accurate.

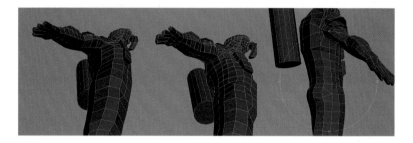

FIG 10.45

Start the hands by extruding a thumb, and cut in some more loops on the fingers to add a slight curve to each finger.

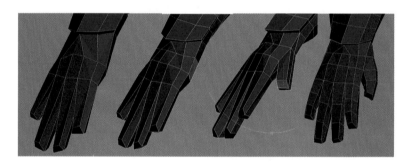

FIG 10.46

As you develop the hand/glove, it's useful to have your reference by your side, so that you can copy the real-life hands/gloves as closely as possible. If you're having trouble making your hand look correct, study your own hand. One of the most common beginner's mistakes is to make the thumb bend like the fingers. The thumb should bend at 90° to the bend of the fingers. It's also very important to build curvature into the palm.

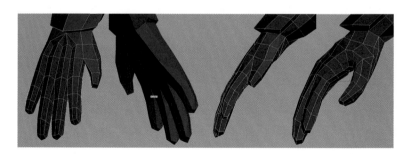

FIG 10.47

Let's make the gaps between the fingers less angular and more natural; select the edges between each finger and chamfer them.

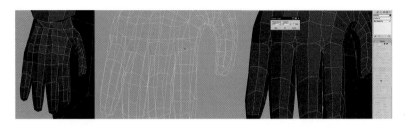

FIG 10.48

Cut some edges and weld (I like to use Target Weld) the rogue points together so that you get a topology something like Fig. 10.49. The aim is to get a smooth loop that flows around the rim of the glove. The glove isn't perfect yet, but let's move up the arm so that we keep an even amount of detail across the body.

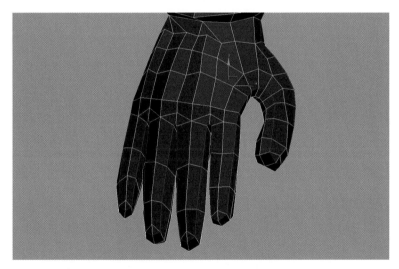

FIG 10.49

Try to improve the look of the arm as much as you can without adding any more geometry. Once everything is in place, cut in more loops to define the straps and pads on his arms. Pay attention to the direction of the loops; they must follow the contours of the outfit.

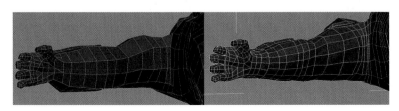

FIG 10.50

When modeling hard-to-reach places such as the cavity near the shoulder pads, you have a few secret weapons in your arsenal. It will be much easier to rotate around your selections if you activate Arc Rotate SubObject near the bottom right of the interface. You can flatten areas by selecting the relevant polygons and pressing the Make Planar button.

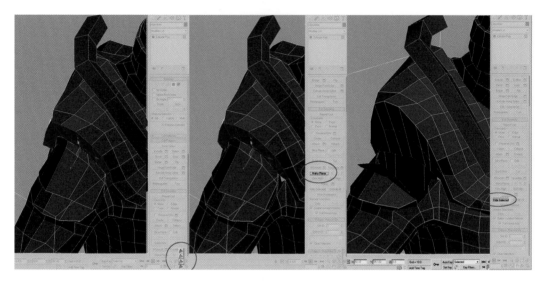

FIG 10.51

If you wish to smooth out a selection of polys, press the Relax button. Another top tip for being able to see what you are doing in difficult places is to hide some polygons. Press the Hide button to hide your selection of polys; Unhide All brings them back when you have finished.

Continue going around the body, looking at it from different angles and tightening things up. Be sure to study some reference material of a suitably tough-looking male, shot from as many different angles as possible. Good anatomical references help you build up the volumes of muscle, bone, flesh, and fat that lie underneath our character's clothing. Again, working from the obscure top and bottom angles really helps give an extra "punch" to the forms.

At this point, you should have all the major shapes modeled in like shown in the following images. The total character at this point contains approximately 5000 triangles.

Once you are happy with the air pipes that you made with the Line primitive, you can convert them to an Editable Poly. The edges are a little sharp, so use the Chamfer function to round them out a little.

Continue to work more detail into the main lines of the mesh, using all our old favorites such as Cut, Move, Loop, Ring, Connect, Extrude, Relax, and so on.

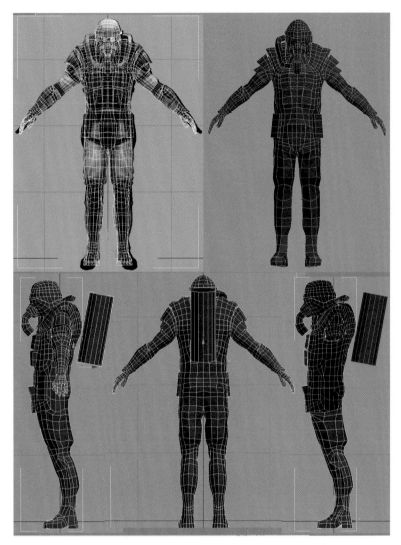

FIG 10.52

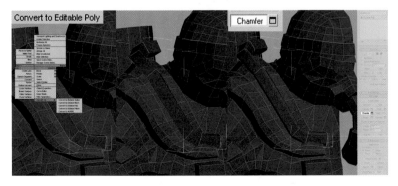

FIG 10.53

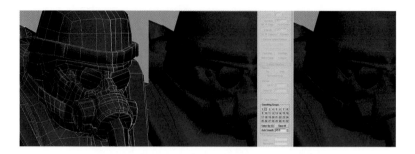

FIG 10.54

I find it easier to work with the mesh if I give each major group of polygons (kneepads, sole, glove, and so on) a different smoothing group; this allows me to better see the boundaries between different areas. A fast way to do this is to use the Auto Smooth button, but you might need to refine its work in places.

Keep adding details until your mesh is about 13,500 triangles; you can use the following images for rough reference. Don't go crazy trying to match my model exactly, but the detail should be evenly spread throughout the body, with a slight emphasis on the face.

Make sure to save your mesh around this point. Although it isn't detailed enough for our high-resolution mesh, it is certainly a good starting point for additional detail. Also, with a little tweaking, it will make an excellent game mesh when we load it back up later on. I call this mesh the "proxy mesh," as mentioned earlier, because it is approximately the same form as both the game mesh and the high-resolution mesh.

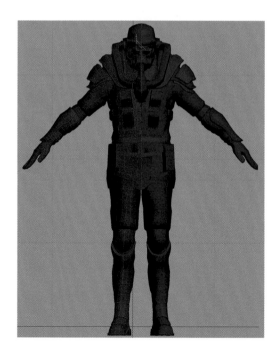

FIG 10.55

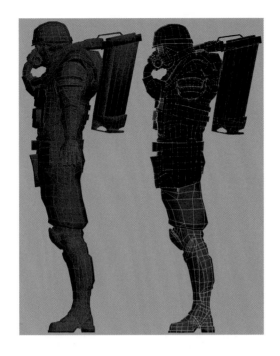

FIG 10.56

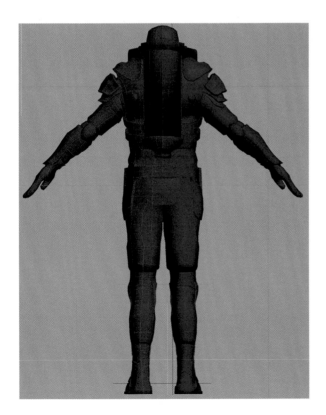

FIG 10.57

The High-Resolution Mesh: Breaking Up the Shapes

Now it is time to start the high-resolution modeling. As the level of detail increases, I find it much easier to work if we break up the mesh into each individual component. Select the polygons for each distinct part of the body and break them into separate meshes using the Detach button. Each mesh can then be isolated if you need to work on the hard-to-see areas.

If the separate parts of the mesh aren't actually welded together, you can easily select them for detaching using the Element selection.

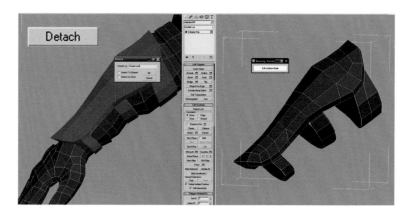

FIG 10.58

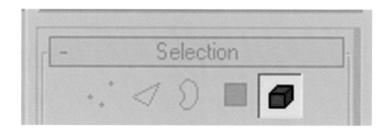

FIG 10.59

The Shell Modifier

It's very important to give even the thinnest shapes some amount of thickness. The quickest and also the most accurate way to do this is to apply the shell modifier and increase either the Inner Amount or Outer Amount parameter. You might want to delete some of the polygons on the inside, as they won't be seen.

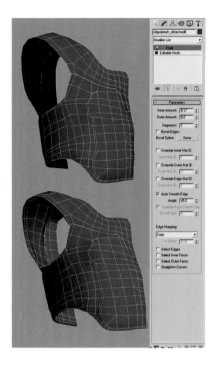

FIG 10.60

The High-Resolution Mesh: Adding More Detail

As you add all the subshapes that make up each piece of the character, you should not need any other tools than the ones we've used already. Just study the concept and the reference material very carefully as you work. Be careful not to get into too much detail in any one area of the character. The aim is to roughly mark in all the shapes until you get to about the level of detail in the following images:

Helmet

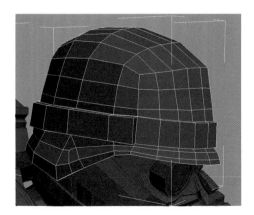

FIG 10.61

Mask

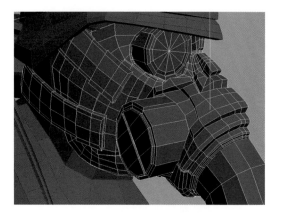

FIG 10.62

Vest

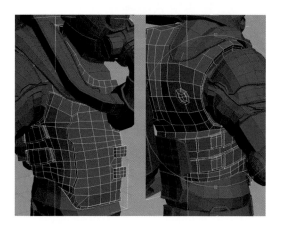

FIG 10.63

Shoulder Pads

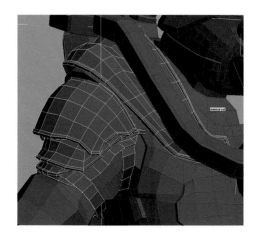

FIG 10.64

Forearm Pad and Kneepad

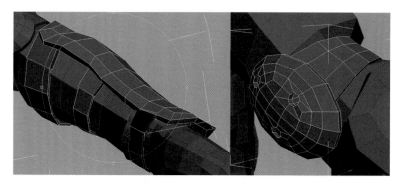

FIG 10.65

Gas Tank

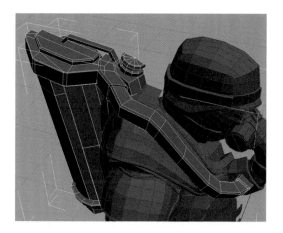

FIG 10.66

Glove

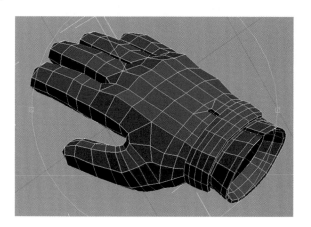

FIG 10.67

Belt and Details

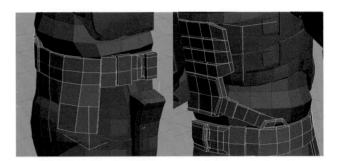

FIG 10.68

Codpiece and Other Details

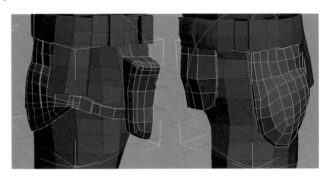

FIG 10.69

Shin Pads

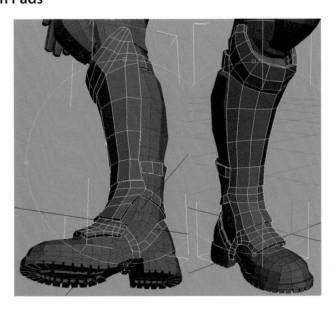

FIG 10.70

Kneepad and Shoe

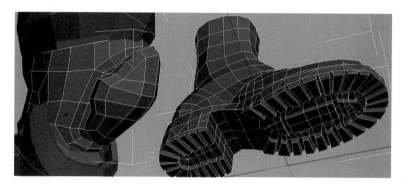

FIG 10.71

Most importantly, the chemical suit is modeled underneath everything. This will make sure that there are no gaps left in our mesh. A common beginner's mesh will have lots of holes in it where the various meshes meet, and this is a great way to avoid that. Don't model any creases or folds yet; we will tackle that later.

Chemical Suit

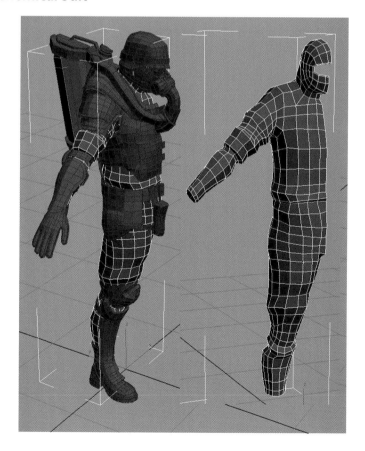

FIG 10.72

Breathing Pipe

An accurate and super-fast way to make the breathing pipe is to use the Loft compound object. Delete the old breathing pipe and in the side view, draw out a rough spline using the Line primitive. I've indicated on Fig. 10.73 the three clicks that I made to draw the line. Be sure to hold the left mouse button down as you drag out each point so that you can control the shape of the line as you create it.

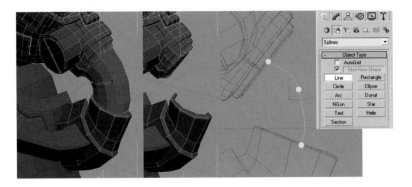

FIG 10.73

If your line is anything like mine, it still looks a little wonky! Go into the Modify panel, select Vertex, and then click on each point and adjust the handles to get a good, smooth line. Also check that your line is correctly positioned in 3D space; it should be centered on the symmetry line of the model. We will call this line the Path of our loft, and it gives the shape to the length of the object.

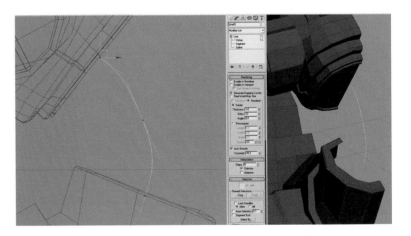

FIG 10.74

Let's draw the shape of the Profile curve that will give the volume to our Path line. For this, we will use a circle primitive from the Splines rollout. Drag out the circle from the top view and scale and position it at the top of the Path curve. Take care to *not* rotate it.

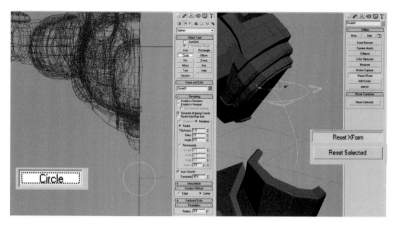

FIG 10.75

The next step is to reset the Xform of these two splines. Reset Xform resets the translation, scale, and rotation information back to how they were when the object was created. Having "zeroed out" transform values is critical for operations such as lofting that rely on this information. Reset Xform can be found in the Utility panel; with each of the two loft curves selected, press the Reset Selected button.

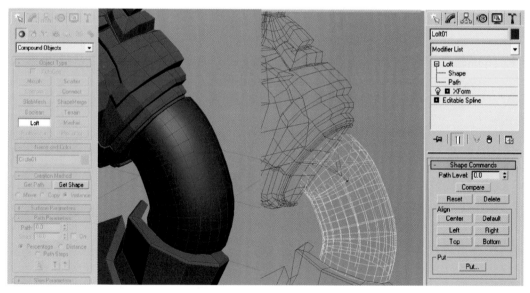

FIG 10.76

Select the Path shape and execute the Loft command, which is hidden in the Create panel's Geometry section (select "Compound objects" from the drop-down menu). Click on the Get Shape button, and then in the viewport, select the Profile circle, and 3ds Max should create a basic Loft shape.

365

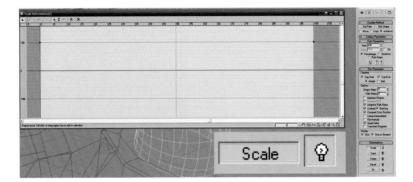

FIG 10.77

We have the basic shape looking pretty good now, but the real power of Loft shapes comes with the Deformation controls. Let's use the Scale deformer to add the ribbed details to the surface. At the bottom of your new Loft object's modifier panel, click on the Scale Deformation button. Adjust the graph that pops up so that it is long and thin as shown in the previous image. You might find that the zoom extends the horizontal button—useful for framing the graph correctly in the window.

Select the Insert Bezier Point button from the Scale Deformation interface.

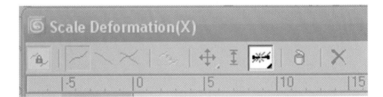

FIG 10.78

With the Insert Bezier Point tool active, click on the red line to add a Bezier point at roughly every four units along the X Axis, across the line; your line should look something like Fig. 10.79.

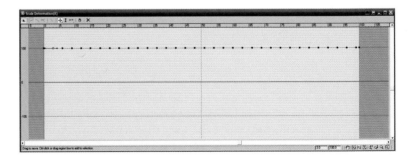

FIG 10.79

With the Move Control Point tool active, select any one point on the graph. You can see the xy co-ordinate of the selected point in the bottom right-hand area of the Scale Deformation window.

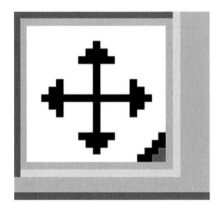

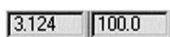

FIG 10.80

The "x" represents how far along the Path we are, and "y" represents the scale (which is constant at 1 the whole way across, at the moment). To get our ribbed details spaced apart with precision, let's type in an exact number into the left-hand "x" co-ordinate box for each point. Here, your knowledge of your "3" multiplication tables will pay dividends! Repeat after me: 3, 6, 9, 12, 15, 18, 21, 24 … 96, 99.

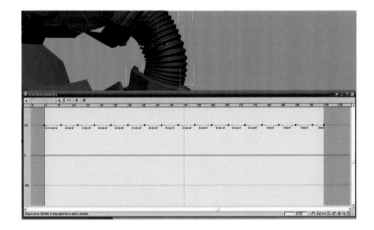

FIG 10.81

To create the bumps in the ribbed surface, select every other vertex (i.e., the ones at 3, 9, 12, 18, and so on), and in the "y" co-ordinate box, type in 90. Boom! The details appear. Open the Modifier panel and check the Generate Mapping co-ordinates option, which will save us time when generating UVs later.

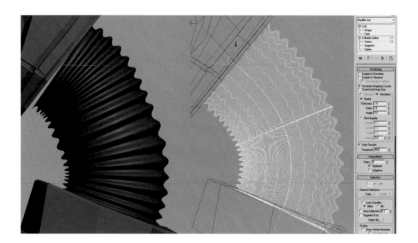

FIG 10.82

Subdividing Your Model with TurboSmooth

The mesh is getting pretty detailed now, but it would take an eternity to keep adding geometry until we lose the harsh, angular look. This is where the TurboSmooth modifier comes in very handy.

Each iteration of TurboSmooth subdivides each polygon into four smaller polygons, relaxing them at the same time. Similar technologies exist in all major 3D applications. These types of surfaces are generally known as "subdivisional surfaces," or SUBDs for short.

The key advantage to using TurboSmooth is that we can make fast changes to a simple poly mesh and not get bogged down tweaking millions of vertices to make a smooth curve. This smoothness is also the biggest drawback; at times it can be very tricky to preserve areas of the model that require sharp edges.

Microbeveling

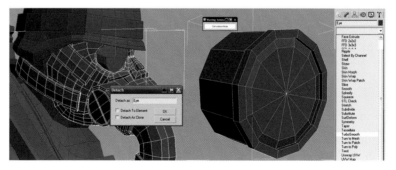

FIG 10.83

Let's start our smoothing process with one of the simplest objects, the lens of the goggle in the mask. Select just your eye geometry and detach it to create a separate mesh.

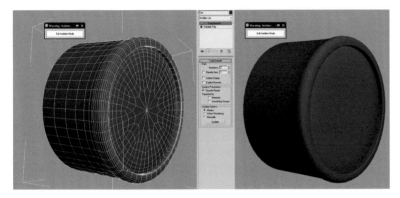

FIG 10.84

Apply a TurboSmooth modifier and push the iterations up to 2. As you dial up the iterations, the circular form of the eye gets rounded nicely, but we lose the crisp edges on the corners.

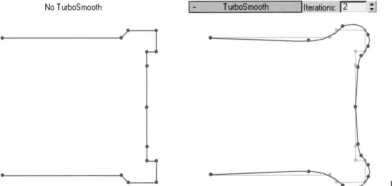

FIG 10.85

We can see the TurboSmooth effect most clearly by studying the side profile. TurboSmooth works by averaging out the positions of the vertices; those that are far apart from each other get moved quite substantially, and not always to your advantage. If you build your models with vertices closer together in areas with drastic changes of shape (sharp edges), they will be less dramatically affected when TurboSmoothed.

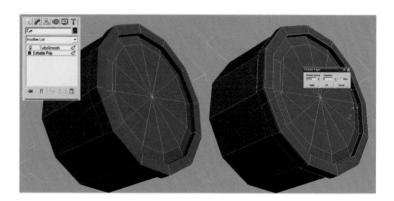

FIG 10.86

Go down the object stack and select Editable Poly. Select all the corner edges that you would like to sharpen up using the Loop tool. Chamfer these edges so that you get a nice corner bevel on each edge; I used the setting 0.012 for the chamfer amount, but this will vary depending on the scale of your scene. Select two segments for each chamfer.

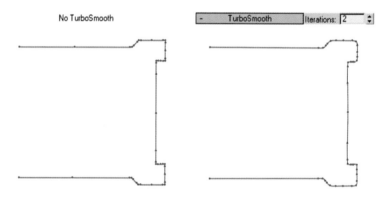

FIG 10.87

Your cylinder should look something similar to this figure from the side profile; the extra geometry locks into place the effect of the smoothing.

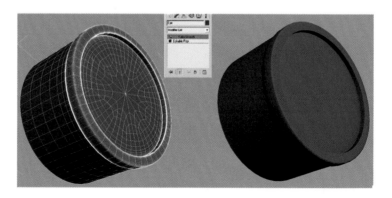

FIG 10.88

The results should be like the previous image: a perfectly round cylinder with hard edges at the corners. This technique is dubbed "microbeveling" in the industry because sometimes the detail you must put in on an awkward corner area gets pretty tiny.

If you build your models with nice, orderly quads, it is very fast and easy to add microbevels by selecting loops and chamfering them. Another advantage of doing your modeling operations on loop selections is that it keeps everything uniform across the edge. Most machined, inorganic forms like this goggle lens are made on a production line in a factory and, as such, are very regular shapes. Unless you want this type of shape to look worn or old, you should try to avoid going in and hand-tweaking individual vertices; it will lead to irregularities that make them look hand-made. Instead, do your inorganic modeling using modifiers and operations on loop-based selections.

Microbeveling the Shoe Edges

The really tricky SUBD stuff comes when we have edges on more than one axis coming together. For example, take the edges of sole of the shoe where the tread pattern might involve beveled edges meeting on all three axes at many corner points. The simple solution is to do all your chamfering at the same time.

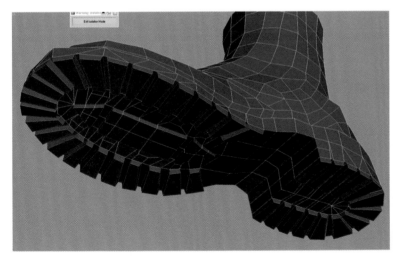

FIG 10.89

First, select all the edges that you would like to perform the chamfer on.

Then use the Chamfer button and tweak the amount to control the roundness of the edges.

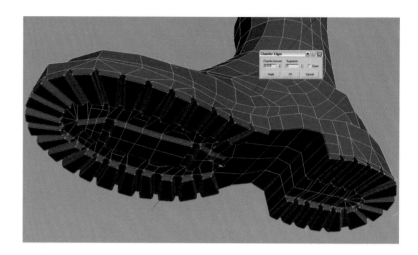

FIG 10.90

This way is much faster and cleaner than doing your beveling one piece at a time. If you select some edges, chamfer them, and then repeat the process for other nearby edges, things quickly get messy. If we perform the chamfer operation to all the edges at the same time, we create a relatively orderly and even topology.

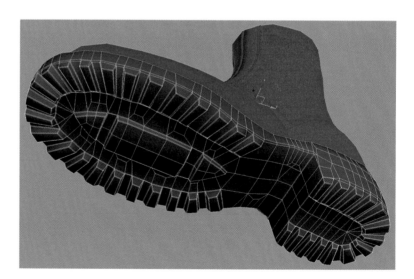

FIG 10.91

The last thing to do is to go through the mesh and reorder the topology to get the nice and clean square-quads look that characterizes a high-quality SUBD mesh. I've detached the sole from the shoe to help keep things simple.

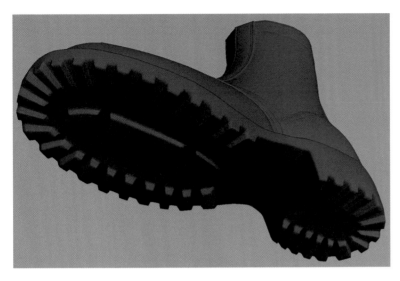

FIG 10.92

Finishing the Symmetrical Details

One by one, work through your objects, adding TurboSmoothing, refining the details, and taking special care with the details of sharp and beveled edges. Avoid creating any asymmetrical details (such as the creases and folds of his trousers); we will tackle these details later on.

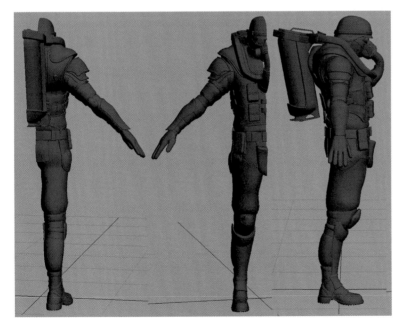

FIG 10.93

Your mesh should now look something like the previous image, with everything apart from the asymmetrical folds and creases of the clothing modeled in fine detail. Once you are happy with your half-character, give it another quick check for holes and other defects. It's much quicker to fix things now, before we copy the mesh across the central line of symmetry and create a right side and a left side that both need identical repair work.

In 3D modeling, it is always beneficial to use symmetry to your advantage. If you take care to get things as good as you can before you mirror them, it will make your modeling almost twice as fast.

Making the UVs in UVlayout

In order to get a texture onto our high-resolution model, we need to give it UV co-ordinates. This procedure can be time consuming and, dare I say it, tedious and boring! Typical high-resolution meshes have polygon counts measured in the millions, so we need every trick in the book to get these UVs done well in a reasonable amount of time. 3ds Max has some fairly good UVing tools for production like the Pelt Mapper and the Relax function, but I've found a small program called UVlayout to be far superior when generating UVs for complex high-resolution shapes. UVlayout optimizes your UVs for subdivision, considering how the UVs will be stretched when subdivided.

The UVlayout interface is not very pretty or intuitive, but if you watch the tutorial videos available for download from www.uvlayout.com, you will see just how amazing the program is. So don't judge this book by its cover! In my experience, unwrapping in UVlayout is more than twice as fast as unwrapping in 3ds Max, Maya, or XSI. The quality of UVs that UVlayout produces is also much higher. The distortion-free UVs generated by UVlayout will save us lots of time and prevent frustration later when we come to texture this object. A trial version of this software is available from the download under Chapter 10\UVlayout\.

To keep things simple, we will import and unwrap each part of the character one piece at a time in UVlayout, so export each part as a separate Wavefront (.OBJ) file from 3ds Max (File > Export Selected). You should now have a list of objects organized in a UVing folder (such as belt.obj, boots.obj, vest.obj, and so on).

In UVlayout, click the blue Load button and browse to your UVing folder where you saved all the OBJ files. Load kneepad.obj first; it's a simple object that will make a nice introduction to UVlayout. Remember to check your Load Options before you load the mesh; UVlayout will take the effect of the TurboSmooth SUBD's into account if you select Type "SUBD." Be sure to select the UV's "New" button too, which deletes any old UVs that might be already applied to your object. Check the Weld UV's and Clean boxes to ensure a tidy mesh, and then, with the correct object highlighted in blue, click the green Load button.

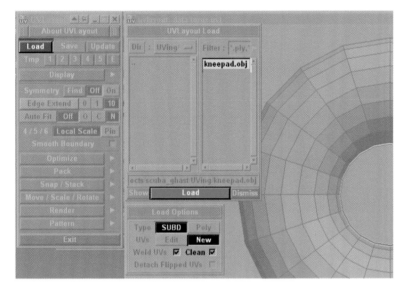

FIG 10.94

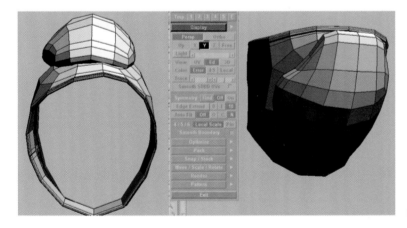

FIG 10.95

The first thing that you might notice is that your kneepads are being viewed from below. Open the Display panel and select "Y" to change UVlayout's co-ordinate system. If you hold the Alt key, you can navigate in the 3D scene using the left mouse button to orbit, the middle mouse button to pan, and the right mouse button to zoom in and out. In the Display section of the interface, there are three different types of views, which you can select quickly using the 1, 2, and 3 keys:

- UV view shows in 2D your unwrapped UV co-ordinates.
- Ed or Edit view shows in 3D only your objects that currently have no UVs assigned yet.
- 3D view shows the original 3D object intact.

375

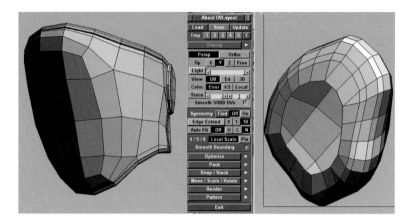

FIG 10.96

When you load the kneecap object into UVlayout, the default view is the Edit view. As you selected NEW when loading the object, it will have no UVs, and therefore its surface should be gray. If you move the mouse cursor over the main plastic kneecap shape at the front of the object and press D, the kneecap will disappear. The shape has not been deleted; instead, UVs have been assigned to it, so it is not shown in the Ed view anymore. Press 1 to jump to UV view and locate your kneecap UVs, which should still be a gray color, as they are not flattened out yet.

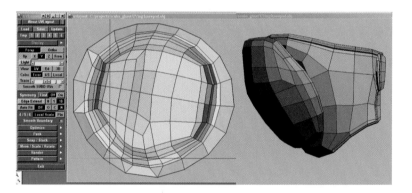

FIG 10.97

While you are still in the UV view, hold your mouse cursor over the kneecap UVs, hold the spacebar, and press F. Watch with joy as the UVs unfold themselves in a weird and wonderful way. Colors appear on the UVs now: red represents areas that do not have their fair share of UV space and blue represents areas that have too much UV space. Both red and blue areas show distortion, and we must seek to minimize that. If you press 3 to jump to the 3D view, you can see the colors now applied to the kneecap, showing in 3D space where the distortion is occurring.

Let's help the UV shell relax a little more by making some cuts; cuts in the correct places will help our geometry unwrap. For most "closed" objects, cuts are mandatory—anything circular like a cylinder or sphere needs at least one major cut in order to be able to unwrap at all. I like to think about unwrapping similar to how a primitive Stone Age hunter might skin an animal to make a cave jacket. A less gory analogy is to compare your final layout of UVs to how a tailor cuts shapes from a blank piece of fabric to make a garment.

Like the seams that a tailor deals with, cutting up your shell generates UV seams in UVlayout. The UV seams are a necessary evil that you must minimize. These could cause problems later if you want to paint your textures quickly and easily in Photoshop. You will need a 3D paint program such as ZBrush or Bodypaint in order to be able to paint continuous textures over seam areas. Furthermore, each UV seam can cause problems further down the line with normal mapping.

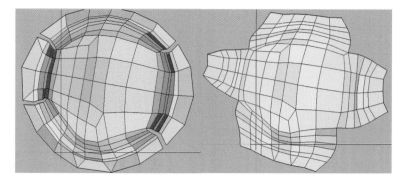

FIG 10.98

Press 1 to jump back to the UV view and then zoom into the top half of the kneecap UVs so that you can clearly see the details of each edge. With the mouse hovering over the relevant edges, press the C key a number of times to make cuts as shown above. Remember that the first cut you make must start from an open edge on the outside boundary of the shell; you cannot start your cuts from the middle of the shell. If you make a mistake, you can weld your cut edges back together by hovering over them and pressing the W key. With the mouse cursor hovering over the object, hold the spacebar again, and press F to unfold the object once more. It should be able to relax much better now with the new cuts, giving you a new relatively distortion-free unwrap.

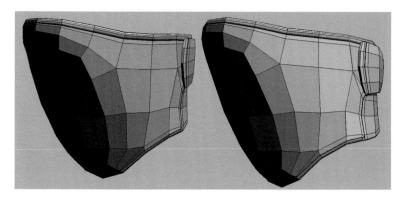

FIG 10.99

In Edit mode, the C and W keys have extended powers, in that they work well with loop-based topology—another great reason to model in clean quads as much as you can. As UV seams hinder our texturing, we must hide them away, thinking carefully about their placement before we draw them.

On character legs, the most unseen areas are the inside surfaces—they are normally hidden by the opposite leg. Go to the inside leg side of the "kneepad elastic" shape, and press the C key on one of the vertical edges. Your "cut" edge is marked in red. UVlayout will try to predict how you would like to continue the cuts along the loop with lines marked in yellow. If you disagree with any of these yellow lines, you can weld them back together with W. It takes only two or three clicks with C and you should have made enough cuts to unfold this area successfully.

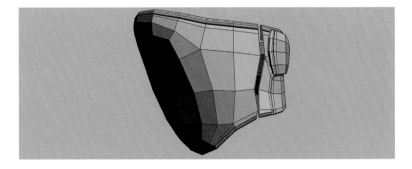

FIG 10.100

As we are dealing with a "closed" shape, before we drop the shell into UV space, we need to "split" the cut edges. Hold your mouse over the red and yellow edges that you wish to split and press Shift + S to use the Split Seams command. The edges should split apart like in the previous example.

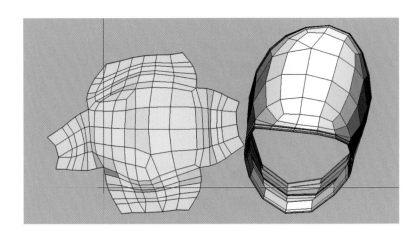

FIG 10.101

Now you can press D on this mesh to drop it into UV space, press 1 to go back
to the UV view, and then unflatten it as shown in Fig. 10.102.

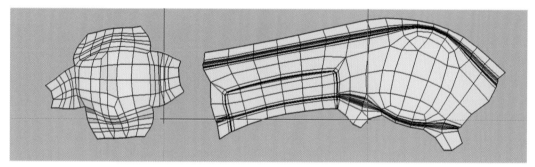

FIG 10.102

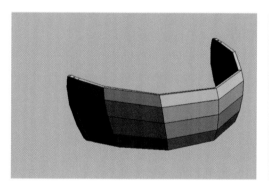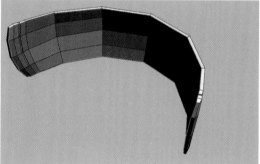

FIG 10.103

Press 2 to jump to Edit view, and you will see that there is now just the strap
which doesn't have UVs. Use the C key to make cuts until you have a closed
loop of cuts going around in a circle. As always, it is best to hide the seam
on the inside surface of the strap where it won't be seen clearly; you will
get an intuitive feel for where to place seams after spending plenty of time
unwrapping various objects.

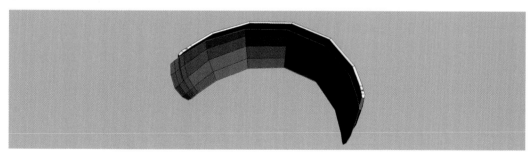

FIG 10.104

Again, press Shift + S to split the seams, and then press D to drop each piece into the UV mode. Press 1 to go back to UV view and unflatten each piece.

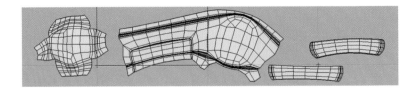

FIG 10.105

If you press W on a few of the shared edges of these two straps, you can see the matching edges turn red to indicate that it is possible to weld them back together. Press Return on one of these shells once you've marked some red weld lines and UVlayout will join them back together. Unflatten the shells again to finish and save your work.

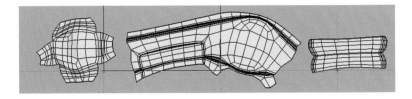

FIG 10.106

For anyone from the old school of UV unwrapping, UVlayout is nothing short of a revolution. It would take me days to unwrap a simple 1000-poly character in 3ds Max 3 with the Unwrap modifier; the same job now takes less than an hour, and I get much better results, too. UVlayout is incredibly powerful software, but I can't hope to cover all the cool features like pinning UVs, straightening UVs, and auto-packing UVs in this chapter. If you want an easy life with UVs, you would be wise to watch all the tutorial videos posted on the UVlayout Web site.

It's essential to unwrap our half-character *before* we mirror over our character; this precaution will make things go almost twice as fast. Once you are happy with your half-character unwrapped, you can add a Symmetry modifier to the mesh, collapse the stack, and then select and flip the UVs from one side to the other. It is then a simple job to weld the left and right halves together to get rid of any unnecessary seams. When arranging my UVs, I start with the largest shapes first; the smaller shapes will fit in the gaps once you have the main shapes in place. Try not to waste big areas of space in your UVlayout because in video games memory is critical and shouldn't be frittered away on half-empty maps.

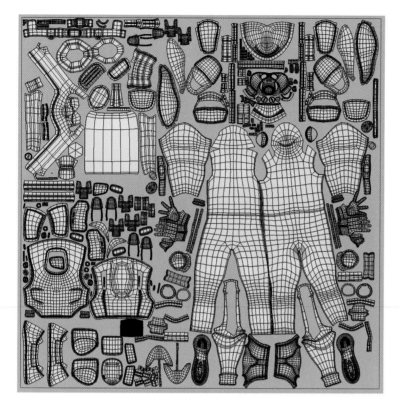

FIG 10.107

I like to lay out my UVs in a meaningful arrangement, with the head at the top and the feet at the bottom, arranged as if the character is looking straight at you. If you pass your work through a production pipeline, anyone who has to pick up your work and make some tweaks to the texture will thank you for making the texture layout as readable as possible.

The Asymmetrical Details: Making the Folds and Creases

It is now very common in professional modeling production pipelines for two or more apps to be used, as each application offers its unique advantages. More and more studios are turning to ZBrush to make the organic shapes that characterize the folds and creases that occur on clothing and anatomy. ZBrush can make the process of organic detailing quick and easy, but as this book focuses on 3ds Max, we are going to make the folds the old way: with SUBD surfaces. Traditional SUBDs take longer to produce, but one benefit will be the efficient use of polygons and system resources. Our 3ds Max clothing will be perhaps 10 times lighter (very high-poly assets are described as "heavy" in industry jargon) than a typical garment detailed in ZBrush, and it is good practice for making flowing SUBD geometry.

On the concept that I have been given, the creases are symmetrical—probably a measure taken by the concept artist to shave some hours off his or her busy schedule. Copying this symmetry into the 3D model is not good for realism, as the creases in all clothing are asymmetrical. Knowing when to follow the concept and when to correct it is very important. Keep a sharp, critical eye on your work so that the mistakes of the concept artist don't get transferred to your models.

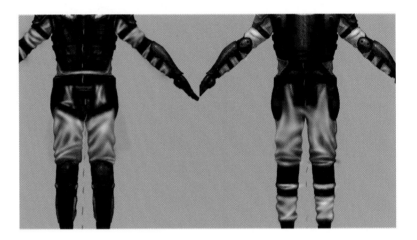

FIG 10.108

As the creases and folds of the fabrics can take a couple of days to model in SUBDs, I've sketched out a quick plan for my creases first. This way, if I don't like the flow of the creases, I can quickly amend them in minutes not hours.

Flow, Flow, Flow!

When modeling organic shapes like the creases, it is critical that each curve flows smoothly into the next; look for unnaturally straight lines and eliminate them. Use Relax to melt the polygons into each other. It makes sense to assign a hotkey to the Relax button, as you should constantly use it.

Take care that your creases don't all point in one direction; study some photos of people in clothing, and you will see the multilateral qualities that creases take on as they try to conform to the shape of the body.

If you use Relax multiple times and the geometry still looks jagged and awkward, the problem is probably your edge flow. Put your mesh in wireframe and adjust any areas where the edges don't run together in nice smooth lines.

Gravity, Tension, and the Feel of the Fabric

Be aware of gravity and how it affects your garments: baggy areas sag, but areas supported by the body remain firm. Imagining the body underneath the clothing is very important. Be aware that protruding parts of the body, belts, and straps pull on the fabric creating areas of tension. I keep lots of reference of the material that I'm modeling handy as I work to make sure that my model has the same look and feel as the fabric that I'm trying to mimic.

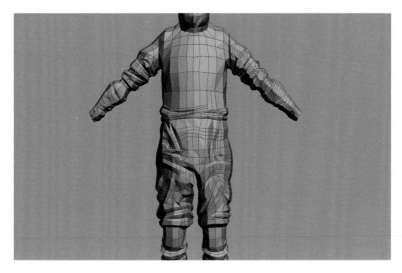

FIG 10.109

To start, just model in all the major creases of the body without too much care for the topology. Try to get the edge loops pointing in the same direction as the flow of the fabric for now—it should look something like Fig. 10.110. I have isolated the mesh for better system performance, but for many areas, it's important to view the rest of the character as you create an NBC suit so that you can really get the feeling of the suit material bunching up in areas where it is restricted by the pads and elastics straps on top of it.

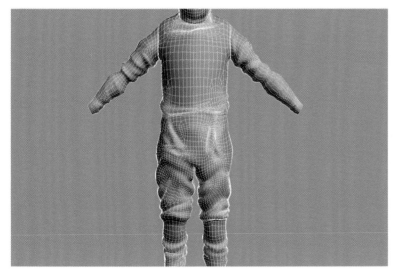

FIG 10.110

Once you have cut in the basic shape of each and every crease and fold, you can add additional details to refine each part. When all the details have been modeled in, it is just a matter of reflowing the topology to eliminate any awkward areas that don't look so smooth and natural. It is good to preview your suit all smoothed out with the TurboSmooth modifier at regular intervals so that you can see how it will look when it is finished.

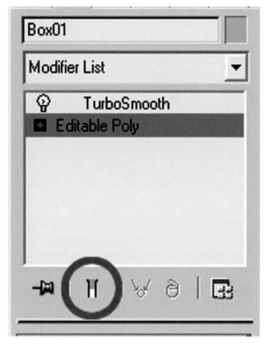

FIG 10.111

Bear in mind that although it is possible to model on the Editable Poly with the TurboSmooth showing further up the stack (using the Show End Result toggle), in the industry, it is generally considered bad practice. Meshes created in SUBD mode like this quickly get messy and tangled up, and they are very confusing to work with if you have to drop back down to the Edit Poly level to make a change. With SUBDs, experience is the best teacher; a few projects down the line, you will be able to accurately predict how your meshes will subdivide. Don't rely on TurboSmooth to create a smooth mesh for you—it's only as good as the base mesh that you feed into it.

Once you've finished adding all the creases, reflatten your NBC suit UVs in UVlayout and make any final tweaks to the layout. It's important to get the UVs as distortion-free as possible to make life easier when texturing.

The Ambient Occlusion Bake

Ambient occlusion (AO) maps are an industry-standard method of baking subtle lighting information into models. AO maps describe how exposed each part of the surface is: the cracks and gaps hidden away in cavities receive very little light and render in dark tones, and the flat, exposed surfaces render in light tones. An AO's soft, scattered light adds a great feeling of depth to your creations. I find it very useful when finishing off my model to render an AO map and apply it to the model. Rendering AO maps in 3ds Max is very simple:

- Apply a white Phong material to your character.
- Go to the Lights creation panel and select Skylight. Click to create a Skylight anywhere in the scene. The placement is not important; anywhere will do.
- Select Render > Advanced Lighting > Light Tracer. Be sure that the "Light Tracer Active" box is checked.
- With the character object selected, click Rendering > Render To Texture.
- Choose an output path for the AO map. Be sure that this render will use the Existing (UV) channel.
- Add a CompleteMap render element. Choose a map size of 2048 × 2048.
- Hit Render and watch as 3ds Max calculates the AO and renders it to a texture.
- Apply the newly created AO map to the diffuse map slot in the character's material and set the diffuse color to white.

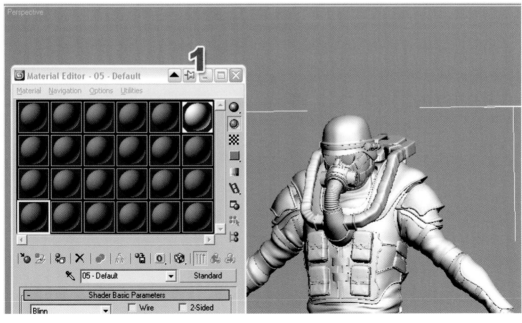

FIG 10.112

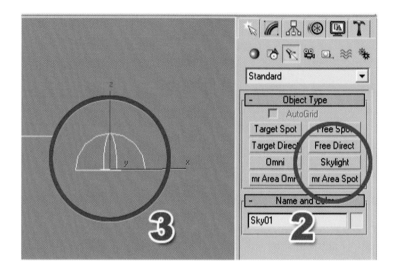

FIG 10.113

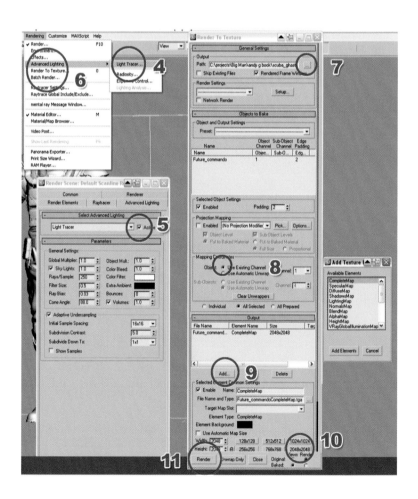

FIG 10.114

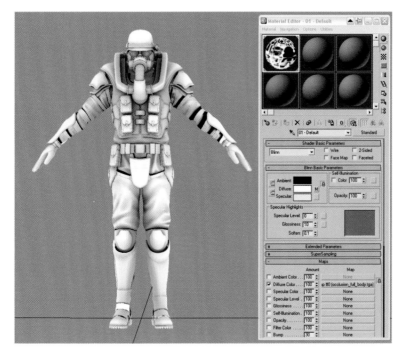

FIG 10.115

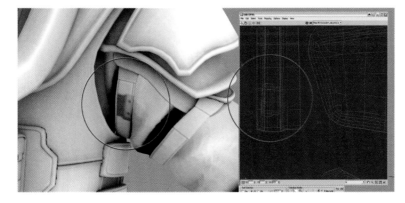

FIG 10.116

With AO applied to the model, it is a lot easier to see where all the overlapping geometry, holes, and other UV errors are occurring.

If you get areas that have rendered with weird-looking patterns on them, the chances are that you have overlapping UVs. Apply the Unwrap UVW modifier and make sure that all the UVs have their own space; get rid of all the overlapping UVs.

387

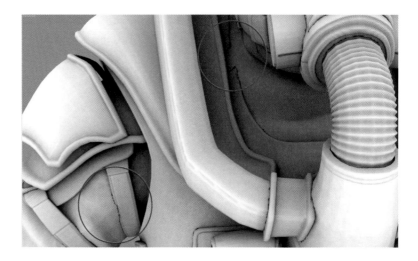

FIG 10.117

AO helps me a lot when fixing overlapping areas, as it really highlights anything that's not right. Have a quick look over your model to see if you have any problems with intersecting geometry.

Once you've fixed all these problems, you can render the ambient occlusion map again; if there are still problems, repeat the process until you are entirely happy with the model and the UVs.

Final Tweaks

So you think you've finished the modeling? I ask you to take another detailed look at your model—you will probably find some mistakes. Perhaps wait a day and come back to your work with fresh eyes. I know some artists who like to flip their work upside down or mirror it horizontally when reviewing their work, as this can give you a different perspective on that model you've been staring at it nonstop for more than three weeks! I like to squint my eyes when looking at the overall proportions, which blurs out the details and leaves me to focus on analyzing just the basic colors and shapes.

Art is subjective, and it is important to note that no artist is perfect; this is why getting other people's opinions of your work is very important. If you have no immediate group of peers, Internet forums can be an important place to get constructive criticism of your work. Good constructive criticism offers ideas for improvement of your work and does not dwell on the mistakes, apart from as a positive way of improving your work.

People make mistakes. This is why the work of companies is often (but not always) superior to the work of individuals, more eyes checking for mistakes—too many cooks don't always spoil the broth! Get opinions from your friends; maybe even your family can help you spot weak areas that need improvement. Everyone is an expert when it comes to looking at people and even your little sister might be able to spot something that you overlooked, like a nose that is too big or legs that are too small.

On my first check of the model, I noticed and fixed lots of little gaps between the objects and added the bumpy creases to the two breathing pipes leading to the mask. I also tweaked a few of the folds on the NBC suit to make them look more natural. On my second pass around the character, I moved the head back and the shoulders forward a little, as his head looked too far forward on the concept. To make the gloves look used, I added some creases and bumps to the gloves. On my third check of the character, I noticed a big gap under the shoulder pads, so I built some geometry to act as the inner padding.

The following figure shows the final high-resolution model.

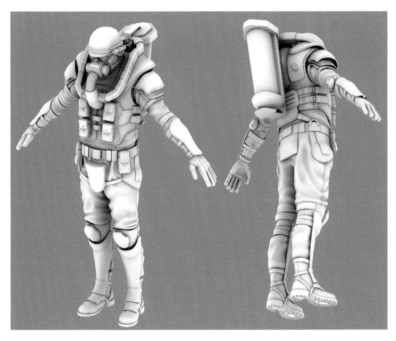

FIG 10.118

Texturing Eats Your RAM!

The texturing process can really put strains on your system, and in particular your RAM, which holds all the texture information in temporary memory. During the texturing process, I sometimes need to use from two to five applications at the same time, which can really stretch the multitasking capabilities of your machine to the limit. If you encounter long periods of down time as you swap applications or perform operations, you probably don't have enough RAM.

To compound the RAM problems during the texturing process, I will be working with a rather large 4 KB (4096 × 4096-pixel) PSD file, even though the final textures will be only 2 KB (2048 × 2048 pixels). Working like this with a higher resolution PSD file ensures that your final textures won't lose clarity after you have resized, warped, and liquefied them several times. Another advantage is that you can use the full 4 K maps for detailed close-up renders of your character—this will win you the dream job for sure!

I recommend a bare minimum of 2048 MB (2k) of RAM in your system, especially on the RAM-greedy Microsoft Windows Vista. There is really no such thing as too much RAM when working in the CGI industry. If you have problems, you could consider networking your desktop to another computer, like a laptop, which you could use beside your desktop computer to run Photoshop and create the textures, freeing up your main system's RAM for the demands of 3ds Max. If you really have problems with texturing on your system, you might want to halve the dimensions of all the textures I use during this chapter; this will make the texture size four times smaller. Instead of previewing my textures in large, uncompressed TIF format, as some people recommend, I prefer to use high-quality JPEGs to save on RAM.

Today's 32-bit operating systems like Windows XP Home Edition register a maximum of only 3.2 GB of RAM; any more than this is wasted, as the 32-bit OS will just ignore it. An emerging solution to your RAM woes is to use one of the new 64-bit operating systems like Vista 64 or XP 64, which theoretically work with up to 16 exabytes of RAM! That's more than enough for your needs.

Baking the Basic Colors

Let's get some colors on the model now. We could paint them on in Photoshop, but I prefer to apply the colors in 3ds Max and bake them onto the texture. Baking the colors is much faster and usually better quality as you don't have to do any fiddly paintwork in Photoshop. Painting the color texture by hand in Photoshop can be time consuming and problematic, as it can be hard to work out what's what in the confusing sprawl of UV shells. I find it much easier to apply the base colors if I assign them to different selections of polygons in 3D, where I can preview the results in real time. What really makes the baking method a winner is that each baked color will generate a coverage alpha channel, which we can use to quickly select and tweak different materials inside Photoshop.

I have identified 13 different materials on the character: gray steel, self-illuminated lights, black leather, dark gray Kevlar, elasticized straps, painted steel on the oxygen tank, black plastic, dark cloth, fire retardant piping, rubber-soled shoes, gray plastic mask, black rubber, and NBC suit.

Break up your model into 13 corresponding pieces using the Detach and Attach buttons in Edit Poly. Each object that you create should be assigned a different colored material. The colors are not important; we will throw them away later. I've used crazy colors just to help myself differentiate between the various types of surface.

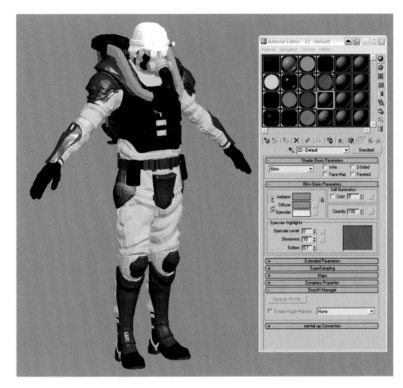

FIG 10.119

Once you are happy with the material groups, bake these different surfaces onto the texture using the Rendering, Render To Texture dialog. For each object, repeat this process:

- Choose the output path and give each file a descriptive name, such as Gray Steel.
- Be sure that "Use Existing Channel" is selected, as it would be a shame to waste those lovingly crafted UVs!
- Add a DiffuseMap output.
- Choose a 4096 × 4096 texture size (4k).
- Hit render.

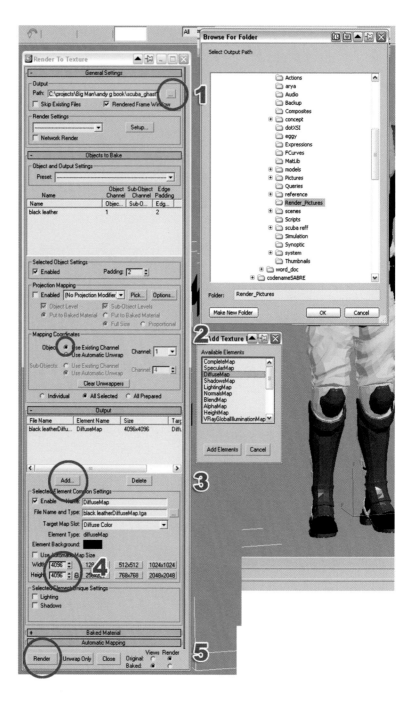

FIG 10.120

If you open up the black leather texture, it's just a black square because we rendered a black material onto a black background! Open up the Channels window, though, and go to the alpha channel to see that we have a map that describes perfectly which areas on our UV sheet are black leather.

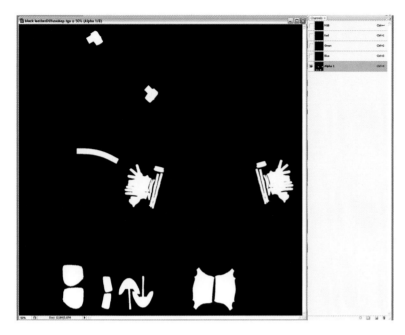

FIG 10.121

Let's make a new 4096 × 4096-pixel (4k) document to collect all these alpha channels together. Save the new document as Future_Commando_01.psd.

One by one, click on the alpha channel of each of your 14 material renders, copy it (Ctrl + C) and paste the channel (Ctrl + V) into a new channel in the Future_Commando_1.psd file. Once you have named each channel accordingly, you will have a collection of channels as shown in Fig. 10.122.

FIG 10.122

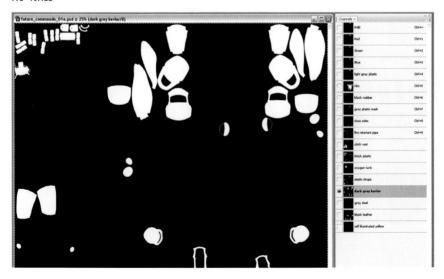

Click on the RGB channel at the top of the Channels window and open up the Layers window again. Let's make a new layer for the NBC suit. Select an off-white color and fill your new layer with this color.

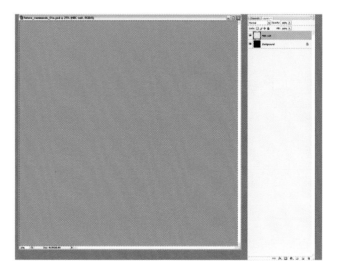

FIG 10.123

Masking Each Layer

Now comes the cool bit: go back to Channels and hold Ctrl as you click on the NBC suit channel to select all the white areas of the channel. Go back to the Layers window and click Create Mask.

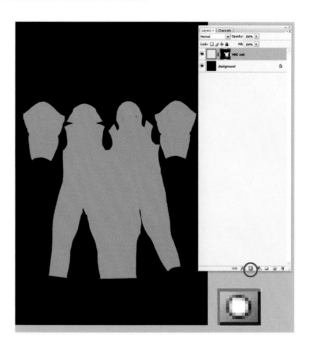

FIG 10.124

If you have done this correctly, the mask will hide the areas outside of the NBC suit UVs. The gray color of the NBC suit layer shows only where the mask is white; areas where the mask is black are transparent, so we can see the Background layer underneath.

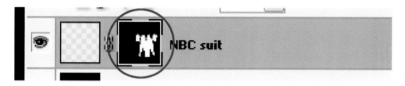

FIG 10.125

A black-and-white mask icon should have appeared in the NBC suit layer. If you hold Alt when you click this mask, it will be isolated so that you can see the mask clearly in black and white. To deisolate the mask, click on the eyeball icon (Layer visibility) of the NBC suit layer.

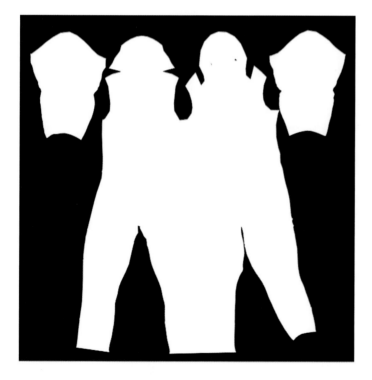

FIG 10.126

Masks and channels are the professional way to edit images in a nondestructive manner; if you want to make changes to something, it often makes more sense to do this with masks. If you don't like your mask, you can throw it away, keeping the original image intact.

As an advanced Photoshop user, it is imperative that you learn all the ins and outs of layers and masks. Masked layers have two thumbnail images instead of the usual one thumbnail. Click the thumbnail on the right to edit the mask, click the thumbnail on the left to return to editing the color layer. You can Ctrl + click on the mask to select all the areas that are white, which can be incredibly useful for making selections. Shift + click on the layer to toggle its effect on or off.

One by one, you can repeat the "fill new layer" with color and then apply the relevant mask process to each of the 13 different materials that we have a channel for. Try to avoid coloring things black or white, as there aren't many things that are truly black or truly white. It's better to settle for off-tones that are more realistic.

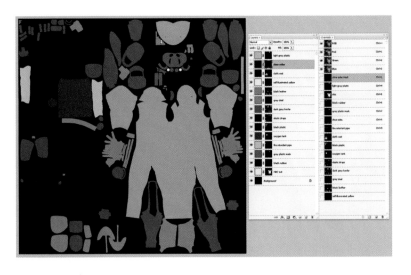

FIG 10.127

When all 13 materials have their own color layer and mask, the texture will look something like the previous figure. I don't like the color of the suit I've applied, but it's too dark, so let's tweak it with levels. Click on the NBC suit RGB color icon (the one to the left of the black-and-white icon) and press Ctrl + L to bring up the Levels command. Move the little triangles in the levels around to adjust the colors. This is a powerful way to make sweeping changes to your layers or selections.

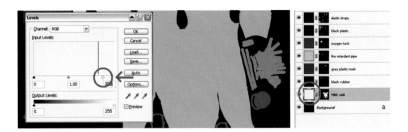

FIG 10.128

Open up the old AO map that we rendered earlier, go to Image > Image size, and convert it into a 4 k map, then press Ctrl + A to select all, Ctrl + C to copy it into memory, and Ctrl + W to close it. We now have the AO map at 4 k in our clipboard.

Select the top layer in your PSD and press Ctrl + V to paste in the AO map from the clipboard. Name the layer AO. With the AO layer selected, select the Multiply layer mode from the drop-down menu. The Multiply command takes the dark parts of an image and multiplies them with all the colors in the layers below, darkening them. Anything that is white in the Multiply layer is invisible and lighter shades have little effect.

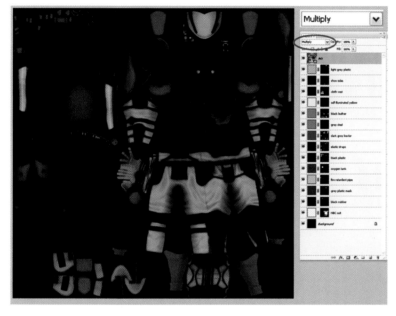

FIG 10.129

To preview the work-in-progress (WIP) in 3ds Max, save out a copy of the PSD as a JPG. Apply a new standard material to your model in 3ds Max and load the WIP jpg into the Diffuse color slot. I like to give the material 100% self-illumination so that I can see clearly every surface on the model—there is plenty of time for gloomy, atmospheric lighting later on. It's also good to raise the Specular Level to about 50; the specular highlights will help us to see some of the details of the surface.

If your colors are anything like mine, you probably made them all too dark, so go back to Photoshop and sort them out with the levels. Keep tweaking until you get something you are happy with. I've put the "Self-illuminated lights" layer above the AO to get the effect that it is lit from within.

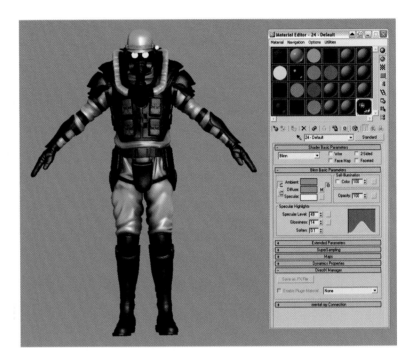

FIG 10.130

Once you are happy with the basic color layers that you just made, it is a good idea to merge them. We still have the channels if we want to make specific selections quickly, and merging all the layers will save us lots of RAM. Select all the layers apart from the AO and the self-illuminated yellow layer (for the eyes and torch), and press Ctrl + E to merge them together. When you have finished, it is a good idea to rename the Background layer: double-click the background layer and type in the name Base Colors.

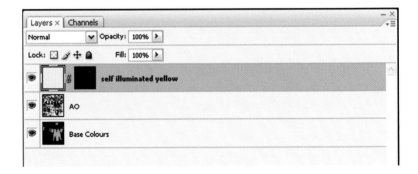

FIG 10.131

3D Paint Applications

When painting textures by hand, it is much more intuitive to use a 3D paint application—you are not faced with the problem of working out which areas in the UVs correspond to which areas in 3D space. 3D paint applications allow us to paint seamlessly across multiple seams, something that is nearly impossible when painting in 2D in Photoshop. Painting in 3D has another advantage in that if you have any distortion in your UVs (sometimes a little distortion is hard to avoid), the 3D paint application will automatically make predistortion adjustments to your 2D texture to compensate for the distortion. The results will look distorted in Photoshop but perfect in 3D— something that you could never do without the 3D paint application.

Bodypaint 3D is a good standalone 3D paint application, but I recommend the use of ZBrush for your 3D painting. ZBrush's ZAppLink feature allows it to plug straight into Photoshop for an unrivaled texturing workflow. Why learn the inferior painting tools of another application when we can use the already-familiar and industry-standard Photoshop tools?

Graphics Tablets

Trying to draw with a mouse is a bit like brushing your teeth with a toilet brush—it's not the ideal solution! Professional texture artists use graphics tablets (digital pens) for any demanding hand-drawn texturing. I recommend the use of the Intuos tablet by Wacom; the pressure sensitivity of pen is excellent.

Rendering the UV Template

If you do not have access to a good 3D painting package, you can render a UV template to help you with your painting in 2D in Photoshop.

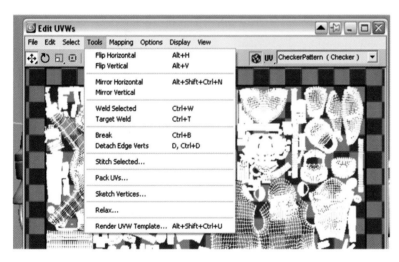

FIG 10.132

Add an Unwrap UVW modifier to your model, and click Edit to open up the Edit UVWs window > Tools ≥ Render UVW Template.

399

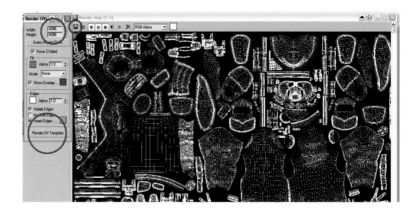

FIG 10.133

Select 4096 for the width and height and click Render UV Template. A Render Map window should appear with your UV co-ordinates nicely rendered; press the Save button (the disk icon) to save the image to a file. Open up this image in Photoshop, select all (Ctrl + A), copy it (Ctrl + C), and close it (Ctrl + W).

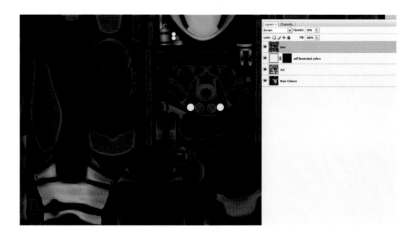

FIG 10.134

Click the top layer in your PSD and paste this image (Ctrl + V) at the top, renaming it "UVs." Put the layer into Screen mode to ignore the black areas. Now only the white areas should show through to lighten the layers below. You can turn on and off this layer as you require while painting your texture; sometimes, it is really useful for seeing the boundaries of the UVs. I often reduce the opacity of this "UVs" layer to something like 20%.

Painting the Dirt Map

Our character is looking pretty good now, but he lacks the small, real-world details that will really bring him to life. I almost always paint some kind of dirt map to give a more realistic look to our characters. If you study anything in the world around you, you will notice dirt and small imperfections on the surfaces of objects.

When creating a texture for a character, I try to imagine his or her history and lifestyle. What does the character do on an average day? Where has he or she been? Has your character been relaxing in a pristine palace all his or her life? Or bathing in mud? When treated with subtlety, the incidental effects will really bring your character to life—the eye of the viewer will pick up on these small details that give credibility to your digital creations.

Many companies specialize in producing photo libraries of dirty surfaces, available for royalty-free use in your textures, but they can be quite expensive. A cheaper solution is to take photos of dirty surfaces yourself. Go to your local industrial area, and you will find an area rich with grime. No one appreciates a good dirty surface quite like the 3D artist does!

Figure 10.135 is an example detail from one of my dirt images that I've collected, before I cleaned it up and adjusted the levels. I like to photograph smooth white surfaces, as it makes it very easy to get just the dirt without any other surface features that will need to be removed to isolate the dirt. Get as many different types of mud, grease, and dust as you can; the more images you have in your library, the more variation you will be able to include on your characters' dirt maps.

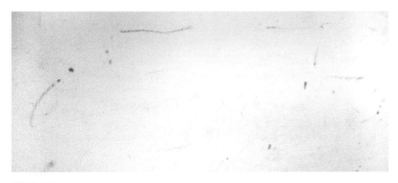

FIG 10.135

I like to paint on the dirt generously to start with, working fast and rough and not caring too much about any specific details. I mix manipulated dirt images from my photo library with hand-painted dirt using the Paint Brush and Burn tools. Next, I go around the model and clean off the dirt with a white paintbrush in the most exposed areas. If an area looks unrealistic, I will give it a heavy blur, paint in more detail, blur a little more, and then add more detail again. It is this iterative process that helps me to build up a history of past incidents on the surface of the character.

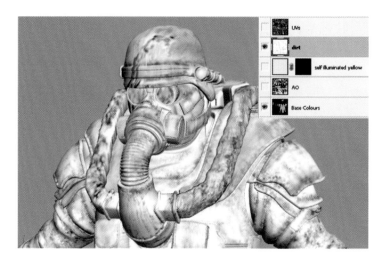

FIG 10.136

Painting your dirt in a 3D application will really make it come alive, as you can see very clearly which parts might not get cleaned as easily and which areas might get cleaned on a more regular basis. Remember that weathering, friction, and collisions will remove the dirt from the most exposed areas, leaving behind the dirt that is protected in the cavities.

If you change the dirt layer to Multiply mode, you will see the dirt on top of the Base Colors and AO layers. If you want a quick and dirty effect, sometimes this is enough, but this technique produces dirt that is only monochrome because of the limitations of Multiply mode. The multiplied dirt layer does not show up very well on any of the darker fabrics, as dark × dark = very, very dark. Dirt usually makes dark objects lighter, so it's a better idea to use another image to create a muddy color and use our dirt map to mask it.

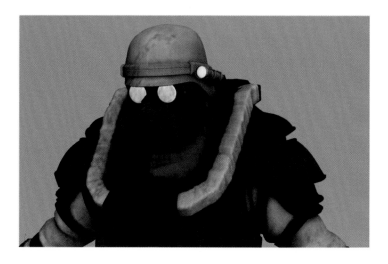

FIG 10.137

Figure 10.138 is a photo that I took of a muddy area of a field; I've used the Rubber Stamp tool to repeat the texture across the surface. This will make a good color for our dirt.

FIG 10.138

To apply our B&W dirt map as a mask to this muddy layer, select the original B&W dirt layer, select it all (Ctrl + A), copy it to the clipboard (Ctrl + C), and then delete the layer. Create a new mask on the color muddy field layer, Alt 1 click the mask to isolate it, and paste (Ctrl + V) in the B&W image from the clipboard. With the mask still selected, invert it (press Ctrl + I) because it is the wrong way around.

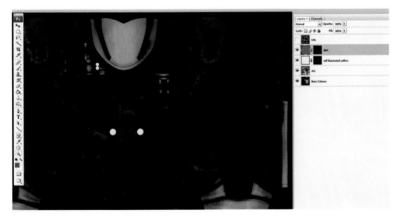

FIG 10.139

Here I've reduced the opacity of this layer to 40%. Subtlety is the key to getting it right, as we don't want the guy caked in mud, but his costume must look like it has been used in a real-life combat situation. We can make certain parts more or less muddy by selecting those areas of the mask with our channels and applying a levels adjustment. I've deliberately understated the dirt here a little because later we will apply the dirt to the specular map, too, to strengthen the dirt effect. In some areas, I have blurred the muddy colors of the layer to get an ingrained, old dirt look, and I have left other areas of the layer quite sharp to get a new mud feel.

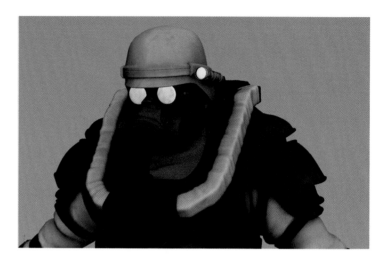

FIG 10.140

Painting the Scratch Map

In the real world, things get scratched in everyday use—especially on the battlefield! On a new white layer, I've painted black scratches; again I've used a 3D paint application to help me get the scratches placed well, with the heaviest ones on the most exposed edges. Like the dirt map, I paint super quick and rough to start with and as I do so I try to imagine how the scratches came about. Maybe the scratches on the helmet came from a fall, so they all go in one direction, maybe scratches on the Kevlar forearm pad have built up over time, so they all point in unique directions. Don't just paint dumb! Think as you paint.

Fabrics don't often scratch sharply like hard surfaces do, so let's blur them out a little.

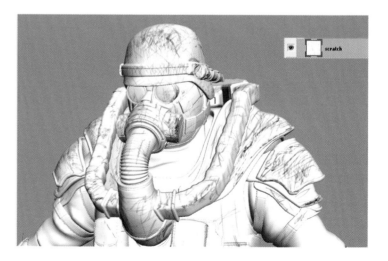

FIG 10.141

Select all the areas where there are soft fabric materials by holding Shift and Ctrl while clicking each of the relevant fabric channels one by one to add them to your selection. Now select Filter > Blur > Gaussian Blur and give these areas a moderate amount of blur. To add more realism, add a mask to the scratch layer and paste in a copy of the AO map, which has the effect of removing the scratches from occluded areas. This newly AO masked scratch layer works well, but we must flatten it so we can use it in another mask—the complexity increases! Add a pure white scratch background layer below the scratch map, select the two layers together, and then merge them (Ctrl + E). Now select and copy the contents of this new merged layer to your clipboard for use in the next step.

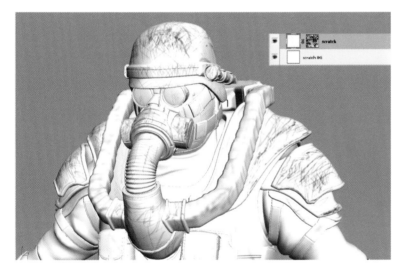

FIG 10.142

Layered Scratch Masks

Many surfaces, such as the gas tanks, have been painted, and they will reveal their underlying materials in areas where they have been scratched. Let's create this layered effect by duplicating the Base Colors layer (right-click on the layer and choose Duplicate). Name the top layer Base Colors and the layer underneath Under Colors. Paste the contents of your clipboard (the merged scratch map from the last section) into a new mask applied to the Base Colors layer.

Now we can paint in the Under Colors layer to create our underlying material colors. The gas tank should reveal bare metal under the paintwork where it has been scratched, so paint a gray color here. Other metals will typically get lighter where they have been scratched, so just lighten those areas. Some plastic areas might be darker where they have scratched and something has created dirt-filled cavities.

405

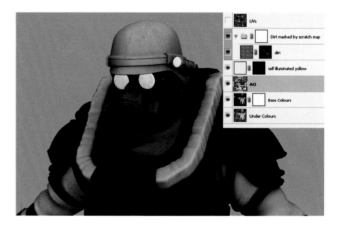

FIG 10.143

If you export the WIP color map to 3ds Max, it should be easier to see how the colors underneath are shaping up. You can use the channel selections to select specific areas and make sweeping changes to many under-colors at the same time. I have also used the Levels command on the scratch mask itself to tone down the effect a little.

For additional realism, let's remove the dirt from the scratched areas, as it would often be removed by friction as the scratches occurred. I have put the dirt layer in a new folder (group) and masked this new folder with a copy of the scratch mask from the Base Colors layer. Nesting masked folders inside folders is incredibly powerful, but can quickly get confusing! Our scratch map will really come alive later, when we can use the specular map to make the scratched areas shinier.

Painting the High-Frequency Detail Layers

Next let's paint the high-frequency (HF) details—the things that crop up again and again across the surface (e.g., skin pores, the pattern of the sole of the shoe, the ribbed pattern on the belt, and so on). Details on this small of a scale are much easier to create using texturing rather than modeling.

I like to create the HF details as black-and-white maps; this means that later we can easily pop out these details in the normal map.

The first step is to gather high-resolution images of each fabric type we will use. Many of the surface types, like the rubber and the plastic, are smooth surfaces that don't require HF detail maps, but we will need images to make the microbumps of the leather, elastic, cloth, NBC suit, and the fire-resistant material on the piping. Like with the dirt, I keep a library of photos of different fabrics; you can buy disks full of fabric textures from the Internet, but I sometimes find it quicker and cheaper to source my own from around the house and quickly take photos/scans of them. Like most reference material you use in your textures, it is much better if it is shot in diffused lighting conditions with no harsh lighting, shadows, or hard contrasts.

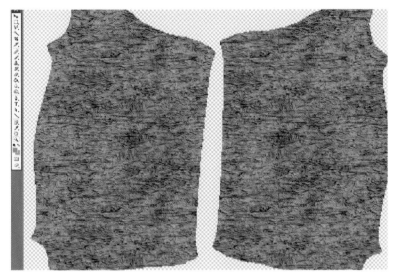

FIG 10.144

Adjust the maps so that they look similar to how the AO map would look if we had actually modeled every HF microcavity in to the surface of the object. Black represents the lowest areas, and white represents the highest points that are more exposed to the light. Figure 10.146 shows my HF detail layer, which describes the creased, wrinkly texture of the leather.

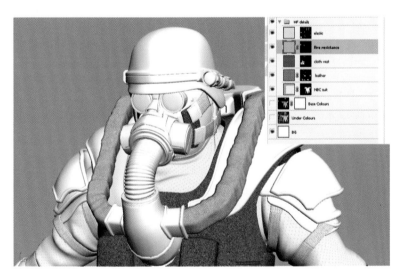

FIG 10.145

Each type of surface should tile to completely fill its own HF detail layer; to keep things tidy, put all the layers in a folder called "HF details." We can use the channels we saved earlier to quickly create a mask for each layer, Ctrl + click the relevant channel to select the areas it masks, and then back in the Layers palette, you can click the "Create mask" icon to quickly mask the active layer with your selection.

Set each of the HF detail layers to multiply, so they have a similar effect to how our AO layer works, darkening the occluded areas.

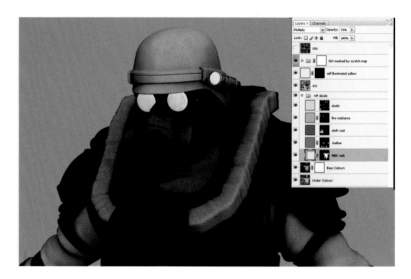

FIG 10.146

Normal and Specular Maps

Let's add another layer of realism to our creation using Normal and Specular maps. Normal maps are used to fool the eye into thinking that there is much more detail than there actually is modeled into the character. They work in a similar way to bump maps, by cheating in the details. Specular maps control how shiny the surface is in different areas: white pixels make the metal look shiny and the black pixels make the dirt look totally matte.

We can see the effects of the normal and specular maps in real time in the viewport if we use a special DirectX shader written by Ben Cloward.

If you visit www.bencloward.com/resources_shaders.shtml, you can see that Ben has created a wealth of different shaders that you can use in the 3ds Max viewport to simulate various surface effects. Read all about these shaders here: www.bencloward.com/shaders_NormalMapSpecular3lights.shtml. He has kindly allowed us to include the "Normal Map Specular Shader—3 Lights" shader on the book DVD. Find Ben's shaders on the DVD ROM here: \Chapter10\3ds Max Files for chapters\10_highres_mesh_textured\directx_ shaders and copy them to somewhere easily accessible on your hard drive. Before we set up the shader, we need to use Photoshop to make some quick, temporary normal and specular maps to plug into the shader.

To make a temporary normal map, use the Paint Bucket tool to fill a new 4 k image with RGB color 127,127,255. This purple/blue tone has the effect of perfect flatness in normal maps; it's the normal map's equivalent of black or zero—it has no effect. Save this as something like Future_Commando_Normals.jpg.

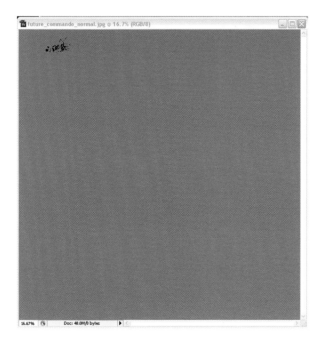

FIG 10.147

To create a temporary specular map, let's use the Paint Bucket tool to fill a new 4 k image with RGB color: 127,127,127. This is a good medium gray color for a moderate level of shininess. Save the image as something like Future_Commando_Specular.jpg.

FIG 10.148

Now we have a color and a normal and a specular map. Let's set up the DirectX shader. In 3ds Max, apply a new material to the character model, and then click on the Standard button in the Material Editor to select a DirectX type of material.

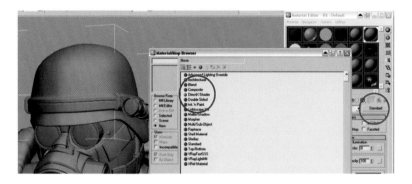

FIG 10.149

Click the top-left box in the DirectX Shader Panel, the one with the long path name in it. This box loads a specific DirectX (.FX) shader onto your material. Browse to the folder to which you copied Ben's shaders and select the one named HLSLnormal_map_specular_3lights_world.fx.

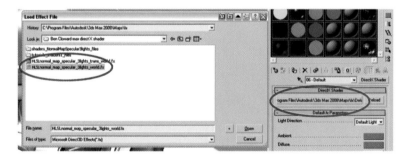

FIG 10.150

Now Ben's shader is applied to your character. Most likely, the model will turn black, as the maps are not loaded in yet. Click on the slots next to Diffuse Texture, Specular Texture, and Normal Map, and load in the relevant maps.

Once you have loaded the three maps into the relevant slots, you should see the shader displaying correctly. The normal and specular maps are just filled with temporary, basic colors, so we are not really getting the benefit from this shader yet. The default settings use the 3ds Max Default Light, but it is better if you make three omni lights that surround the character and load each one into the Light Position slots, as explained below.

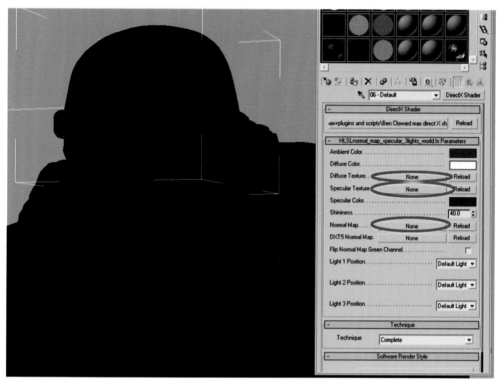

FIG 10.151

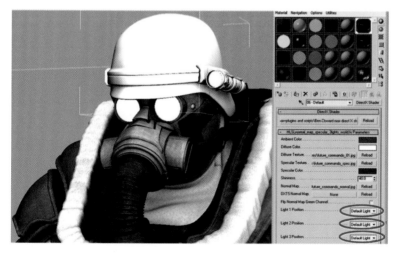

FIG 10.152

Using Create > Lights > Standard Lights > Omni, make one Key light that has an intensity of around 1 and is positioned at the front of the character, but a little to one side. At the other side, make a Fill light with an intensity of about 0.5, and at the back a Rim light with an intensity of around 0.5, too.

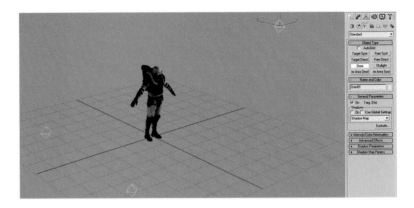

FIG 10.153

You can tweak the light settings to your own preferences; it's all just to help you see what is going on with the normal mapping later on. You can even animate the intensity and positions of the lights so that you can play the time line to see the character in different lighting conditions.

Normal Mapping the High-Frequency Details

We can really give the HF details much more punch if we pop them out using a normal map. As it is just a texture-mapping effect, this illusion breaks down when viewed up close, especially when seen at angles perpendicular to the viewing angle where it is obvious that the details are not truly 3D. Normal mapping does not work well as a replacement for modeling the larger geometry, as it does not affect the silhouette of the shape in the way that modeling does.

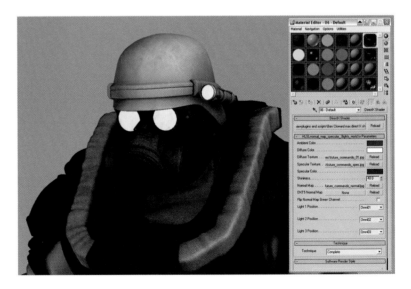

FIG 10.154

To follow my style of normal mapping, you will need to install the NVIDIA Normal Map Filter for Photoshop, which is available for free download from here: http://developer.nvidia.com/object/photoshop_dds_plugins.html.

One by one, feed the contents of each of the HF detail layers to the Normal Map Filter. The Normal Map Filter does not work on PSDs with more than one layer, so one at a time, copy the contents of each HF detail layer and paste each one into a new document, being sure to flatten each image down to just one background layer.

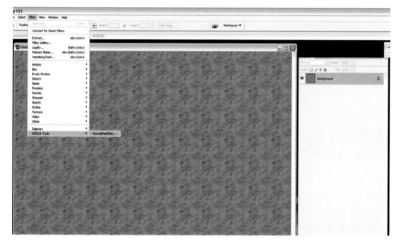

FIG 10.155

With one of your temporary, one-layer HF detail documents selected, choose Filter > NVIDIA Tools > NormalMapFilter to bring up the options for our normal map.

Although there are lots of options here, all you really need to do is type different numbers into the Scale Box. The Scale setting describes how powerful the effect of the bumpiness of the surface is. I find that 6 works well for me most of the time. You can also press the 3D Preview button if you want to see how your normal map will look in real-time 3D. Press OK to create your normal map.

Create a new PSD file called Future_Commando_01.psd and one by one, paste in the normal maps that you have generated for each HF detail layer.

To blend all these maps together, copy over the masks from the original HF detail layers in the color PSD (Future_Commando_01.psd). Your Future_Commando_Normals_psd should look something like the Fig. 10.157. I've zoomed in to 300% to show the details. I like to add a little note for myself on the name of each layer: L3 means that I generated the map with a scale of 3, L6 a scale of 6, and so on. These notes will help us if we decide to tweak the strength of each one later on.

413

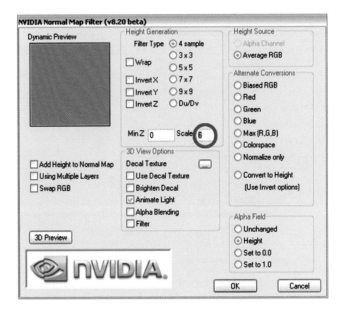

FIG 10.156

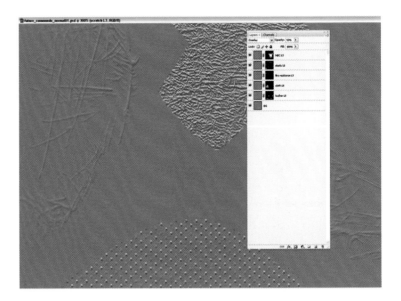

FIG 10.157

In the normal map PSD document, select "Save As" and overwrite the temporary Future_Commando_Normals.jpg map that we made earlier. If you go back to 3ds Max now, the new map should have automatically loaded into the material and the normal map should be displaying nicely now. You should export your normal map to 3ds Max frequently as you work because reviewing the normal map applied to the character in 3ds Max is much easier than staring at a bunch of blue colors in Photoshop.

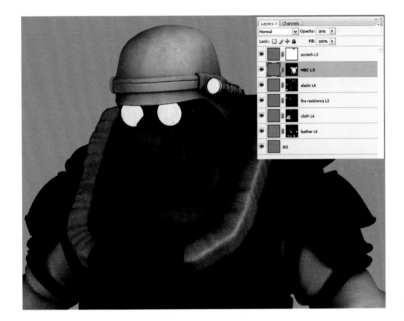

FIG 10.158

In the previous figure, I've decided that the NBC suit material is too bumpy, so I've toned that down by changing the opacity of the NBC L3 layer to 6%. I've also gone back to the color PSD and made his vest a little bit lighter.

Adding More Small Details

Before we finish the texturing with the specular map, there are a few finishing touches to add to the color and normal maps. As these details are all very flat, we won't be generating normal maps from them, so they can all be painted on the Base Colors layer.

The Danger Label on the Gas Tank

I drew the shapes for the Danger label using the Rectangle and Polygon Selection tools, using the Brush tool to fill the selections with color and the Edit > Stroke command to outline them where needed. I used the Text tool to create the typography, and then merged everything down onto the Base Colors layer, making sure to preserve the (scratch) mask. Be sure to make the yellow tones a slightly desaturated yellow; in the real world, most things are not completely saturated with color, but usually faded from weathering.

Metal Textures

At the moment, your metal areas are probably looking a little flat and boring; better that we give them an interesting texture. To build up the texture, use Filter > Add Noise, and then Filter > Blur > Gaussian Blur a number of times, entering smaller numbers into the Size parameter on each iteration.

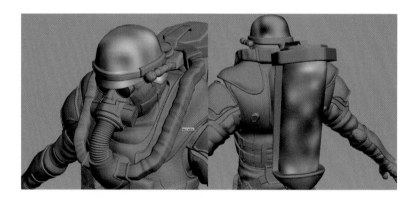

FIG 10.159

Glowing Bulbs

If we were working on a character for a feature film that would be viewed close-up, I would probably model the inner workings of the glowing eye and torch, and add some cool render effects. However, as this texture will eventually need to be baked down onto a 1-k game mesh, it is probably too much work on this project to get bogged down in this level of detail. In production, you have to draw a line somewhere on the level of detail or you will make too much work for yourself and miss your deadlines.

I drew the glowing torch and eye lenses by hand using the Brush tool, and then overlaid a grid image in Color Burn mode. When I was happy with these layers, I merged them together onto the self-illuminated yellow layer to save a little RAM.

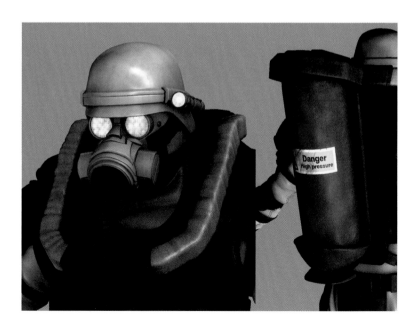

FIG 10.160

Microbumps Layer

Many surfaces are not as perfectly smooth and flat as you might assume. Accidents, daily use, weathering, factory defects, and warping caused by sun exposure all lead to small imperfections on surfaces.

To create this effect of less-than-perfect surfaces, let's paint another black-and-white map that we can feed into the NVIDIA Normal Map Filter. Starting with a mid-gray background, you can use the Burn tool to darken areas that you would like to push down in the normal map. If you hold Alt when using the Burn tool, it will dodge instead, lightening the areas, and thus raising them in the normal map. You can paint these micro bump dings onto the helmet, gas tank, shoes, and anywhere else where you'd like to make the surface less regular. Generate a normal map from this black-and-white image using the NVIDIA filter and place it in the top layer in the normals.psd. If you put this microbumps layer into Overlay mode, it will blend over the top of the existing normal map layers.

The High-Resolution Specular Textures

Creating the specular map is fairly straightforward; for the most part, we will use already-existing elements from the color PSD. We will create a number of new "Specular" layers that we can turn on to convert our color PSD texture into a specular map.

The adjustment layers (icon shown in Fig. 10.161), which are found at the bottom of the Layers window, are great for making nondestructive changes. Adjustment layers can be turned on and off and masked, and if you don't like them, you can just delete them to return to how things were before.

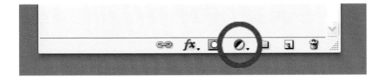

FIG 10.161

Select the top layer in your PSD (probably the UVs layer), click the "Create new fill or adjustment layer" icon, and Select Hue/Saturation. Drag the Saturation control down to −100 to totally desaturate everything underneath this adjustment layer and press the OK button. Right-click on the new adjustment layers mask and choose "Delete layer mask"; this step will save a little of our precious RAM, as we don't need the mask. Now give the layer a meaningful name, like "Specular Desaturator."

Create a new layer above the Base Colors layer called "Specular Colors." One at a time, select each channel that we saved earlier and fill that selection with a color. Fill Specular Colors with black for nonreflective (specular is just a

417

cheated reflection, really) things like cloth. Fill Specular Colors with medium gray for things that have a moderate amount of shininess, like the NBC suit and plastics, and fill it with white for very shiny things like metal. This layer should completely block out any layers below it.

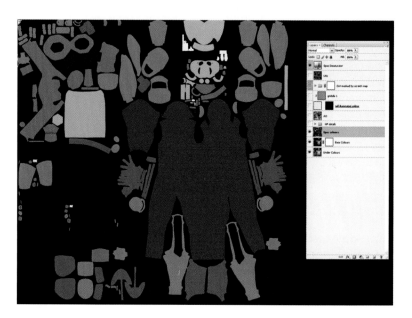

FIG 10.162

My aim when creating the specular map is to break up the highlights; the specular map is where I concentrate the majority of the grime and dirt in the textures. As I've mentioned earlier, if you look at even the newest objects around you, you will notice that the reflections on their surfaces are broken up by imperfections, fingerprints, dirt, and scratches.

Let's improve our specular texture by making the dirty areas less shiny and the scratched areas shinier. Copy the dirt and scratch masks that we made earlier and paste duplicates of them at the top of the Layers window next to the Specular Desaturator layer. Name them "Specular–dirt is darker" and "Specular–scratches are lighter," respectively. Now if you put the "Specular–dirt is darker" layer into Multiply mode, it will make all the dirty areas not shiny; if you put the "Specular–scratches are lighter" layer into Screen mode, it will make all the scratched areas shinier. (You might need to invert it, too.) I also adjusted the levels of these maps to amplify their effects.

Right-click on all the new specular layers one at a time, selecting Layer Properties and applying a gray color. It will now be easy to identify which layers are for the specular map, an ability that will reduce user errors when we toggle our PSD between color and specular modes. If you use Save As and save this image over the temporary Future_Commando_Specular.jpg texture, you can check the new specular map in 3ds Max.

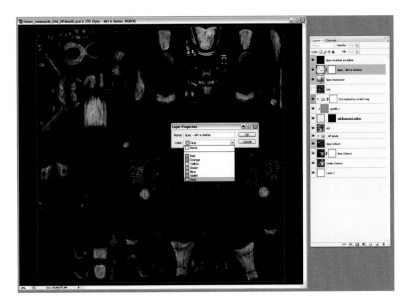

FIG 10.163

In the DirectX shader, make sure that the Specular Color is set to white, so you can accurately tweak your specular map. It's now just a matter of tweaking the three textures to your taste. When you are finished, you can re-export the textures in TIF format to increase the quality.

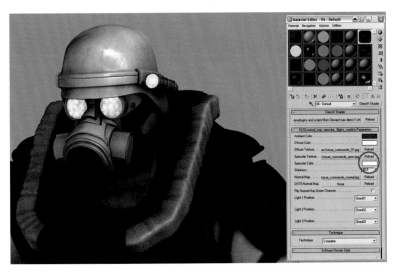

FIG 10.164

The Gun

After a discussion with the team, it was decided that an over-the-top, multifunction gun would best suit the battlefield needs of our soldier. As we didn't have a concept image for the gun, I blended together elements from several existing weapons into one design, mixing together a flamethrower and a chain-gun. It had to be big, as we didn't want our soldier to feel inadequate on the battlefield! The weapon required additional fuel tanks to be fitted to the existing gas tank to supply the flamethrower with fuel. As these are detachable items, the gas tanks and the weapon both have their own separate texture sheets.

In-Game Mesh Modeling

For our game mesh, we have been allocated a polygon budget of 12,000 triangles. This is a reasonable amount for a prominent game character for a first-person shooter on the Xbox 360 or the Playstation 3. Background characters that don't receive all the limelight might get only 2000–5000 triangles, but lead characters that are designed for talking in close-up shots might get 15,000 or more polys.

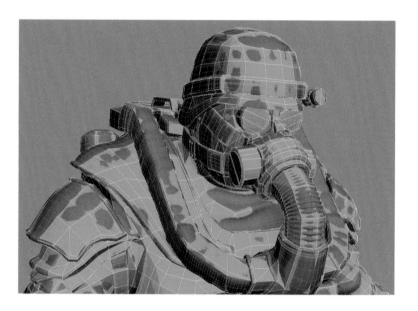

FIG 10.165

Earlier, during the modeling of our high-resolution mesh, we wisely saved a copy of our work-in-progress proxy mesh when it was around 6000–7000 triangles (for half the mesh). This basic, approximate form will make an excellent starting point for our game mesh. If we load up this old .OBJ mesh (File > Import), it should fit perfectly over the top of our high-resolution character. Add the Symmetry modifier and give this proxy mesh a green material with opacity of 50% so that we can clearly see the high-resolution mesh underneath it.

Using all the familiar Edit Poly tools, we now need to optimize this mesh for use in videogames, aiming to get the half game mesh to around 6000 triangles. The core idea when creating real-time assets such as this is that each triangle/polygon is precious. If we can reduce polygons in one area without any detrimental effect, we can spend these elsewhere in the model to improve the overall appearance. Ideally, we can keep a clean, quad-based topology, but a few triangles here and there are fine.

The way I construct my game meshes owes much to my previous experience with using normal maps. Normal maps are great at representing the many small details, but they are very poor when used to fake the larger features, which should always be modeled in. Sometimes, we can delete many polygons from a relatively flat area and let the normal map do the work instead, without the surface looking much different.

I spend lots of polygons on creating a detailed silhouette because only geometry can give us a detailed and interesting profile. Sometimes I change the material so that it has 100% self-illumination, which makes it easy to focus on just the silhouette. View your game-mesh model from every angle and see whether its silhouette looks correct. If you press F4 to toggle edged faces, you can see whether there are areas with lots of polygons that are contributing very little to the silhouette, and then track them down and delete them.

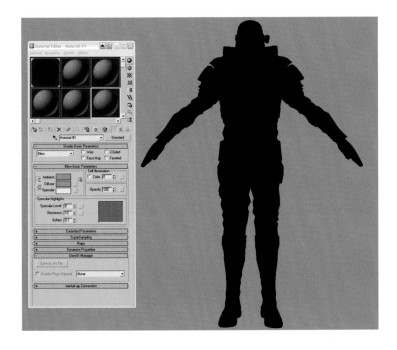

FIG 10.166

Typically, an in-game character will be rigged and animated through a wide range of poses, so we must take care that the geometry we build around areas that bend (knees, elbows, shoulder, wrist, and so on) has enough detail to support a full range of movement. The best way to get a feeling for this is to rig your own meshes and test-animate the rigs so you can experience firsthand exactly where geometry is needed and where you can scrimp on it.

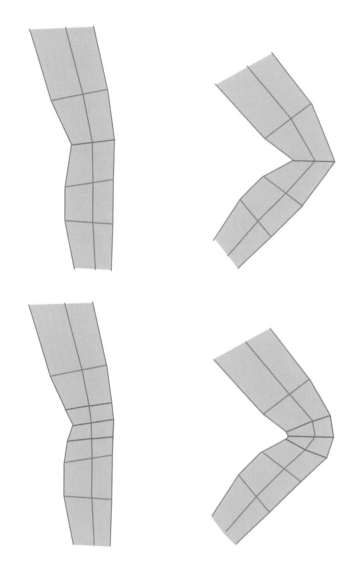

FIG 10.167

FIG 10.168

One edge loop on a joint is often not enough once you start animating the character.

When in doubt, a good rule of thumb is to have at least three edge loops around each joint to allow for correct deformation during animation.

Modeling for games sometimes involves using some low-down dirty tricks! Knowing when you can pull these off and when to do things the proper way is an art form in itself. Some people might tell you to make sure that all areas of your mesh are welded together. Granted, this approach works better in some situations, but we can save lots of polys in some areas if we disregard this advice. Andy Gahan showed me the following trick when I first started to work on PS2 games, but it's as relevant as ever for the current generation of games.

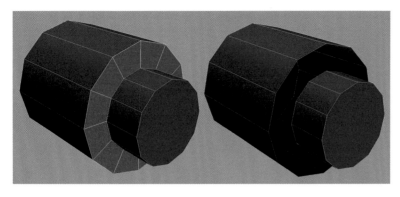

FIG 10.169

As an example, take a typical cylindrical object with some beveled detail like the one in the following figure. The highlighted polygons here contain 24 triangles; let's delete them.

Select two opposite edges and use Edit Polys Bridge command to join them together; repeat the Bridge operation for each set of opposite edges.

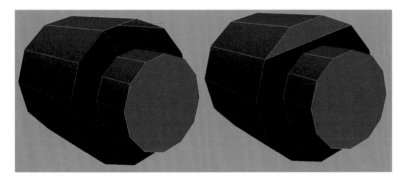

FIG 10.170

Now we have two overlapping shapes rather than one whole mesh. The new polygons we have added contain only 10 triangles, a savings of almost 60%!

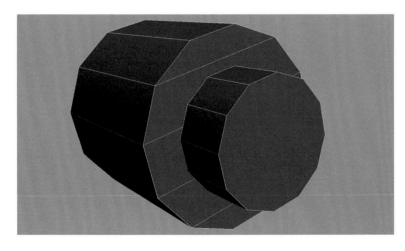

FIG 10.171

423

If we use this trick on the ends of each cylinder on the gas tank valves, we can make substantial savings. Here I saved 30 triangles by deleting the old welded ploys and replacing them with new bridged edges. There is a gas tank valve on each side of the character, so this is a total savings of 60 triangles. Look for other areas to perform this trick and save additional polys that we can use to improve the detail in complex areas, such as the creases and folds of the NBC suit.

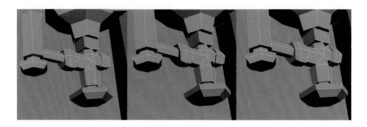

FIG 10.172

You should avoid the use of this trick in certain deformable areas, as the open edges may get exposed during animation. The only way to get a good feeling for how far you can push this is to get firsthand experience with rigging and animating game meshes.

When finishing off the model, I like to turn on the Edged Faces in the viewport and squint my eyes at it so I get just a hazy general impression of the mesh topology. This makes it easier to see areas where the polygons are denser and areas that are relatively sparse. Unless there is a special reason (animation, silhouette, or mapping), all the meshes should have similar levels of detail. Sometimes I rob from the rich to give to the poor, taking polygons away from areas that don't need them.

Many games give a bias to the head when it comes to detail. The viewer's eye naturally focuses here, so it is worth spending a bit more of your budget here. Some games feature the characters up close in animated dialog shots, so they are built with lots of detail in the face, designed to smoothly morph between different emotions and mouth shapes.

In-Game Mesh UVing

Like the high-resolution mesh, it's good to UV the half game mesh before you mirror it. You should try to minimize the number of UV shells. The fewer shells, the fewer seams, so join them together whenever possible.

When you have the Unwrap UVW modifier applied to your object, the seams show up as bright green lines. I try to hide the UV seams in areas that won't be seen easily, like the inside of the legs or the inside of the arms. Better still, I line up the seams with areas where there are already fabric seams in the high-resolution mesh (the areas where the garments are stitched together or the intersection between two different surfaces).

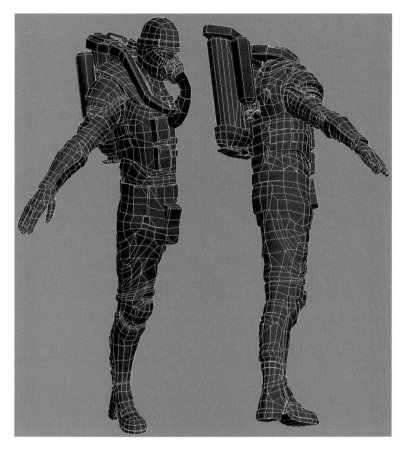

FIG 10.173

It's worth noting that sometimes developers give a bias to the UVs of the head and the eyes; that is, they make them larger to fit in more detail. But as our character is intended for a fast-paced arcade game with few dialog scenes, this won't be necessary.

Once you're happy with the UV seams, add a Symmetry modifier and collapse the stack into an Editable Poly to create the full mesh.

Now that we have the whole mesh, we can create the creases and folds that are unique to the left-hand side of the NBC suit. It is also possible to save some more polys by deleting any edges on the line of symmetry that aren't contributing to the character's form. Once you have finished modeling, select the new half of the mesh and horizontally flip the UVs. In UVlayout, it is now straightforward to complete the UVs by welding all the seams that run up the center line and reflattening all the pieces. In the previous figure, I have cut off the codpiece as a separate UV shell to avoid having a seam that runs down the line of symmetry. As always, remember to pack your UV shells as tightly as possible.

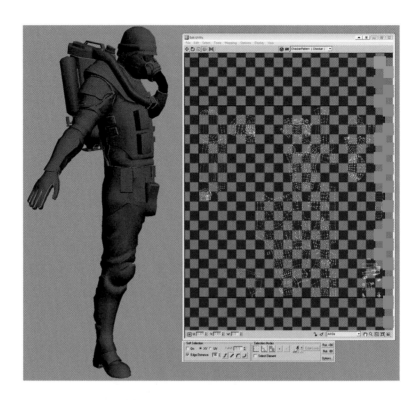

FIG 10.174

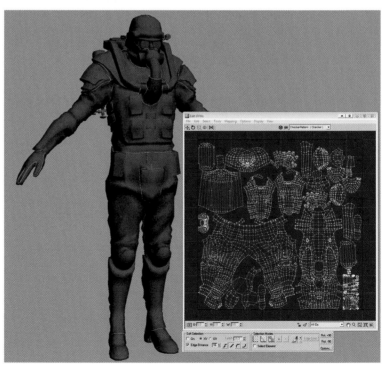

FIG 10.175

Baking Down the High-Resolution Details

To produce the highest quality meshes for Playstation 3 and Xbox 360 games, the colors and details of the high-resolution mesh are often baked down onto the comparatively low-polygon game mesh. The game mesh's normal map does a great job of faking the high-resolution details, giving us almost the same effect for a fraction of the system resources of the original multimillion-polygon mesh.

The high-resolution and in-game meshes should now sit perfectly over the top of each other like the following figure. Be sure that the high-resolution meshes have standard 3ds Max materials, with the color, specular, and normal maps applied to the relevant map slots. Make sure that no DirectX materials are applied to the high-resolution objects, as they cannot be baked down onto the game mesh.

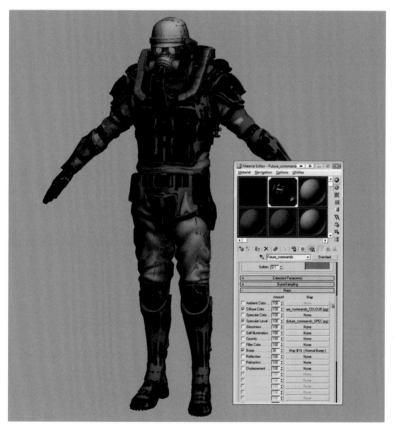

FIG 10.176

We could go through and bake our maps one by one, but it is easier to bake all three maps (color, specular, and normal) at the same time. Select the game mesh and select Rendering > Render To Texture. In the General Settings tab at the top of the Render To Texture settings, choose an output path for the textures.

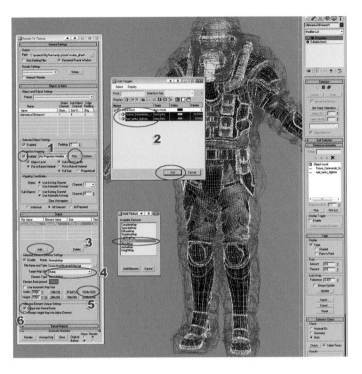

FIG 10.177

Be sure to check the Enabled box in the Projection Mapping section and click the Pick button to bring up the Add Targets menu.

In the Add Targets pop-up box, select all of the objects that make up the high-resolution mesh; in my case, this is the main body of the future commando and the gas tanks. Click Add and a Projection relationship will be set up between the game mesh and the high-resolution objects.

To set up the normal map output, click Add in the Output section and choose a NormalsMap Texture element. Choose Bump for the Target Map Slot to ensure that Render To Texture will plug our new normal map into the bump slot of the new material that it will apply to our character. Click the 1024 × 1024 button to choose a 1 k map size. Be sure that "Output into Normal Bump" is checked, so that the normal map gets plugged into bump slot through a Normal Bump node.

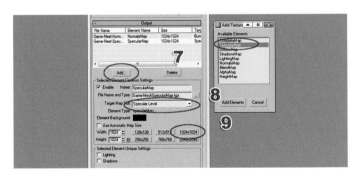

FIG 10.178

Now we have the NormalMap output all set up, let's configure the specular map bake. Click Add and choose a SpecularMap Texture element. Choose Specular Level for the target map slot. Click the 1024 × 1024 button to choose a 1-k map size.

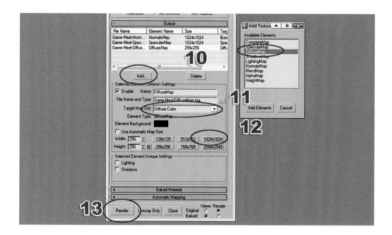

FIG 10.179

Finally, let's set up the diffuse/color map bake. Click Add and choose a DiffuseMap Texture element. Choose Diffuse Color for the target map slot. Click the 1024 × 1024 button to choose a 1-k map size. Click Render to render out all three maps at the same time and apply them to a new material.

Isolate the game mesh or hide the high-resolution mesh to view the work so far. In Photoshop, browse to the location where you saved these textures, and open them up to take a look at them.

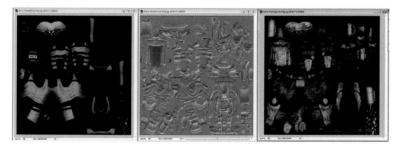

FIG 10.180

Back in 3ds Max, you will notice that a blue cage has appeared around the game mesh and that a Projection modifier has been added to its stack. The blue Projection cage is a visual tool to help you control how the information is baked down from the high-resolution target mesh onto the low-resolution one. During a render, rays are fired out from each point on the game mesh until they get to the cage, from where they take the information from the nearest high-resolution surface.

429

When baking from high- to low-resolution, there are often some problems. Cavities and other complex areas with overlapping details cause problems for the renderer because when there are many high-resolution surfaces close to each other, the renderer doesn't know which one to take its information from. The Projection cage is designed to solve this problem, as each vertex in the cage can be tweaked by hand, but because we have more than 6000 vertices in this mesh, the prospect is daunting!

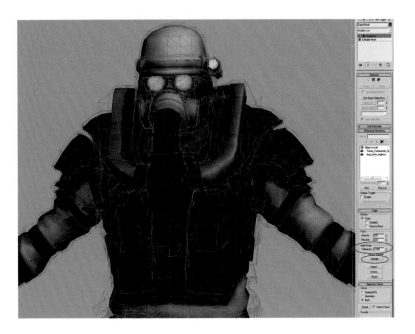

FIG 10.181

Luckily, there are controls in the Projection modifier that can move each vertex on the cage all together at the same time. If you type various values into the Auto-Wrap parameter and hit the Update button, you will see the cage recalculate at different distances from the game mesh.

My favorite and fastest way to get perfect game-mesh maps is to bake each of the maps a number of times, each with a differently sized cage. Often I will bake a small, medium, and large version of each map, which I blend together in Photoshop using masks.

To fix the color map, I rendered first with a small cage and then in the areas with missing information, I painted in (using a mask) another version of the map I had rendered with a larger cage. To quickly finish it, I used the Brush tool, Rubber Stamp tool, and Healing Brush tool to make a few quick and dirty fixes on the layer that was corrected by hand. I fixed the problems with the specular map using exactly the same techniques.

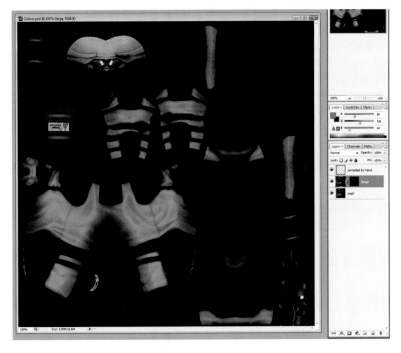

FIG 10.182

To fix the normal map, I used the same process as I did for the color map, with a couple of additional techniques. I corrected some of the areas that had rendered incorrectly by painting the blue/magenta color R127, G128, B255 on the hand-corrected layer.

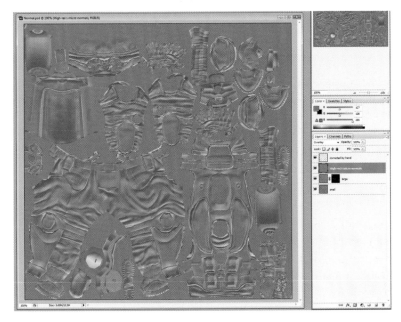

FIG 10.183

The low-frequency normal maps that we obtained from the baking process do not include all the high-frequency details that are in the normal map of the high-resolution version of the character. To add these details to our mesh, apply the normal map of the high-resolution character to its diffuse color channel instead of its usual bump channel assignment. Then when you bake the maps again, the high-resolution normal map has been baked into the DiffuseMap texture. Copy and paste this map into our game-mesh normal PSD and put it in Overlay mode to blend it over the top of the other normal map layers.

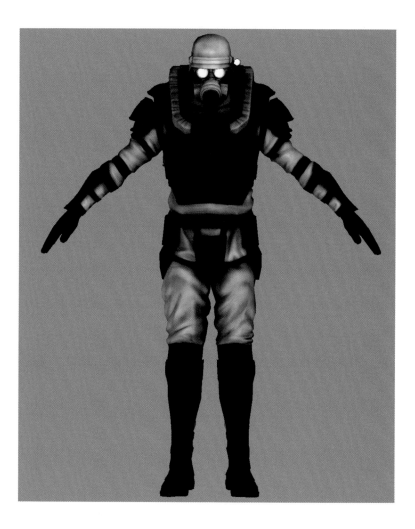

FIG 10.184

It is very useful to apply the DirectX shader that we used earlier so that we can preview the effects of the specular, normal, and diffuse maps all working together in real time. If you keep a sharp eye out, you can make the game mesh incredibly similar to its original high-resolution counterpart.

Rendering Your Character

So we've finished the character now, and although he looks pretty darn good in the DirectX shader in the viewport, we can make him look nicer still if we render him using the Scanline renderer. True high-end rendering is beyond the scope of this chapter, so we will use specular highlights to approximate blurry reflections and AO maps to approximate the diffuse scattering of light.

I will show you how to render the high-resolution asset, but I recommend that you render the game mesh, too; potential employers are keen to see what you can do with a restricted polygon count. Dramatic, shadowy lighting looks cool but doesn't give a detailed view of your model; perfectly flat, even lighting looks unrealistic and doesn't show off the contours of your model. Here we will create a lighting scheme somewhere between these two extremes. To start, delete any old lights from the scene and apply a blank, gray material to the character.

The Studio Wall

Although it will not be the focus of the renders, a simple and well-lit scene can help show off our character and put him in a real-life context. I used the Primitive Plane object and a couple of bend modifiers to make a primitive photography studio wall like you see below. Gradually curved wall-to-floor backdrops like this allow photographers to get the most minimal backgrounds possible, with no hard corners or other visual distractions. To add a little real-world believability to the studio floor, I've added a color texture with some marks on the floor where people have been standing with their dirty shoes on.

Be sure that the Studio Wall object and the soles of the character's shoes are exactly touching, without penetrating or crossing each other. A floating character or one that sinks through the floor will destroy the illusion of realism.

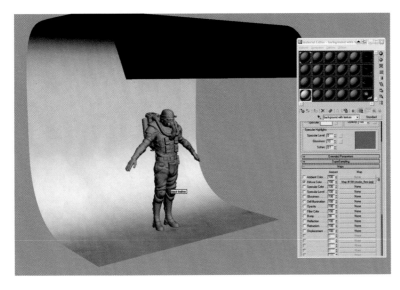

FIG 10.185

Using the AO baking, like we rendered previously for the character, we can calculate the lighting for the studio wall. Render the AO map and apply the texture to the diffuse slot of the Studio Wall object.

The AO shadow texture on the floor will add a subtle "this character is really standing here" ambient shadow effect. If you take this AO map into Photoshop and multiply it over the top of the dirt-textured floor, you will mix the two for a nice-looking background.

FIG 10.186

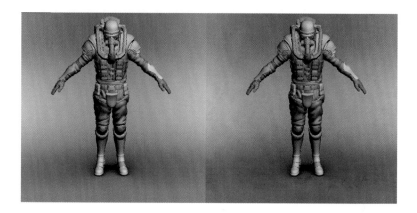

The Camera

Create a camera a good distance away from our character and point it at him. Now zoom in until he fills the screen in the Camera viewport. Remember, the further away the camera, the less perspective distortion. We will be doing square renders, so in the Render Scene options, set a width and height of 512 pixels for our test renders. Right-click on the camera name in the viewport and turn on Show Safe Frame in the options so that you can see the proportions of the camera in the viewport.

Creating the Lights

When creating lights, it is essential to add them one at a time so that you can see the effect each one has on the scene. With lighting, more is less, so make sure that each light you create has a purpose.

To create our key light, go to the Create > Lights panel and choose a Target Spot light; drag to create the light and point it directly at the character—the default intensity of 1 is usually okay. Normally, key lights are in front of the subject, often to one side to help show off the form of the shape. Lighting that is too close to the camera makes your objects look flat, so it's better to have this main light off to the right-hand side.

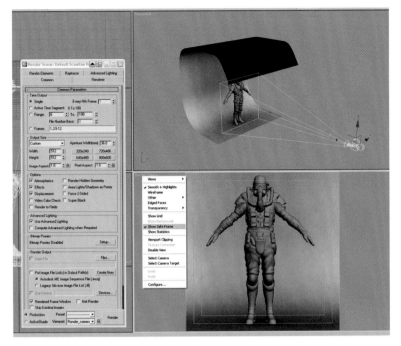

FIG 10.187

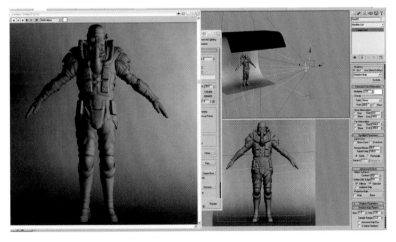

FIG 10.188

Be sure to check the Shadows On box to turn on the shadows. If you were to render now, you would get the hard-edged shadow look so common in CGI (Computer Generated Images). Interior light is usually quite soft, as the light bounces around quite a lot compared with outdoor scenes. Photographers often use silk or other translucent materials in front of their harsh studio lights in order to spread out the light and soften the shadows. We can simulate this effect by changing the size of the Shadow map to 128 pixels (a very rough setting) and the Sample Range to 12 (to smooth out the effect).

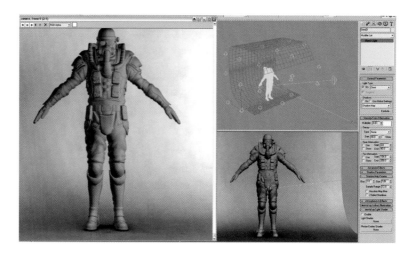

FIG 10.189

In the Spotlight parameters, you might also want to increase the Hotspot and Falloff of the lamp. Do a test render and you should get something like the previous image.

Photographers often use fill lights to fill in the shadowy areas of their subjects; in CG, we use fill lights for similar purposes and also use them to simulate the effect of bounced light from the environment. Add lots of Omni lights around the character, each with no shadows and a tiny Multiplier value like 0.03. You might want to give the lights to the left a slightly blue tint to simulate the ambient light of the sky coming in from a large window. It is also a good idea to give the other Omni lights and the main key light a slightly orange tint to simulate the hue of a light bulb.

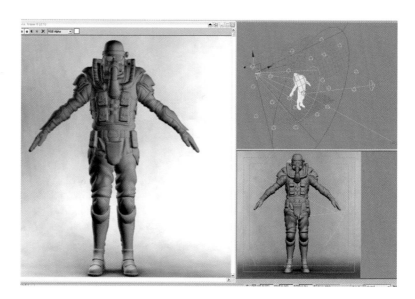

FIG 10.190

Rim lighting is used in photography to really pop subjects out from their background. Make a copy of the key light and move it to the other side of the character. This process should wrap up an interesting lighting scheme, which shows off the complex modeling we have done.

Materials in Theory

An object's reflective qualities are dictated by how rough or smooth the object is on a microscale.

Diffuse reflection occurs when light hits a rough surface and is scattered in many directions. Surfaces with 100% diffuse reflection look the same no matter which angle you view them from. A good example of a surface with pretty much 100% diffuse reflection would be a dirty, old cardboard box.

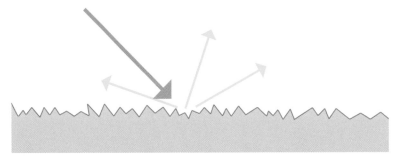

FIG 10.191

Specular reflection occurs when light hits a smooth object and bounces off at a perfect right angle. Specular reflection is easy to identify because it changes depending on the viewing angle. A mirror is a good example of an almost perfectly 100% specular reflective surface.

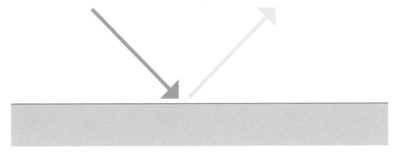

FIG 10.192

Different ratios of mixed diffuse and specular reflection occur on most surfaces. These surfaces are not flat enough to show perfect reflections like a mirror, but they are smooth enough to ensure that most of the light bounces off in a consistent direction to create blurred reflections. A good example of this would be most metals; they are very shiny, but the details of the reflections are blurred.

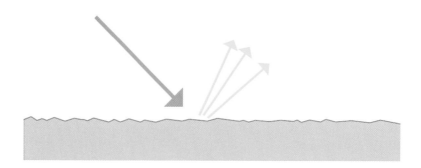

FIG 10.193

Materials in 3ds Max

To simulate these different types of surface in 3ds Max, we will split up the mesh into a number of smaller meshes, each with its own material:

- Blurred Reflections should be applied to all the objects with hard, shiny surfaces like metals and plastics. This material uses the standard Specular effect to fake the look of blurred reflections; true blurred reflections are very computationally expensive and available only on the more advanced renderers, but this cheat will suffice for us here.

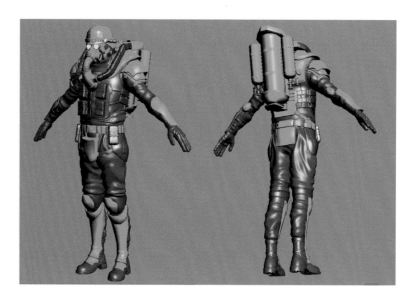

FIG 10.194

The micro roughness as I talked about earlier can be achieved using the Glossiness control; a value of 37 will give tight, smooth highlights.

- Blurred Reflections Rough should be exactly as Blurred Reflections, but with a tweaked Glossiness value of 11. This material should be applied to all the fabrics with fairly rough surfaces, like most of the fairly matte clothes and straps.

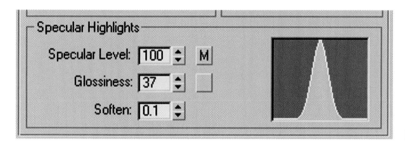

FIG 10.195

- Blurred Reflections Mid represents the medium-roughness areas and should have a Glossiness of something like 21. Apply this material to the NBC suit and leather areas.

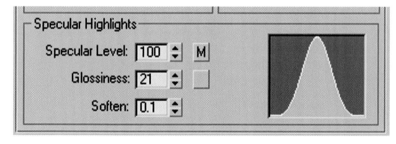

FIG 10.196

- Self Illumination should be applied just to the eyes and lens of the torch; it will be just a regular texture, but with the Self-Illumination setting at 100%.

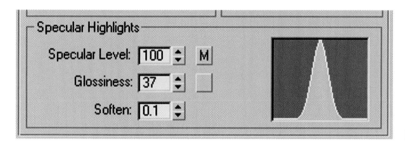

FIG 10.197

Now all that remains is to plug the relevant color and specular maps into the Diffuse Color and Specular Level slots of these four materials. To apply the Normal Map click on the Bump Slot and choose Normal Bump, and then click on the Normal slot to apply your bump map.

Back in the Maps section of your material, take care to change the Bump value from its default of 30 up to the full strength of 100.

439

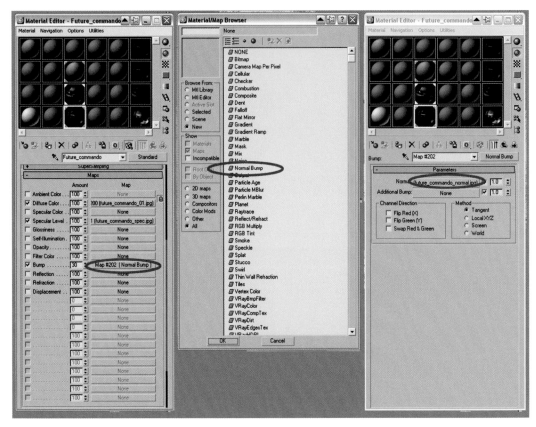

FIG 10.198

The Final Renders

For the final renders, increase the resolution to 1024 × 1024 or more pixels. In the previous figure, I have linked all the objects of the character to a dummy so that I can easily rotate the character (by rotating the parent dummy) for different renders.

As we have modeled some pretty awesome detail into our soldier, you might also want to do some close-up renders to showcase our attention to detail.

The renders I have produced here have a kind of stylized, cartoony feel to them because of the manual cheating we have done in the lighting. Quite often in videogames this is a good thing, as many projects require a stylized effect. Setting up the lighting manually like this gives you ultimate control.

We could have gone further with the rendering to achieve a higher level of realism. To improve the quality of the light, we would have to discard the AO layers from our texture maps and use a true "global illumination" renderer such as Brazil, Mental Ray, or V-Ray. These high-end renderers can accurately

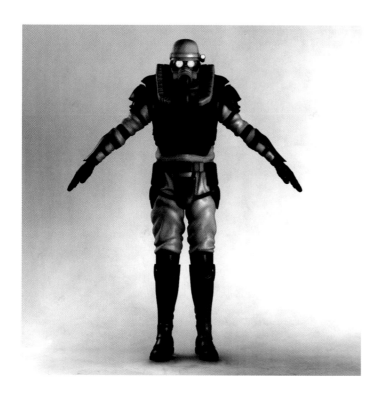

FIG 10.199

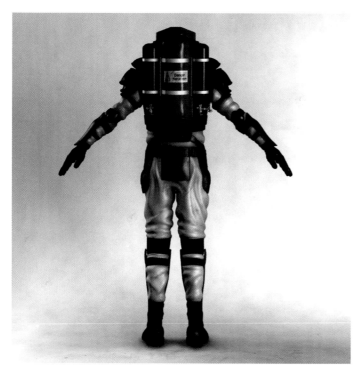

FIG 10.200

441

render real-world lighting effects such as color bleeding, caustics, area lights (3ds Max's standard lights are infinitely small), and blurry reflections.

As a 3D artist, you must constantly improve your work to keep up with the rapid pace of change. And at the end of a project (after a good rest, of course!), it's a good habit to perform a little postmortem on your work. What could you have done to make it better? How could you have made the process faster? How does your work compare to that of your peers? If you learn from your experiences, you will build your next character faster, and it will be of higher quality, too.

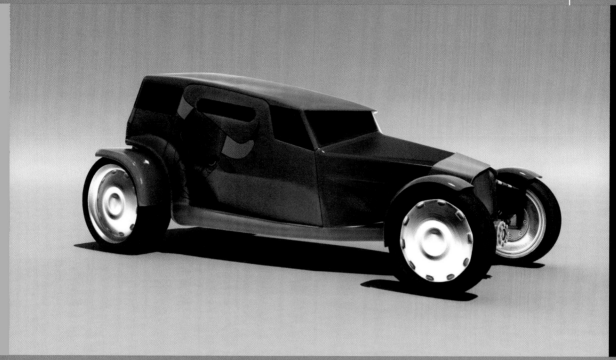

CHAPTER 11

Portfolio and Interview

Portfolio

If you've been through the whole book, you've created some images and learned how to render them, so you've got yourself a portfolio, right? Wrong! The first rule about putting a portfolio together is that *the work must be your own*. I've put this in emphasized type because it is the single most important rule when sending off your portfolio and applying for a job.

It's okay to show your friends and family all the great renders that you've created by working through this book, but if you're going to send work off to a professional reviewer, you'll have to throw it all out and start again, from scratch—sorry! The main reasons for this are as follows:

- Although you technically completed the projects in each chapter, don't include them in your portfolio, as it's not all your own work. You'll need to create similar pieces of work based on the skills you've learned. That way, the projects won't be recognized by anyone as a tutorial and will truly be your own creation.
- If the reviewer recognizes one piece of work in your portfolio from a tutorial that they know or a book they own, they will most likely throw

the whole portfolio out and you'll never get another chance with them, or possibly even that company, ever again.

- It's important to be original. Recruiters get sent lots and lots of portfolios every day. Although you need to demonstrate that you can do the basics (as covered in this book), you'll need an edge to impress them. Also, if you've bought this book and created a portfolio from it, you probably won't be the only one. So take what you've learned, apply it to a few different models, themes, and subject matter and create a stunning portfolio of your own work, which you can be truly proud of.

If you feel that you've gone through this book and completed some or even all of the tutorials but you're not quite ready to apply for a job (or don't even want to), then there are a few things that you can do next:

- You can go back through the tutorials that you enjoyed and redo them, this time creating something similar using your own reference or concept material.
- You can browse the texture and reference photo folders included on the DVD and build something from those.
- You can take some of your own reference photos and build something completely new, from scratch.
- You can even create something completely new that you can't take reference photos of; for example, something futuristic, some inner workings of a machine or animal, or even something fictional.

Your portfolio is your advertisement of your work. It highlights your skill and talent, as well as your problem-solving abilities, so have some fun with it. Just remember to include enough of the basics to satisfy the employer. If you're not sure what to include, here's some advice.

What to Include in Your Portfolio

I'm assuming that you want a job in the games industry (or a related industry) due to the title of the book, so I'll base my advice on that assumption. When deciding what people look for when looking at portfolios, I asked a number of industry professionals what they look for. Here are a few things that came up a number of times:

- General artistic ability and command over traditional art principles (drawing and sketching, especially)
- Creative ability
- Strong original ideas
- Controlled and manageable topology and good UV layout
- Attention to detail and good observational skills (including technical details: naming conventions, pivot points, file formats, and so on)
- Good variety of work

The bottom line is to include only your very best work. If you have only five good pieces of work, then that's all that should be in your portfolio. Padding your portfolio out with everything you have ever done not only reduces the overall quality of your portfolio but also advertises every single mistake you've ever made—not what you want to be doing. So, be strict and include only work that you believe to be flawless. Ask yourself, "Is this the best I can do, or are there any small improvements that I can make?" If there are, do them; it's really important not to rush getting this together. A rushed portfolio can hold you back for many years. If you've included only your very best work so far, you may have only a few renders. As you flick through them, the small number of pieces may be the catalyst you need to buckle down and produce some more work. If not, it should be. If your portfolio is brimming with everything you've ever done, you won't feel the same sense of urgency, so try to be aware of what you *really* have and what you need to do about improving it.

How do you decide what to include? Well, it all depends on the job you want. If all you want to do is model cars and other vehicles, then your portfolio should include a lot of good examples of that—one or two just isn't enough. However, if you're happy to do anything, then you'll need to have a good variety of work. If you're not sure what position you'd like to apply for, here are a few of the more common roles:

- 3D artist (does a bit of everything). This tends to be a more junior role.
- Vehicle artist (depending on the company, this can cover aircraft, military, cars, trains, and sci-fi).
- Character artist (these range from photorealistic, real world, cartoon, alien). This role can include weighting and rigging, as well as modeling and texturing.
- Environmental or level artist (real world, alien, cartoon, fictional).
- UI (User Interface artist: the selection screens you navigate between game levels).

If you're still not sure whether you want to specialize in any of the specific roles, keep everything generic at this point and do a bit of everything. Remember that originality is king here. You should create brand new conceptual forms if it allows you to flex your artistic muscles. I would much rather see a beautifully dirty and damaged vehicle for an imaginary sci-fi scene than yet another shiny Ferrari.

Ask for help if you're not sure what your best work is. Luckily, there are lots of forums and galleries to post your work for your fellow artists to critique for you. Two of the most popular are www.deviantart.com and www.cgsociety.org

Some of the best artists in the industry post work on these Web sites, so brace yourself: this is who you're competing with for work. Also, some of the best artists will routinely comment on your work or works in progress and offer valuable advice, which you'd struggle to get anywhere else—and the best thing is that it's *free* advice.

Let's move on to the more difficult question: what you *shouldn't* include.

What Not to Include

First and foremost, don't include any sloppy work (unmapped polygons, stretched UVs, holes in geometry) because the mistakes will stand out from a mile away, and if you haven't spotted such errors in your portfolio, then the reviewer will wonder what your mistakes will be like from day to day and you'll probably be rejected.

Don't include old work. For some reason, a lot of artists feel the need to sign and date their work, especially life drawing. If I see a date on a portfolio piece that's more than a few years old, it makes me wonder, "What have they been doing recently?" If all the work is old, it puts me off. If you must include old work, make sure you remove any dates, or better still, don't add them in the first place. Again, if all your work is too old, you will most probably be rejected.

Unfinished work should not be included, unless it's your latest piece and it's looking really good. I love it when an artist comes for an interview and shows me a piece of work that he has been working on specifically for Evolution Studios or one of the projects we're developing. It's great when a piece of work has been created just for the interview.

Artists do this a lot if there are gaps in their portfolio, when the work they have been doing is a different style or subject matter than the company or role they are applying for, to prove that they can do the job or even to show how much they want the job. If you do try something like this, casually drop it in at the end, saying something like, "And there's this, which I was working on last night/week while preparing for today; it's not finished, but …" (and then point out what you need to do to round it off). Obviously, only do this with work that is close to completion; otherwise, it will have a negative effect.

I spoke to some of my lead artist contacts in other companies about what they really don't want to see in interviews. Here are some of their responses:

- Clichés (spaceships, Amazonian beauties, churches)
- Sloppy work (unmapped polygons, stretched UVs, poor quality)
- Unfinished work
- Scenes or exercises from books or (worse) from the 3ds Max tutorials

Overall, get as many people to look at your work as you can and listen to what they say to you. If you really like a piece but no one else does, drop it from your portfolio. By all means, keep it in a personal portfolio but don't send it off to companies or take it to the interview.

One very important point to note is that you should not send original pieces of work under any circumstances—that is, your only hard copy of something you've drawn. These will not be returned to you, and you'll lose them forever.

Now that you have an idea of what you want to do, you have to produce the work, or, if you already have it, you get to organize it.

Producing the Work

If you feel that you might not have enough good work in your portfolio, you'll need to plan what you need to do. It's really important that you make a plan and stick to it. Some people create lists and work through them from top to bottom, but I prefer to use S.M.A.R.T goals. S.M.A.R.T stands for Specific, Measurable, Achievable, Realistic, and Timed. For example, if I'm applying for a new role, I might identify four new pieces that I need to produce for my portfolio, aimed at this new role. Here's how I work out what my goals should be:

- Specific: I want to create four new pieces of work similar to (for example) my first portfolio page.
- Measurable: I identify the target quality from an existing portfolio piece. I then need to list everything I need to model, texture, compose, light, and render in the scene to hit this level of quality.
- Achievable: I take each set of time estimates for the four pieces of work that I intend to build and add rough estimates for each task, in hours. I then add all the estimates for each piece of work and see roughly how long it will take me to make all of them. Once I have this total, I can compare it to the total amount of time that I think I can spend on this work (maybe five hours a day, for example). Comparing these estimates shows me how much work I have to do and how long I have to do it in.
- Realistic: If the total of amount of work is less than the time I have to do it in, it's a realistic goal. If it is slightly more, I may decide that if it all goes well, I can probably still do it, so it's still fairly realistic. If the amount of work to do is far more than the amount of time you have, it's an unrealistic goal and you should probably reconsider the amount of work.
- Timed: The closing date for applicants for the new role is (in this example) six weeks away, so to be sure I make it on time, I'll plan out four weeks of work.

For this example, if I think each piece will take me approximately two weeks of work, then it's obvious that I don't have the time to do the four pieces I wanted to. In this case, I'll opt for doing two of the pieces or re-plan the whole lot using a simpler piece of work as the quality bar.

This technique is extremely important when planning any work. Breaking down the tasks into smaller actions makes it easier to estimate accurately, which is very important for hitting deadlines, and also really useful for pricing freelance work as a contractor. To find out more about SMART goals and other planning techniques, try an Internet search—there are plenty of resources that go into planning in a lot more detail.

Now that you have your work, let's organize it.

Organizing the Content

If you're sending your work in to studios via e-mail or disc or if you're compiling a printed portfolio, you must put your very best work first. In a lot of cases, a reviewer might look only at the first couple of pieces, so you have to blow them away with the very first piece. If you don't, you'll be in the trash—it's as simple as that. You can organize your work as simply as a set of images, or a movie, but keep it simple. Finding and downloading strange codecs to view someone's work really puts me off. A lot of people present their Web site portfolio, but clearly labeled folders of JPEGs work just as well.

This is how it works in some companies. A well-known developing company that makes great games and is advertising for staff might get 10 or more show reels or portfolios a day from independent applicants (the number can be even higher if recruitment agencies are involved). If the Art Manager or Recruiter looks at these once a week, they'll have more than 50 show reels to look through; if they're really busy, as most are, and do this only once a month … well you can do the math.

Whenever I'm faced with such a task, I know that I can spend only a small amount of time on each. If the first few images are well below the standard that we require, I'll make a note "thanks, but no thanks" and move onto the next one. However, if the first few images are good, I'll look a lot further through the portfolio, even if I see a few poor pieces of work, just to make sure that I'm not making a mistake or missing out on finding a good candidate. Often slightly junior members of the team are tasked to filter the applicants first. This may improve your chances if your first few pieces aren't the best, but don't risk it.

As well as putting a few of your best pieces at the start of the portfolio or show reel, you'll need to put some of your best at the end. This will leave the recruiter with a good feeling about your work, improving your chances. I prefer to use fully rendered scenes containing lots of models for the start and end of my portfolio and then focus on individual assets in the middle. I often include wireframes and texture pages as half of the portfolio, so that it is clear how efficiently the models are built and rendered. This is just my preference—have a look at some online portfolios and try to work out why the artist has organized them the way they have.

Final Presentation of Your Portfolio

Once you've produced and organized the work, you need to present it, as well as you can. If you are sending in a show reel on disc, it must be in a box, with a cover, and the disc should be either printed or clearly labeled. Both the cover and disc should have your name, your contact details (e-mail and phone number), and also your Web site address. If you are taking in a paper portfolio to show, it should be in a clean binder of a suitable size for your work. I always use two matching leather portfolios for interviews. One is 17 3 220 (A2) with all my illustration, life drawing, pastel, charcoal, and painting, and the other is 11 3 170 (A3) and has all my 3D modeling shown as full-color renders. The smaller portfolio sometimes has magazine scans of articles and high review scores of the games I've worked on, depending on the role I was applying for. If you're sending a demo reel, always remember to name your files properly—for example, AndrewGahan001.jpg, so that your work can be easily identified if it gets mixed up with someone else's.

If you are scanning or copying work to include in your portfolio, remember to do everything in color. Even pencil drawings should be scanned or photocopied in color, as all the gray tones will be lost if you just use the black-and-white settings.

Now you have your portfolio sorted out, go ahead, and apply for that job.

Applying for a Job

I recommend that you look for your first (or next) job in these two main ways. The first, and the one I recommend the most, is to apply directly to companies that are hiring. To do this, look at the relevant magazines for your country (or the country you want to work in) and browse the advertisements from the companies looking for staff. In the United Kingdom, one of the best for this is *Edge* magazine, which is readily available in newsagents. You can also try looking on the Web sites for companies that you'd like to work for—often, there are positions advertised that have not been in the press yet, which might get you a slight head start on the position. There are also a lot of advertisements on various Web sites such as http://www.gamasutra.com and http://www.gamesindustry.biz; just search for "games industry 1jobs" in any major search engine, and you'll find lots of positions advertised.

This leads me to the second method of finding out who's hiring and the approach to take if your direct applications don't get you the results that you want. Again, look through the relevant trade magazines or Internet search engines, but this time, concentrate on all the recruitment agencies. You will probably find these a lot easier to find than the actual companies. Browse through their listings. If there is something specific that you like the look of, drop them a line or apply direct through the Web site. If there isn't, send an e-mail with the sort of position you're looking for.

You'll find that the second method might get you more responses, but possibly not be for the exact job you want. The recruitment agencies will often fire off your CV and show reel to every company on their books and get you lots of interviews. On the other hand, you might end up in a pile of other artists while the agency does all the hard work to place the more senior jobs. Remember, interviews cost money to attend, so take care how many you agree to attend, and if you are invited to one, ask if they'll pay your expenses. In a lot of cases, they will.

The recruitment agencies work on commission and they will charge from 10% up to 30% of your starting salary to the company hiring you. For this reason alone, a lot of companies will not use them, so do your research and find out which companies do.

The most important thing you need to do with recruitment agencies is to keep calling them every week and ask for an update. If you don't, you might get lost in paperwork.

Finally, if you're going to start applying, you're going to need a resume or curriculum vitae.

Resume or Curriculum Vitae and Cover Letter

Every good job application should come with a cover letter, a resume, or curriculum vitae (CV) and a show reel or demo disc. Let's look at them in a little more detail.

A Cover Letter

The cover letter is your way of introducing yourself to the company and should explain why you want this particular job. It should give the employer some insight into your desire and your personality. It should be no more than one page long and should describe how you are qualified for the position. This is a good opportunity to make an impression and maybe stand out from the crowd. This is also a good opportunity to make a bad impression, so be careful what you write. A letter that lacks specifics about the position or company that you're applying to will look like a mass mailing and will show lack of effort and thought. Always use a spell-checker on all your text; spelling mistakes show that you have poor attention to detail—this really does matter. Also ask someone you trust to proofread your letter, as they may see grammatical errors that you missed, which must be corrected.

Resume/CV

A resume or curriculum vitae (CV) is a list of your skills, experience, interests, and successes; nothing more. It should not contain page after page of details about your hobbies or spare time, and it should not be used as an opportunity to hype every single thing you've ever done. A good resume will be easy to read and no more than two pages (maybe three if you have had a lot of relevant experience). It should have lots of open space and be presented in a clear, easy-to-read font such as 12-point Arial. You should print it on good-quality paper and put it in a matching envelope. Recruitment agencies routinely take personal information off CVs when they send them out; this often messes up the formatting, making them difficult to read. Obviously, if you apply for positions personally, you get full control over how you are presented. Also, it's important not to go mad with jazzy paper and gimmicks—we've seen them all before and are not usually impressed by anything that is supposed to shock or amaze us.

You can use the following checklist to produce a good CV directly:

- Contact information (phone numbers, e-mail address, and mailing address)
- Objective (the exact position to which you are applying)

- Experience (employment dates, job titles, and brief descriptions of responsibilities)
- Skills (Maya, 3ds Max, Photoshop, Illustrator, and so on, including version numbers)
- Education (degrees, certifications, and additional training)
- Other relevant skills (related skills, personal successes)

There is also a mountain of free advice on the Internet for creating good CVs and resumes. Just search for "CV or resume" and you'll find a lot more detailed advice.

One important point about your contact information is that if you are currently using an e-mail address that you set up in college that is something like biggy69@hotmail or sexyboy1980@yahoo, then you'll need to change it to something more professional. You should definitely have your own Web site when looking for a job, even if it's just a one-page resume that you're putting online. It is so cheap to create and maintain a Web site these days that it's pretty much a no-brainer. In addition to letting you circulate your name and qualifications worldwide, it's also a permanent e-mail address for life, which is important: you're permanently reachable through you@you.com instead of having to rely on a hotmail address. It comes off as very professional and shows good thought and consideration.

The best thing to do is to register a Web domain that is your name or similar and generate a new e-mail address using the new domain. You should also get a Web site hosted on this domain showcasing your best work (your portfolio) and any new work that you complete. There are loads of cheap Web hosting organizations (I use http://www.streamline.net), and if you're not a Web developer or don't know anyone who is, you can get cheap Web sites done for you by using http://www.elance.com or by getting your local Web developer to put together a single-page site. If you do put your own Web site together, always remember to use images to show your e-mail address or contact number—this will cut down on the amount of spam you get from bots searching your site for contact information.

At the Interview

There is a wealth of advice available about interviews, techniques, and what you should and shouldn't do, but here are a few key points directed to the creative industry in general, and more specifically, the games industry:

- Preparation: Preparation is extremely important and will give you some confidence in the interview. Know the company you are applying to. Find out what games they've made, who the key staff are, and especially, what they are working on now. If you can't find out what they are currently working on, the project must be unannounced, which gives you a great question in the interview.
- Arrive on time: You're going to meet some very busy people and they will not be amused if you're late. If you have to be late, make sure you that

451

telephone in as soon as you know and give them a realistic time when you're going to arrive. This will give them time to reschedule. If you're late and you don't call, you may miss your slot completely, and it will be a wasted journey. Also, don't arrive too early. I've had applicants turn up one and a half hours early, which really put me on the spot. Do I leave them sitting in reception for 90 minutes for a receptionist to look after or do I reschedule half my day? Either way it is a hassle that you don't want to cause anyone.

- First impressions are lasting impressions: You will never get a second chance to make a first impression, so try to get it right. First, smile when you are introduced; it will get you off to a good start. A firm handshake is next—not a vice-like grip or a clammy wet lettuce, just short and firm. If you're really nervous and your hands are sweating, ask the receptionist where the restrooms are and freshen up before you meet anyone. Dress is also important. You'll need to look professional. Wear a nice long-sleeved shirt, some smart or casual trousers, and some clean shoes. As it's the creative industry, most people will be very casual, but don't assume that the people interviewing you will be. They are likely to be fairly senior staff and may well be very tailored. You can dress down once you have the job. Finally, use eye contact, but don't glare. Keeping eye contact will make you look more confident than you may feel. If two people are interviewing you, it's easier, as you can switch between them. If you talk to people while looking away, they might think that you lack confidence or even interest.

- Listen: I realize that this sounds obvious, but it's really important to listen to the questions you are being asked before you answer them. Wait until the interviewer has finished speaking and then answer that question only, without waffling. Your answers should probably be only a couple of minutes long. Remember not to talk too much, too.

- Stay positive: Sometimes an interview feels like it's not going well, but as you can't be sure, you need to stay positive and enthusiastic. It's okay if you're asked a particularly difficult question and you don't answer it very well; just move on and focus on your successes and all the great work in your portfolio.

- Ask questions: If you can get a couple of good questions in early, without coming across as pushy, you will be able to tailor some of your responses to suit what the interviewer is looking for. Here are two good examples of questions you could ask:
  - What would be my responsibilities if I were to get the position?
  - What qualities are you looking for in the ideal candidate?
  - Try to keep a good dialogue going, as well as answering the questions, and try to ask some of your own—don't just leave them to the end.

- Be honest: It's very important to be honest in interviews, as well as on CVs. A lot of companies check references and career histories to make sure that candidates have actually done what they say they have. A friend of mine told me that he did a background check on someone he had just interviewed and discovered that he's lied about a role on his CV. Although the candidate was very talented and would have got the job without the lie, my friend could not trust him and didn't make him any offers. It's a common myth that most people lie on their CVs; they don't and you shouldn't either. If you lack experience, then your work must stand out on its own. If it doesn't, keep working hard, posting on forums, and learning as much as you can. What we do isn't rocket science, and if you persevere, you'll get your break into the industry.

There are also a number of things that you shouldn't do, but (skipping the obvious), here are a few essentials:

- Don't disrespect previous employers, tutors, or colleagues: One of the best ways of talking yourself out of a job is by saying negative things about previous employers, professors, or colleagues. It won't help you in any way if you do it—so don't.
- Salary and holidays: This question comes up more than any other when I ask junior artists if they have any questions for me. Obviously, salary and holidays are important, but don't bring it up unless they do. Besides, you can always call the HR representative of the company or whoever booked the interview once you know that they like you or in the second interview.
- Have some questions prepared: It is not a good sign when I ask a candidate if he or she has any other questions, and the candidate says, "No." If you've prepared for the interview, which you definitely should have, you should be able to ask the interviewer a series of good questions about the company, the direction it's going in, expansion, new projects, or whatever. If you have nothing to ask, it shows that you haven't done your homework, you're not interested enough in the job, and that you're wasting everyone's time.
- Don't forget to follow up: Even if you think that you made a complete disaster of the interview, don't forget to follow up with a written note thanking everyone for the interview and reiterating your interest in the position and the company.

If after doing all of this, you are still rejected, don't take it too personally and don't see it as failure. It's just a result; not the result you were looking for, but a result that you can learn from. I have had artists apply to me more than once, and in some cases, I have hired them the second time around. There are a number of reasons why you weren't picked for the role, but if you keep improving and working as hard as you can, you'll get there.

Congratulations on completing the book! Good luck, and don't forget to check out more advice and tutorials on www.3d-for-games.com, and be sure to use the forum; it is a wealth of valuable information for amateurs and professionals alike.

Index

Page numbers followed by *f* indicates a figure and *t* indicates a table.